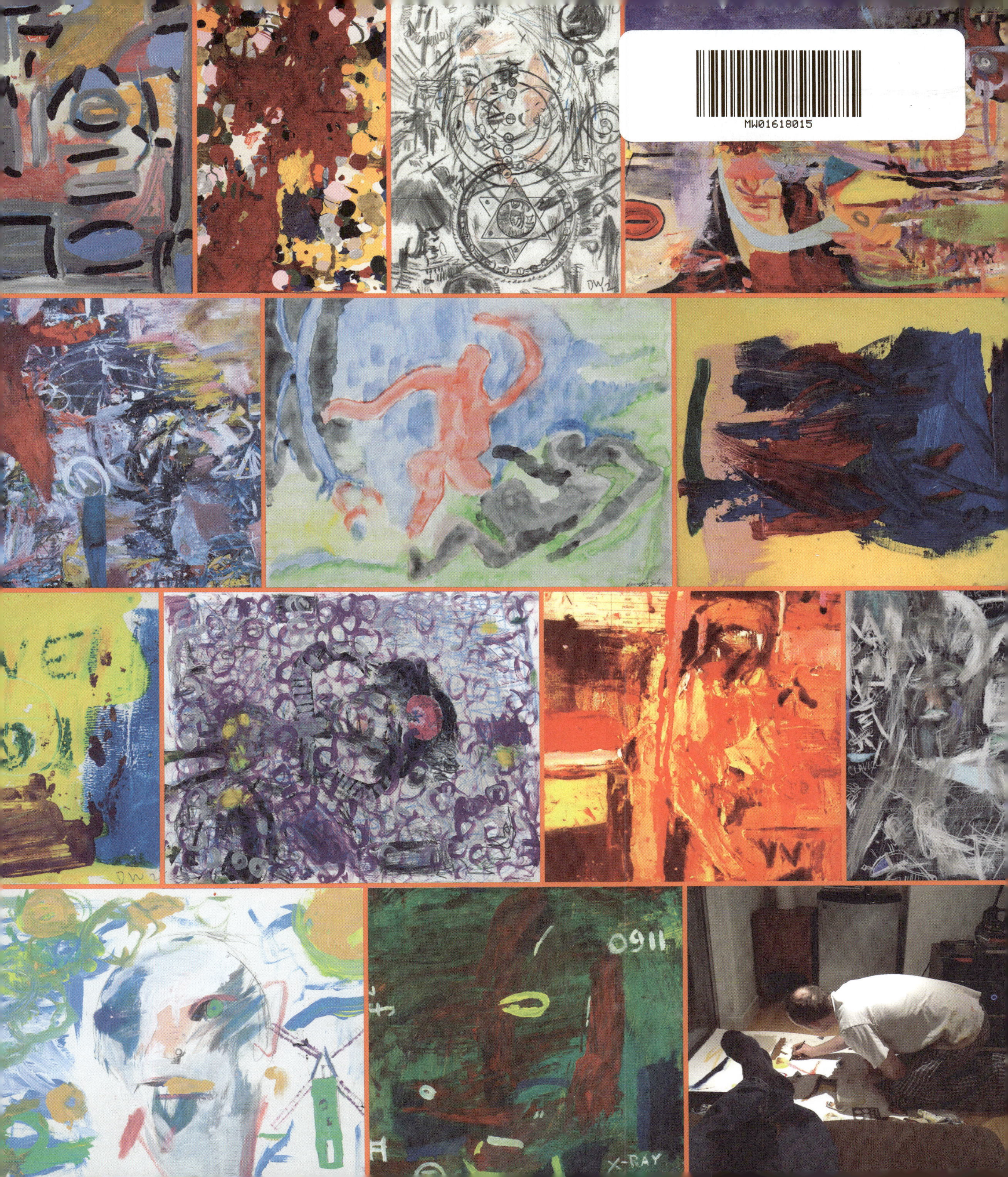
MW01618015
0911
X-RAY

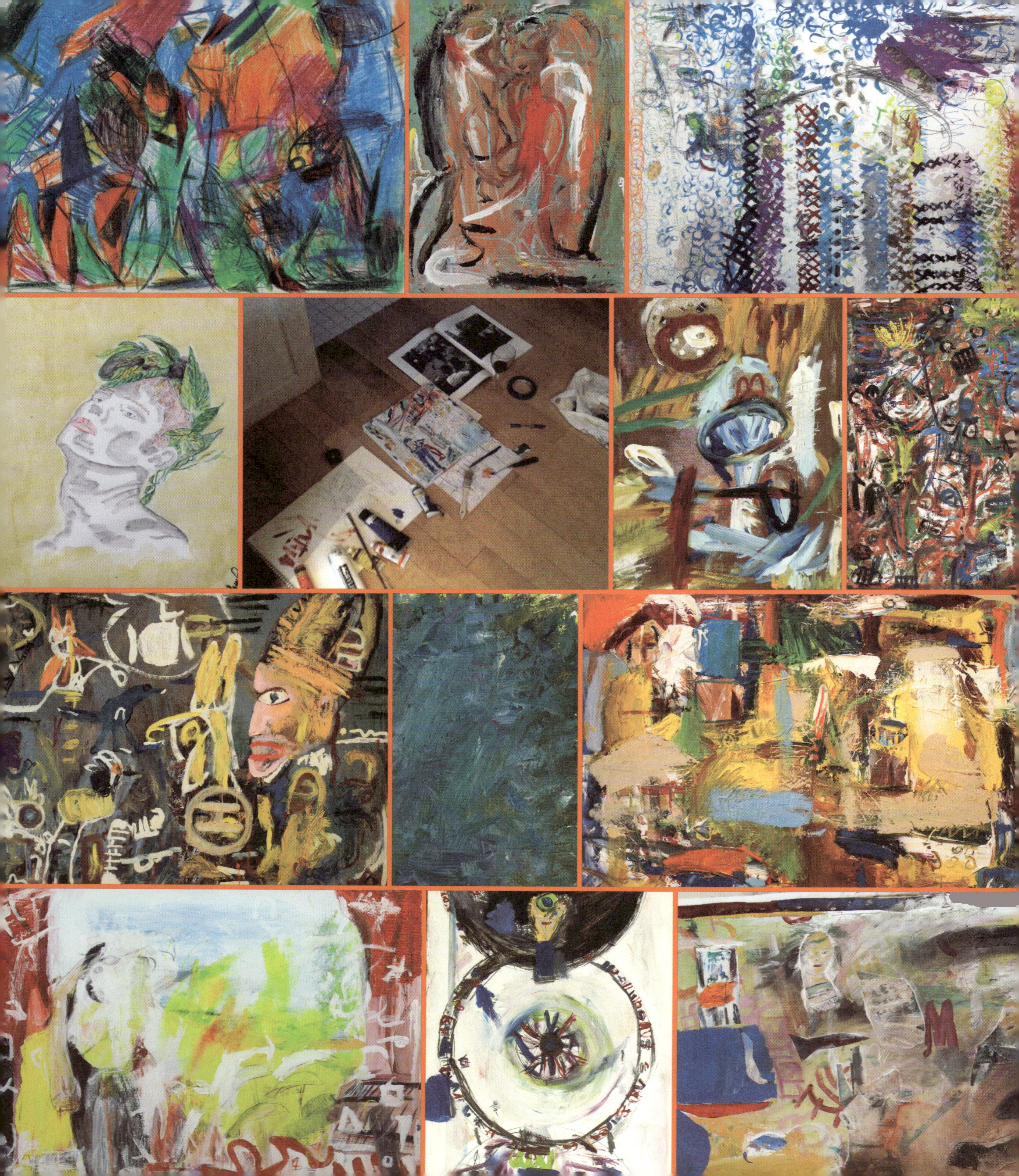

"He smelled like turpentine, oil paint, and fresh flowers.
His favorite color was orange and it went well with his blue eyes."

—DAVYD WHALEY, describing himself.

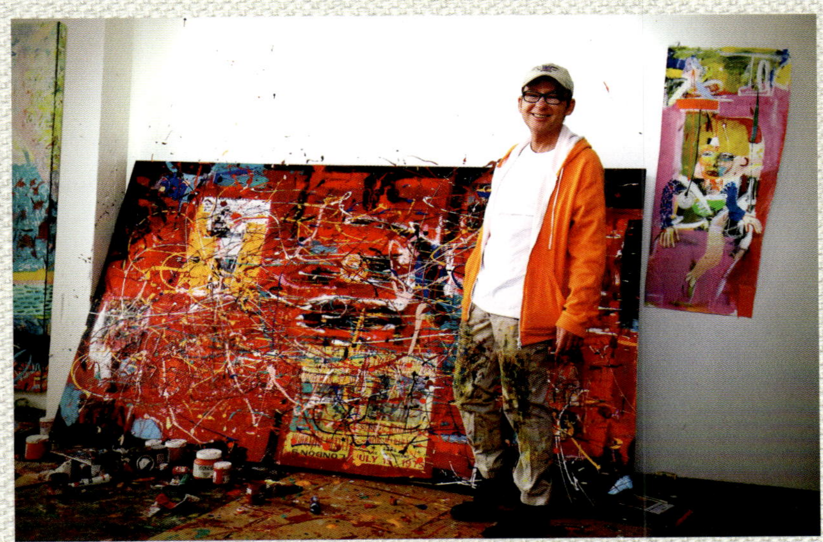

Davyd in his studio with his painting, *75*.

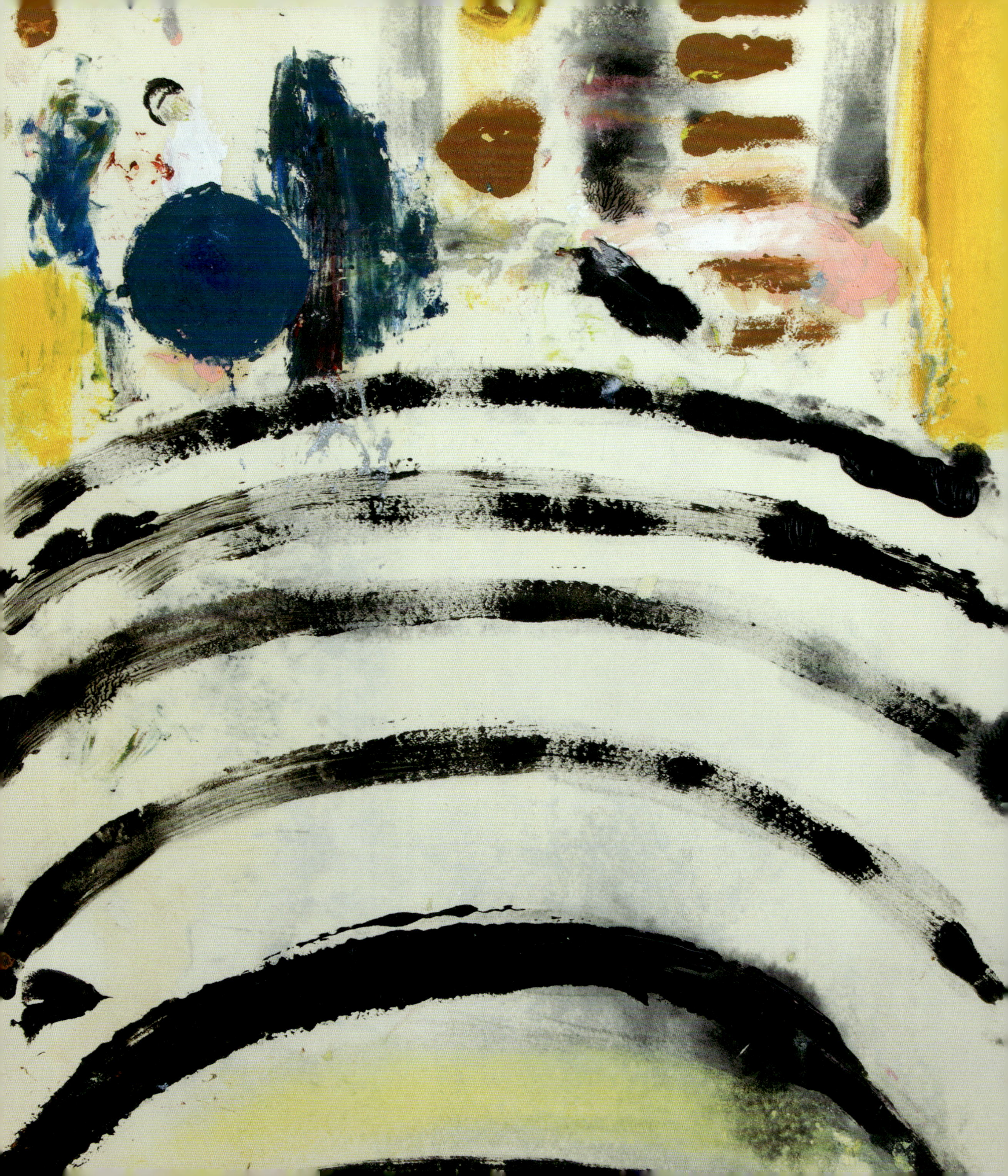

DAVYD WHALEY

"A Hero's Journey"
essay by Peter Clothier

Edited by Norman Buckley

Opposite: *Read Between the Lines*, 2012

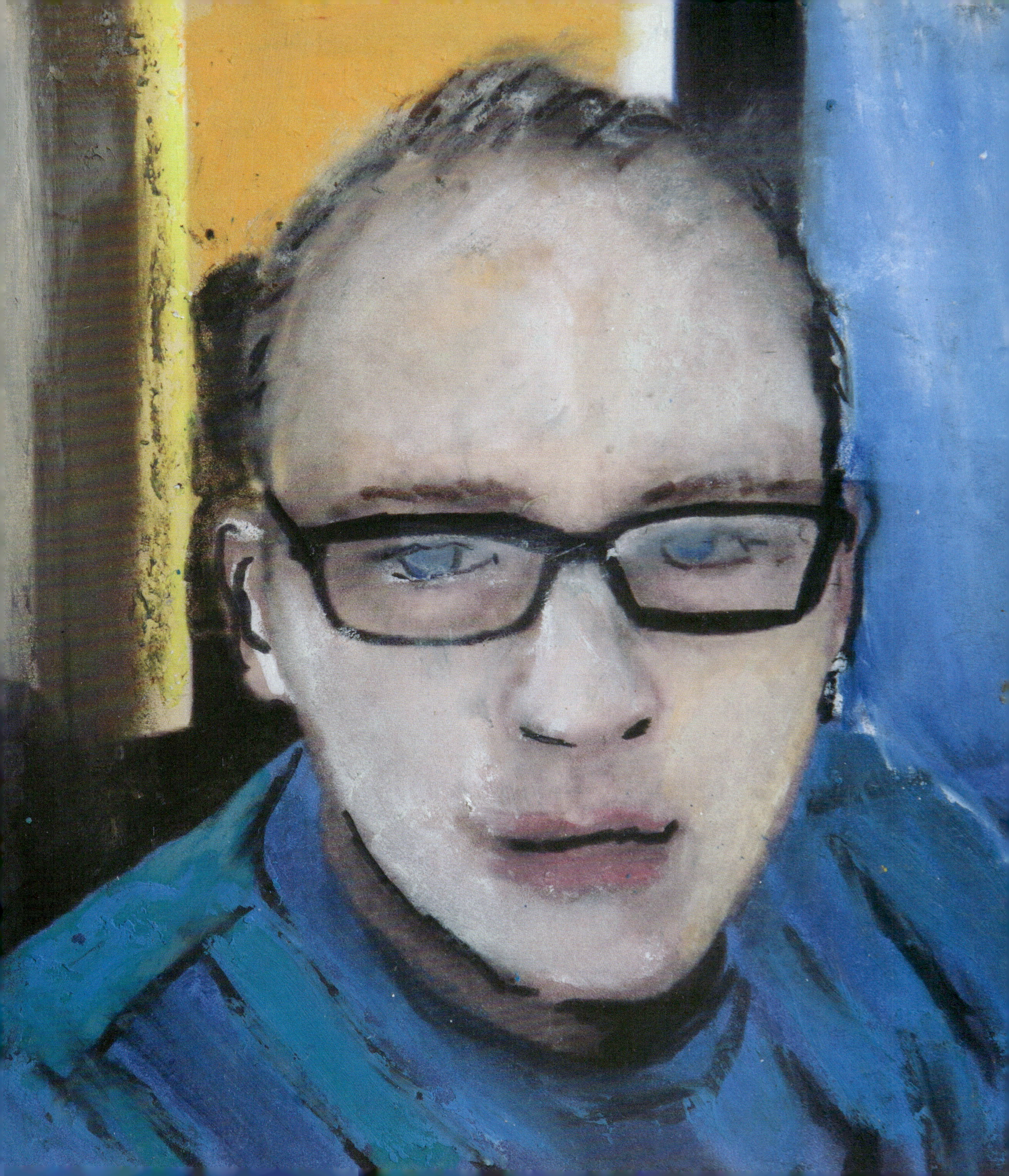

*"What matters is right in front of me.
There is nothing else."*

—DW

Opposite: *Self Portrait*, 2008

Contents

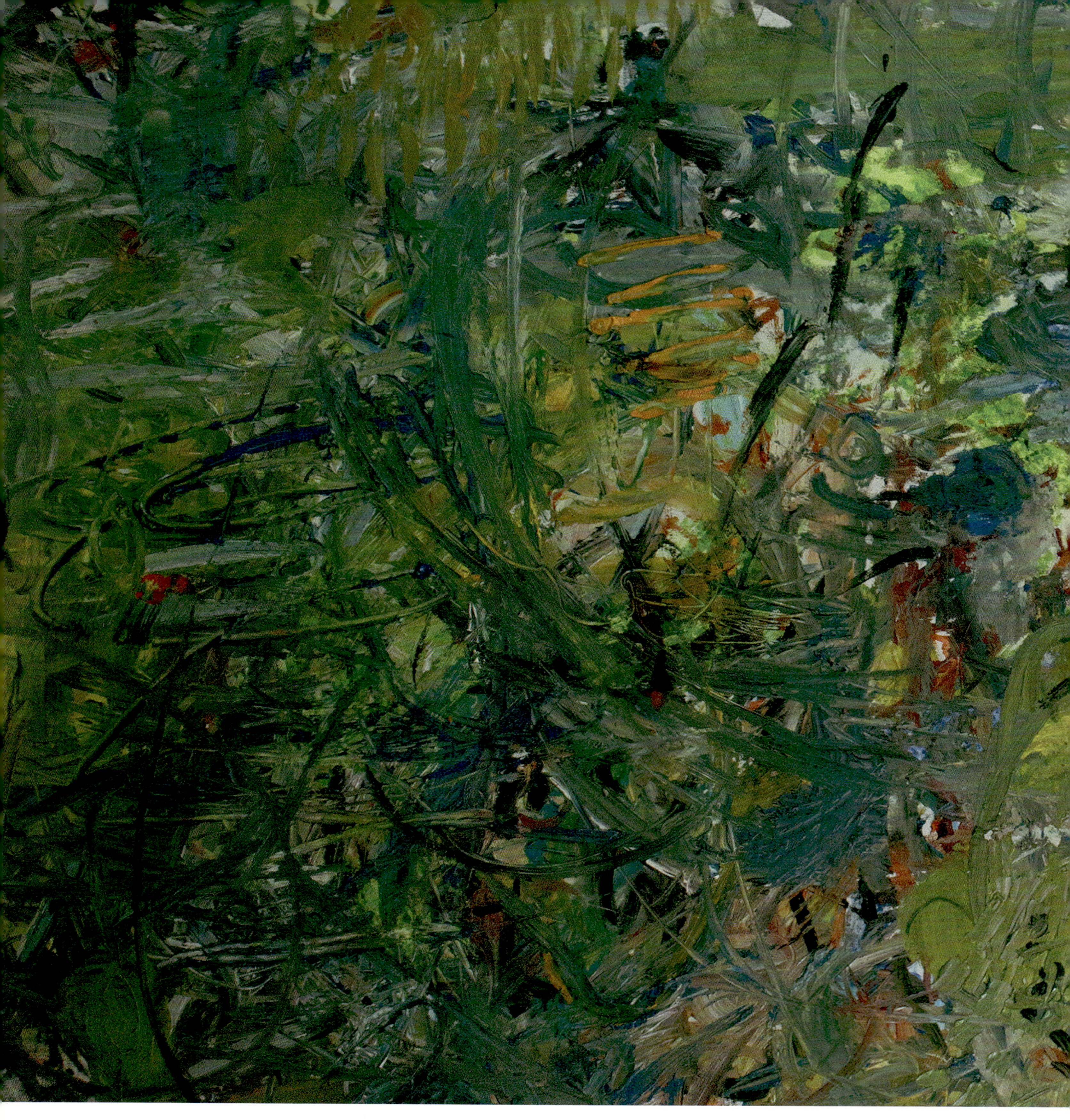

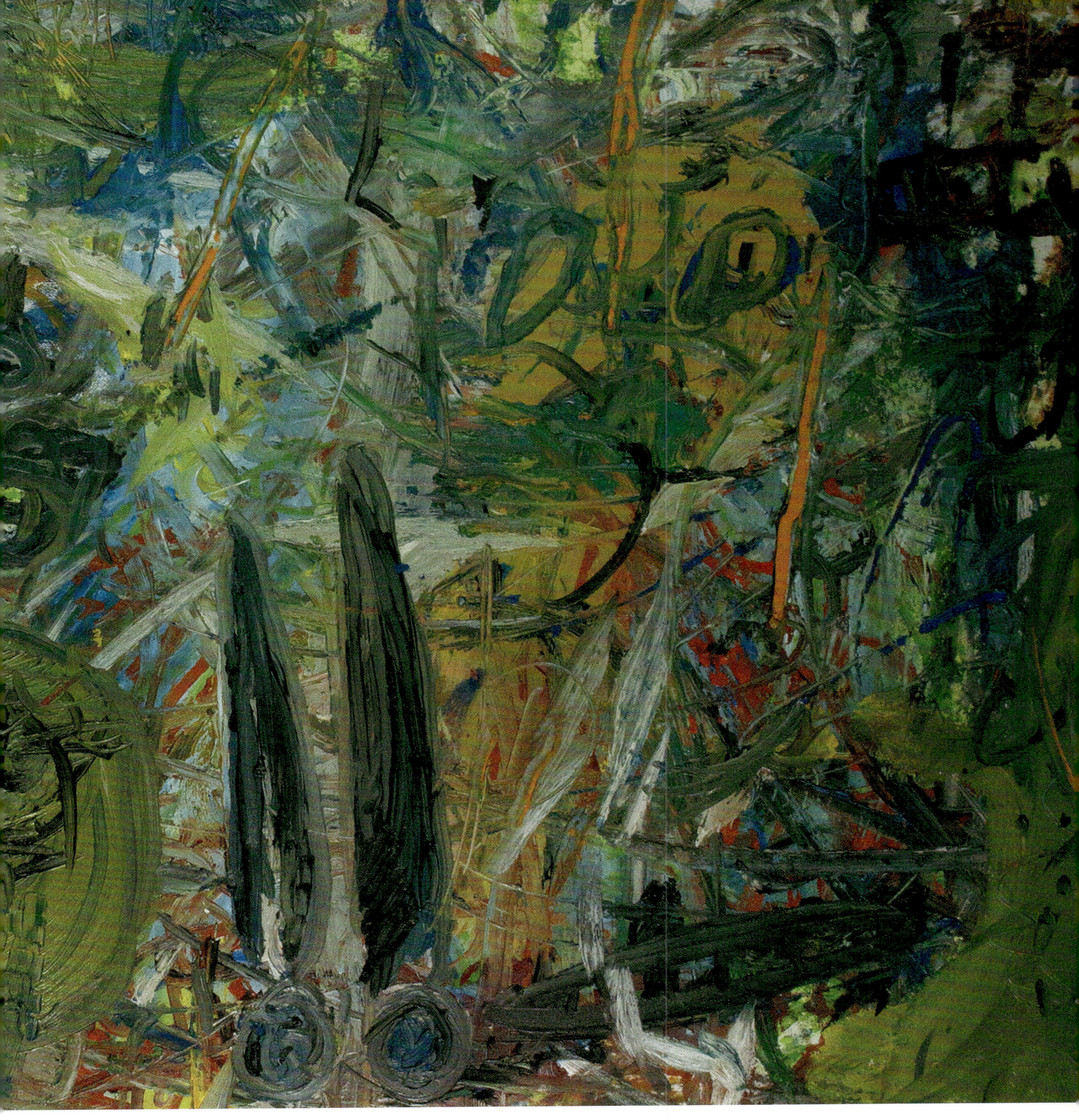

Relative Peace, 2010

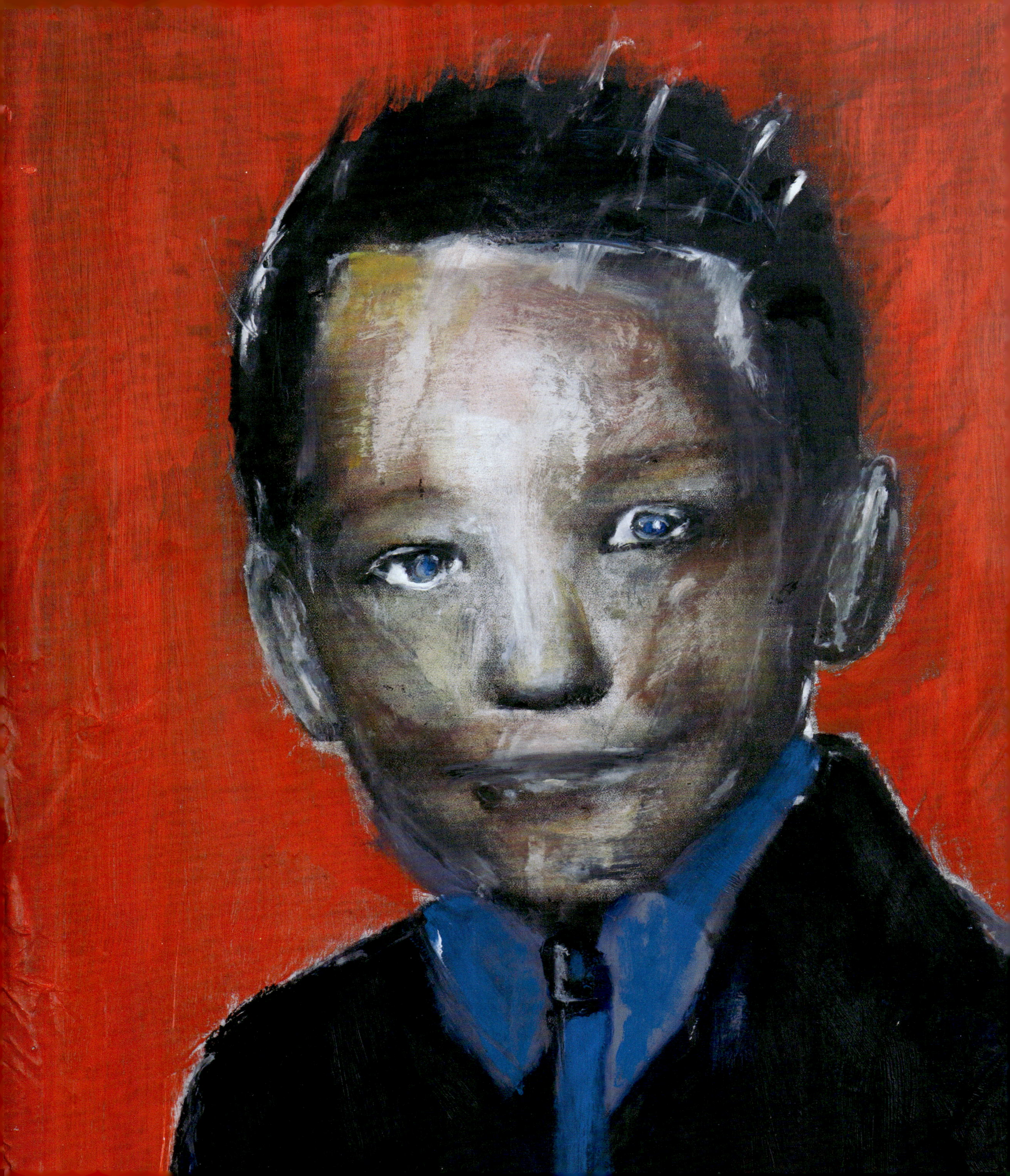

Preface

Shortly after Davyd Whaley died, a friend said to me, "Davyd always saw things the rest of us don't." And indeed it was true. He had a quiet watchfulness. He was intensely curious about other people and the world around him. And yet he also had an otherworldly quality that everyone who knew him seemed to recognize. It almost seemed he was visiting this physical plane from somewhere else. He was wiser, kinder, and more deeply spiritual than anyone I have ever known.

These qualities are reflected in his work; his multitude of paintings and drawings, his journals, and his photos. It is impossible to include all of them here—there are hundreds—but the ones included in this book speak to Davyd's preoccupations. These are the paintings that were important to him. He showed a remarkable empathy, an understanding of the difficulty of the human condition, as well as its joy and ecstasy. His paintings burst with light and life, but also circle back to life's shadow. Since his passing, it has become important to me, his husband, to have a record of his work, to preserve his legacy, to honor the extraordinary person that he was.

I miss the physical presence of Davyd Whaley so very much, but he is not gone. I look at what he has left behind, and I commune with the wonderful spirit that still is. I remain grateful to Davyd for illuminating my life, for allowing me to see what he saw, for giving me a concrete vehicle—his art—to take me deeper into myself and my continued experience of him. I take comfort in what I find there; in the insistence that there is more to existence than this dense manifestation of matter; that we are only energy, here briefly in a physical form, reflecting the scattering of light.

Norman Buckley
May 2016

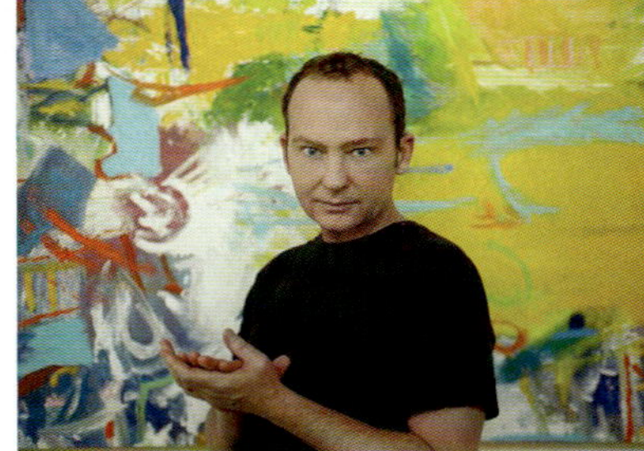

Davyd Whaley, 2011

Opposite:
***Boy in Uniform*, 2013**

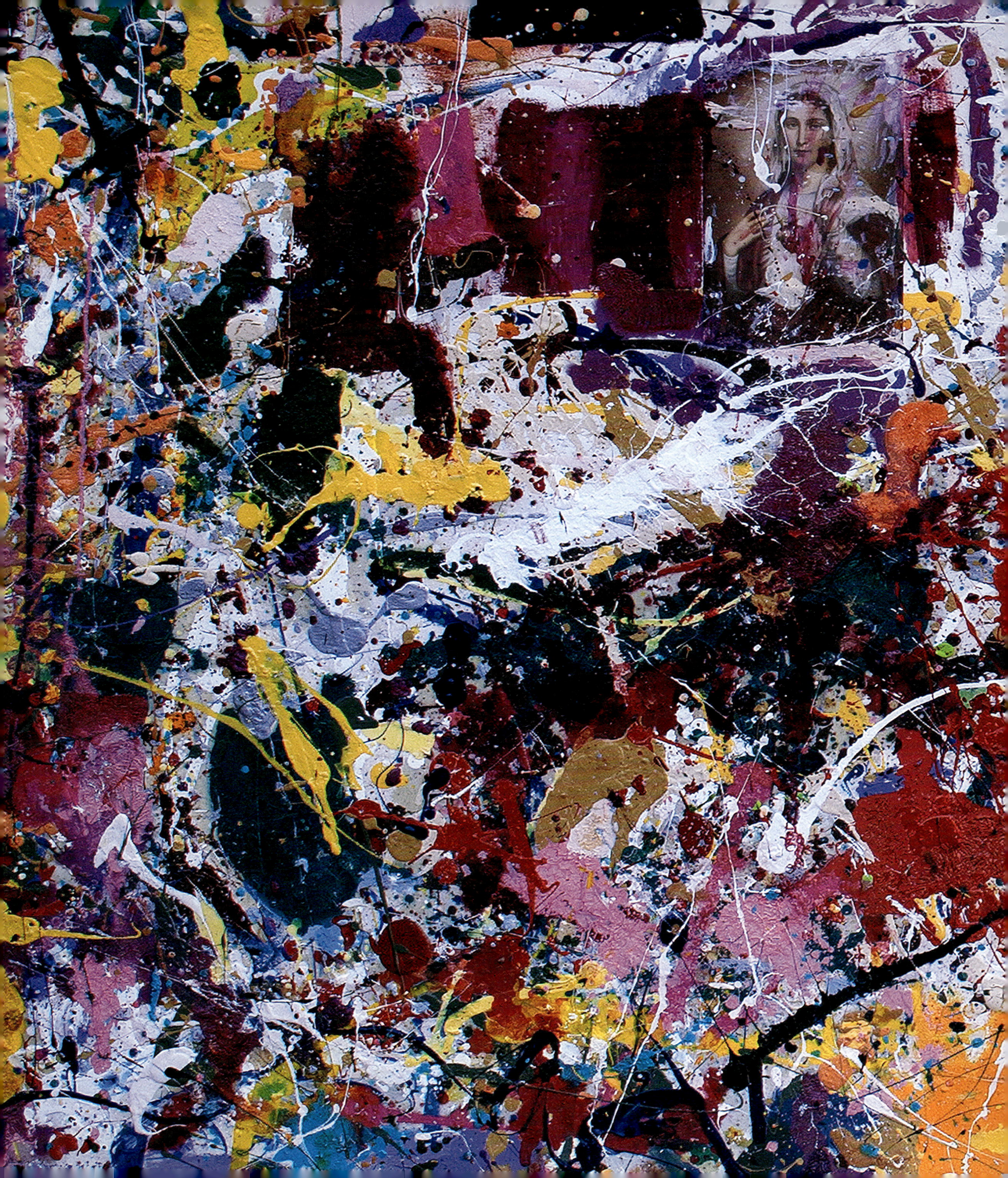

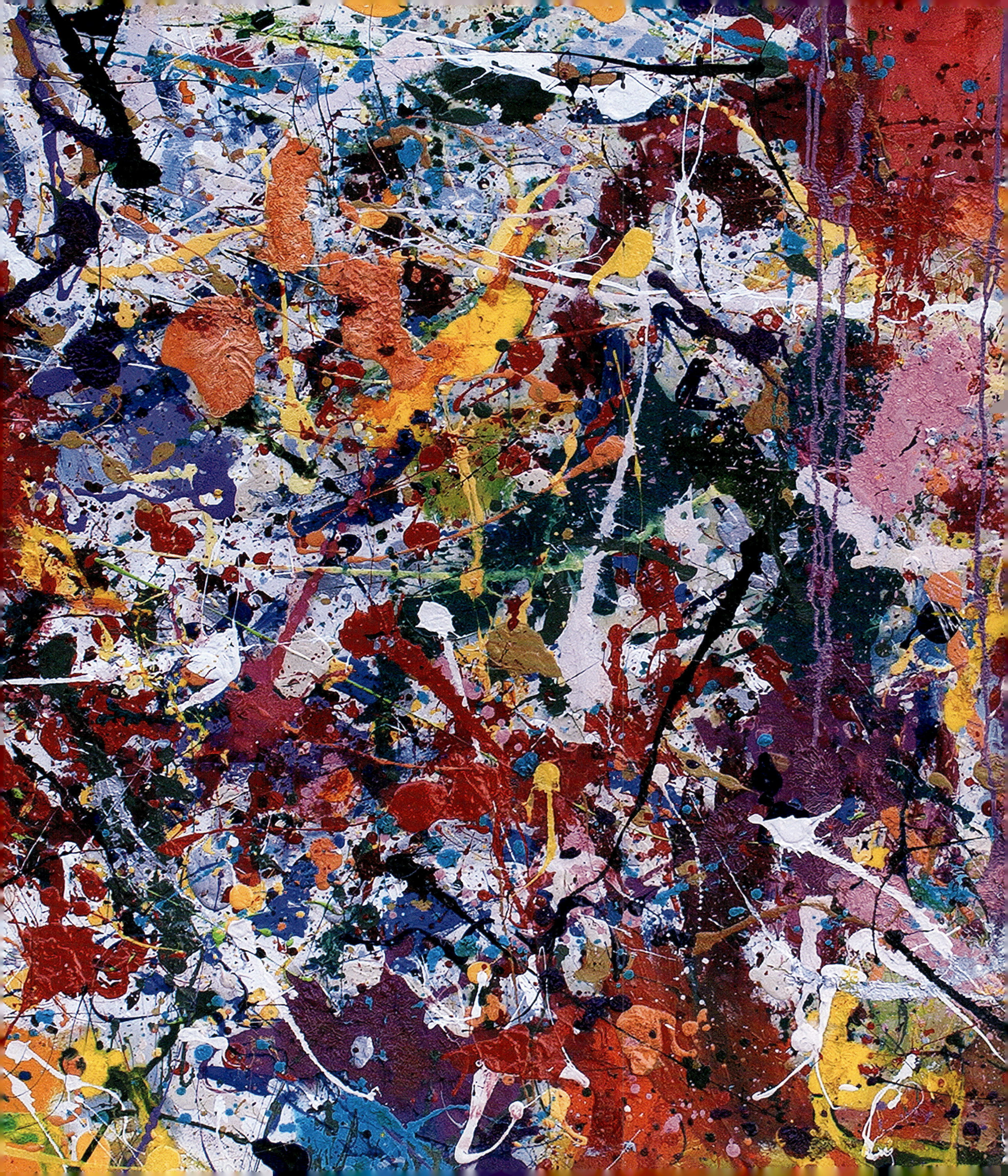

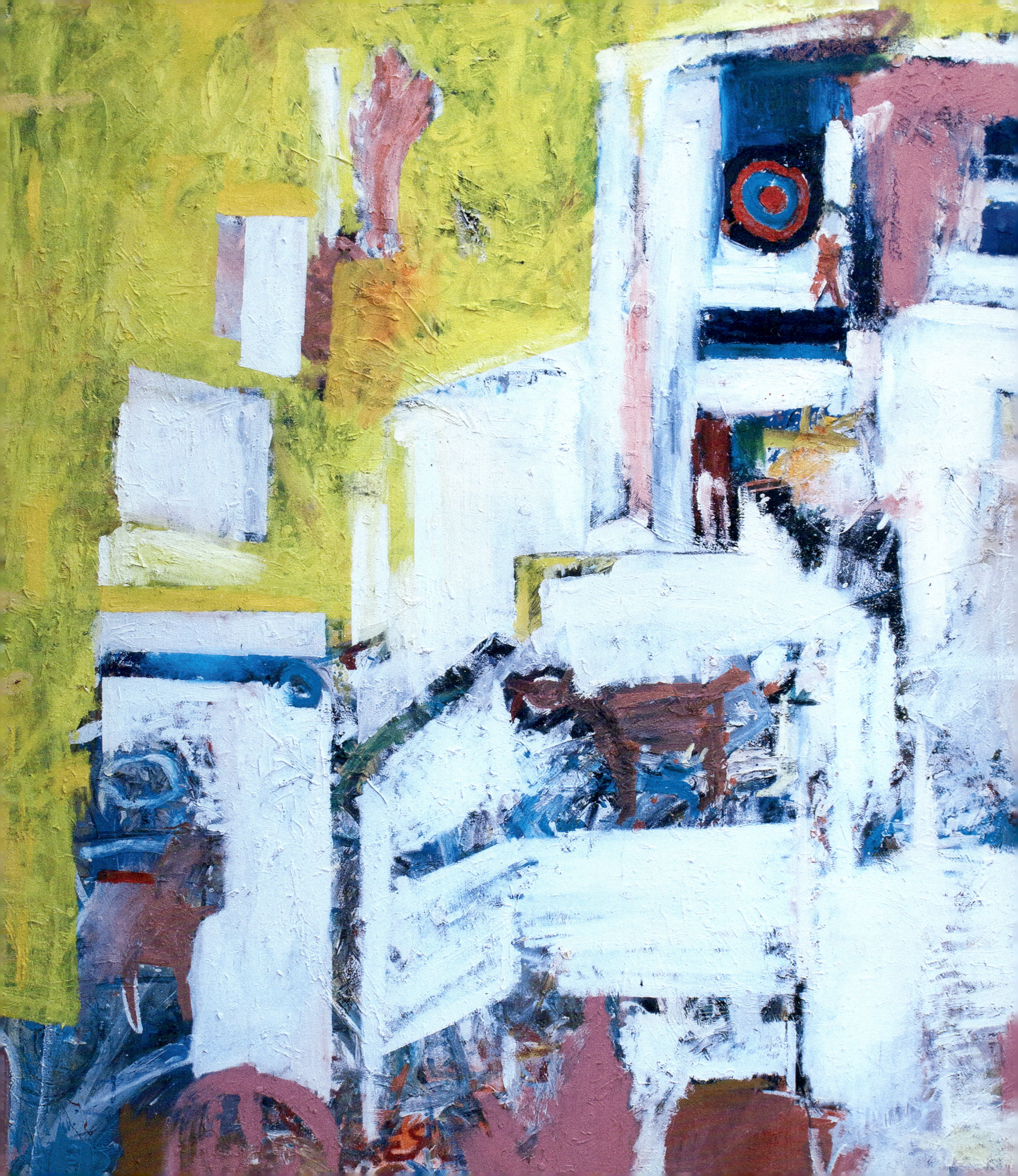

DAVYD WHALEY
A Hero's Journey

Davyd Whaley's paintings offer an exceptional insight into the heart of human creativity at its most impassioned. He came to serious art-making relatively late in his short life, plunging into it with every ounce of energy and skill, and reached the end of his life—and his artistic career—at a tragically early age. In the mere handful of years allotted him as an artist, he progressed with astonishing speed from enthusiastic neophyte to accomplished painter, leaving behind a body of work that is testament to a natural, raw talent, a persistently inquiring mind, and a relentlessly exploratory spirit.

Given the often quirky, peripatetic brilliance of Whaley's creative vision and the intensity of his brief career, it is hardly surprising that some parts of his story, both as a man and as an artist, remain unresolved, sometimes even contradictory. The chronology of his works, for instance, produced for the most part over a period of no more than five years, lacks the more clear-cut "development" that we usually find in the work of an artist, progressing from phase to phase or period to period over many years. In Whaley's *oeuvre*, the practice of representation and abstraction coexist, as do fervid expressionist abandon and obsession with the human figure. Dates, too, are often muddled. Many paintings are undated, and the artist sometimes misremembered or misassigned dates in retrospect. Chronology alone, then, is not a particularly useful guide to an understanding of this work. Because he died before achieving conventional art world recognition, there is also little to draw on in the way of written critical response; the artist's own comments on his paintings are often the best and only resource available.

Eye on Ewe, **2012**

Pages 10–11:
Sacred Heart, **2013**

The biographical information normally available in tracing the maturation of an artist's intellect and skills can also be confusing. Whaley himself reported different versions of his childhood, his memory perhaps distorted by the trauma of those early years. Born on December 6, 1967, he was brought up in the Appalachian Mountains of Eastern Tennessee, where his family life was beset with poverty and ignorance and his childhood scarred by physical, sexual, and emotional abuse. The details are uncertain, but the big picture is clear—and painfully ugly. Even the person closest to him later in life, Norman Buckley, the man who became his partner in marriage and with whom he spent his happiest years, was never fully able to unravel the mystery of his past. "From what I understand," wrote Buckley later, after Whaley's death,

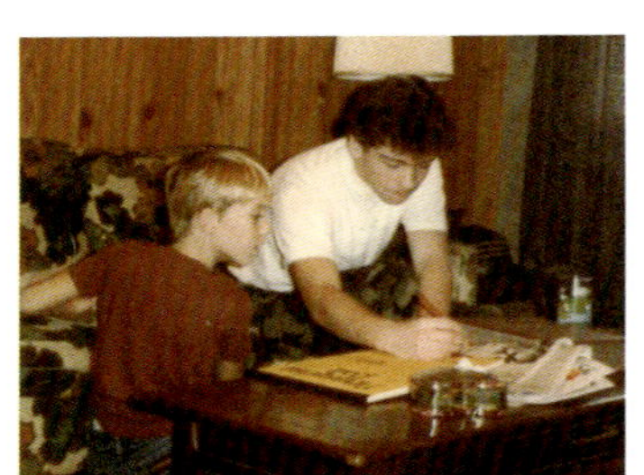
Davyd sketching, with his younger half-brother David, 1986.

> he was abandoned at 3, moved from relative to relative, [and] spent time in various foster homes, before ending up again at some point with his mother and stepfather. In our ten years together he never once mentioned the words "my mother," instead only ever referring to her as "the woman who bore me" or "the female caretaker." As far as I know he never spoke to her while I knew him. He also never spoke to his older siblings. He did speak with affection of a younger half-brother, his father's son by another marriage (also curiously named David, which was why Davyd changed the spelling of his own name) and also some various cousins. But he seemed frightened of re-engaging with any of his relatives, because it seemed to bring up too many painful memories.[1]

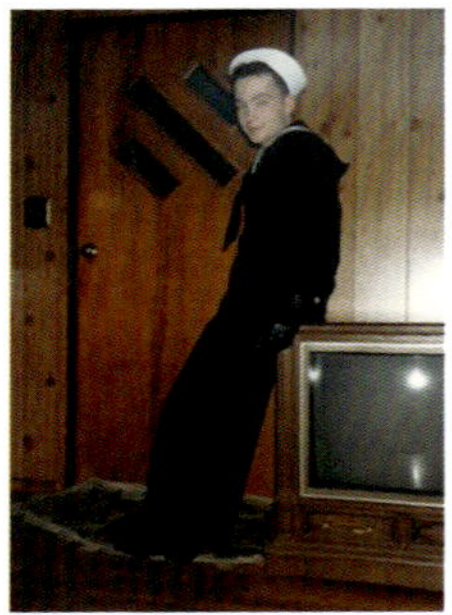
Davyd, 1986

Young Davyd was attracted to art-making at an early age, but his innate talent was neither recognized nor encouraged in an alien, even hostile cultural world, in which he knew that such behavior was regarded as effeminate, therefore reprehensible.[2] For a young gay adolescent beginning to acknowledge his sexual identity, this would have been yet another source of anxiety and self-doubt. After high school graduation, had he been able, Whaley later said he would have wished to go on to college or art school, but such a course was unimaginable to a person coming from his impoverished background. Instead, at the suggestion of the only positive masculine role model in his young life—the caring father of a high school friend, Alesia Leingang—he enlisted in the military. "Knowing that I had few choices out of high school," Whaley later told an interviewer,

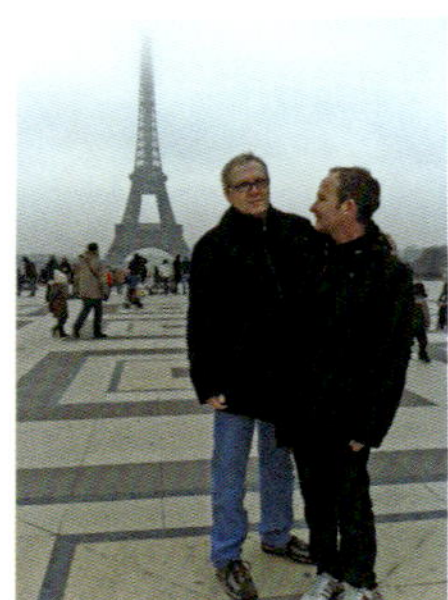
Davyd with his husband Norman Buckley, 2010.

> he encouraged me to join the U.S. Navy, as a way of getting money for college, and he advised me to pursue electrical engineering. [...] My Chief Petty Officer in the Navy was another big influence; he was a figure I idolized and he was also an electrical engineer. The training helped me as an artist, especially the drawing. I became familiar with perspective, line, scale and dimension. It also taught me precision and discipline.[3]

Whaley served in the Navy from 1986–1990, and Alesia, whose father had pointed him in this direction, was to remain his loyal friend for life.

With the discipline, along with the greater social and financial security afforded by his naval training, Whaley enrolled at East Tennessee State University in 1990 and completed a bachelor's degree in Business Administration in 1993. He found employment in the business world and spent ten years working as a successful electrical engineer in the field of information technology. It soon turned out, however, that his life goals and personal ethical standards were not a good match with those of the corporate world—a mismatch that was compounded by the unhealed wounds of his dysfunctional childhood. Confused and distressed by the mismanagement, fraud, and corruption he witnessed in the workplace, he gradually slipped further into a period of physical and emotional turmoil, leading to a serious health breakdown in 2005 and effectively ending his business career.

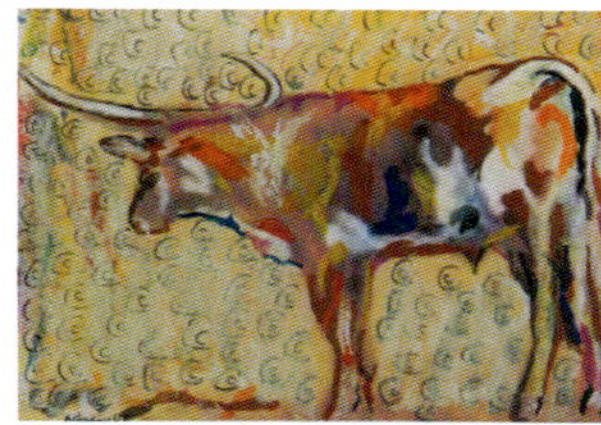

***Longhorn*, 2008 (88)**

By good fortune, already in 2004, he had met and formed what was to be a lifelong relationship with Buckley, who stood by him through two more difficult years of persistent health problems that included seizures and convulsions and necessitated the use of psychotropic drugs. The crisis led Whaley not only into Jungian therapy but also, propitiously, into art. It was in 2005, Buckley notes, that Davyd "started painting, and finding peace."[4]

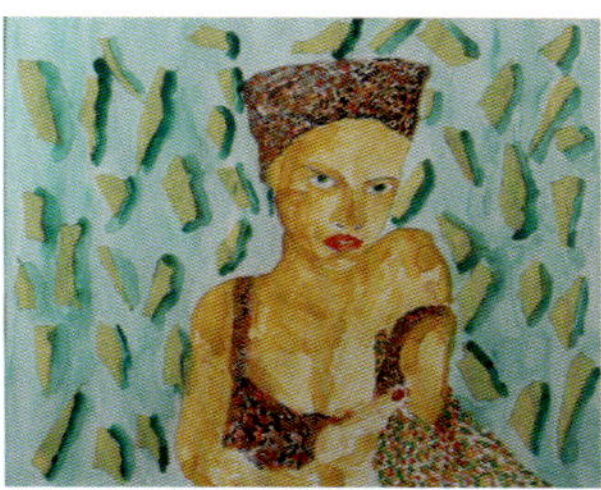

***Green*, 2008 (88)**

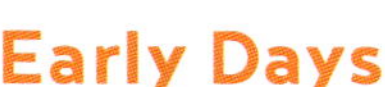

Early Days

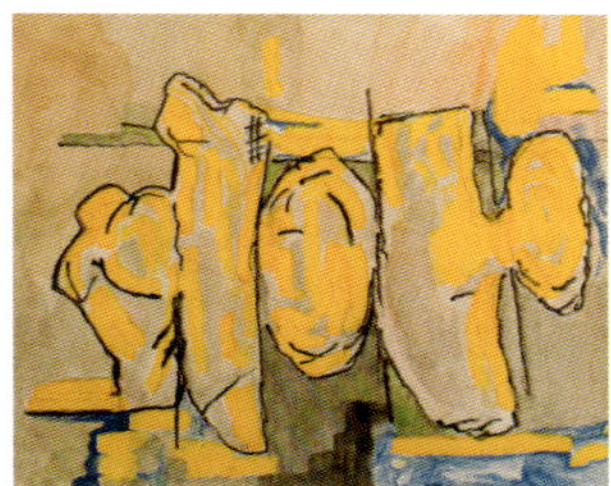

***Elegy*, 2008 (89)**

There remain a good number of surprisingly accomplished, boldly colorful pastel drawings and portraits from sketchbooks that Whaley kept in the years before he began to seriously consider himself an artist. Starting in 2005 and continuing through 2008, it's clear from the sketchbook pages as well as a handful of remaining larger works that he is beginning to explore the skills and sense of purpose that it would take to move from casual, if obsessive and clearly talented amateur, to dedicated painter. He is working in these years not only on paper in graphite, pen and colored pencil, but also on canvas, in oil and acrylic paint. There is a series featuring longhorn cattle—a subject that may seem peculiarly chosen, in the light of his later themes—along with numerous smaller, more intimately scaled works that often focus on other animals, quite frequently on cats. It is not surprising to note, in the images created around this time, that he is also taking a good look at the work of earlier artists. In the drawing *Green* (2008, watercolor on paper), for example, in what he designated as his *Watercolor Series* of 2008, we see the unmistakable influence of Matisse; in *Elegy* (2008, watercolor on paper), a tribute to Robert Motherwell; and in the small oil painting on paper, *Three Heart Chakra* (2008, oil pastel on paper), a clear debt to Jim Dine.

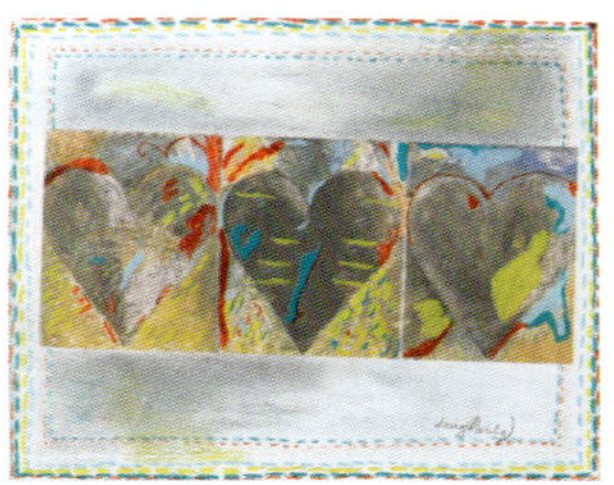

***Three Heart Chakra*, 2009 (123)**

A year later, in *Bathers* (2009, oil on canvas), a group of dancing figures reads like explicit homage to Cézanne and Matisse. These are signs of the thoughtful apprenticeship that every serious artist undertakes, studying and emulating the work of those who inspire him and help cultivate his sensibility.

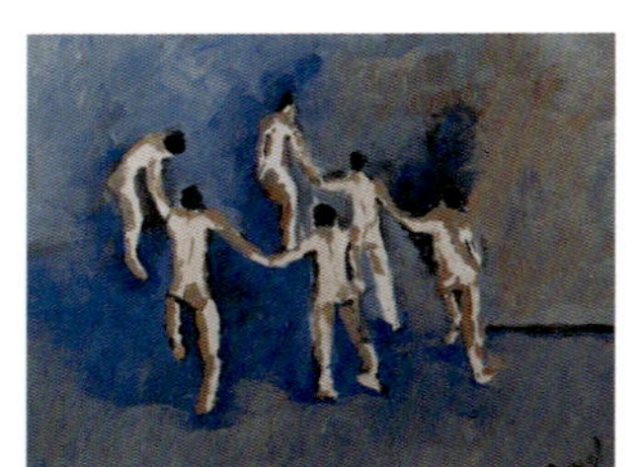

The Bathers, 2009 (88)

Among the most original and ambitious of Whaley's works from this period is *Black Man* (2008, acrylic on canvas), a small 12 × 36 painting that manifests a raw, even passionate engagement with its subject, the naked figure at the center—a figure that reportedly appeared to the artist in a frightening dream. The yellowish-white "shadow" emanating from the nude black male, together with the subtle pink surround, evokes a numinous, somewhat threatening radiant energy, a spiritual presence intuited in an empathetic gaze that engages the viewer in contemplation of the masculine figure's quasi-primitive and commanding sexual power. The delicate touches of coloration—blue, yellow, orange—and the seemingly casual, spontaneous quality of the telling detail of scratched and scribbled lines announce an artist already in command of his medium and capable of authentic emotional engagement. We sense him looking at once into himself for his own emotional response and out, toward his subject, with a serious, sensitive, and objective eye.

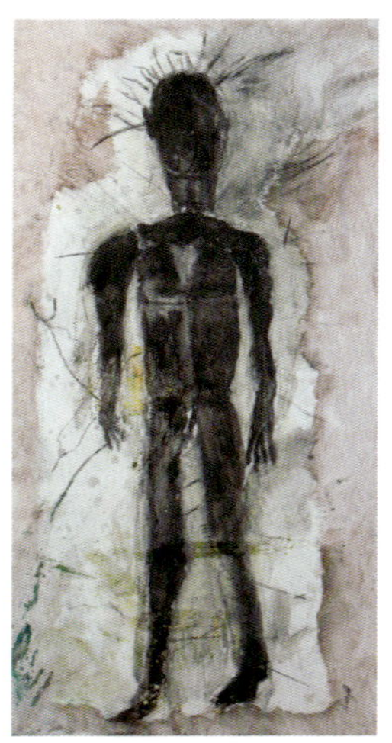

Black Man, 2008 (page 35)

Black Man was painted before Whaley started to attend art classes at New York's Art Students League. In the years 2008–2010, during trips to New York City necessitated by his partner's work as a television director, Whaley found his way to this venerable atelier school to enroll in painting classes taught by Larry Poons and his colleague, Ronnie Landfield—both established professional artists known for their post-Abstract Expressionist work in abstract and color field painting. Under their influence, surely, Whaley's paintings from the period show signs of an increasing sophistication and awareness of modern and contemporary art. They also begin to address some of the themes that will preoccupy him for the rest of his career. *Provider* (2009, oil on canvas) is one among a good number of his paintings that wrestle with the trauma of early family life. Writing about it in retrospect, the artist noted that the image represents "the nuclear family," where "the mother and father are shown as prehistoric caregivers"—an ironic comment on the lack of care that he himself received. For him, "it evokes one of the first paintings I did at six years of age. There is a fair amount of tension in the lines of the figures as I look back at it several years later. It's dynamic, but withholds a lot of information from the viewer. I see myself as the child, not fitting in with this family."[5] The "father" has just killed the bird—the symbol, perhaps, of the child's freedom and creative potential—and the child looks on in terror as this "sacrifice" is about to become the provider's source of sustenance. Associated with young Davyd's classroom collage of a Thanksgiving turkey, this image will recur in later paintings. The vivid neon pink scratch marks between the figures are a dramatic evocation

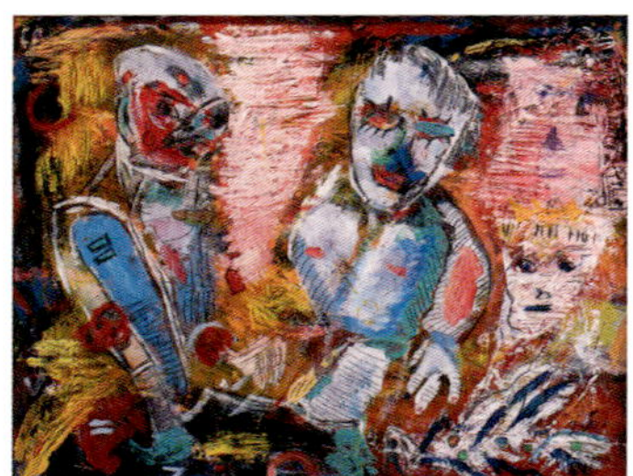

Provider, 2009 (78–79)

of the tension and the threat of violence between husband and wife, father and child. It is a radically disturbing image in its archetypal representation of the human family in a state of primitive, Oedipal tension.

If *Provider* is still an essentially representational painting, it comes at a time when Whaley is starting to move—presumably, again, due to the influence of Poons and Landfield—away from the skill with figurative images acquired in earlier years, and into a highly personalized combination of representation and abstraction. Looking closely at these works, as well as at many of those that follow as he matures, it's tempting to see the abstract surfaces as a cover-up for the pain that continues to preoccupy the artist's attention in many of his paintings. From now on, hints or glimpses of the figure will often reappear behind an agitated abstract surface, as they do in the hidden portrait in *Retrograde* (2009, acrylic, ink and enamel on canvas), for example, and in the suggestion of an eye in the top right corner of *Mayhem* (2011, acrylic on canvas). As Whaley himself put it, he strategically "withholds a lot of information from the viewer," even as he prompts our narrative curiosity with visual clues.

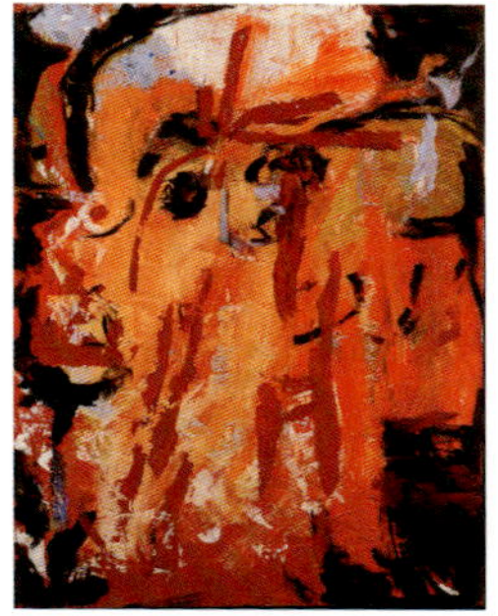
Retrograde, **2009 (115)**

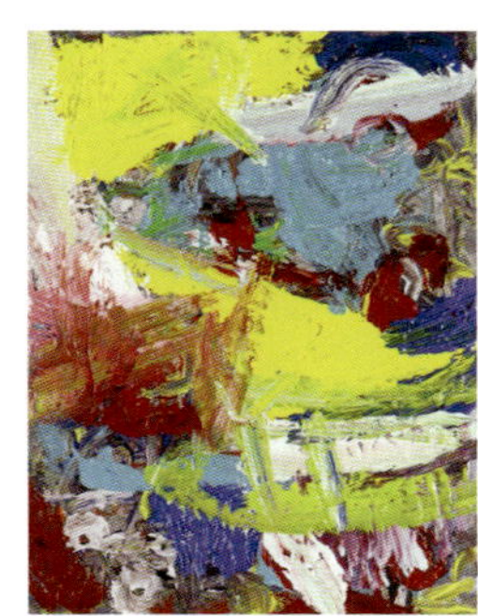
Mayhem, **2011 (57)**

His commitment to art was reinforced in October, 2009, by another severe health crisis, when Whaley's complex of physical, emotional, and psychological issues reached its climax in a major grand mal seizure that culminated in a coma lasting several hours. This crisis, however, proved a watershed moment, a catharsis that irreversibly changed the way he saw himself as an artist. "This period of unconsciousness changed everything," he later wrote, "my relationships, how I viewed the world, and how I wanted to *exist* in the world. My willingness to explore deeper meanings and the connection they had to my day-to-day life became extremely tangible and omnipresent. After that last seizure, I had an epiphany. I woke to the realization that painting was what I was meant to do."[6] He expressed a belief, too, that his work "became bolder and originated from a deeper place" as he "moved away from figurative painting and more into the world of the abstract."[7]

The "deeper meanings" he alludes to were further clarified in an interview for *Artworks Magazine* with the writer Erin Clark. "Before the seizure," he told her, "I was one of those people who looked at people who claimed to be 'spiritual' and said, 'Yeah, right.' Now I get it. I have an appreciation for truth, beauty, and deeper meanings."[8] He came to understand, too, that his dream life offered him access to those deeper meanings.: "I was never interested in dreams before the bad seizure," he told Clark, "but I'm grateful for it."[9] The plethora of journals from this period of his life, disorganized and mostly lacking even the semblance of chronological sequence, are evidence of Whaley's growing obsession with his dreams, and what they have to tell him about his inner life. Part scribbled scraps of storyline, part hasty images sketched out—one suspects—in that state of hazy half-consciousness to which one awakes in the middle of the night, these journals are a mine of insights into a mind that was unquestionably brilliant and, at the same time, profoundly troubled. They are the active seedbed of the artist's creativity and the source material for all his paintings. "The journal," Clark noted in her essay, "is a roadmap of sorts; small snatches of the artist's subconscious brought forward through Whaley's dreams, [...] when pieced together, give him clarity and direction in his life and art."[10] "I wake up with half a thought," Whaley told her, "or a full thought about something, or some image that I just dreamed about. I'll draw it, or write it all down, and from there I go to my dream analyst who helps me figure it out."[11]

Studio

Davyd Whaley in his studio at the Santa Fe Arts Colony, 2010.

This is the springboard, then, from which Whaley launched what was to be the barely five-year period of frenetic creative activity that was the sum of his career as a full-time, fully dedicated artist. It was in the summer of 2010 that he made the commitment to rent a studio at the Santa Fe Art Colony in downtown Los Angeles. He also enrolled in painting classes at UCLA extension. Among his teachers were Max Maslansky and Nick Brown, both of whom were impressed by his raw talent. Aside from Whaley's curiosity and passion, Maslansky wrote in answer to an interview question, "his other strength was his ambition. I got the sense that he couldn't make work fast enough to please his 'muse.' He was incredibly open and receptive to critique and thus willing to try new things, to push himself. He seemed completely unafraid of tackling large-scale paintings, and lots of them. He was constantly evolving." Whaley's painting, he added, "was unique, and it had a certain brutal, but sensitive force to it."[12]

The Santa Fe studio had the space and light the artist needed to put that "brutal, but sensitive force" to work. His process was a ritual. "He rolls out large pieces of unstretched canvas on the floor [...]" wrote Erin Clark, "mixes eight to ten different paint colors and places them in small plastic bowls around the canvas, turns on his music, usually jazz but when he's really feeling it he sometimes opts for the energy of groups like Nine Inch Nails. With everything in reach, brushes in hand, and a Trent Reznor serenade turned up to full volume, Whaley settles in for a 12-hour painting marathon—trying to catch a dream."[13] The artist himself describes his process in these words:

> In [...] technical terms, I am drawn to asymmetrical forms and the energy and power provoked from the contrast of light, depth and color. I paint by building up thick layers of pigment with a palette knife to more effectively achieve special color effects. A raised surface is important in my paintings to convey feelings and contribute a three-dimensional effect to the overall piece. My finished pieces contain meandering strokes, thick with color and texture. I paint in episodes,

> each work expressing a moment; each canvas a spiritual sequence, like dreams linked in our subconscious by ethereal themes or meanings.[14]

Poons was particularly influential. He encouraged him, Whaley noted, "to be very physical. He encouraged me to add more color. He kept asking how one could know what one wanted to paint until one had covered the entire canvas. He kept saying that a painting must have symmetry and it must have light."[15]

These became the principles that freed Whaley from conventional restraints and guided him in his new period of frenetic activity. Aside from the physicality involved in the act of painting, the strategy of working from above and from all four sides of the canvas also erodes the rational, quasi-narrative constraints of horizontality. By the same token, it tends to free the artist from interference from the rational, conscious mind, enabling him to project his energy exclusively into the physical action of applying paint. It is notable, of course, that Jackson Pollock worked precisely in this way, allowing himself the spontaneity and unfettered freedom of expression that he modeled for so many artists who came after him. The dream images, so important to Whaley as he worked, could be allowed to emerge and be subsumed into the surface of the painting as a part of the action through irrational, non-narrative impulse. Noting Whaley's "very strong intuition for putting things together poetically," his teacher Nick Brown encouraged him "to explore these approaches and attitudes with even more vigor, making the materiality more visceral and creating more contrast between the elements."[16] Throughout his career, Whaley felt free to combine graphite drawings and found objects with paint, his primary medium, especially where they helped, in Brown's words, "to create dynamics and poetic relationships."[17] It is this interplay with images, some evident on the surface of the painting, others partially or wholly hidden, that contributes to the cryptic lyricism of much of Whaley's work, often flirting with explicit meaning, often rejecting it, often simply dancing with its possibilities.

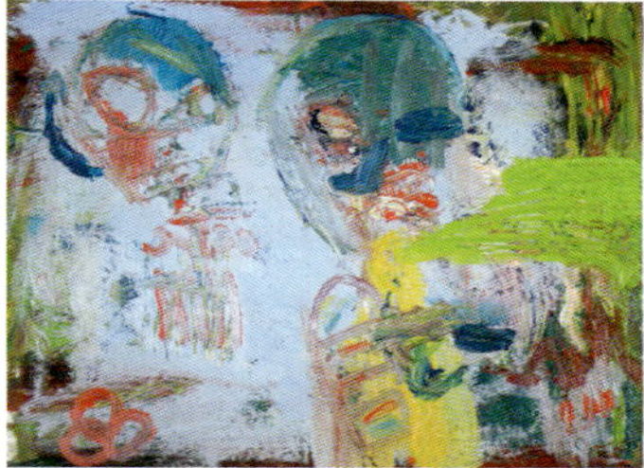

***Guardian*, 2011 (70–71)**

In this direction of his work, Whaley was profoundly influenced by his meeting in early 2012 with the painter Franklyn Liegel. Liegel was teaching at the time at Otis College of Art and Design, and chose Whaley's *Guardian* (2011, oil on wood) for inclusion in an exhibition he curated at Topanga Canyon Gallery. "When I saw your pieces in the slide registry," he later wrote in the email correspondence that followed their meeting at the show's opening. "I was intrigued. I felt the work was very poetic."[18] In a later email, he added, "May I be presumptuous in saying that we both love paint? [...] We seem to love the same artists [...] how they make their work, the process. It's a kind of madness... This love of paint is truly wonderful."[19] He shared with Whaley his enthusiasm for the avant-garde, neo-surrealist European art group COBRA (for COpenhagen, BRussels,

Amsterdam), comparing his (Whaley's) work to that of a Belgian artist known by the single name, Corneille, a painter much influenced by Joan Miró and Paul Klee. Whaley also relished a gift from Liegel, a copy of James Elkins's *What Painting Is*—a book in which the author likens the painter's work to that of the alchemist, spinning one substance, his raw material, paint, into something entirely new. "The book took me out of my head and into a new place with my studio practice," Whaley wrote later. "I began to think about paint differently. To me, the book seemed like a history of paint in an alchemical sense. It went way beyond painting as a creative process and took it into the world of medieval chemistry."[20]

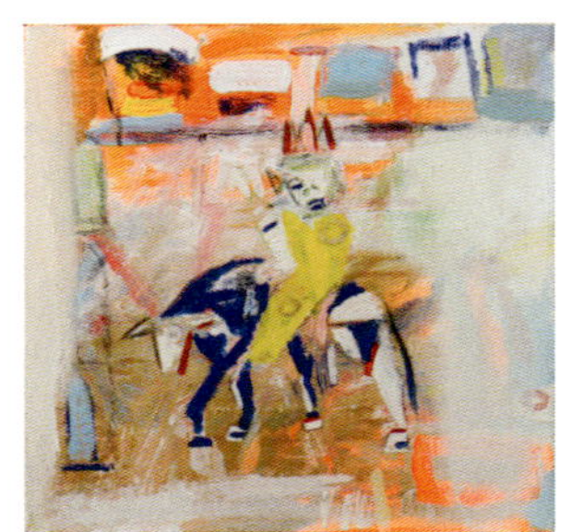

***Hero, The Fool*, 2011 (129)**

Deeply affected by Liegel's sudden and premature death in March, 2012, after what was for him an exhilarating but too short a mentorship, Whaley came away from it with a new sense of encouragement for his love of the sheer materiality of paint, for the poetic vision that guided him in his work, and for an understanding of the creative process as a transformative one: "The lessons I learned from Franklyn and the book are about the hard transformation that physical paint must go through. All the chemical bonds and reactions are similar to the transformations which people go through when experiencing transference and psychological growth."[21] Above all, with Liegel's express encouragement, he insisted on the freedom to create as he saw fit. "I am motivated in my art-making process," he wrote, "by a rejection or refusal to accept the norms. I consider myself to be self-taught, with many non-traditional methods, including: Let's break it and put it back together."[22]

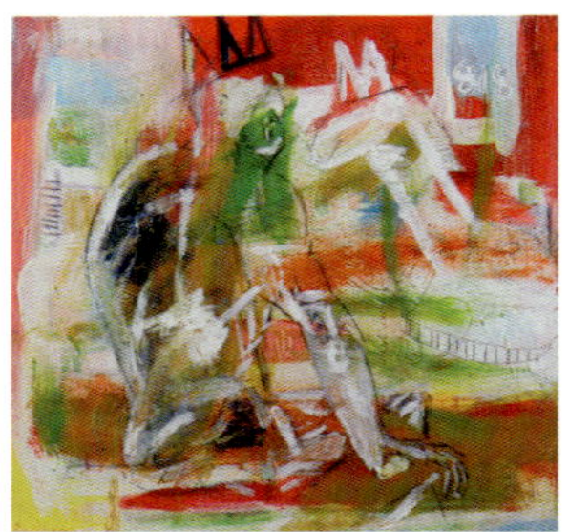

***Hero I*, 2011 (130)**

Hero

If there is a trajectory to the path that Whaley followed between the years of 2010 and 2014, the year he died, it is that of the Jungian hero's journey. *Hero*, indeed, is the title he gave to a series of paintings that, despite their small size (each is no more than 10″ × 10″), offer a significant clue to an understanding of his work. The image in several of them is the same—that of a strong male torso in an attitude reminiscent of Rodin's *Thinker*, turned away from the viewer, seemingly lost in contemplation of either a mirror image of the self or, in one case, a sun, the source of light. Each one is adorned with the childishly sketched, three-pointed crown that so frequently recurs in Whaley's figurative work, evoking at once both the hero/king and the king's fool, the court jester. One of the unnumbered series, indeed, presents the hero as a Don Quixote figure, astride a skeletal horse. It is subtitled "The Fool."

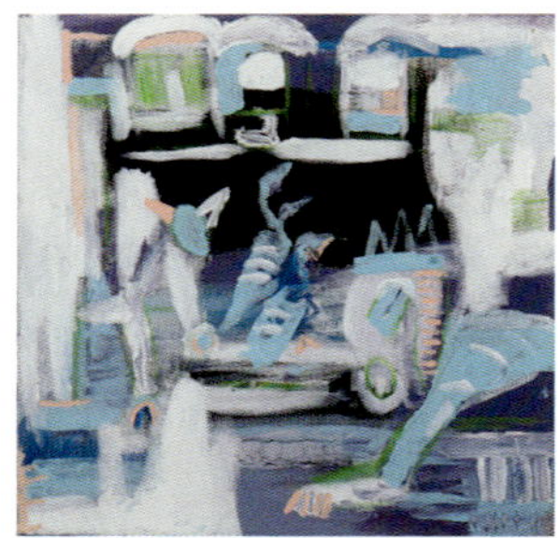

***Hero, Enki*, 2011 (135)**

If we are puzzled by this association of fool and hero, a theatrical analogy may be helpful. In classical tragedy, the hero is inevitably seen in mortal conflict with the gods—

forces representing a rule of absolute and unchanging order beyond human experience or comprehension. In a post-Nietzschian world abandoned by the gods, the existential reassurance of that order is supplanted by its opposite, chaos, and tragedy by farce. (Think Beckett, Pinter, Ionesco...) The hero's journey, however, remains the same, the mythical pattern of descent, ordeal, and return, the quest to escape the darkness and confusion of the human experience and emerge into clarity and light. It is the *Journey* (2011, oil, acrylic and enamel on canvas) to which Whaley's painting of that title refers, with its dark drama, its lightning highlights, its intense blue depths of hope. Looking back on this painting, he recalled, the black and yellow elements reminded him "of two crows, who I call Blackie and Pearl... [who] often appear in my dreams and also on the roof of my house. I think of them as messengers on my life's journey."[23]

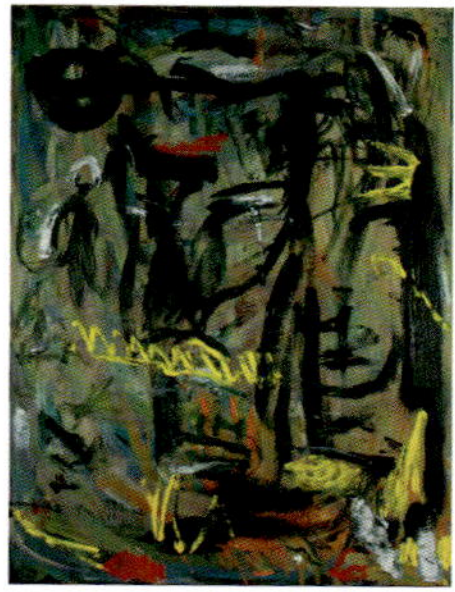

Journey, 2011 (115)

For an artist immersed in Jungian therapy and the world of archetypal dream imagery, this is the essential journey; for one haunted by the chaos of a tormented childhood and still struggling with his demons, it seems inevitable that it be seen in terms of nightmare, inner turmoil, and dark humor. In this light, each one of his paintings is a hero's journey, a quest involving conflict and the resolution of that conflict. In psychological terms, it is the conflict between the chaotic experience of the fragmented child and the adult striving to achieve integrity, maturity, and freedom from the dark side of his nature. In artistic terms, it is the practical, ongoing conflict between artist and medium—the chaos that only the successful painting can resolve.

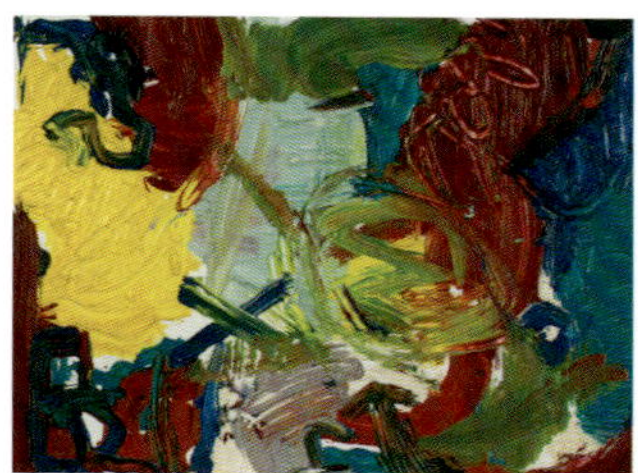

Six-Dollar Water, 2011 (56)

At times, Whaley challenges head-on the persistent memory of childhood neglect and abuse, much of it recalled in dreams and subsequent therapy sessions and noted down in journals. It is the text or subtext in many of his paintings. The titles alone make some of these themes quite explicit. According to notes written by the artist, for example, the early triptych, *Six-Dollar Water* (2011, oil on masonite) recalls the embarrassment and humiliation he felt, with parents unable to make the payment on a water bill. One of the panels, he noted, "shows a green six, the amount of the unpaid water bill, while the white shows the void, the nothingness where the water used to be, our empty faucets, water hoses, kitchen sinks, and dried up bath tubs."[24] In other works, including the pivotal *Child's Play I* (2012, acrylic and oil on paper) and *Child's Play II* (2012, oil on foam board), the imagery of conflict is expressed in representational form on the surface of the painting, along with the suggestion of a narrative content. In a long note written to accompany an exhibition that included these works, Whaley vividly recalls the cowboys-and-Indians play with a neighborhood boy that sparked the memory on which they are based. The paintings themselves are on first impression filled with the drama, the energy and excitement, and the sheer fun of boyhood play; but there is also a disquieting suggestion of terror behind

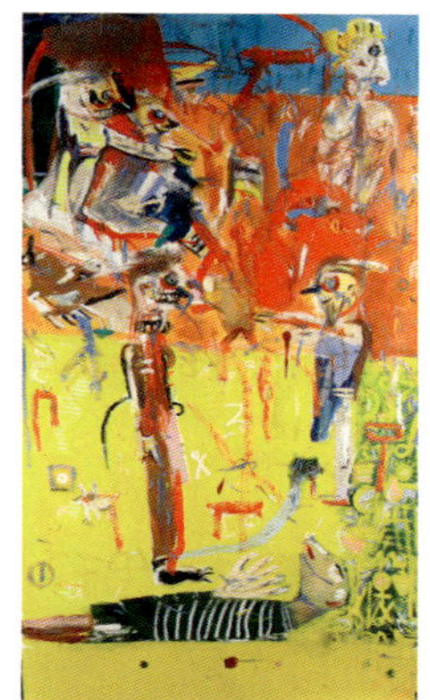

Child's Play I, 2012 (108)

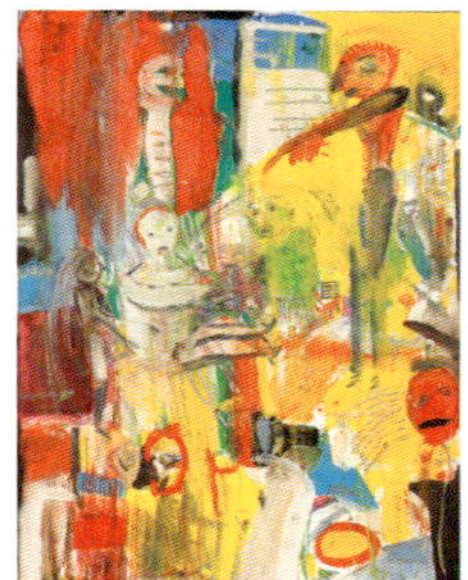

Child's Play II, 2012 (111)

the play, in the grotesque facial expressions and masks of the participants, their sometimes spectral appearance, their threatening gestures, their oppositional distribution in the proscenium of the picture frame. In the larger of the two, *Child's Play I*, we note the looming presence of the "mother" in the background, her attention turned elsewhere, beyond the painting's edge. These action-packed pictures, with their distortions and their agitated surfaces, transcend the "bang-bang, you're dead" fantasy of actual child's play and lead us, instead, into the realm of nightmare. To return to the language of theater the sensibility that informs these paintings—as in so many of Whaley's works—is a combination of theater of the absurd and theater of cruelty.

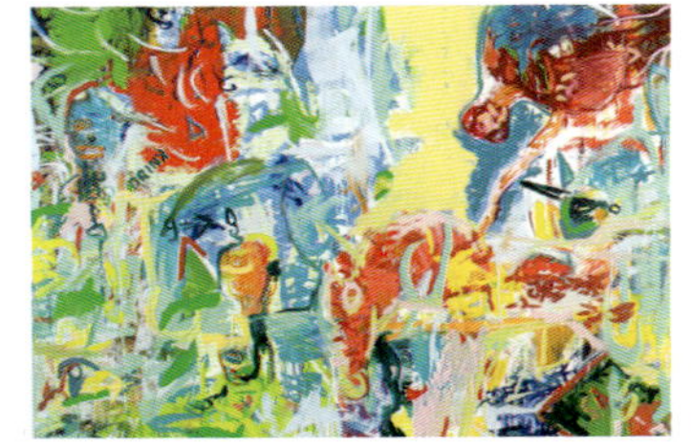

***Angels and Horses*, 2010 (116–117)**

A corollary to the child's insecurity and dread of violence is the longing for protection, which Whaley expressed in several of his paintings, as for example in *Angels and Horses* (oil on canvas, 2010) and *Guardian*. In the former, a careful scrutiny of the surface reveals the vestigial shapes of both angels and horses, but much of the representational imagery remains hidden beneath the urgent, brightly colored, gestural brushwork. Its theme harks back to a popular sentimental print, *Guardian Angel,*[25] that Whaley recalled hanging in the family living room when he was seven years old. "I visualized myself," he wrote, "as the young capped, shoeless boy crossing the bridge,"[26] protected by the looming image of a winged angel. The second, somewhat later *Guardian*, is the image that was juried into the Topanga Canyon Gallery group show by Franklyn Liegel. The painting features dual heads, one of them the spiritual dopplegänger of the other, and a motif of repeated circles—Whaley's symbol for unity and completion. With its muted palette, this image has a less agitated, less fearful feeling than *Angels and Horses*, and Buckley has kept the small, 16 × 20 painting in his own collection as a reminder that "the concept of a guardian—a guardian angel, a parent, a friend, a teacher, a spouse—was something Davyd frequently pondered in his work. [...] We are all surrounded by forces visible and invisible that watch out for us and encourage us on."[27]

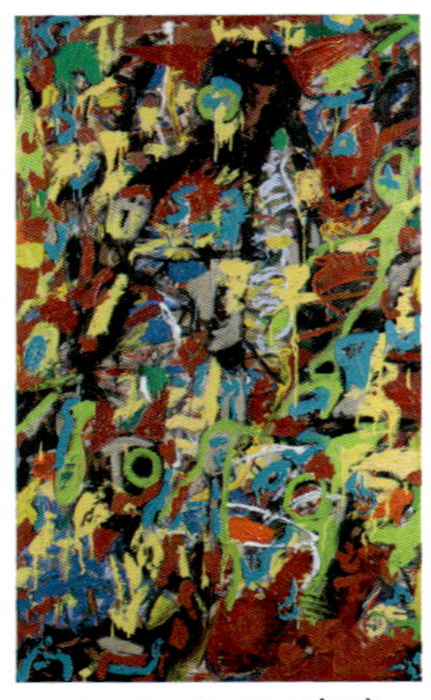

***Nuclear Family*, 2011 (52)**

Other images and symbols associated with childhood memories are buried deeper in the surface of the paintings whose titles alone tell us they address them. *Nuclear Family* (2011, oil on wood), is one such painting; the edgy ambiguity of its title suggests, at once, a necessary cohesion and the potential of massive explosion. Whaley noted that this was "the first time I let everything come out on the canvas about my childhood."[28] In this picture, he wrote, black represents "submission to the father or authority. Red is the color of blood, and expresses the survival instinct. Green is the color of fertility and balance. Blue represents spirit and yellow is the color of wisdom."[29] (Here, as elsewhere, Whaley's notes on his paintings are certainly useful indicators of the artist's intention, but they are highly personal, and generally available only when the viewer is prepared to do some research beyond the actual visual experience of the painting. All artworks must eventually speak for themselves, without requiring explanation or interpretation. In the case of a work like *Nuclear Family*, it is useful to think of the notes as Whaley's way of talking to himself about the painting rather than as an exhaustive or reductive way of looking at them. The child's struggle and its emotional impact are more immediately evident to a patient and observant viewer in the surface of the paint than in words used to describe them.)

There are a number of other paintings made around this time that evoke the darkness into which the hero's journey must descend, and which we may safely associate with the artist's painful past. *Shadow* (2010, oil on wood) is perhaps the darkest of them; from right to left, we move gradually through the turbulent surface to the visceral, blood-hued tumult on the left. Does the clear, white "W" evoke the artist's name, a small voice calling out for refuge from the storm? We may imagine so. Certainly, at the center of the painting, we can discern the outlines of a female figure—the "mother"?—and a skeletal head gouged into the surface of the paint. Emotionally, at the primitive level of the shadow life, the overall image powerfully evokes anger, fear, uncertainty, inner turmoil, the terror of the unknown. From the following year, though less dark, *Cthonic Elements at Play* (2011, oil on wood) is, as its title suggests, another exploratory descent into the underworld; the word "chthonic" derives from the Greek *khthonios*, meaning "subterranean." And the theme of conflict and the search for its resolution is pursued in other paintings of the period. The stark dualism of *Heaven and Hell* (2012, oil and mixed media on paper), for example, makes explicit the struggle between the forces of light and darkness to which the artist seeks to give expression. Here, a blood red sky looms over a chaotic scene in which multiple figures—saints and sinners—vie for space with scumbled or heavily layered passages of paint and scrawled words, some of which are barely legible and others, like "BOY"—a word we know to be fraught with parlous significance—quite legible off to the right edge of the painting. Occupying its own prominent space, "MONET SAYS" reads like one of the notes scribbled in Whaley's journal, a thought or reference passing through the artist's mind as he paints. It's as though he spontaneously spilled the contents of his mind—dream images, mini-portraits, fantasies, scraps of thought—out onto the surface of the paper. We might think the "hell" of the title refers to the experience of inner pain and anger, the "heaven" to the cathartic effect of creating the work of art, with Monet as Virgil to the artist's Dante.

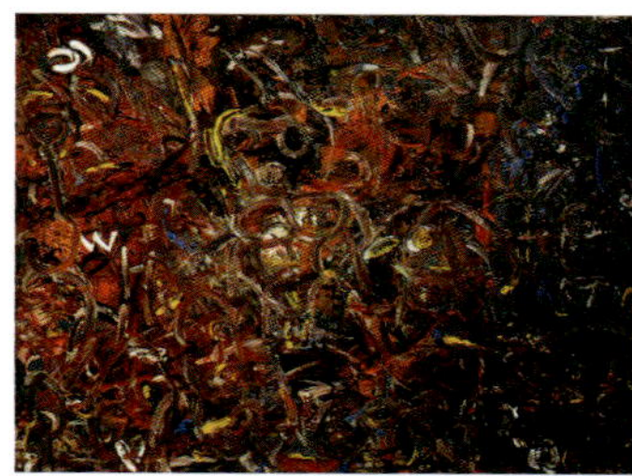

***Shadow*, 2010 (104)**

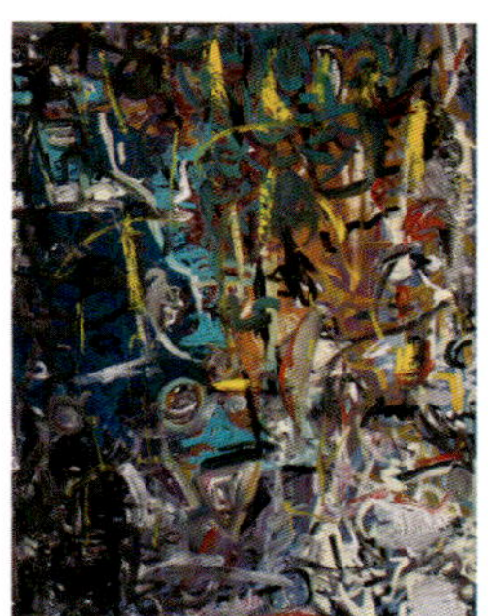

***Cthonic Elements at Play*, 2011 (55)**

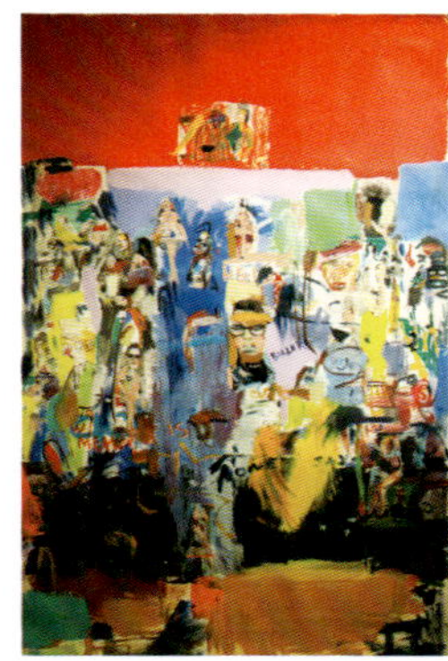

***Heaven and Hell*, 2012 (170)**

The hero's journey is above all a spiritual quest, whose ordeal is the battle with the dark side of one's human nature, and whose grail is "enlightenment"—finding the light, the self-knowledge that leads to inner peace and the recognition of one's place in the world. The emotional turmoil that has its source in Whaley's childhood experience begins to find resolution in the recognition of his "true self" as an artist. As Buckley noted, once he starts painting, he starts finding peace. While we know from his notes that *Relative Peace* (2010, oil on canvas) refers specifically to an episode of personal contention with a security guard and former student at Art Students League, it seems legitimate to see this painting, not as a final resolution of the inner turmoil—the artist is not given to find this in his lifetime—but at least as a step toward inner tranquility. He also notes that he has recently been awed by Monet's *Water Lilies* at the Metropolitan Museum of Art, and the predominance of blues and greens in this painting suggest that he is borrowing not only from the palette of that monumental masterpiece, but from its disorienting inclusiveness. It provides perhaps the earliest example of the kind of "overall" painting approach embraced by Pollack and succeeding artists. Whaley had already discovered in the abstraction taught by Poons and Landfield a method that allowed him to drown his demons, as it were, in a sea of paint. From that same year, the smaller, beautifully executed *Meditation* (2010, oil on masonite) also suggests the trope towards a discovery of inner peace.

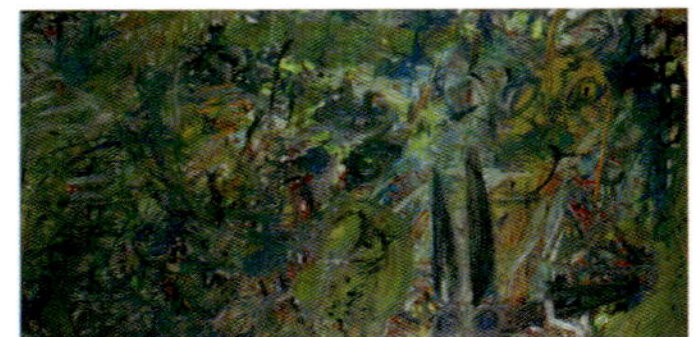

***Relative Peace*, 2010 (6–7)**

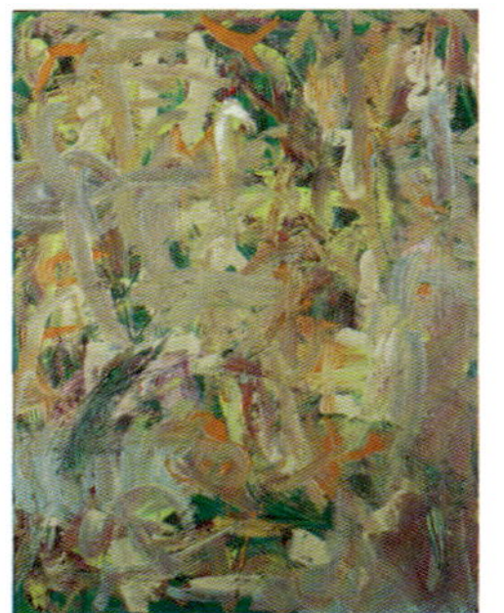

***Meditation*, 2010 (162)**

There is, however, a particular triad of paintings that, for Whaley, represented his most intense and conscious approach to the spiritual quest: *Atonement* (2010, oil on canvas), *Jiva and the Goddess* (2011, oil on canvas), and *Salvationist* (2011, oil on canvas). Originally, the artist tells us, these three were a single canvas, which he cut into separate pieces. He was inspired for the series by the El Greco painting, *Christ on the Cross* in which, he writes, "Christ is portrayed as a sacrifice [...] willing to die for the sake of mankind."[30] We may think Whaley identified with both the artist and his subject, whose vulnerability in the painting appealed to him so powerfully. An exceptionally large canvas in itself, *Atonement* is divided structurally into a number of asymmetrical areas of color, graffitied over with a plethora of inscrutable marks and symbols. What is the sin that needs atonement here? We are offered only a clue in the suggestion of a figure, running as though to escape some unrevealed pursuer—perhaps, we may think, in the attempt to escape his past. In the second canvas, *Salvationist*, seen adjacent to the first, a gun appears to point back at the running figure, and offers a view of him, now crucified, a victim and sacrifice as is Jesus in the El Greco painting. This center panel—if we view the sequence as a hero's journey—is the ordeal, and *Jiva*, the third painting, is the salvation, the ascent. In this third part, Whaley observes in a note, the running figure "is reborn and lives again as a female goddess named Jiva. Jiva refers to the immortal essence or soul of a living being which survives physical death."[31]

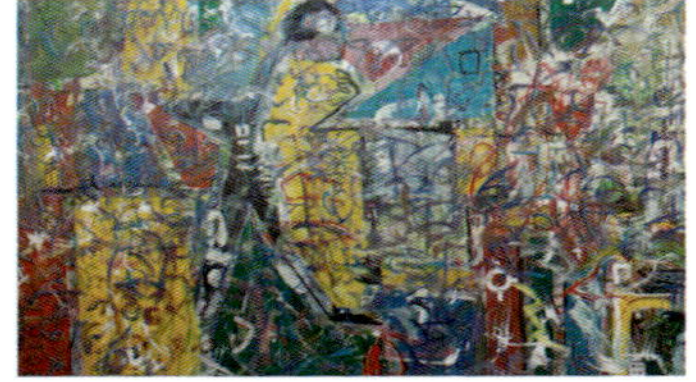

***Atonement*, 2010 (36–37)**

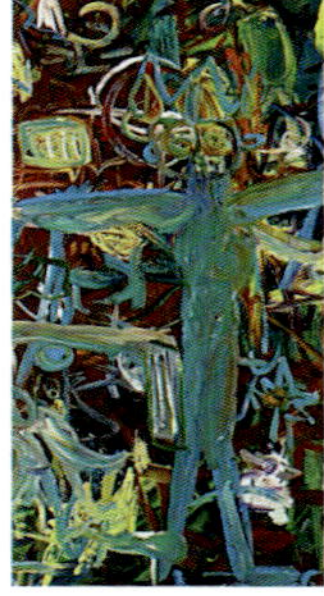

***Salvationist*, 2011 (38)**

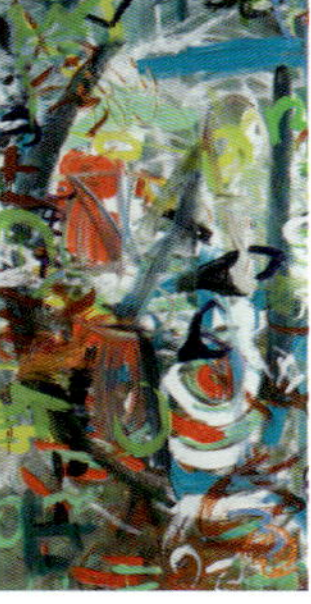

***Jiva and the Goddess*, 2011 (39)**

We may also see in the figure of Jiva the representation of the Jungian anima, the eternal feminine principle, with which Whaley identified strongly in his own psyche and which he explored extensively in his work as the source of his creative impulse.

Anima

No matter the isolation and introspection required by studio work, Whaley never abandoned his artist's curiosity and observation of the world out there—nor his concern for his fellow human beings. As might be expected in a person who had experienced more than his share of suffering in life, he had a highly developed sense of compassion. Outside the

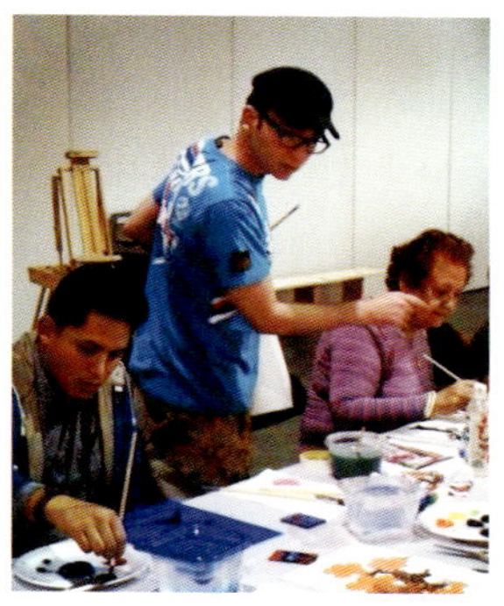

studio, once having concluded that the business world was not for him, he turned his attention to the more humanitarian field of health care, enrolling in nursing school in 2006. The following year found him volunteering at Kaiser Permanente, working to aid and comfort the families of patients in intensive care. He contributed his largest canvas to date, *Fields of Play* (2011, oil on canvas), to a group exhibition in Beverly Hills benefiting The Art of Elysium, a foundation for critically ill children—and it was the favorable response to this painting that opened the door for future gallery representation and the beginnings of a financial return on his paintings that took even the artist by surprise. That same year he was named Volunteer of the Year by Los

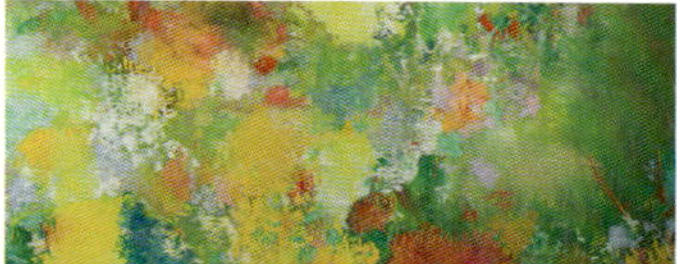

***Fields of Play*, 2011 (44–45)**

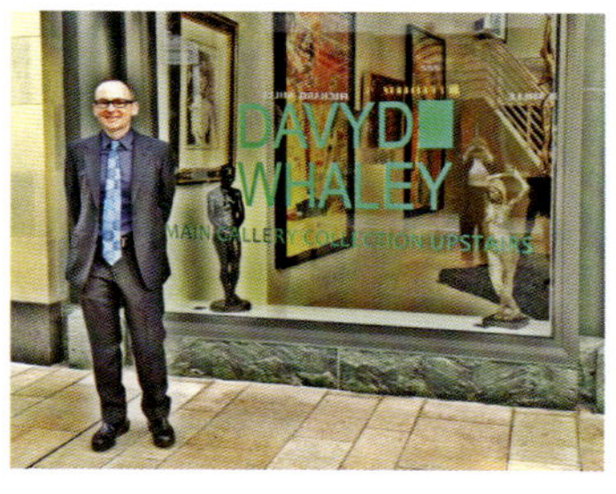

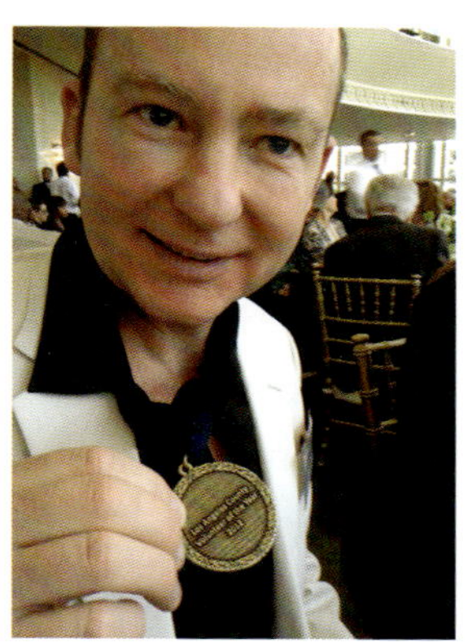

Angeles County for his volunteer work instructing art classes for seniors and underprivileged children at a community center in East Los Angeles.

Whaley cared deeply about people, then, with all their quirks and suffering, and found outlet for that passion in sketchbooks, drawings and other, usually small-format artwork made concurrently with his big paintings. Always ready to probe the depth of his own feminine energy, his anima, he was particularly drawn to women—as they were to him. Fascinated by feminine beauty, he would frequent Fashion Week runway shows on his visits to New York. His *Beauty Series* gave expression to this fascination, exploring both the delights of physical attraction and its attendant emotional cost. Beauty, as he portrayed it, often brought with it pain and conflict. *Beauty 6* and *Beauty 7* (both 2012, acrylic and mixed media on canvas), for example, offer a study in contrast. In *Beauty 7,* the emphasis is on the physical appeal of the model's external appearance, though the expression in her eyes leaves us intuiting a deep inner conflict of emotions. In *Beauty 6*, we see the face of perhaps the same woman, or one remarkably similar, now seemingly bruised and damaged. We find a tantalizing clue to the source of her distress in the prominent police department tag at lower left. In a note he wrote about this series, Whaley said he wanted to

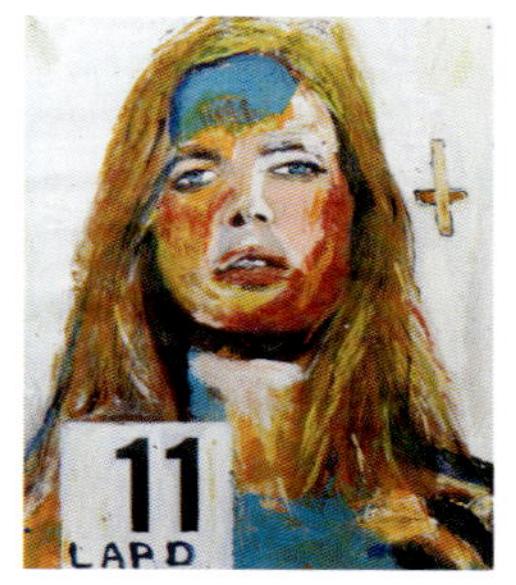

***Beauty 6*, 2012 (94)**

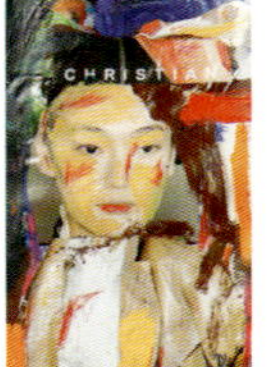

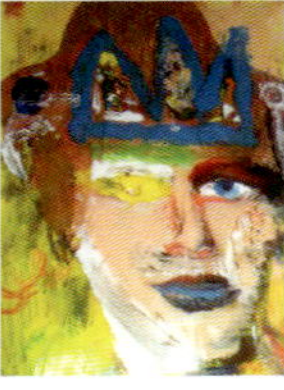

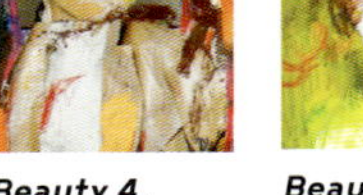

Beauty 4, 2012 (93)

Beauty 2, 2012 (93)

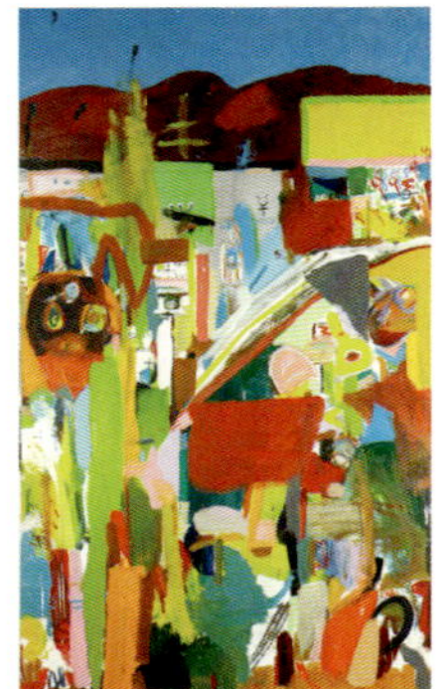

Santa Monica VII, 2012 (168)

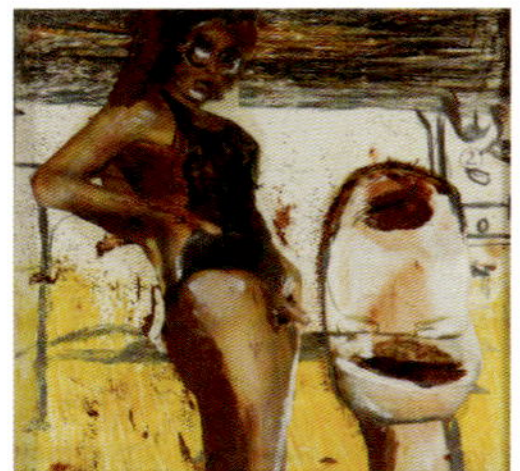

Santa Monica I, 2012 (166)

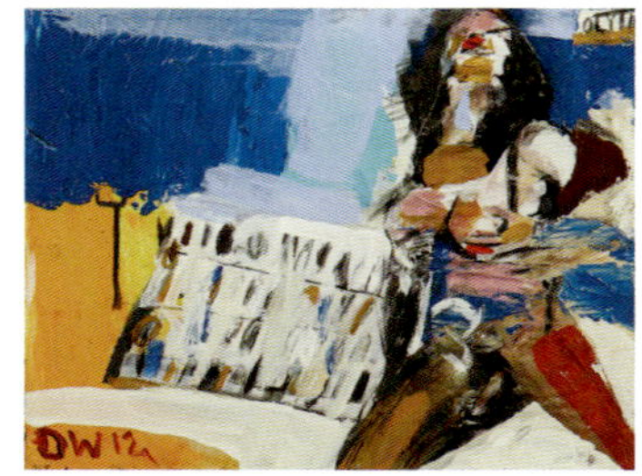

Santa Monica III, Arena, 2012 (166)

address "the misunderstandings that occur in our society, when people assume that beautiful people are perfect."[32] Thus, these small images celebrate beauty even as they seek to humanize and place it in a meaningful social context. Typically, as in *Beauty 4* (2012, acrylic on paper), Whaley embellishes collaged photos clipped from a fashion magazine with acrylic paint marks that are used to alter, enhance, or sometimes deface the socially sanctioned definition of feminine allure, replacing it with something more real, more disturbing, and more emotionally complex. That familiar, awkward three-pointed crown from the *Hero* series appears again on the subject's head in *Beauty 2* (2012, acrylic on paper), suggesting that this woman, too, lives in a world where the purely beautiful and the grotesquely comic coexist. This clumsy crown transforms her from fashion icon into a figure of quasi-tragic farce.

Also from 2012, the *Santa Monica Series* is a related series of, again, mostly small-scale paintings. The "Santa Monica" of the title is not the upscale beach city where Los Angeles sprawl meets the Pacific Ocean; this is the Santa Monica Boulevard of West Hollywood, a bustling, racy mecca of the gay community. Whaley writes about his inquiry into its diversity and excitement in graphic detail:

> I studied people of interest, interviewing them, making many sketches, photographing them with a Polaroid camera and set up story-boards in my studio [...] I also photographed interesting buildings and landmarks which caught my eye in the evenings as I walked my dog, being most interested in the transgendered females wearing brightly colored clothes, small boutique buildings, [a] Spanish colonial apartment building painted in muted pinks and greens, which repeated along the boulevard like cloth sewn on a blanket.[33]

Santa Monica VII (2012, oil on canvas) is by far the largest image in the series. It invites the eye to explore the visual patchwork of shape and color he evokes so expressively in words. "I want the viewer to travel when they see the painting as a whole picture," his notes tell us, "[and] let their eyes move over the painting without fixating on specific forms."[34] With its clear blue sky, its mountainous horizon and its brightly colored buildings, *Santa Monica VII* summons the aura of West Hollywood with the delighted observer's eye of a David Hockney—an artist to whom he also alludes in his contextual note. Significantly, too, he refers to the painting's "push and pull," the trademark teaching of Hans Hoffman, whose influence is evident in both the coloration and the composition of this lively painting.

Appropriate to the culture of its particular urban setting, the *Santa Monica Series* also explores the theme of sexual ambiguity with playful curiosity. For all their small scale, the paintings addressing this theme are assertive, even aggressive. The first in the series, *Santa Monica I* (2012, oil and mixed media on clayboard), features a coyly posed figure of mixed gender, breasts prominent and sexually suggestive, with a penis pointed into an open toilet bowl. Numbers *III* and *IV* in the series similarly feature exuberant female figures flaunting male sexual parts. These works suggest that ambiguity and the conflation of male and female identity is an important part of Whaley's own psychic core—not as emotional conflict, in this case, but as the object of continuing interest and investigation. In *Anima* (2010), oil on canvas), we revisit the two crows—he frequently refers to them as ravens—in whom he sees companions on his life's journey; here they attend the central, androgynous figure that might double as the artist's self-portrait, given the urgency of the palette knife and brush strokes and the intense, painterly scrutiny of the face, all of which suggest a passionate and personal engagement with the subject. Red—the color of blood and passion in Whaley's lexicon—and blue, the color of spirit, blend into an evocation of body and mind together, the integrated psyche that includes, in all of us, the female energy along with the male, or, we might say—particularly in view of later works—earth along with sky.[35]

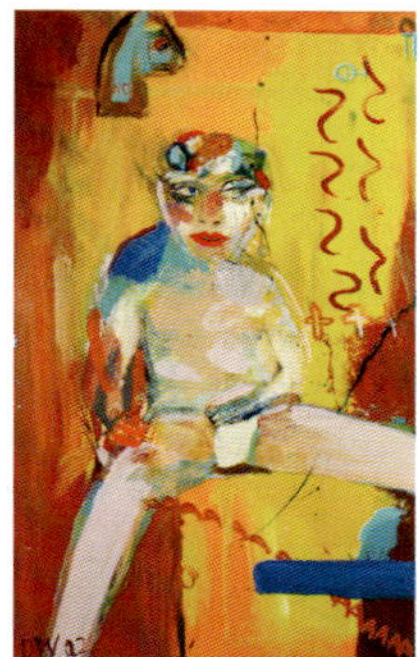

Santa Monica IV, 2012 (165)

Fertile Instinct (2013, oil and objects on canvas), made in the course of a stay in New Orleans, represents a different manifestation of anima. Again, the artist tells the viewer more about the painting's history in a note: "The doll in the top right section [...]," he writes

> has been sewn onto the canvas. It is a ceremonial voodoo doll, a totem for success, which I bought at the Marie Laveau House in New Orleans. The wooden doll in the center of the painting is from the Ghana Ashanti tribe. I found it one day while walking through the French Market. The person I bought it from explained to me that Ashanti women carried this paddle with them in hopes of having a child. I instinctively put these objects in the painting, where they logically made sense without any preconceived notions. It is a very innate archetypal image of the mother.[36]

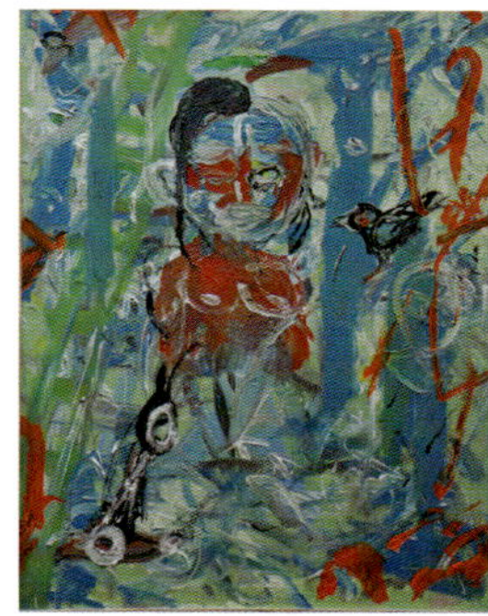

Anima, 2010 (59)

The emphasis in the painting then, with its tribal attachments, its confrontational predominance of blood red color and its prominent, visceral drips of paint, is on the primal stage of anima, fertility and birth, rather than on the nurture and mothering that follow. It is a different manifestation of anima entirely that appears in *Sacred Heart* (2013, oil, enamel and mixed media on Arches paper), also made in the New Orleans studio. It combines a collaged image of that archetypal, compassionate "mother," the Virgin Mary, amidst a spectacular display of color. Represented here, Whaley's accompanying note tells us, is the maternal principle that was absent from his life, the one that involves "sacrifice, protection and unconditional love for all people."[37]

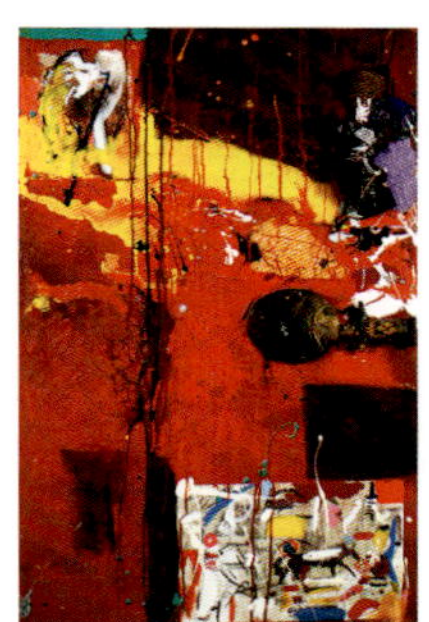

Fertile Instinct, 2013 (120)

That universal embrace finds visual expression in the painting's overall, edge-to-edge quality. Save for the collaged photographic image, there is no up or down, no left or right in the way the paint is applied to canvas; and in a good number of other works of this kind, we find Whaley engaged in exuberant, even joyful painterly action. There is an early manifestation of this mood in the monumental scale of *Fields of Play*. This huge, 64 × 149

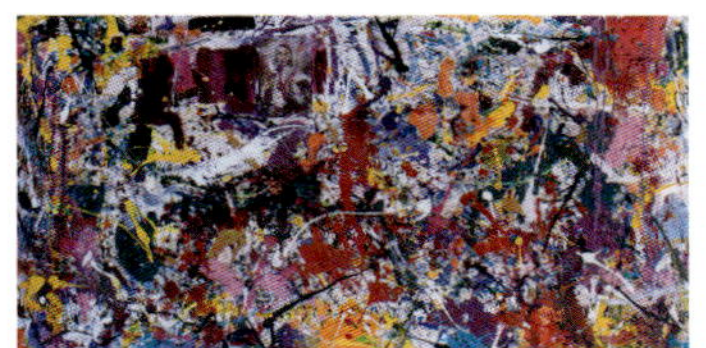

Sacred Heart, 2013 (10–11)

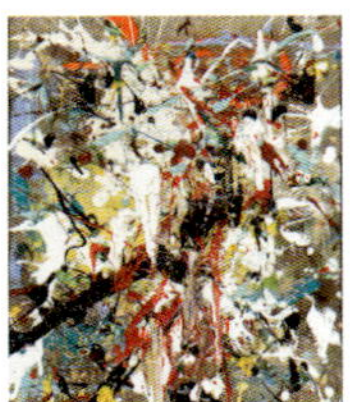

Triumph, 2013 (53)

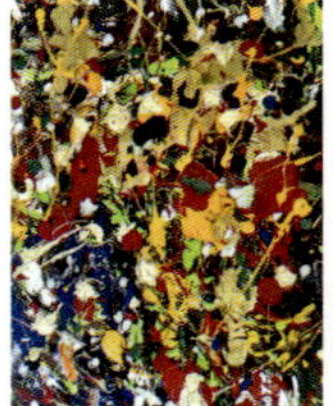

Tomahawk, 2013 (57)

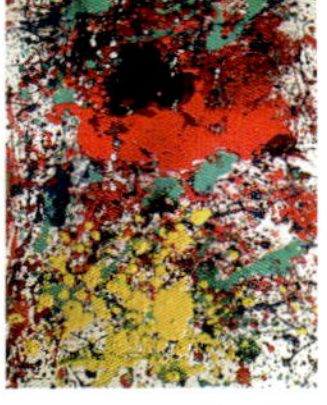

No. 9, 2013 (57)

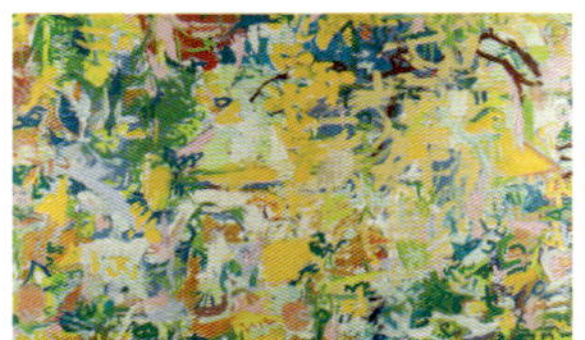

Cadence, 2011 (66–67)

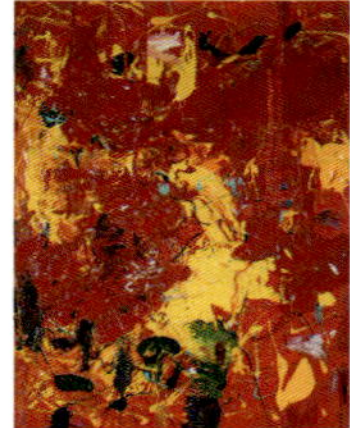

Insistent Rhythm, 2013 (119)

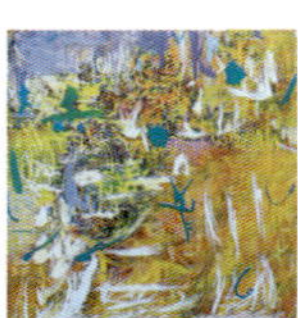

Sunflower, 2012 (145)

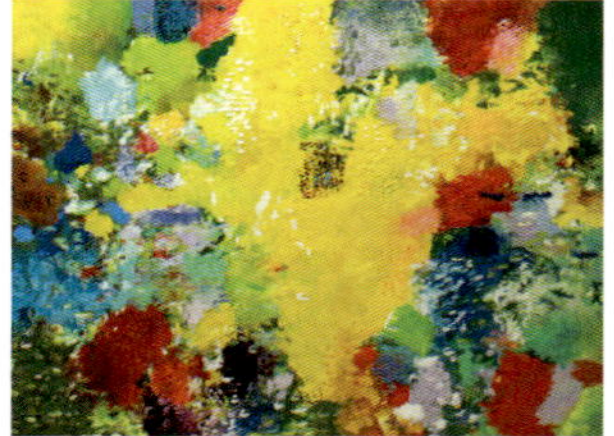

Narcissus, 2012 (46–47)

painting was created in the Santa Fe Avenue studio in Los Angeles on a cold and rainy winter's day. "I painted away the negative aspects of the environment," Whaley notes. "I would take breaks and read my dream journal about grassy plains, meadows, flowers, and things I saw in the water"[38]—another implied homage, surely, to Monet's *Water Lilies*. As its title suggests, there is a light, playful quality to this work—a quality that also characterizes the emotional freedom of a number of similar paintings that are to follow in 2012 and 2013. Some of them are quite small, but still manage to share in the exuberance. *Triumph* (2013, oil and enamel on canvas), for example, catches the mood suggested by its title. *Tomahawk* (2012, oil and enamel on arches paper) and *No. 9* (2013, oil on arches paper) share the same energy—the latter painted with the music of the joyful iconoclast John Lennon in mind. Whaley's delight in music is expressed in similar large-scale works, the relatively early *Cadence* (2011, oil on canvas) is a beautifully modulated painting, using color and line to mimic the rhythmic patterns of music. In the later, bolder *Insistent Rhythm* (2013, oil on canvas), bright areas of yellow paint pool, drip and fork off across the bright red surface with the lyrical abandon of jazz. And along with music, the titles of a number of these large abstract paintings let us know that they are inspired, like *Fields of Play*, by that other "mother," nature. *Sunflower* (2012, oil on canvas), with its bold gold, yellow and orange brush and palette knife strokes and its impromptu highlights of green puts the viewer in mind of the great painting by Van Gogh. The central yellow shape and core of dark dots in *Narcissus* (2012, oil on canvas) evoke the image of that graceful flower in a colorful garden bed. Such paintings as these reflect in nature itself the recurrent theme of Whaley's work, the struggle between order and disorder, and the life-enhancing journey out of darkness and toward the light.

Illusion

WHILE *SACRED HEART* SHARES its all-embracing, colorful enthusiasm for the creative act with a good number of such ecstatic moments, the contemporaneous *Fertile Instinct* reminds us that Whaley continues to address the darker, existential questions that obsessed him. Each of these two paintings demonstrates in its dramatic way that in his quest to explore the depths of the human spirit he eagerly absorbed the occult aspects of New Orleans' culture along with its uninhibited embrace of religious iconography, from African-influenced voodoo to Catholic hagiography. His inner belief in psychic reality and his personal experience in the dark life of the soul find their outward, emotional complement in his compassion for human suffering. Having watched the city of New Orleans battered, years earlier, by the onslaught of Hurricane Katrina, he was appalled by the still-evident extent of the storm's devastation and the memory of its toll on human life. This potent mix of thoughts, memories and feelings began to come together in the New Orleans studio in a new canvas, originally entitled *Hurricane*. Later renamed *Your Mental Illness Is an Illusion I* (2013, oil on canvas), it turned out to be the first of three paintings of that title completed during Whaley's New Orleans stay. The change in title reflects a shift in focus from the particularity of the one, terrible event to the broader context of victimized humanity. For him, this was personal as well as universal. The painting referred, Whaley notes, "to a certain archetypal personality; someone who is victimized often, although there is no real assailant." In the collaged figure of Christ (center left) he sees the Jungian "philosopher archetype [who] holds the painting together."[39] He continues:

> This work deals with the illusion of mental illness in the face of an ever-changing reality. The painting has direct relation to the Dionysus archetype, the mystery of religion, as in "spiritual intoxication," and is also inspired by the colors of Mardi Gras. When I created the work I was thinking about how people often hide behind a mask instead of showing true feelings. The red in the painting represents the tendency to easily fall in love. The deep purple represents justice, and gold represents power.[40]

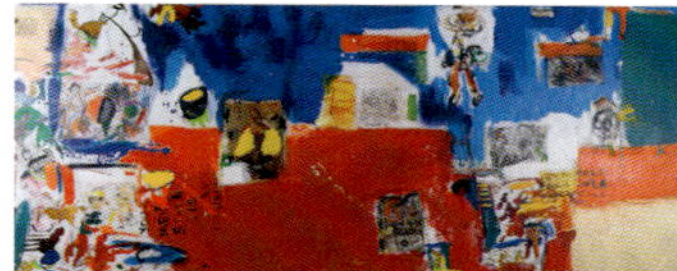

Your Mental Illness Is an Illusion I, (aka *Hurricane*), 2013 (72-73)

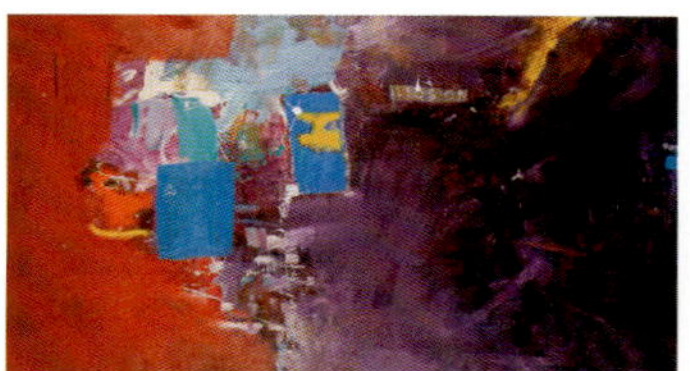

Your Mental Illness Is an Illusion II, 2013 (74-75)

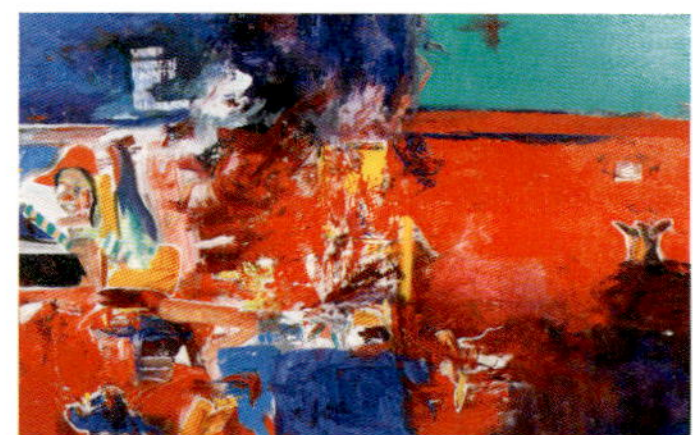

Your Mental Illness Is an Illusion III,2013 (76-77)

There is, then, a "story" in the painting—a story told in fragmented images and color, in opaque or sometimes explicit references and layered textures of medium, in mood and metaphor. But beyond the artist's personal attempt to understand and explain what he has more fully laid out on the canvas, the viewer must inevitably come back to the experience of the painting itself. Our eye is left to travel through its surfaces as on a journey, beguiled by details—here, the hanging man, the "Coca Cola" child, the confusion of images, symbols and shapes on the left side of the painting—and our minds register a shifting range of thoughts, associations and emotions as we go. We understand that everything might work out differently for us on our next trip around. What is there, emptied out on the canvas, is not limited to his intention, but rather the totality of the artist's being at the moment of its creation.

The mind creates its own "illusions" as it travels, then, a phenomenon that Whaley's painting invites us to consider. Here, as in the other two paintings in the triad, we find him not only consciously creating a visual illusion with his medium, but also asking us to explore how that illusion plays out as we experience it. He confronts us with the stark reality of illusion—there's the paradox!—in the second painting, where the word itself appears as a glowing banner against a deep purple background. In the third, above the figure of what appears to be a tumbling clown—in this instance, perhaps, the victim—he writes these words: "your mental health is an illusion." The paradox between this inscription and the title underscores their identity; not only mental *illness*, mental *health* is also an illusion that our minds create—as indeed is everything we experience. The artist's spouse reports having pointed out what he saw to be this contradiction in the painting, and to receiving this response: "It's both, Norman," said Whaley. "Don't you see that? Neither health nor illness is the thing that defines a person. Those are only temporary states. The essential self is beyond the contradictions."[41] Buckley also tells us this about the artist: "Davyd believed in the idea that there is a deeper, more substantial reality beyond that [which] we can see or acknowledge." All we have to go on, in this mode of thinking, is what we happen to be experiencing in this moment—and for *Mental Illness Is an Illusion*, this is quite simply the painting in front of our eyes.

No wonder that Whaley found in art a means of healing. As a way to discover that "essential self" somewhere beyond suffering, it put him at each moment in touch with the ephemerality of existence. It was a means of "identifying and befriending [his] own unconscious behavior [...], a way of healing and having a richer experience of reality."[42] In the Jungian perspective, it could "heal the illusion of separateness." Through the act of painting, he could create the illusion of oneness, and therein find release from suffering.

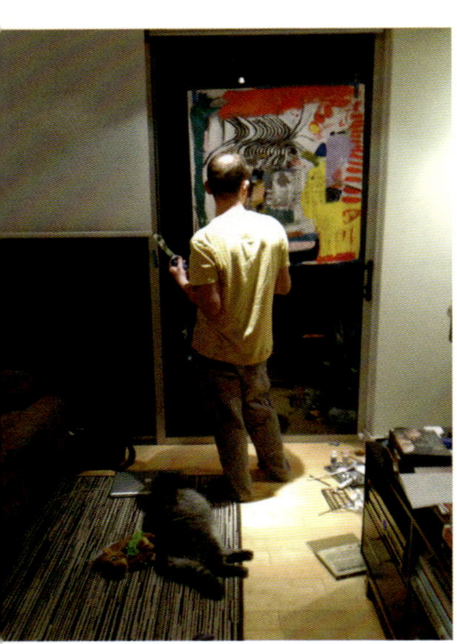

Through Darkness, into Light

> *"Do you realize that if you fall into a black hole, you will see the entire future of the Universe unfold in front of you in a matter of moments and you will emerge into another space-time created by the singularity of the black hole you just fell into?"*
>
> —Neil deGrasse Tyson

This needs to be said: David Whaley died by his own hand on the night of October 14 or the morning of October 15, 2014. Like so much else about his life, the date could not definitely be established, and no amount of rational analysis can fully fathom the act he chose.

With the *Mental Illness* triad and several other important works completed in New Orleans, he returned to Los Angeles early in 2014 and went back to work in the Santa Fe Avenue studio. Later that year, he signed up for further painting instruction, this time at Art Center College of Design in Pasadena. But as those closest to him began to realize, a profound change had occurred in his psychological and emotional life. His work had begun to manifest the change. "I think one might argue," Buckley noted subsequently in his blog, "that he was already moving away from his connection to this planet. He was moving into the mystery; his preoccupations were no longer with the dense manifestation of matter, but in the ways in which light defines our existence, makes us see objective forms, and the true nature of our very physical presence.... He was trying to make sense of the universe."[43] Already in March, Buckley noted in the same blog entry, "he became more quiet and reflective and then slipped into depression in the early summer." He suffered from severe headaches and insomnia, and exhibited symptoms of paranoia. "It felt as though he'd become completely uncomfortable in his physical shell," Buckley added. "It almost seemed his body didn't fit him any more, in the same way that we outgrow clothes."[44]

Yet Whaley continued to show up in the studio. His impressive production in the final year of his life includes, amongst other significant works, the *Blauw Series*, the *Sky Series*, and the magnificent, monumental, and poignantly entitled painting, *Four Last Songs*.

The paintings in the *Blauw Series* are problematic because they are quite different from anything Whaley had previously attempted. (Why he felt the need to add that "w" to the German word for "blue" is yet another mystery! Could we understand it as a reference to the initial of his own last name, an oblique reminder that so much of his painting is an act of self-discovery? We find it, prominently, in the earlier *Shadow*; and even a casual search will find the letter buried in the surface of many other paintings.) In the large-scale *Blauw* works, painted in March of that last year, he seems to have largely abandoned the brush and palette knife in favor of a large roller, applying thin layers of paint in wide swaths and allowing, in places, the light to shine through from behind the veils of color. It is as though his new goal was to paint light itself, in all its purity. "Larry Poons told me," he wrote once, "[that] any good painting must have light."[45] And light remained an enduring, primary concern for him. But light is paramount here, to the exclusion of all other concerns. Whaley's blue is reminiscent of the renowned "IKB"—the "International Klein Blue" claimed as his invention by the French *nouveau réaliste*, Yves Klein. Klein also died young. He famously sought in his art to create what he called "zones of immaterial sensibility." Seen at a casual glance and in gallery lighting, Whaley's *Blauw* paintings might seem, by contrast with earlier work, to be relatively flat and lifeless. However—and there is no way to know if the artist intended this effect—they come unexpectedly to life in *low* lighting, which is how the painter Mark Rothko—to whose ethereal paintings the *Blauw Series* might best be compared—preferred his work to be seen. In low light, these canvases exude a quietly thrilling, vibrant glow that can transport the viewer into something akin to those "zones of immaterial sensibility" to which Yves Klein aspired. Seen thus, their peculiar, otherworldly aura is a manifestation of that disconnect with the physical world of which Buckley writes, an impulse to move beyond the personal story that has obsessed the artist in much of his life and work to date, and into a transpersonal world of light and space.[46]

***Blauw III*, 2014 (62)**

***Blauw IV*, 2014 (62)**

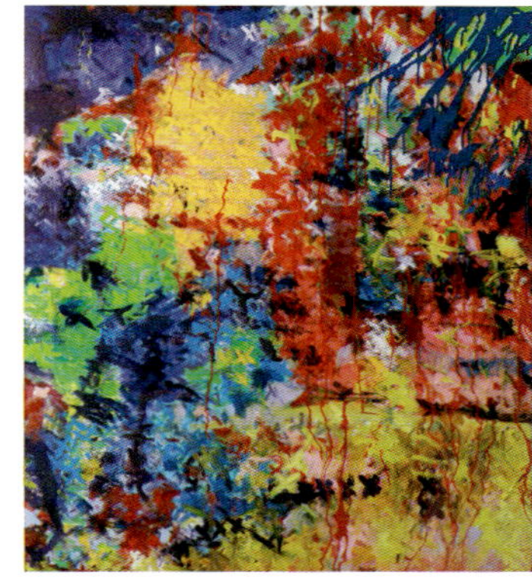
***Grand Nebula (Key Hole)*, 2014 (187)**

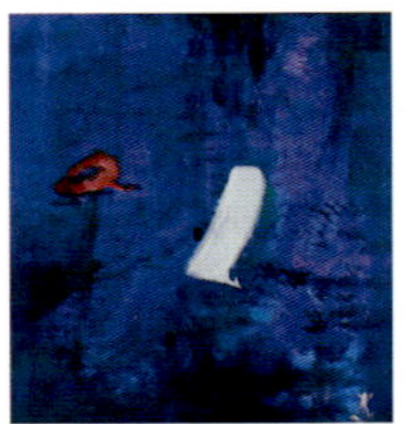

***Diamond in the Sky*, 2014 (190)**

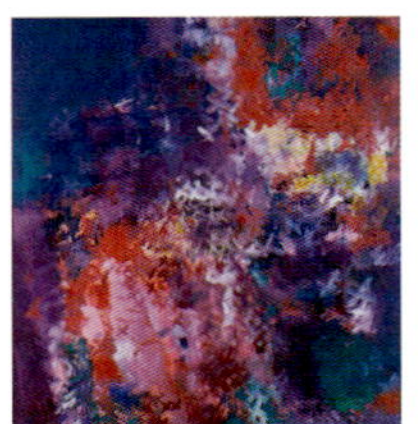

***Reinventing En Plein Air*, 2014 (179)**

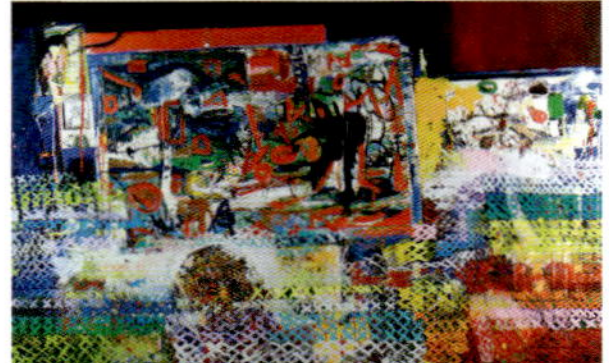

***Insomnia*, 2014 (192–193)**

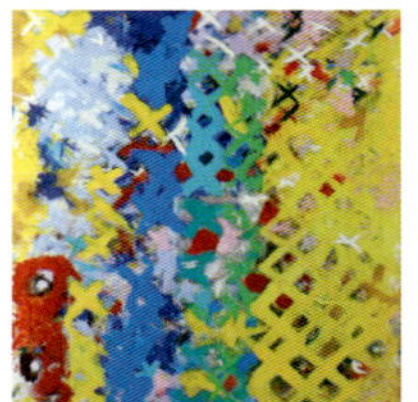

***Horizon*, 2014 (182)**

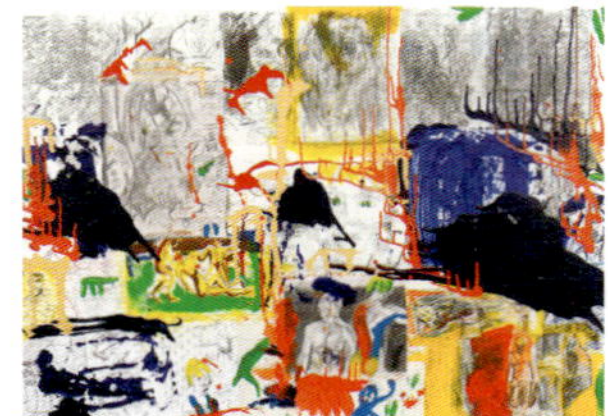

***Be Devil*, 2014 (159)**

That there are no more than four paintings in the *Blauw Series* suggests that the artist himself was not entirely convinced by this direction. Light and space, however, remained Whaley's central preoccupation in the twelve works in the *Sky Series*. With a single exception, the paintings in this series reach out, a sense of passionate ambition, beyond the artist's personal struggle and into broader questions about the nature of the universe. The exception is *Insomnia* (2014, oil, bed sheets and wood painted on linen), the largest and the most disturbing of the twelve, whose only apparent connection to the rest of the series is the bold cross-hatching that predominantly occupies the lower half of the work. Painted in oil on bed sheets—perhaps the very sheets between which the artist struggled for sleep—the greater part of the picture plane is kept tight, crowded, claustrophobic, noisy with clashing color and buzzing with the energy of a circuit board. It evokes the familiar torment of sleeplessness with immediate and dramatic intensity, and offers an intimate glimpse into a mind filled with restlessness, confusion and a longing for escape into that elusive serenity beckoning in the deep space at the top edge of the painting. Its seemingly anomalous inclusion in the *Sky Series* serves to accentuate the spacious, expansive vision of its neighbors and to suggest that the physical turbulence of the universe is a reflection of the inner turmoil of a human mind now under severe stress. In this, it more closely resembles *Be Devil* (2014, mixed media on canvas), another large canvas from the period, which combines Whaley's accomplished draftsmanship with his acquired painterly skills in a tumult of dream-like activity. Far from the edge-to-edge, painterly quality of the *Sky Series*, this one is fragmented into multiple, intimate glimpses of the memories, obsessions, desires and fantasies that pervade a human mind. The haunting gaze of the half-hidden, green-eyed figure—male or female?—at the center of the picture is suggestive of the self intensely observing its own chaos of inner fears and impulses, an orgy of sexual fantasy, primitive urges and conflicted emotions. It's a descent into what Freud identified as the id, or a dark stage in what Jung called the hero's journey.

Other than *Insomnia*, though, the *Sky Series* looks beyond the confines of the earth and out into the universe. The title of each painting refers to a specific physical or astrophysical phenomenon, as though the artist were now engaged on a project of scientific and philosophical research—searching the universe itself for answers to those imposing questions that remain insoluble in the human mind. What is the nature of reality, and how do we perceive it? And is there, anyway, an objective reality that exists outside ourselves, or is what seems so real to us no more than the illusion created by our minds, a play of light, a fabrication? Completed in April, May and June of 2014, these essentially abstract works are executed with more effortless assurance than we have seen in Whaley's work before. The leitmotif of criss-cross marks—starbursts, we might say, in the context of the overall theme—gives cohesion, ground and balance to the chaotic, sometimes conflicting surfaces of color, the spontaneity of washes, scratches, drips and splashes, and the broad, gestural brushwork. The paintings radiate with a kind of nuclear energy, offering an ecstatic, richly imaginative vision of the far reaches of an ever-expanding universe. They seek to replicate that sense of awe we feel in the presence of the images that reach us now from outer space—those images of majestically rotating galaxies, collapsing or exploding stars and vast, polychromatic gas clouds that manifest in staggering time-space distances from our planet.

Twelve canvases, none of them so monumental in scale as a good number of Whaley's earlier paintings, are hardly sufficient to account for such a vision. A line from the poet Robert Creeley comes to mind: "What I come to do/is partial, partially kept."[47] In this sense, the *Sky Series* must inevitably be seen as partial, offering us a few random, tantalizing glimpses into a vast realm of visual possibilities. Given the scope of the ambition, it could hardly be otherwise. Then, too, it is often enough to see one tiny corner of the carpet in order to grasp the latent existence of the whole. The gift of this series of remarkable paintings, as with so much of Whaley's work, is to withhold the ultimate secret of its mystery, and to leave our minds in a state of open-ended speculation--as does, indeed, the universe itself.

But if we can never know, we can always celebrate. This, I think, is what Whaley does in his towering, thirteen-foot high paean to the beauty of pure color and light, *Four Last Songs*. It is not his last painting, but among the last, and for so exuberant a painting, it is not without a note of poignancy. The title refers to a song cycle by Richard Strauss—the last of this composer's works—based on three short poems by Hermann Hesse and one by Josef von Eichendorff.[48] Each poem is no more than the space of a breath, a serene anticipation, almost a longing for death. By contrast, though also anticipatory of Whaley's own imminent death, his painting is a vast, soaring expression of lyrical intensity. It is composed of successive bursts of color and light, a fireworks display of exultation and delight in the sheer pleasure of paint. A sunburst of yellow holds the center, surrounded by explosions of pinks, reds and blue. At the top and bottom, the passages of green bring the mind back to the Earth we are given to live on. In Whaley's last symphony of explosive images, I'm tempted to call *Four Last Songs* his "Ode to Joy." It remains a fitting tribute to his work, and to his memory.

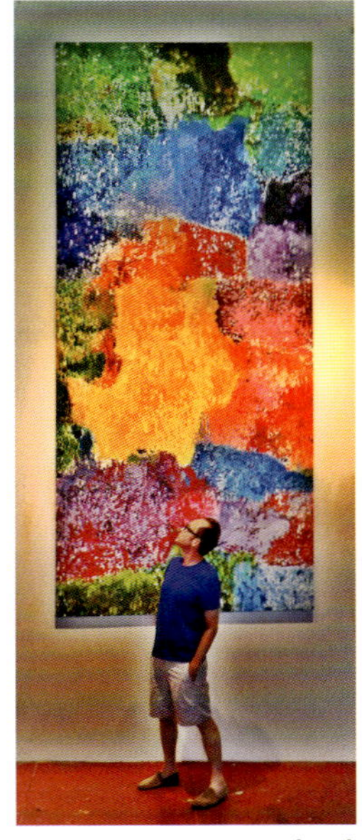

***Four Last Songs*, 2014 (195)**

PETER CLOTHIER

PETER CLOTHIER, PH.D., is a poet, novelist, and art writer. He is the author of *David Hockney* (1995, Abbeville Modern Masters), two books of poems, two novels, a memoir, and three recent collections of essays: *Persist* (2010), *Mind Work* (2012), and *Slow Looking* (2012). In his academic career, he served as Dean of Otis Art Institute (1976–1979) and Dean of the College of Fine & Communication Arts at Loyola Marymount Universtiy (1982–1986).

From Davyd Whaley's Journal

June 25, 2012

"I'm an artist who truly listens to my subconscious and dreams, and is working from a level that is personal, yet also pushing forth something deeper than most could ever comprehend or will be understood in my lifetime. I paint what I dream, or things shown to me by my subconscious. It's for someone else to sort out. Without this journal how could you understand my paintings? You would consider me mad."

Opposite: ***Black Man*, 2008**

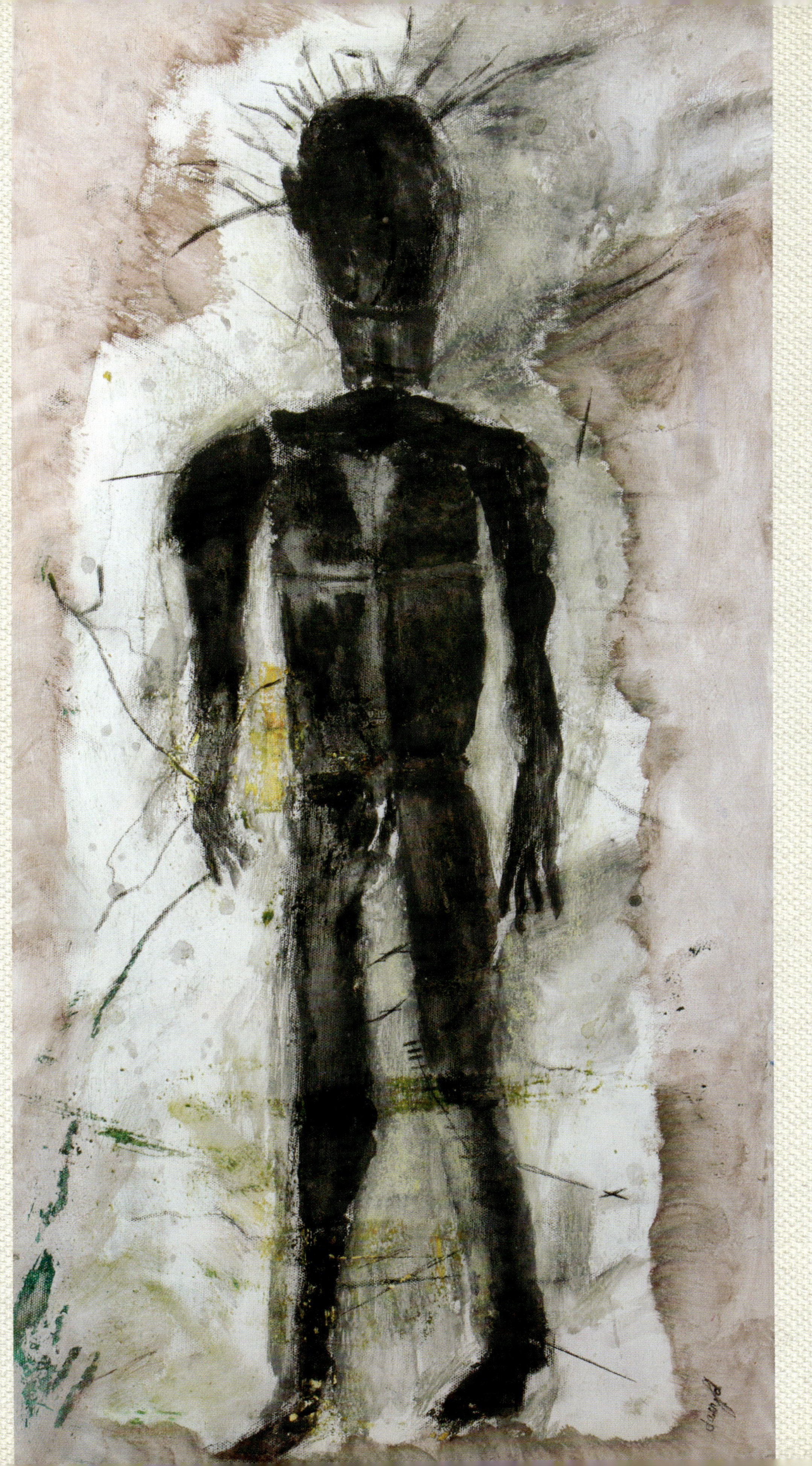

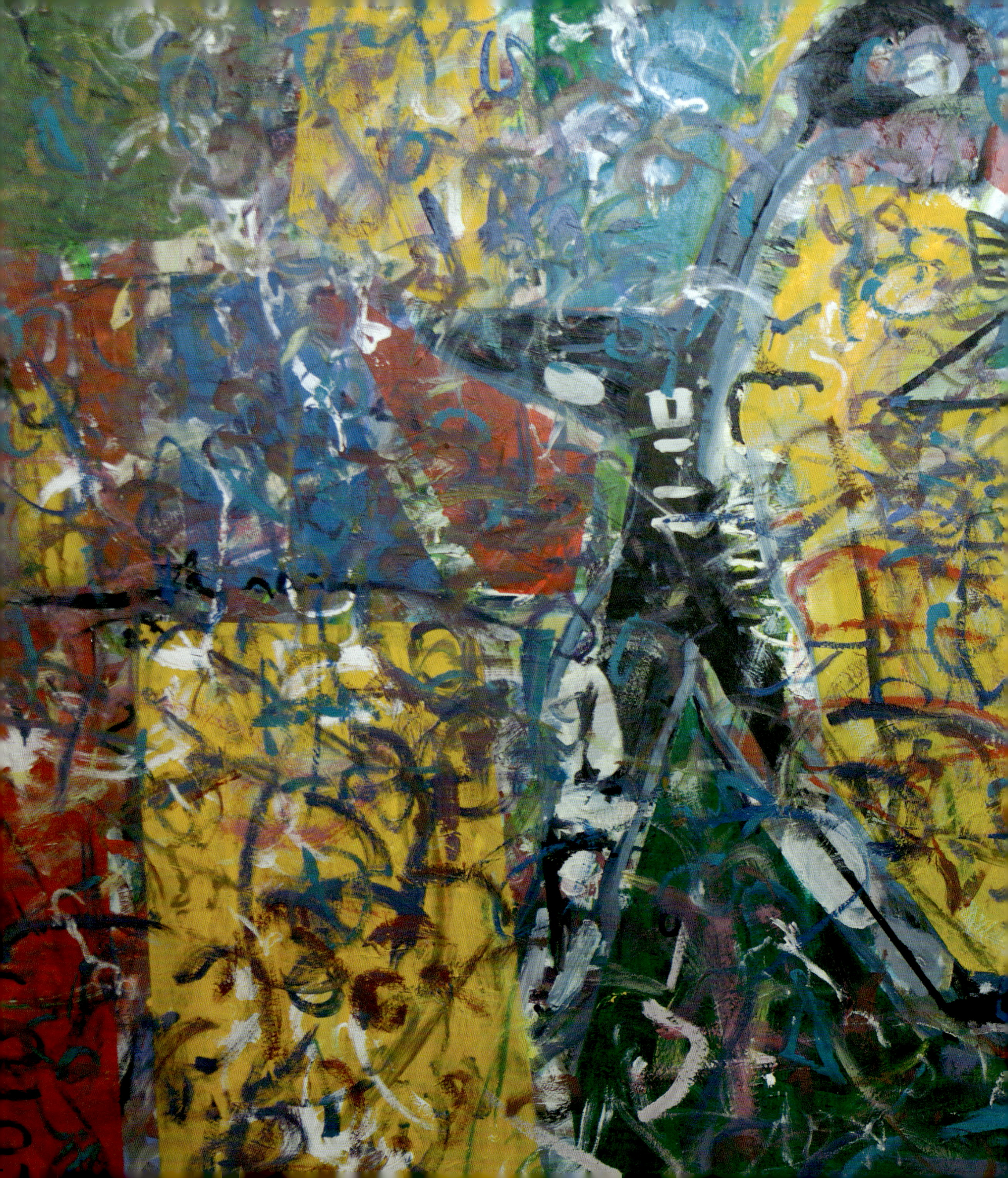

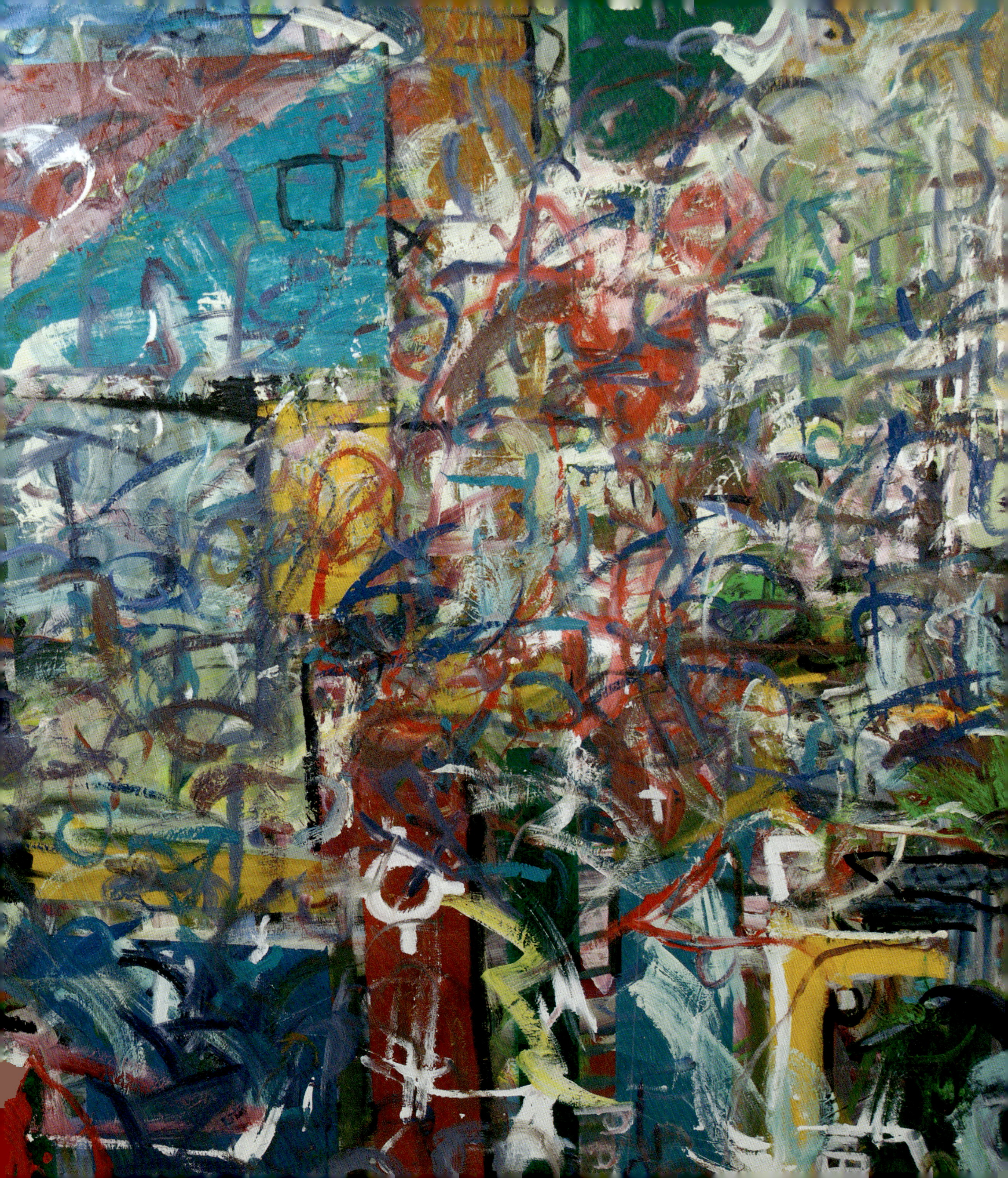

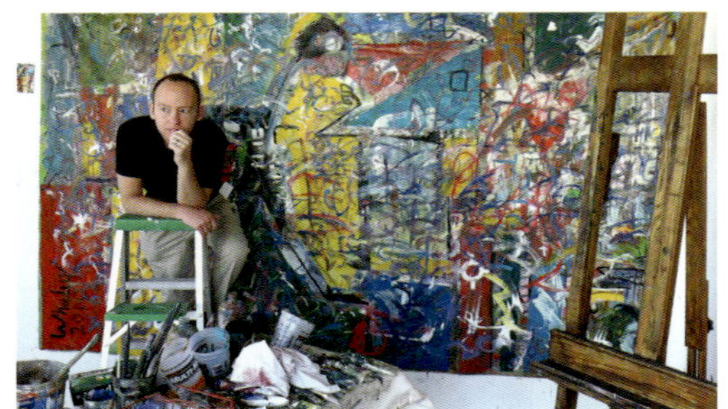

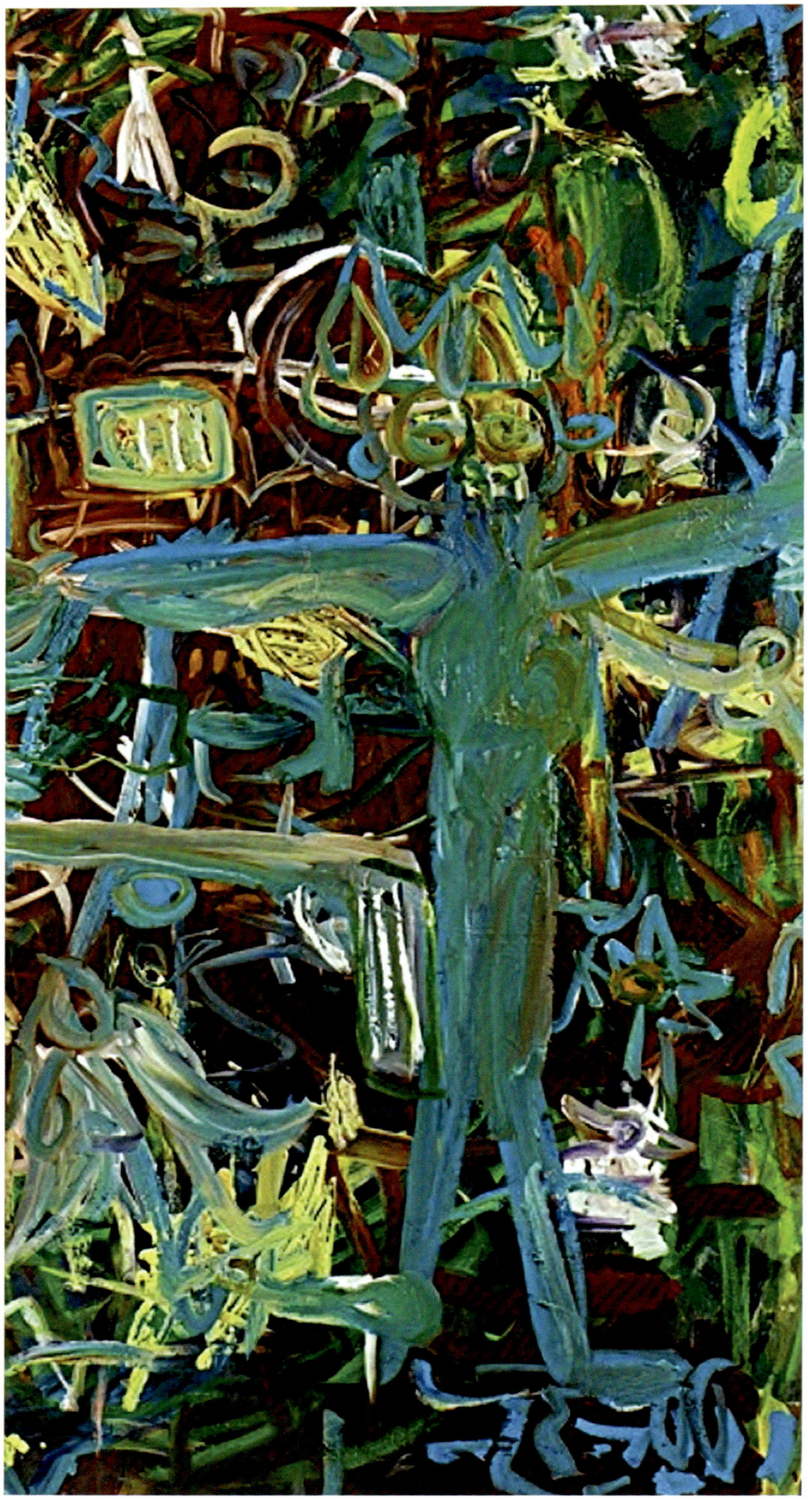

***Salvationist*, 2011**

Overleaf: *Atonement*, 2010

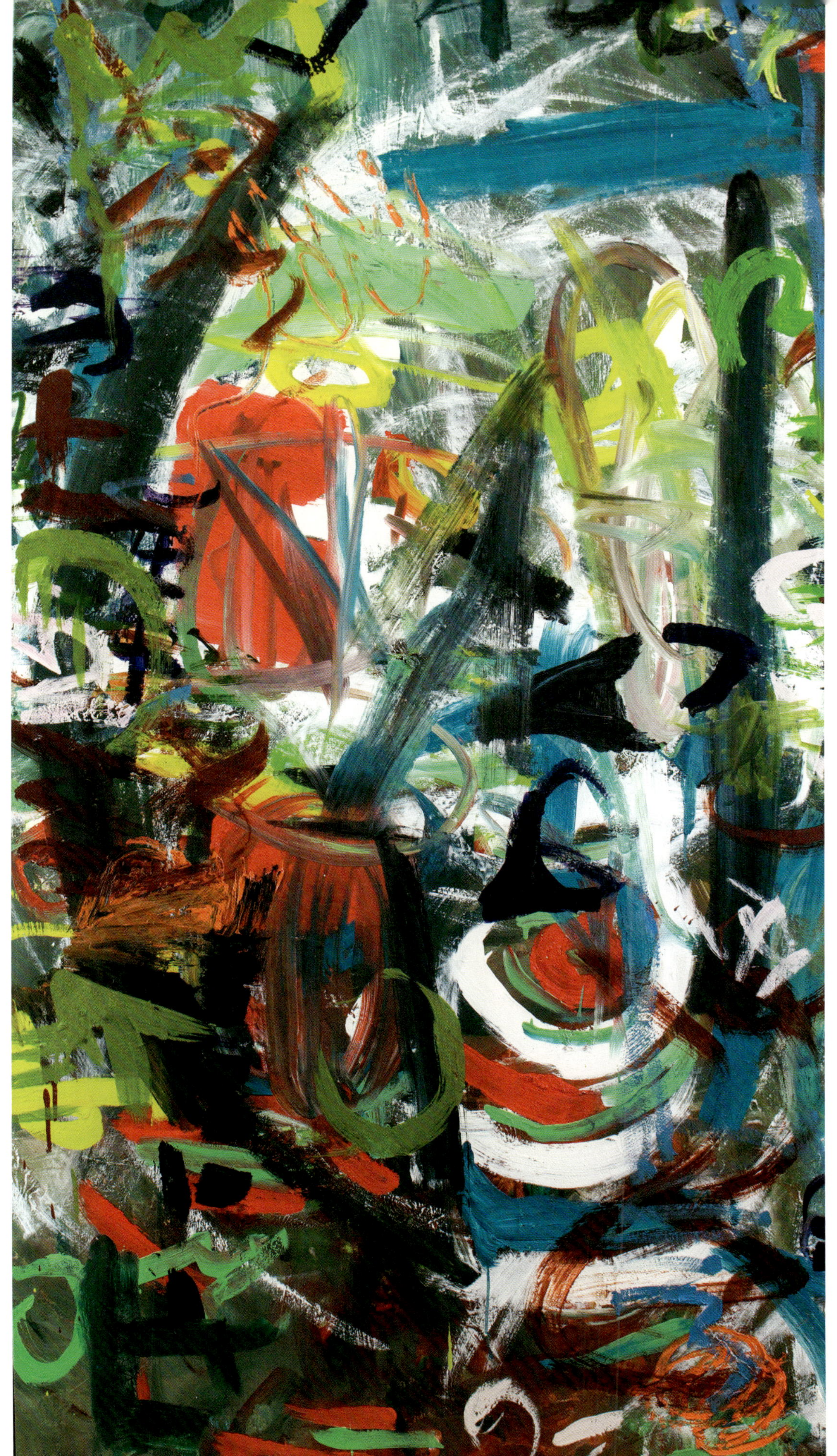

Jiva and the Goddess, 2010

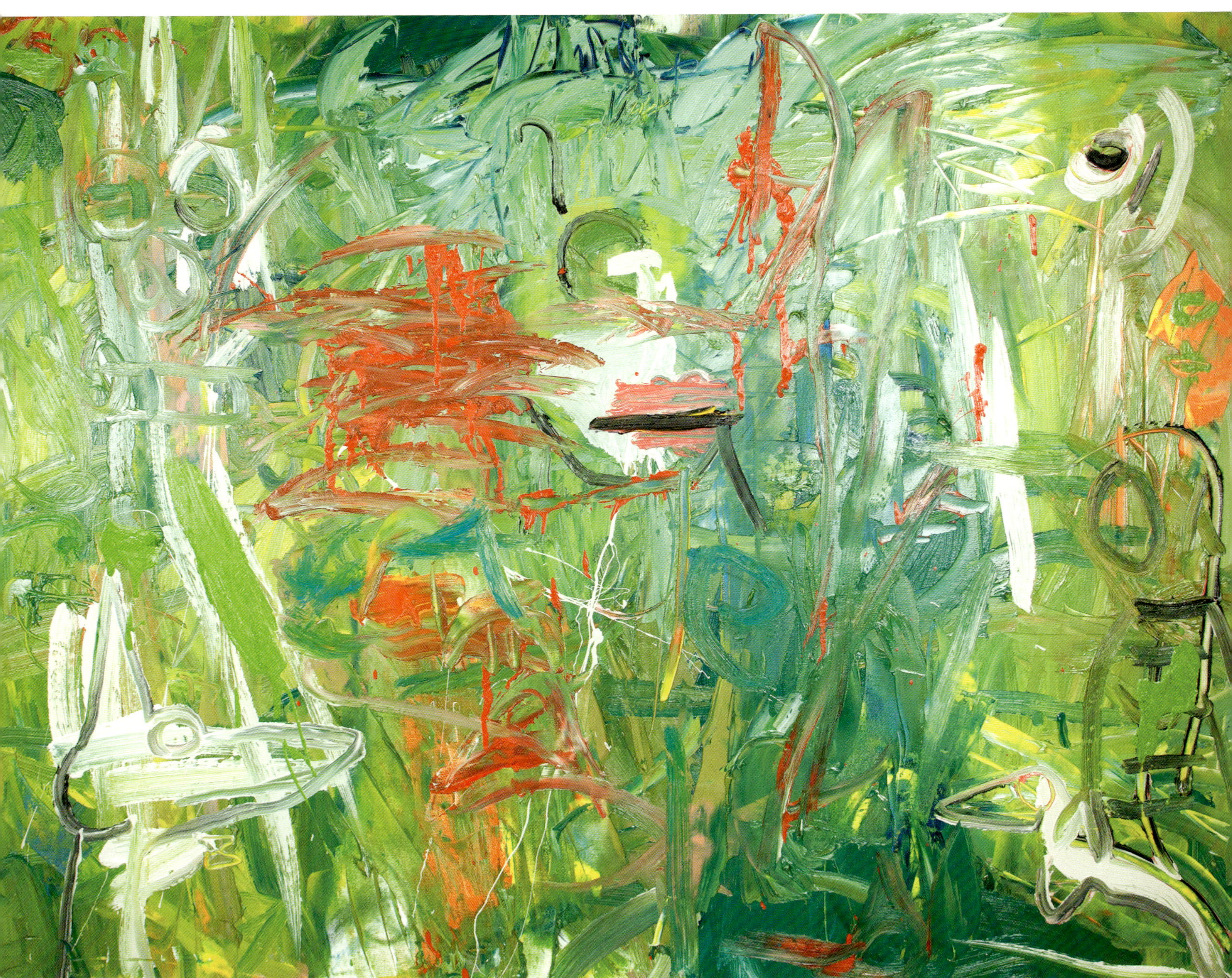

Initiation, 2011

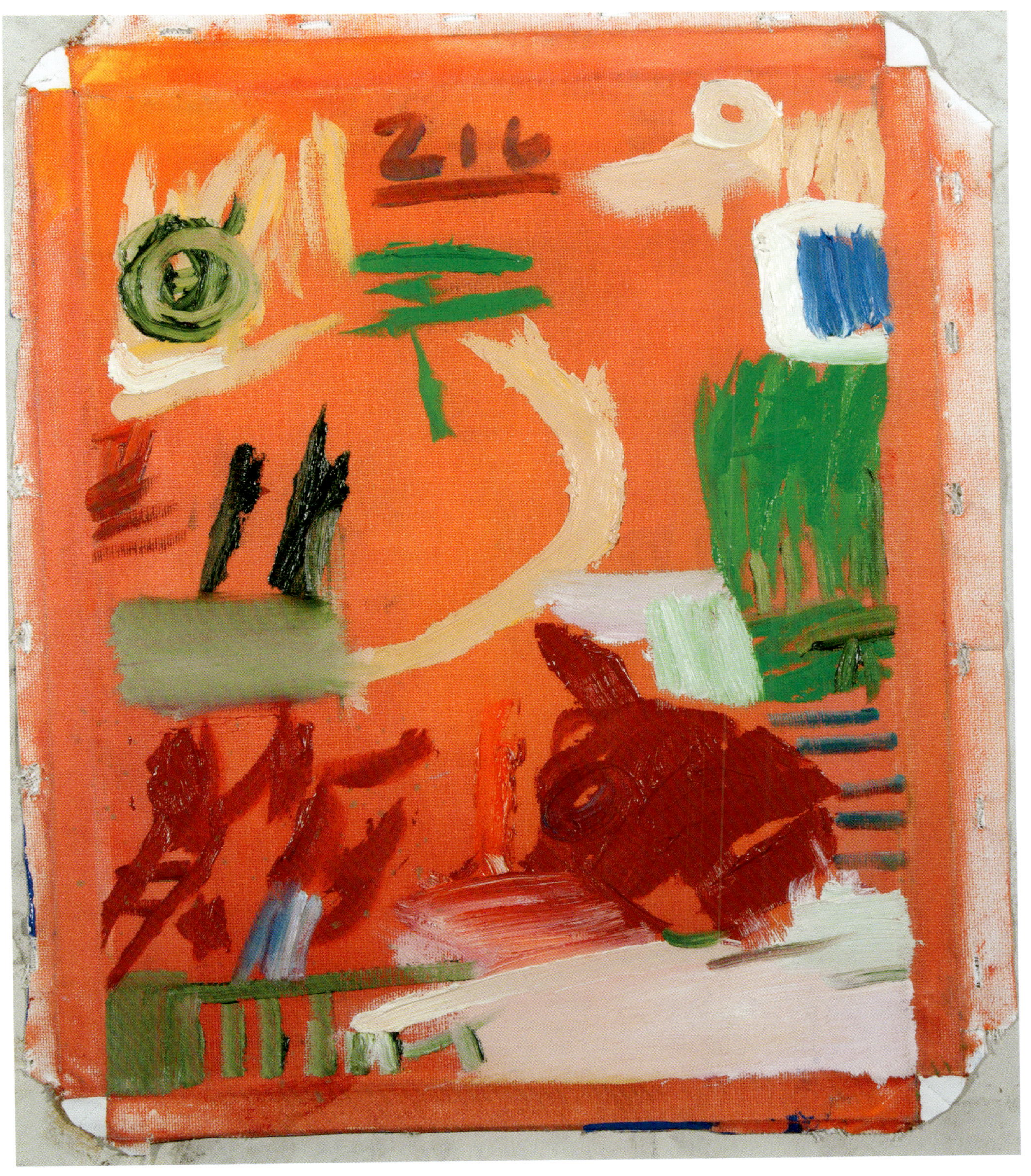

216, 2011

"Some have a flair for it. I just have a love affair with color."

—DW

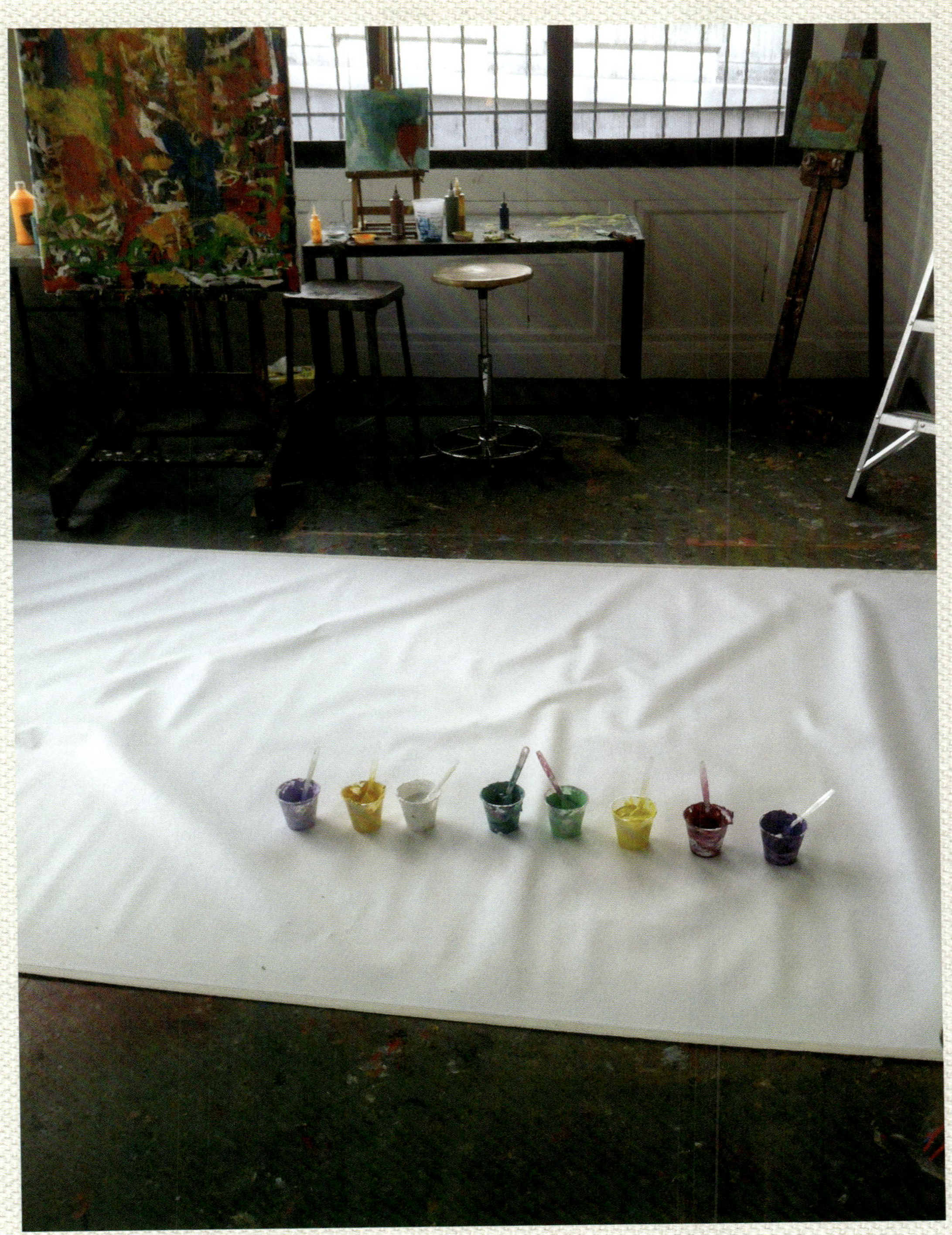

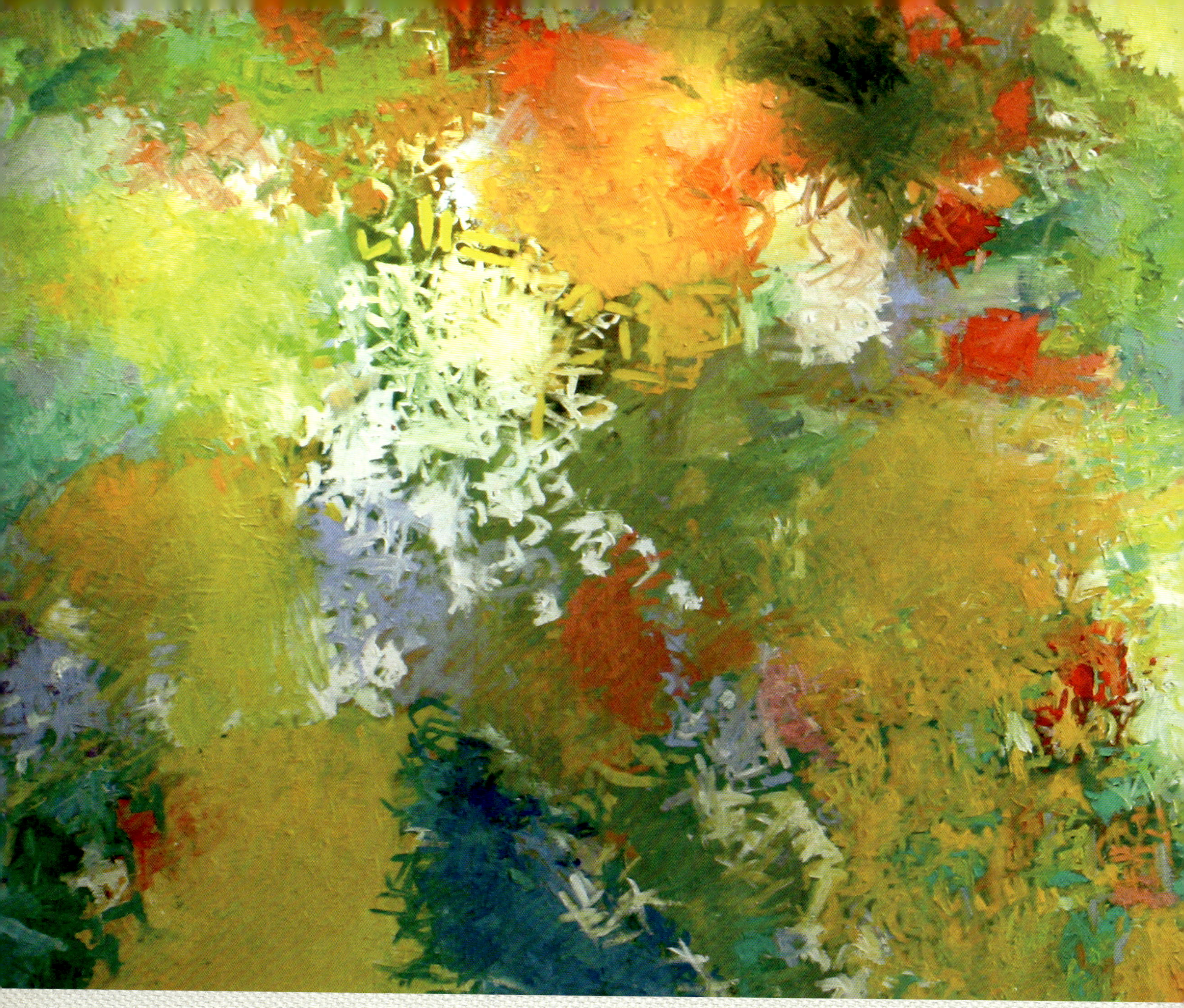

"Fields of Play is an oil painting on canvas, which I worked on during the rainy season in Los Angeles, California. It began as an experiment with color. I rolled out as much canvas as possible along my studio floor, working the flat surface on my hands and knees. I used mixing bowls to mix various colors. I sat mid-canvas, on the edge of the canvas, and also laid down horizontally to create it. I would listen to the trains go by outside during the rainy afternoons and feel a draft come through the windows of the studio, wishing it were

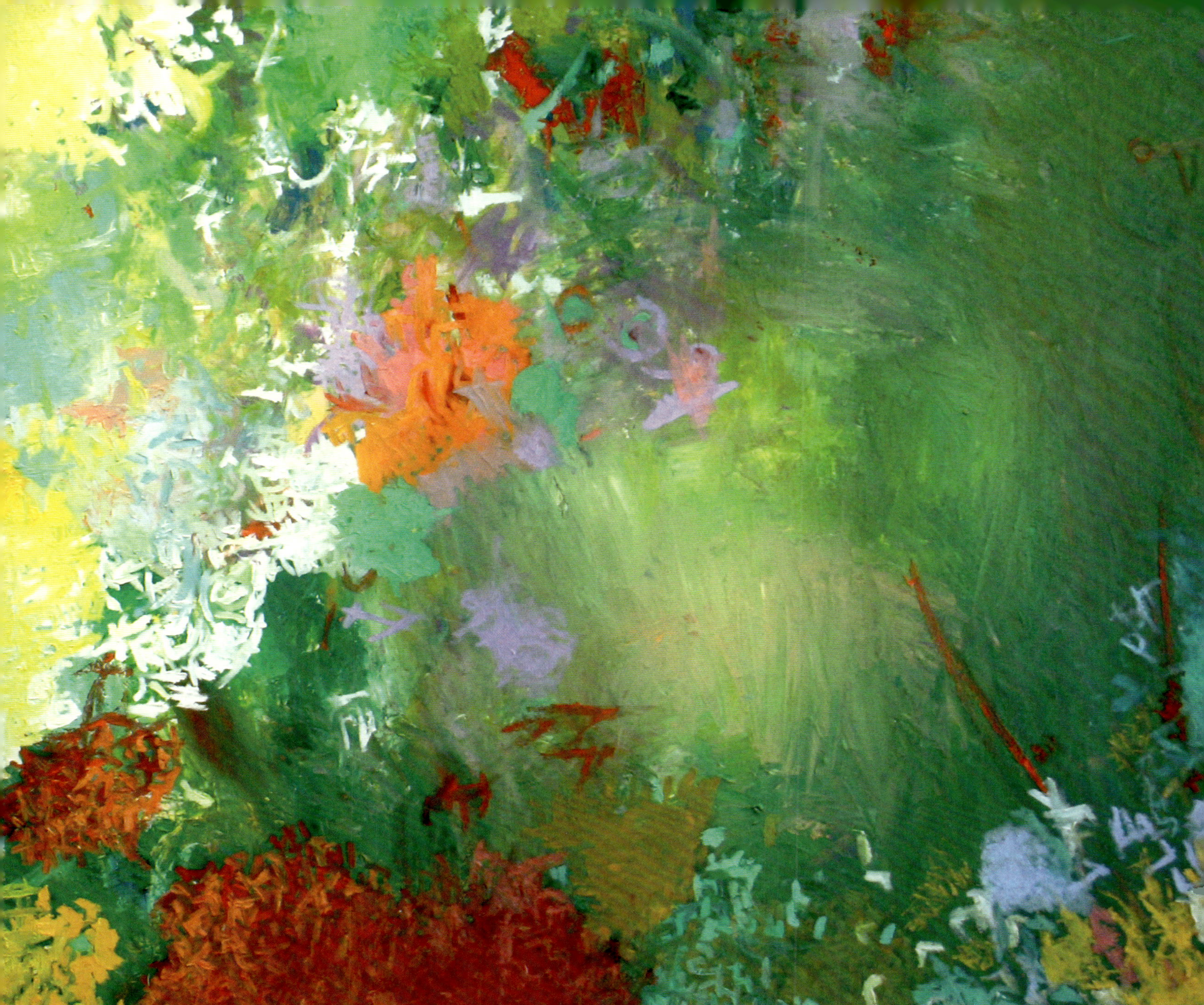

***Fields of Play*, 2011**

warmer and that the sun would come out and be brighter. I painted away the cold. I painted away the negative aspects of the environment. I would take breaks and read my dream journal about grassy plains, meadows, flowers, and things that I saw in the water. Figures would appear and then I would paint over them, shadows hiding behind light. The texture in the painting is very elaborate. An entire under-painting exists underneath. *Fields of Play* was created as an expression and meditation. Our environment is always a factor in what we create, or can be—sounds, temperature, light. This is the bigger picture of my work." —DW

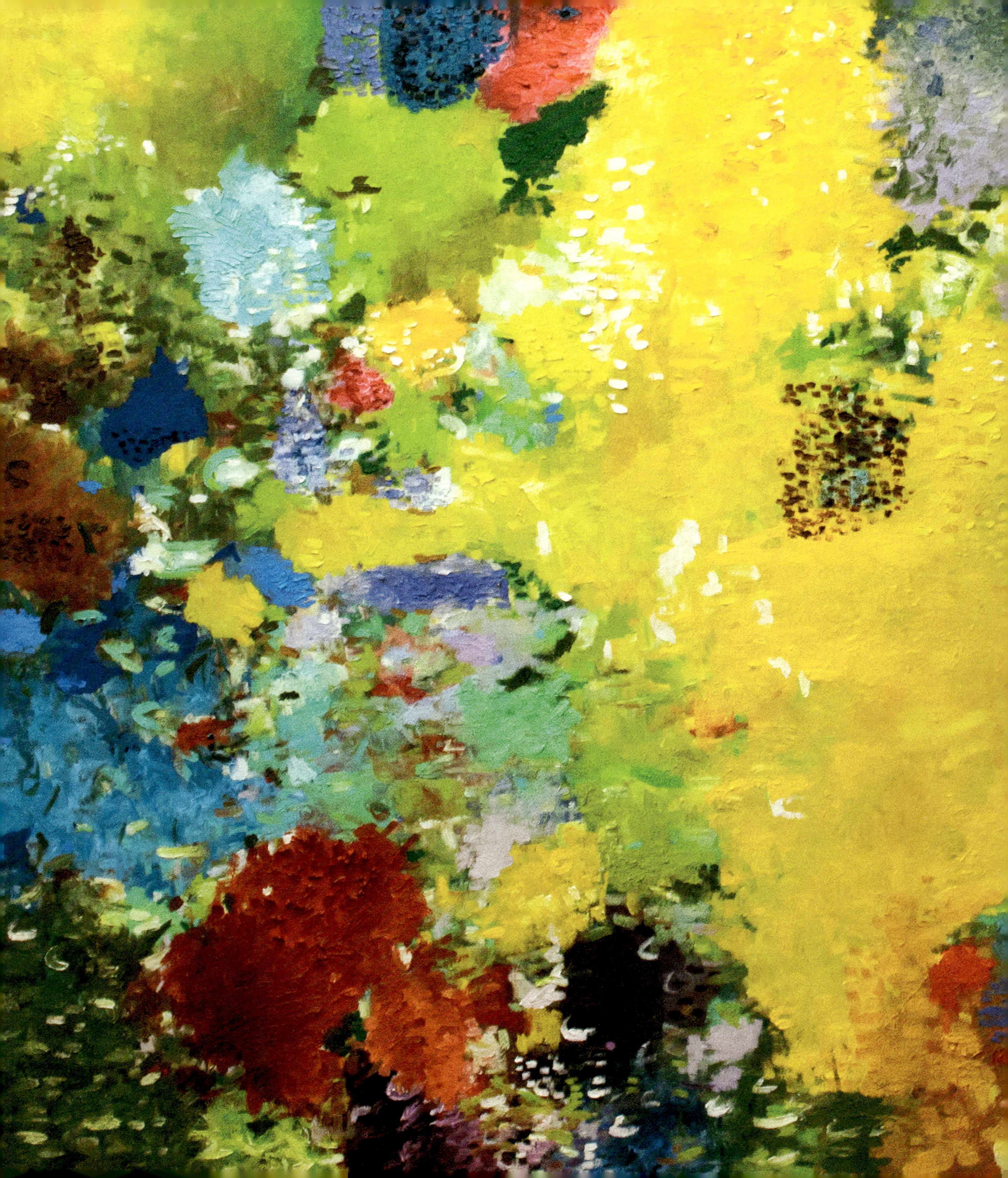

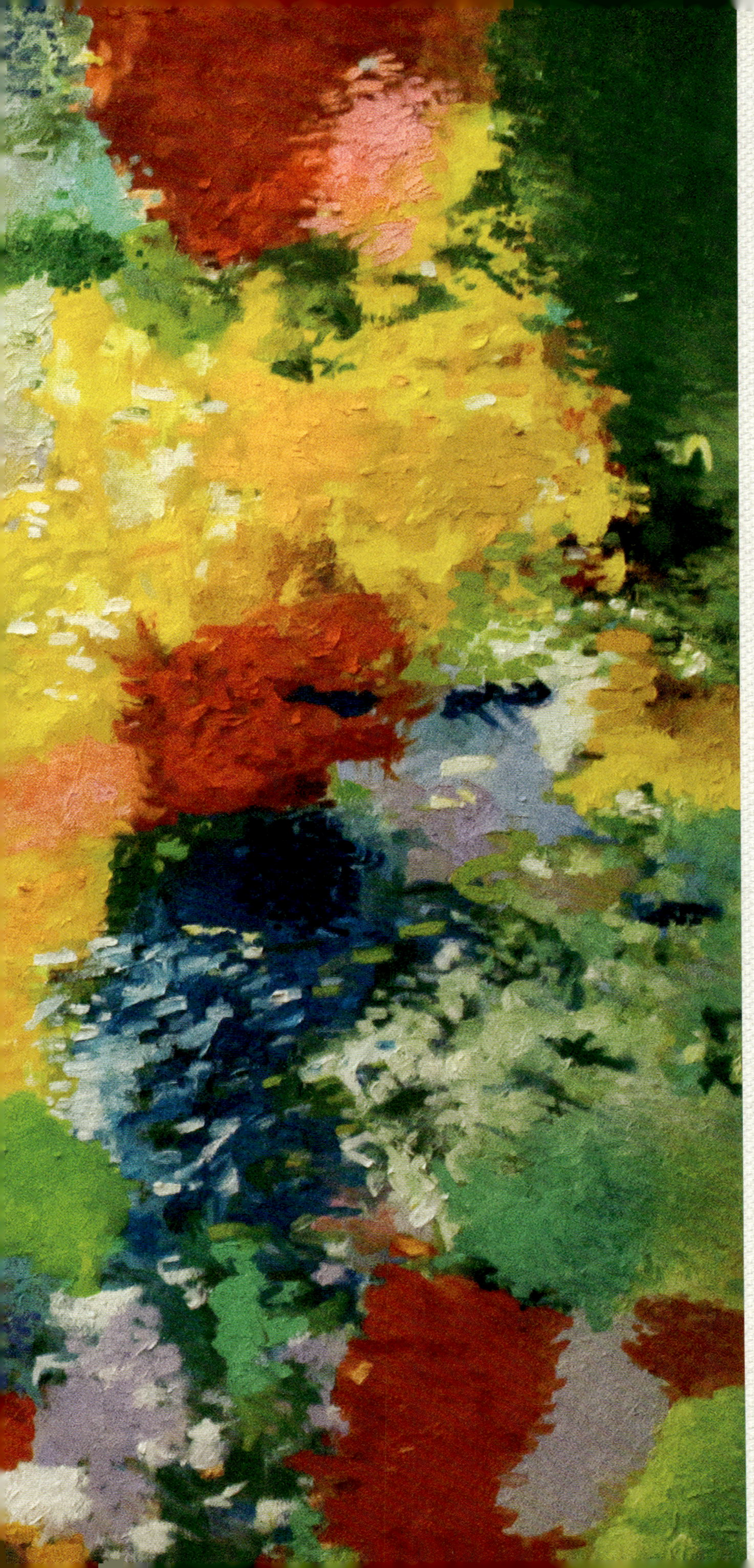

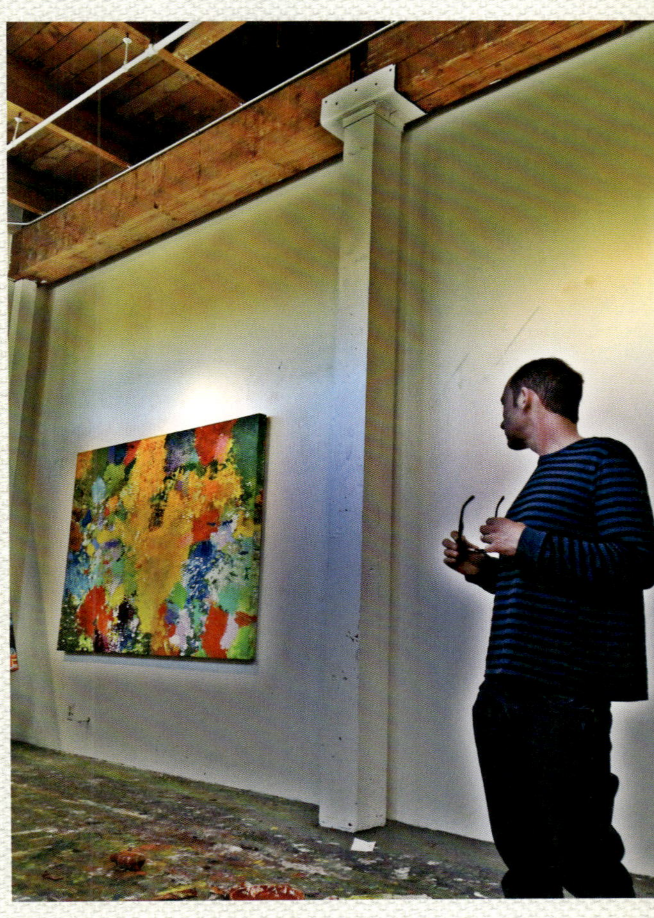

Narcissus, 2013

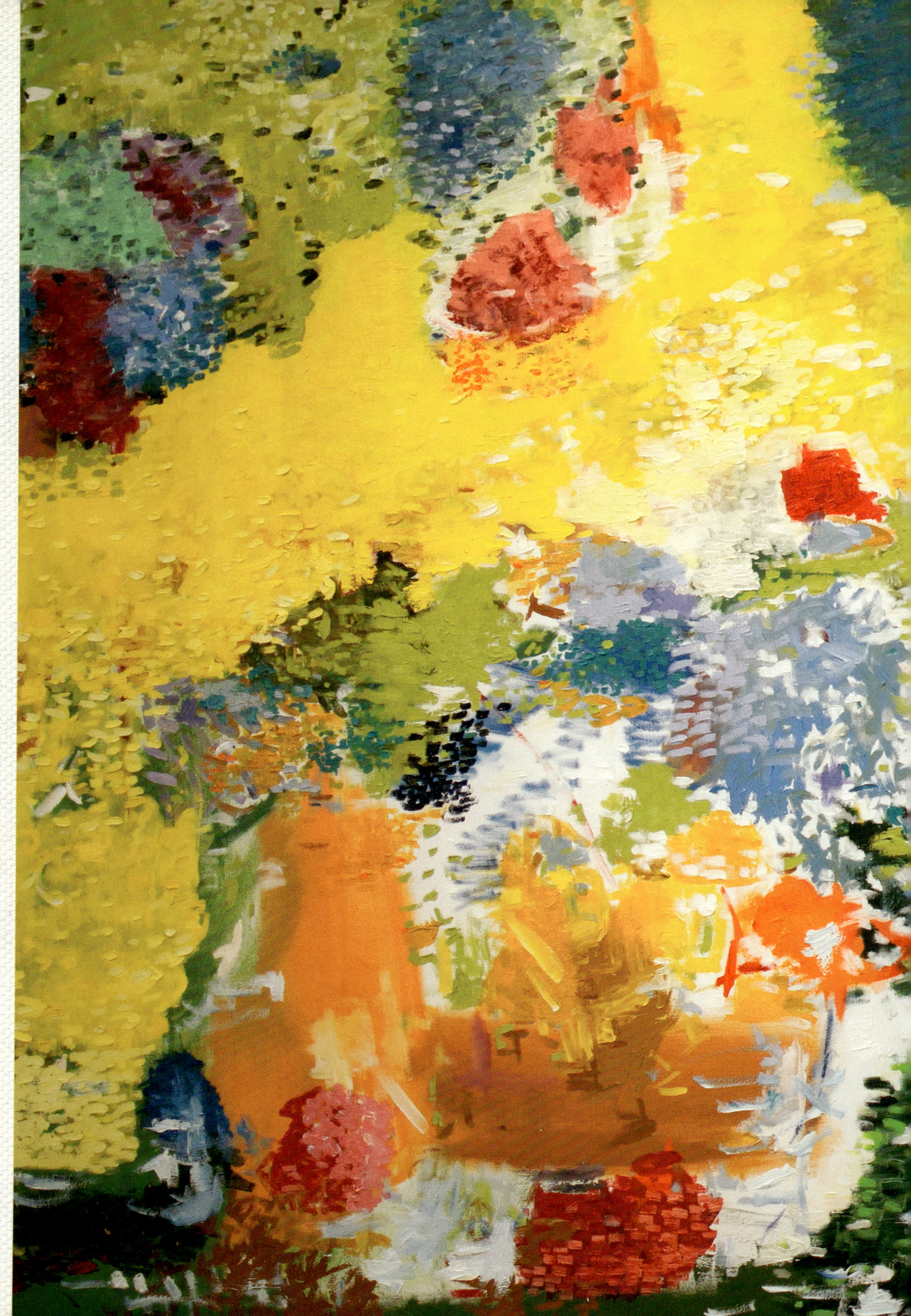

Columbines, 2013

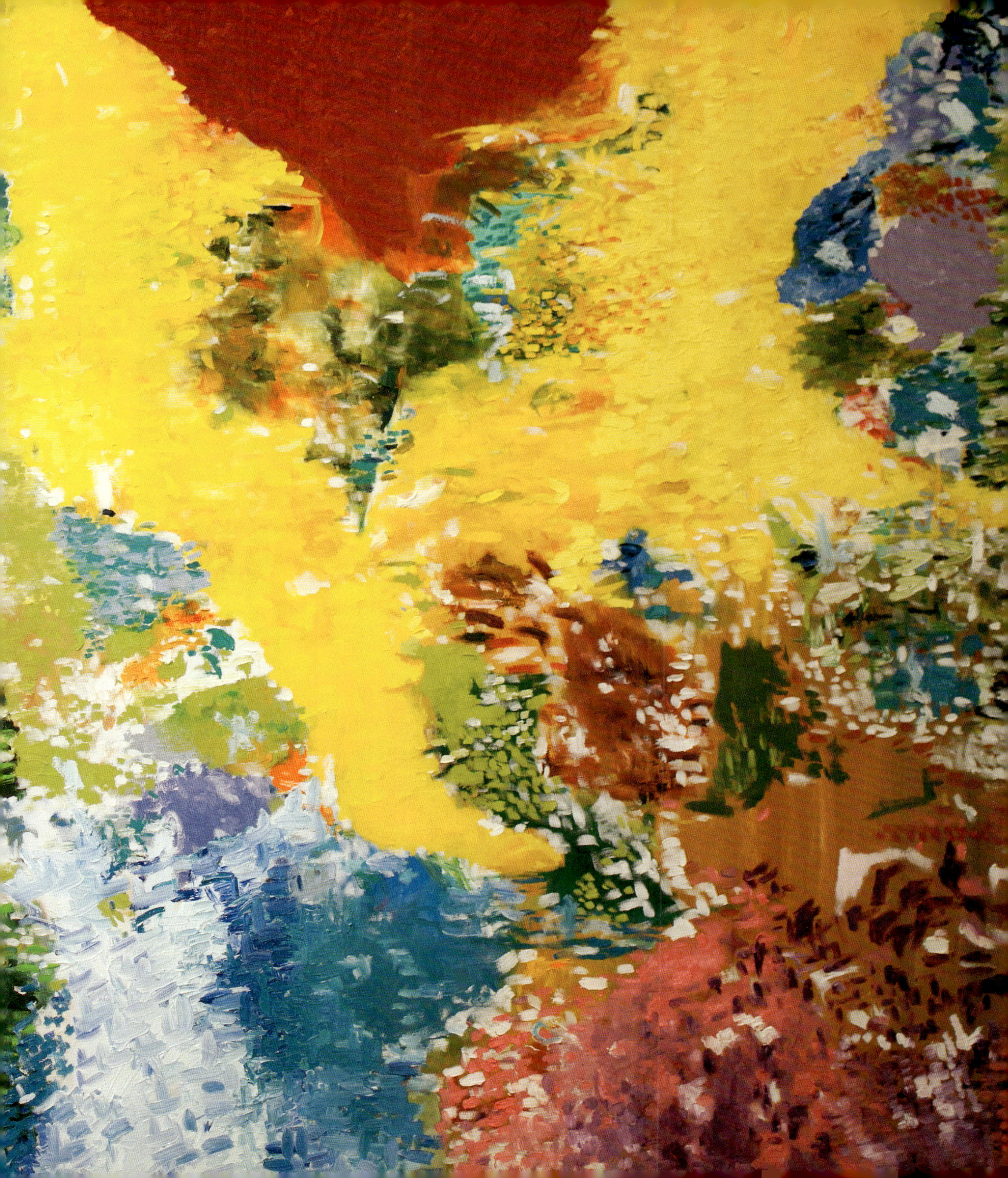

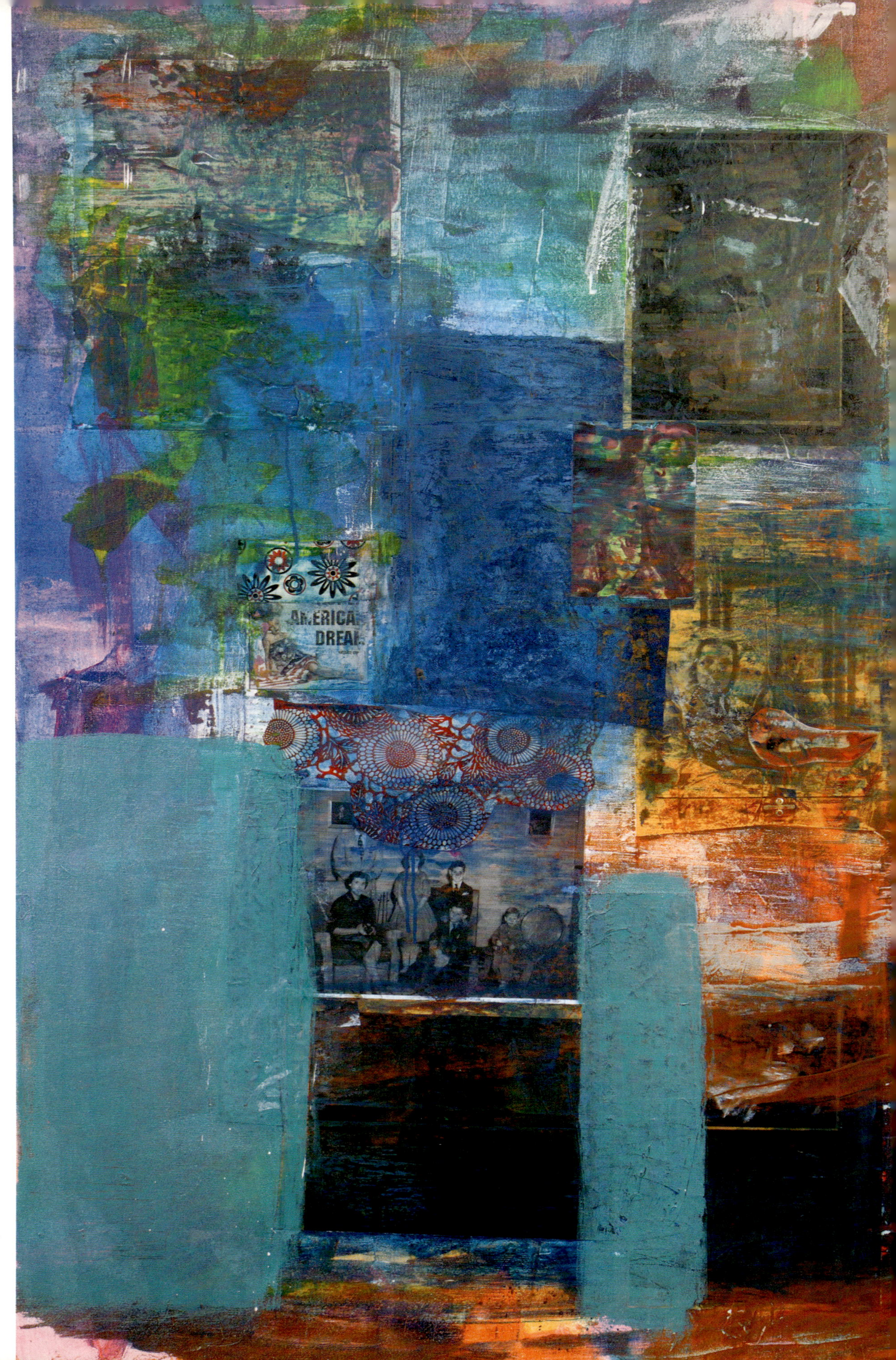

***Family Tree*, 2014**

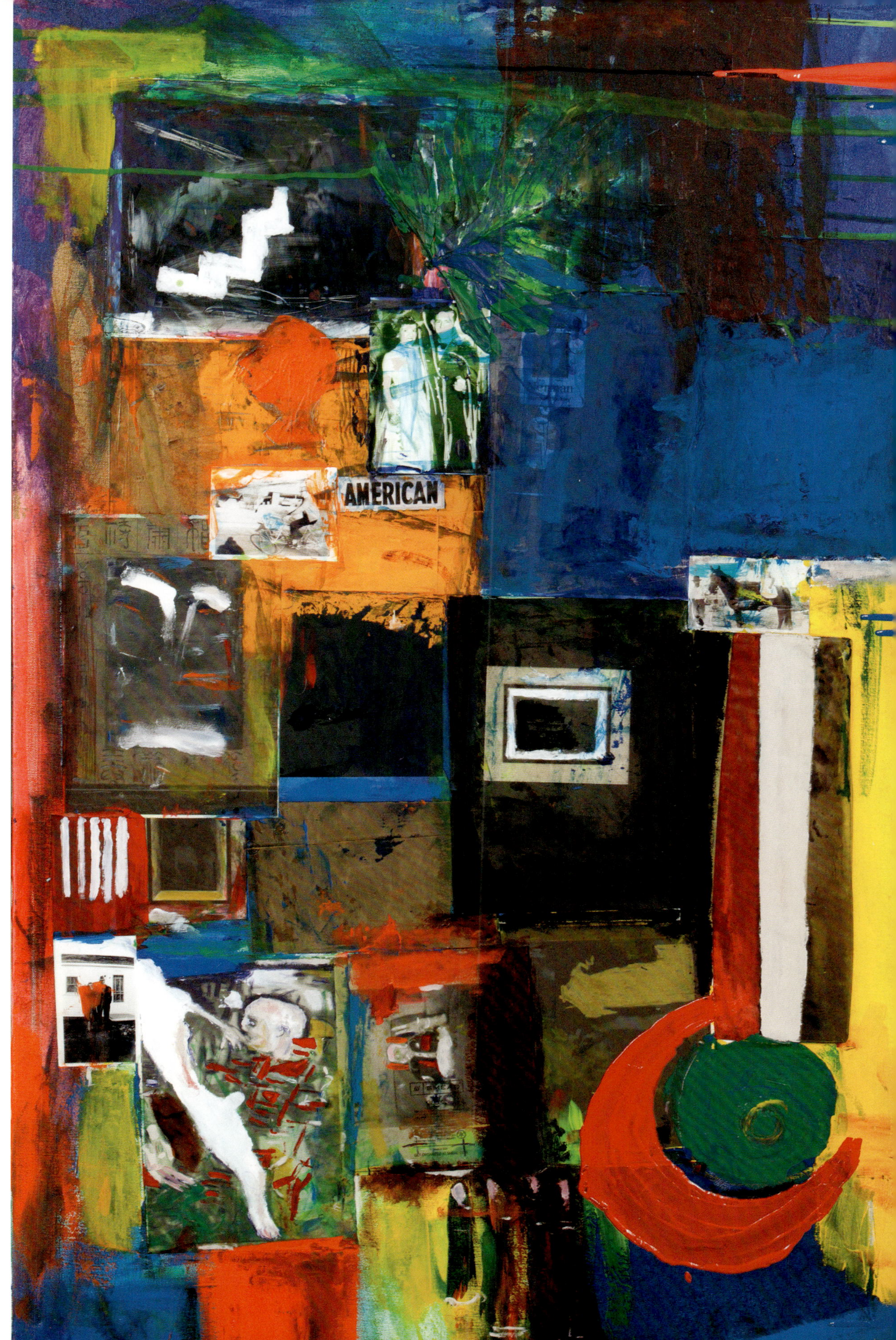

American Dream, 2014

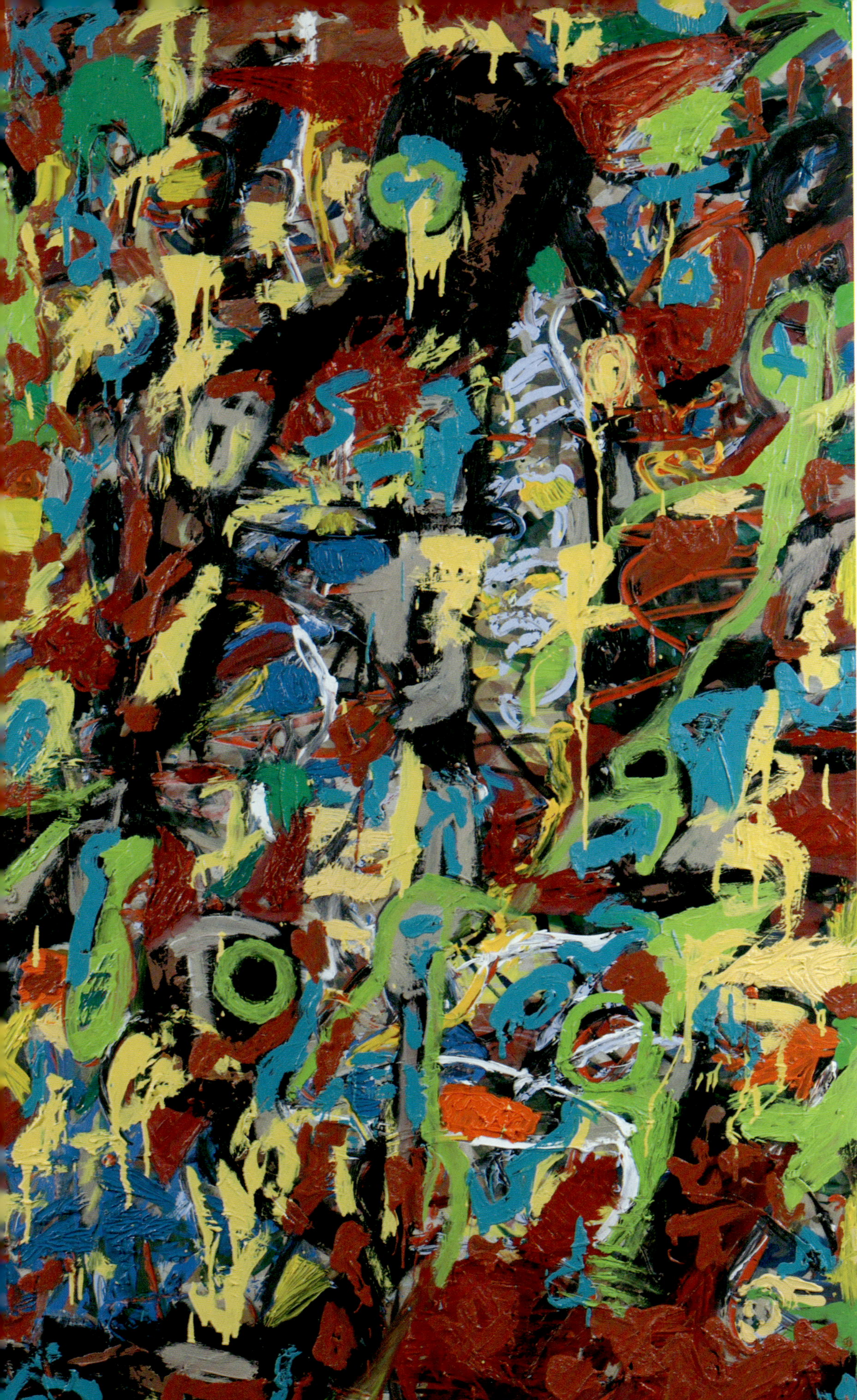

Nuclear Family, 2012

Opposite: *Triumph*, 2013

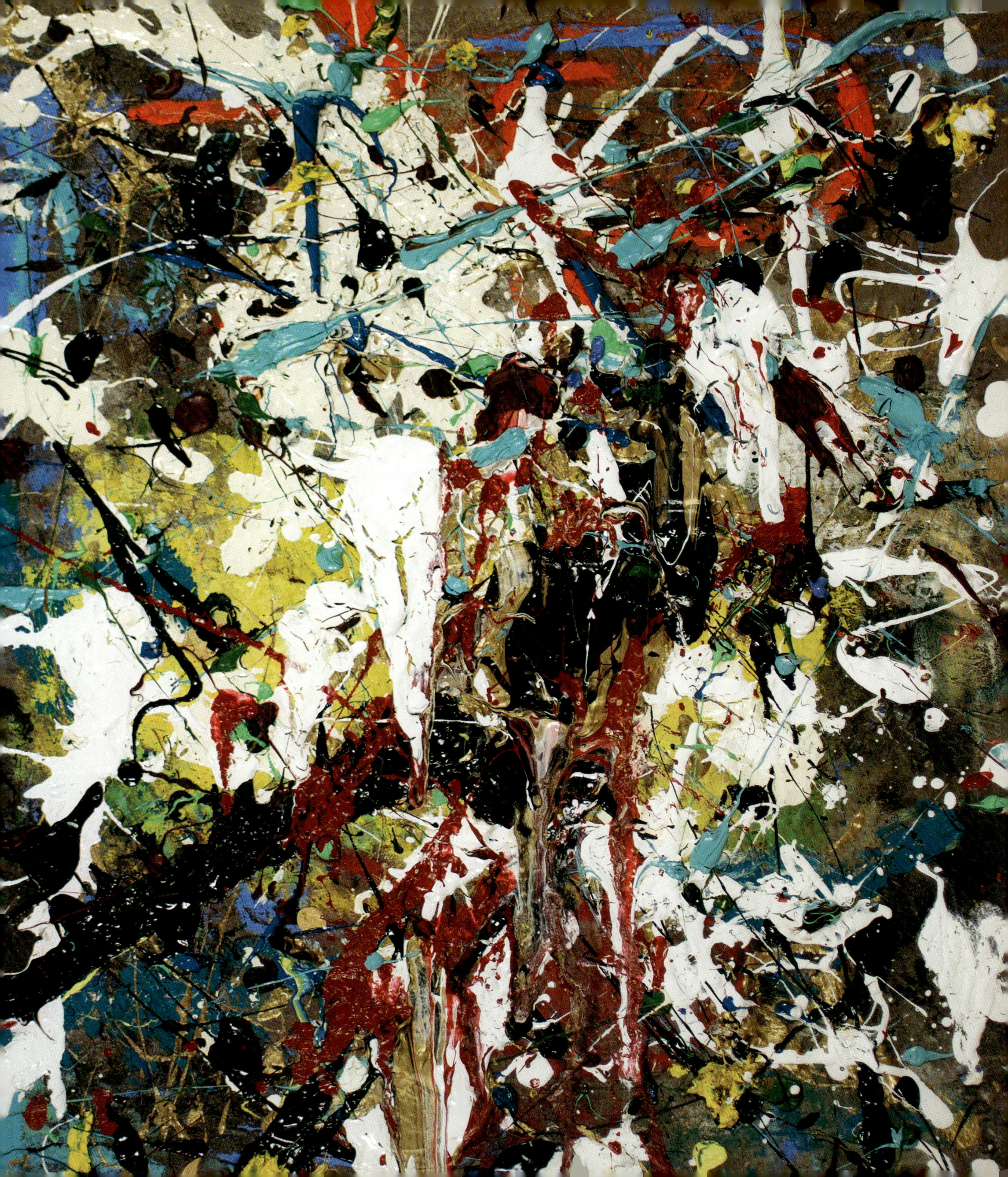

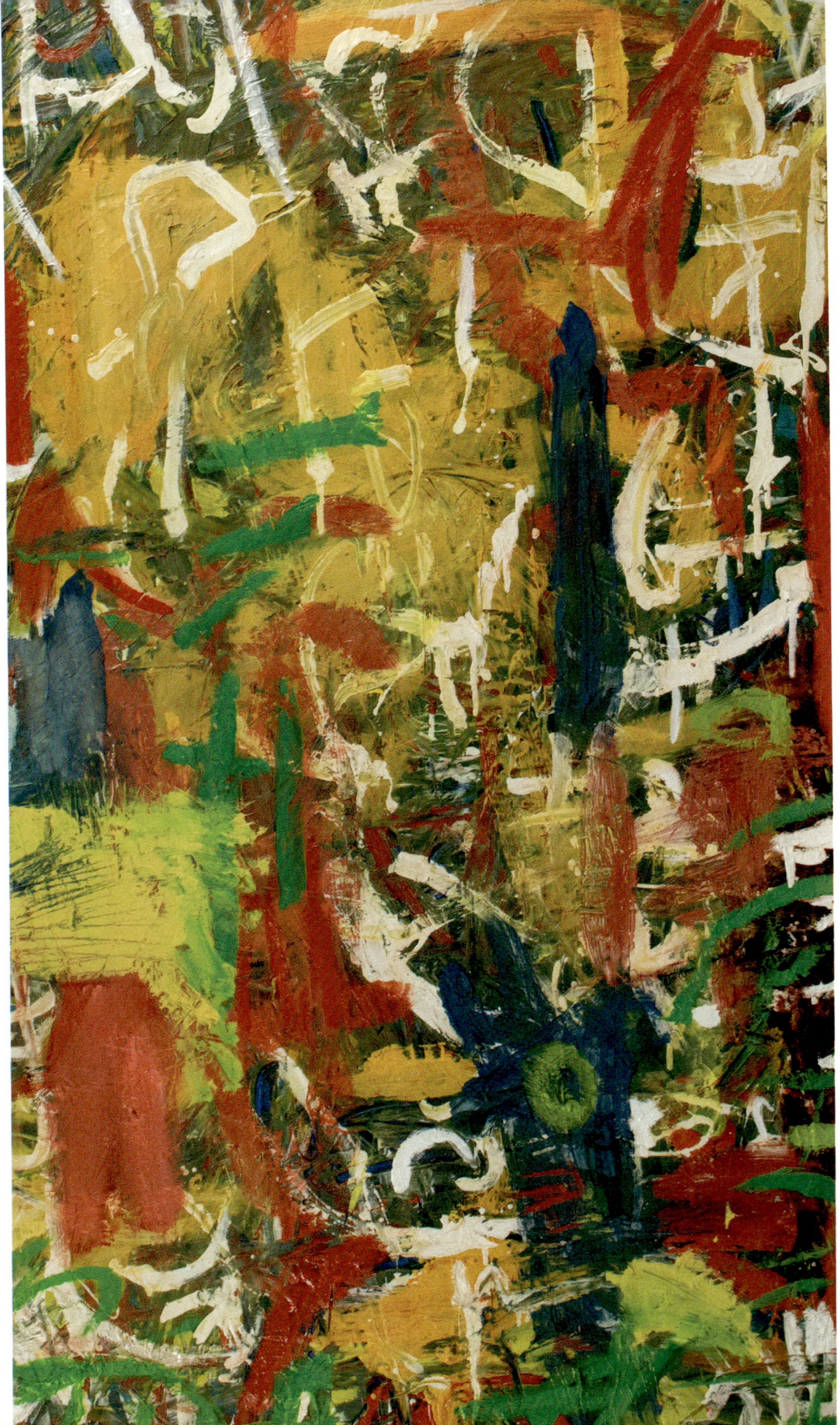

***Howl*, 2012**

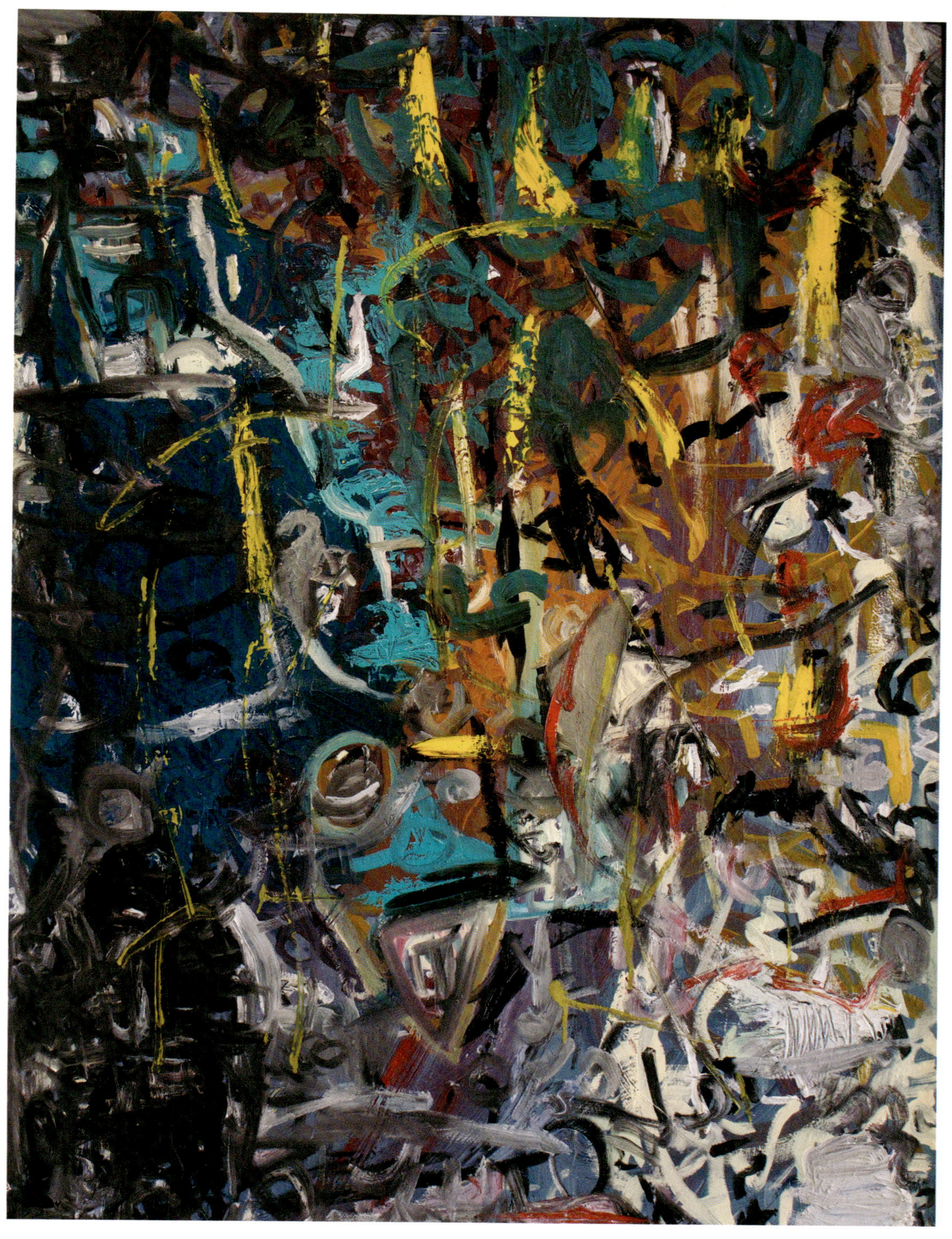

Cthonic Elements at Play, 2011

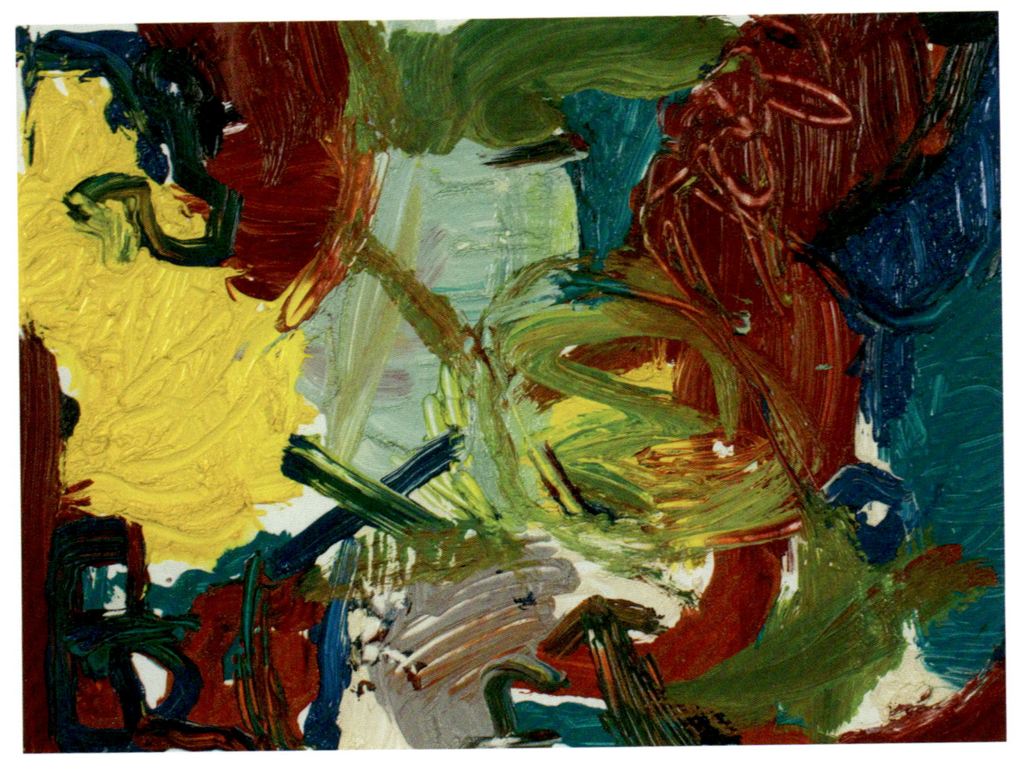

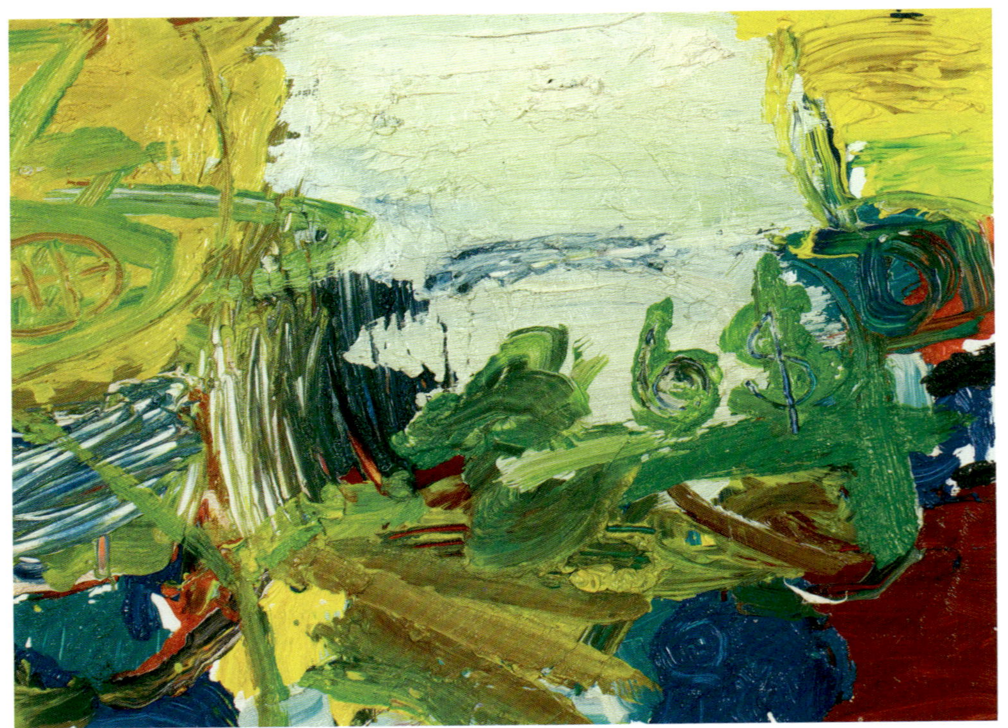

Six-Dollar Water, 2011 (two paintings from triptych)

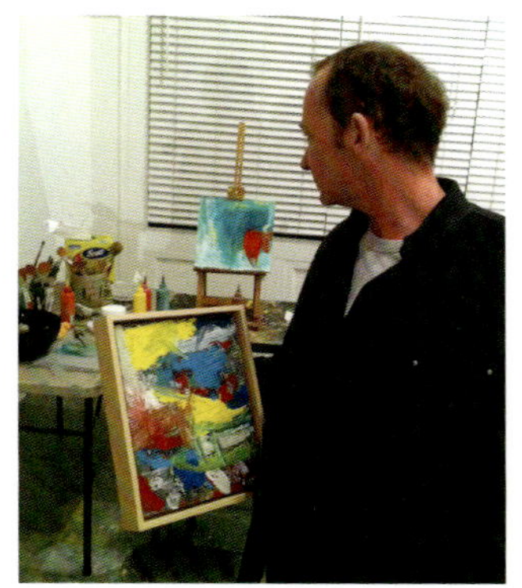

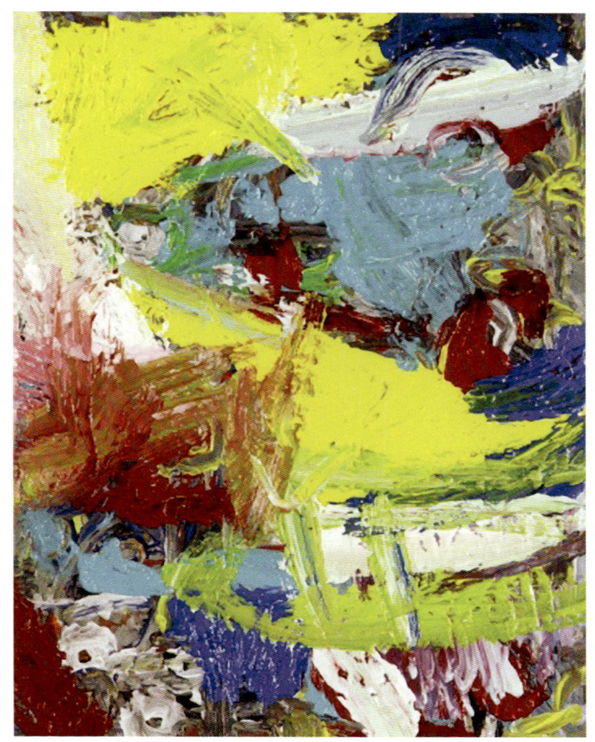

Mayhem, 2011

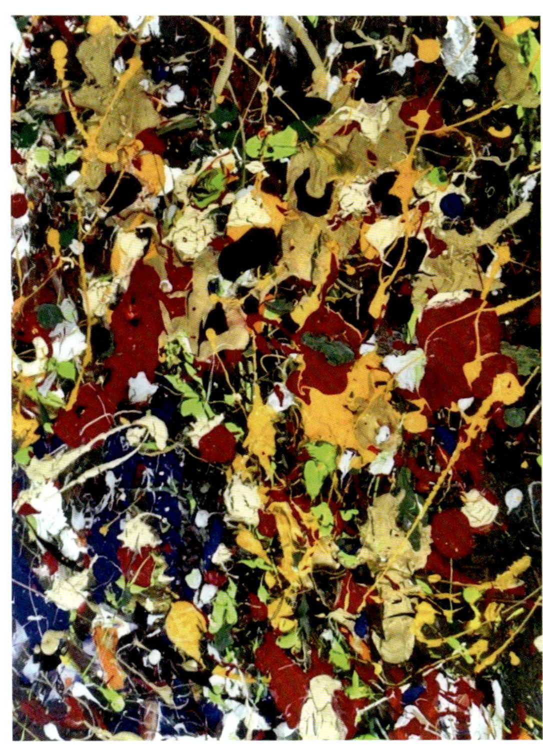

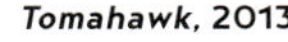

Tomahawk, 2013

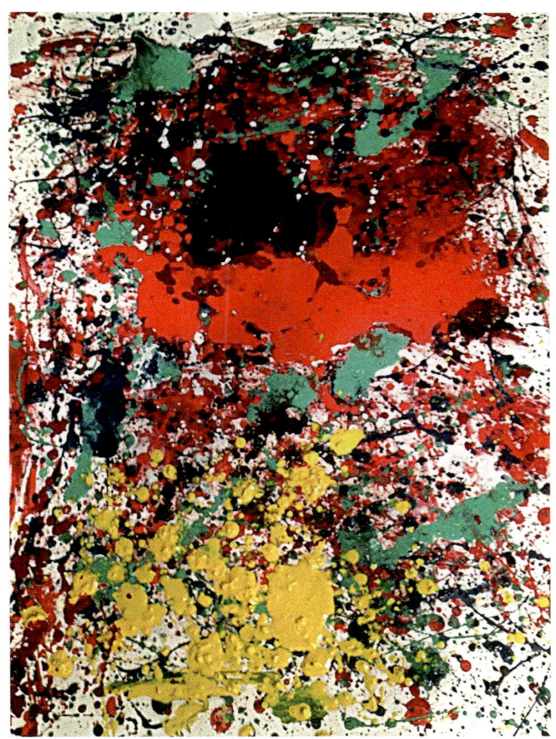

No. 9, 2013

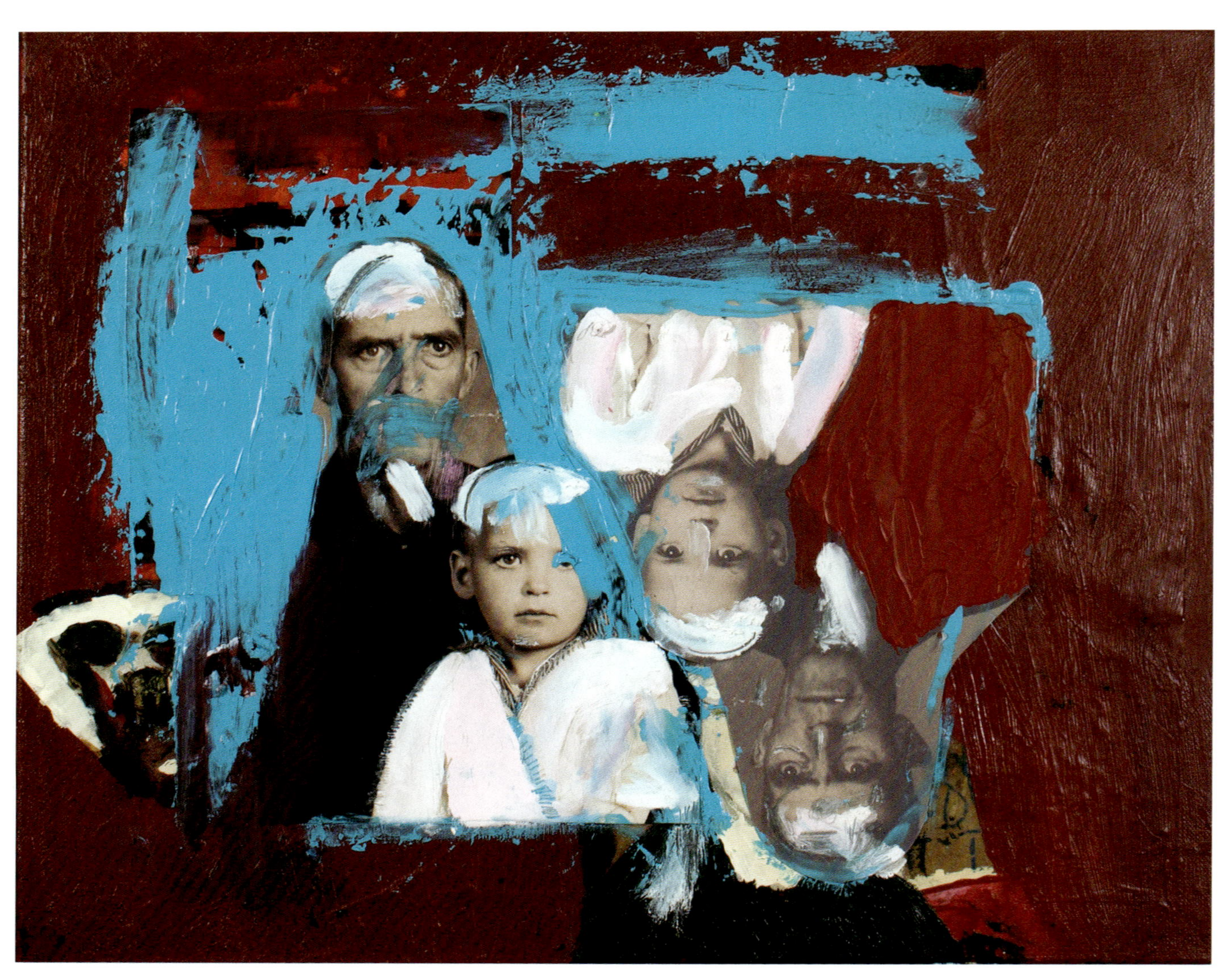

Familie Portrait, 2013

Opposite: *Anima*, 2010

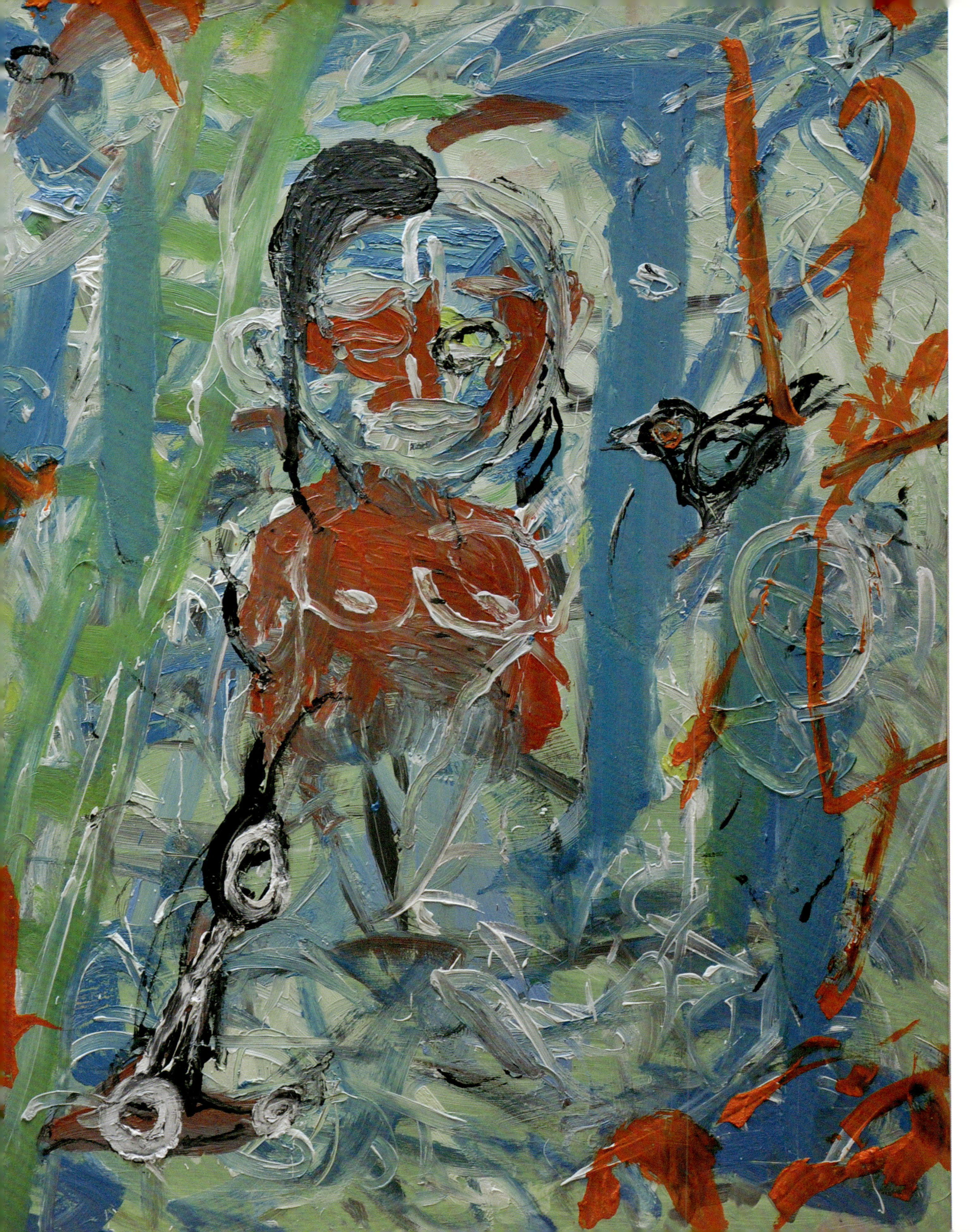

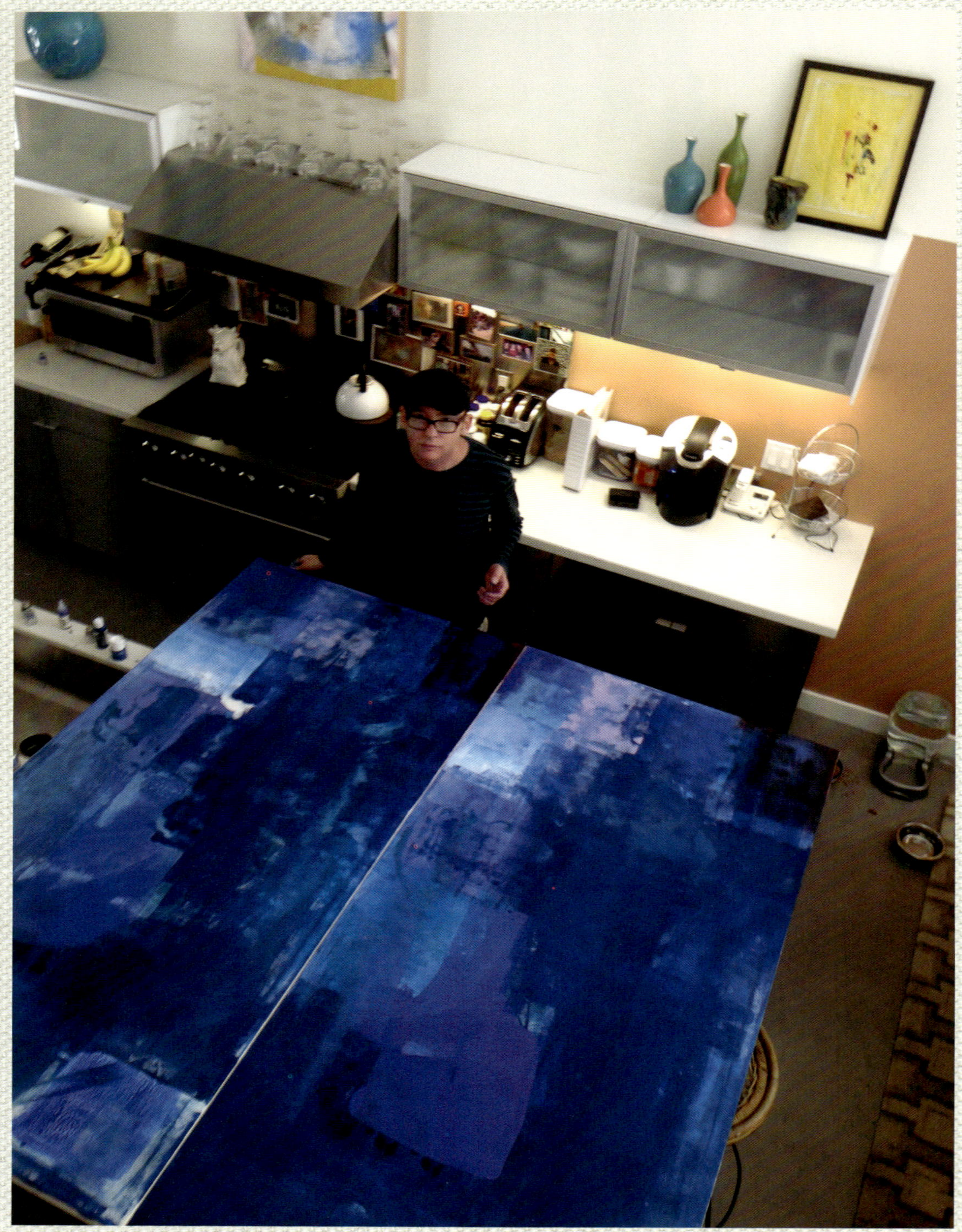

Blauw I, 2014

Blauw II, 2014

Blauw III, 2014

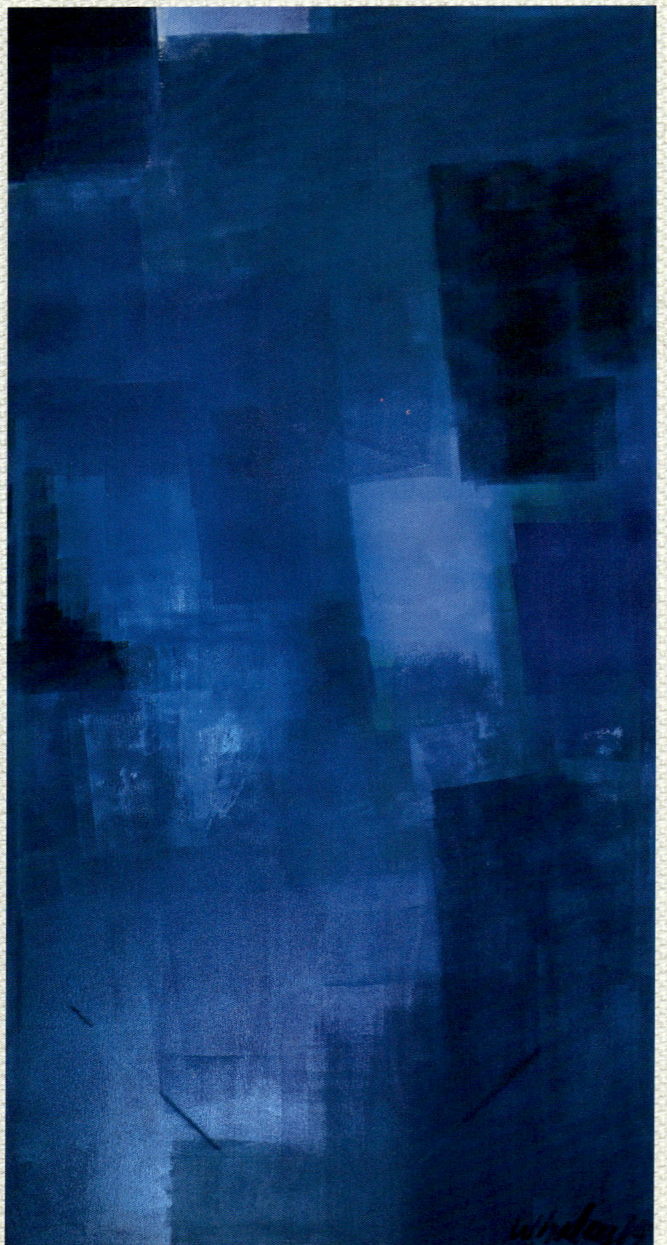

Blauw IV, 2014

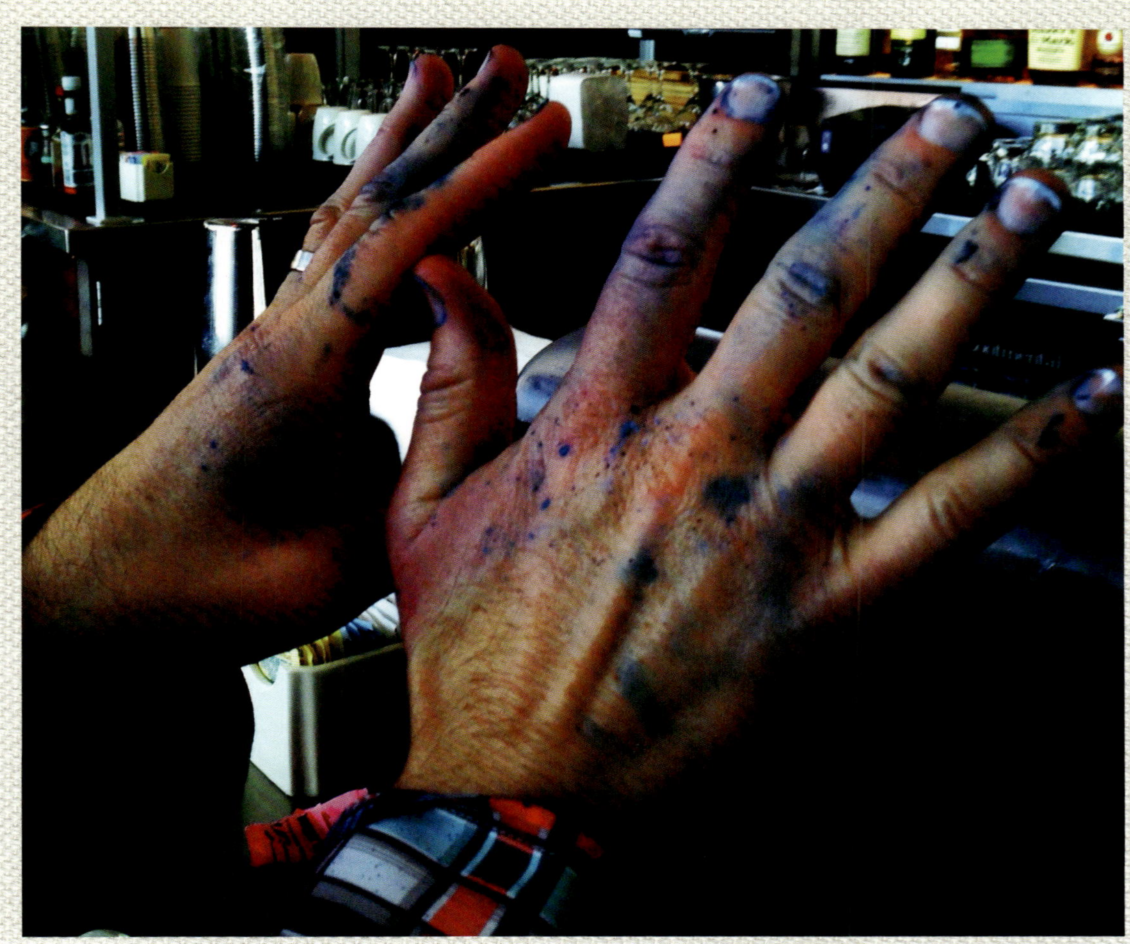

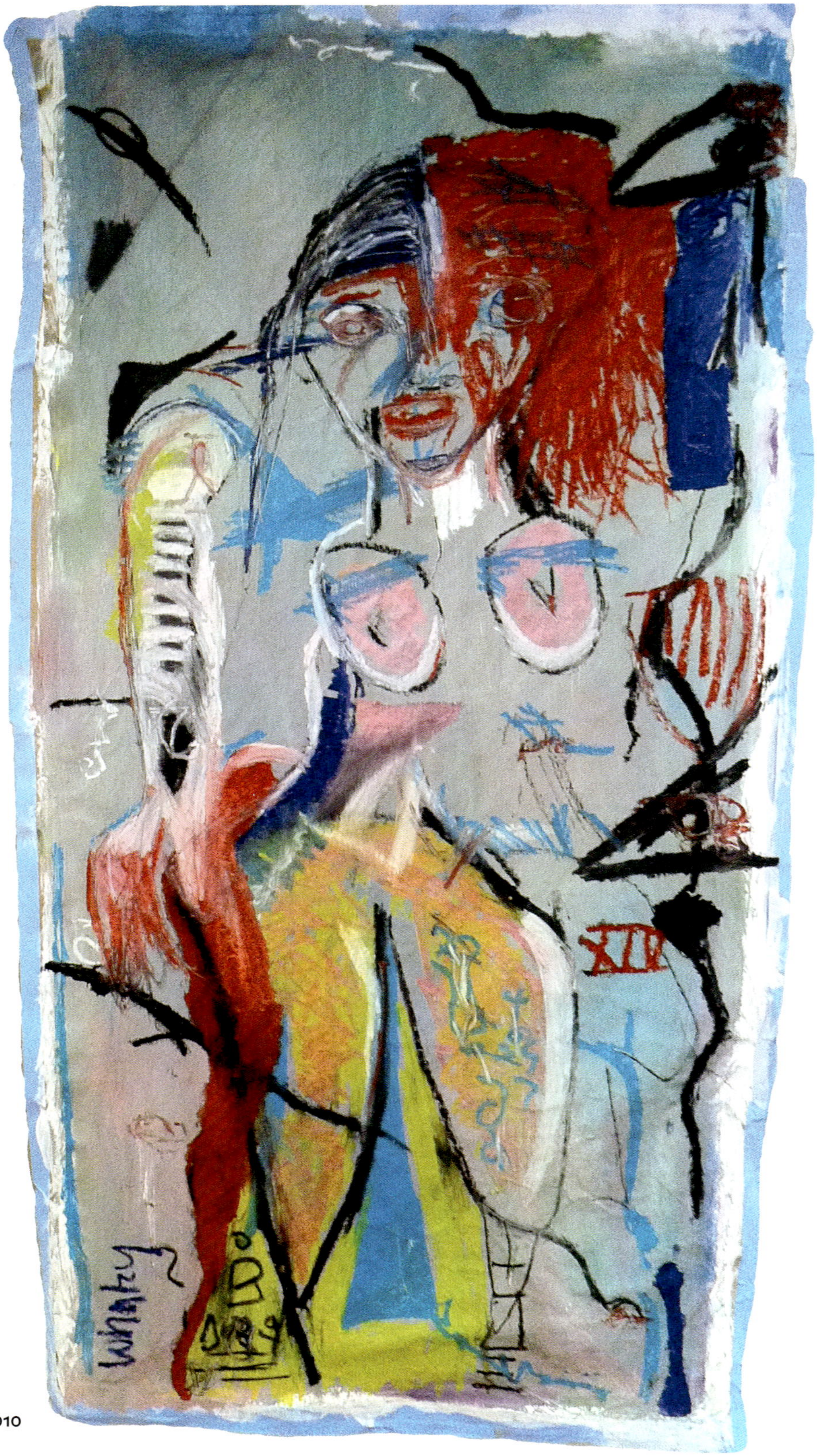

She AKA, 2010

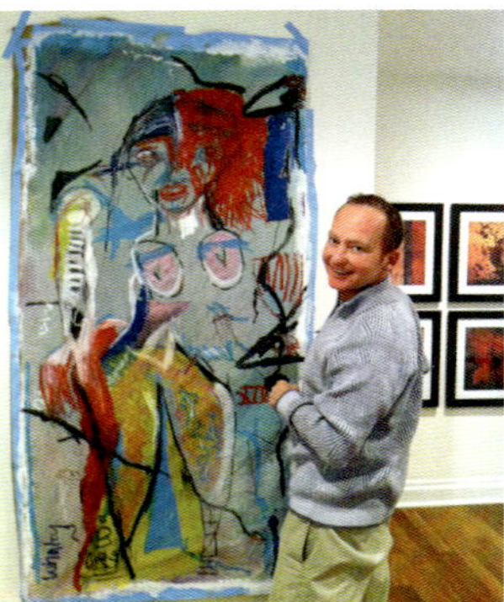

Painted during a stay at the AKA Times Square Hotel, New York City, 2010.

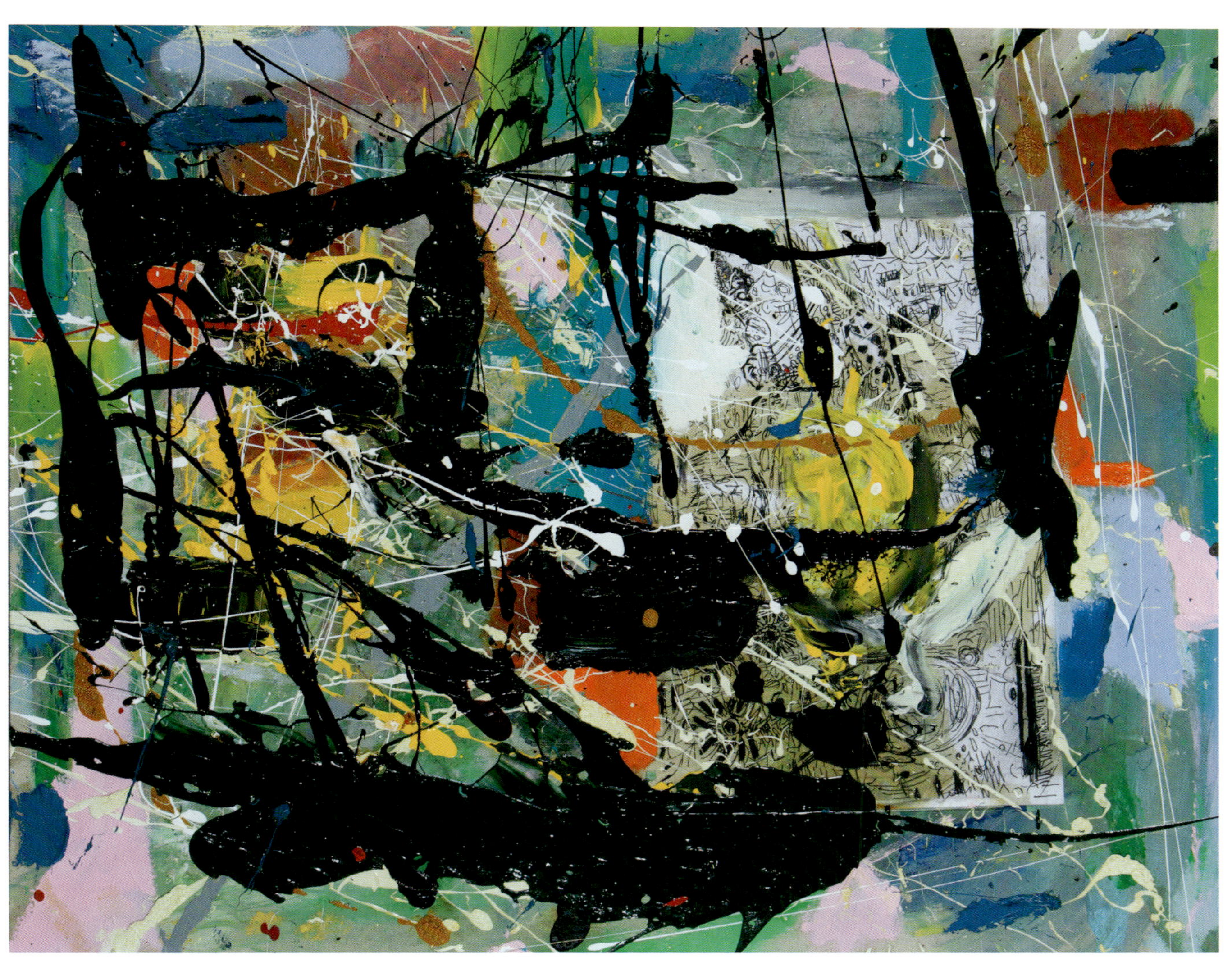

***Woman with Crane*, 2013**

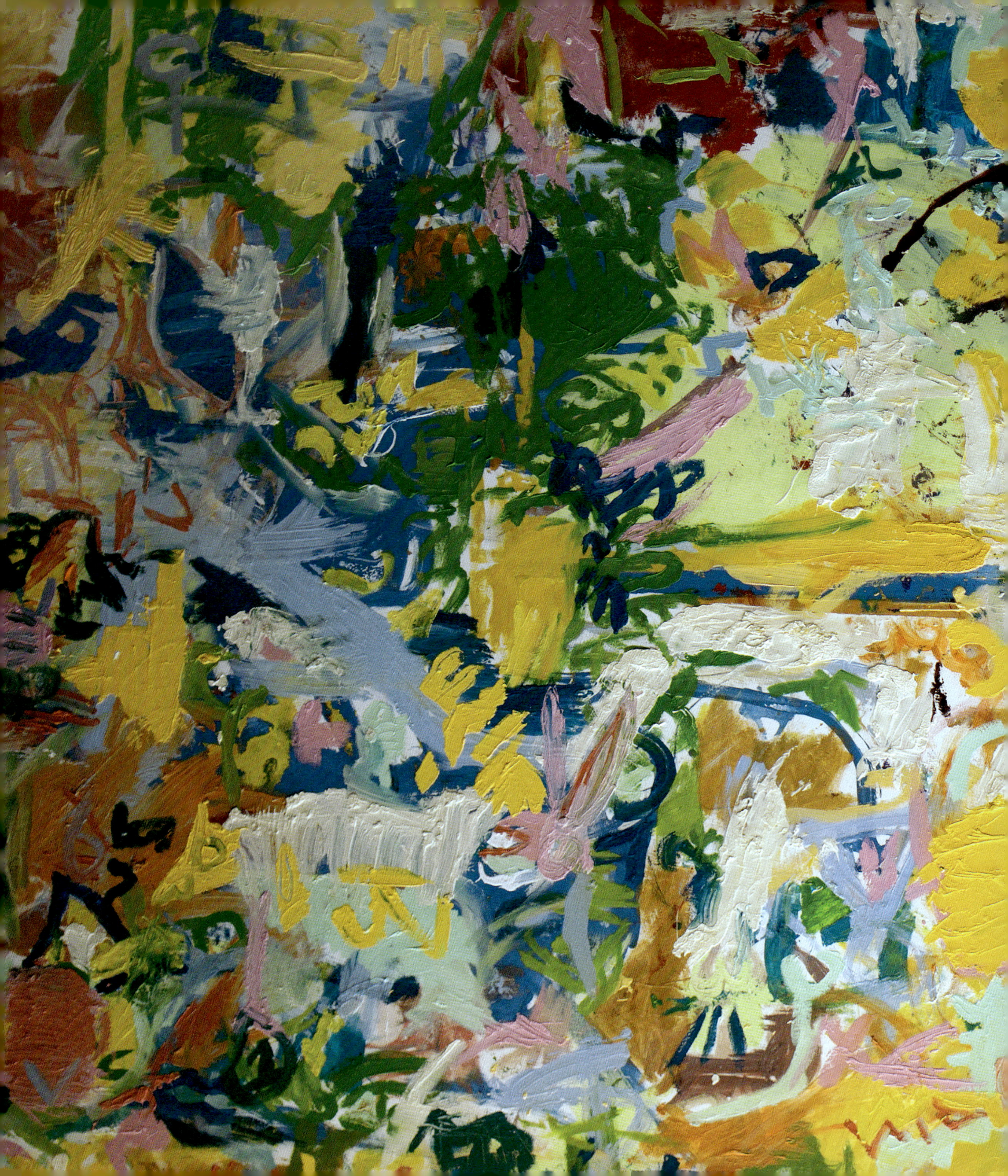

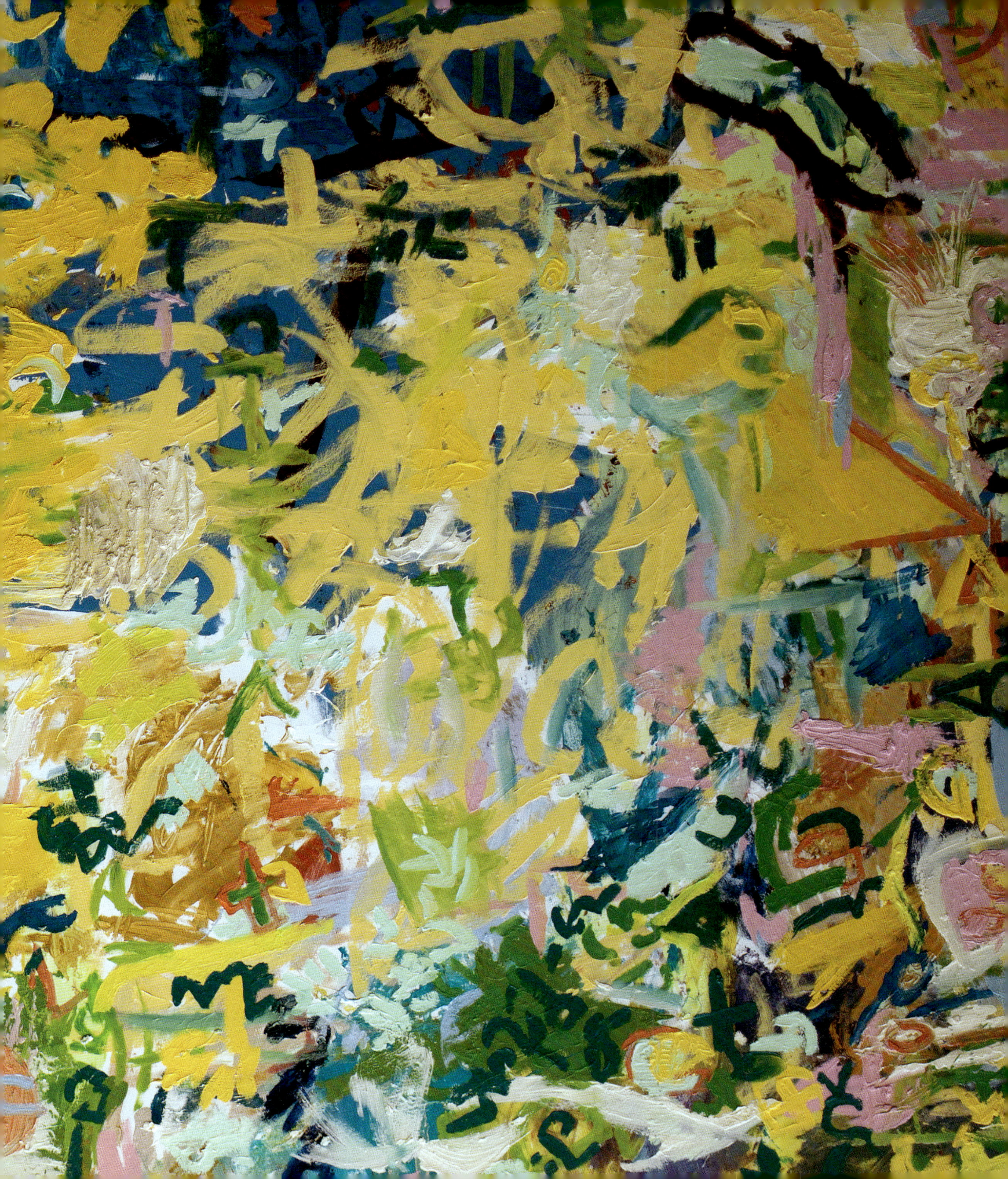

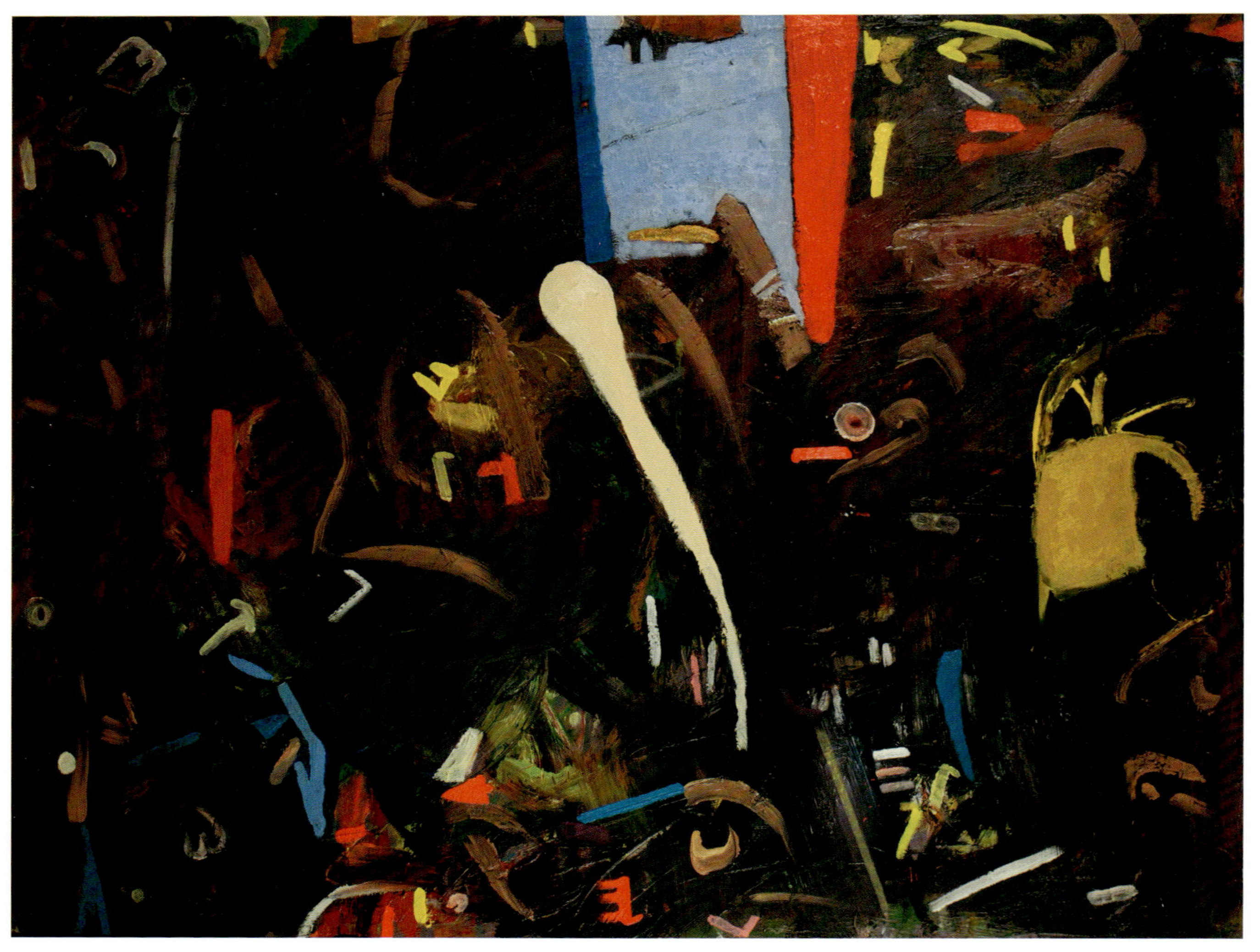

Rubedo, 2013

Overleaf: *Cadence*, 2011

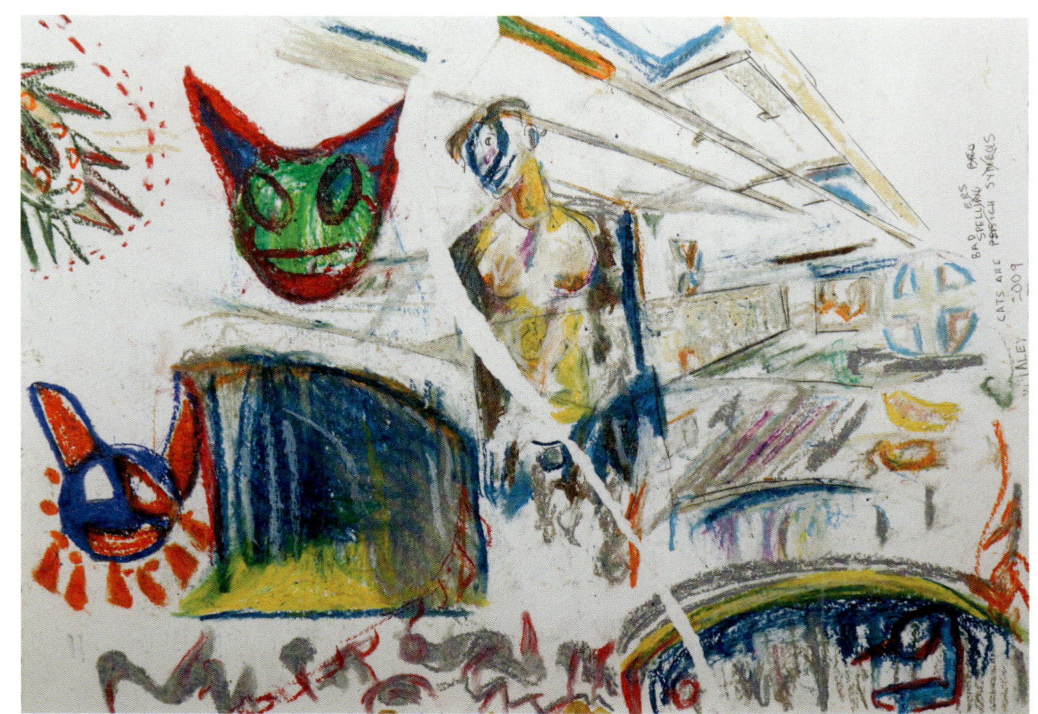

***Cats Are Bad Spellers*, 2009**

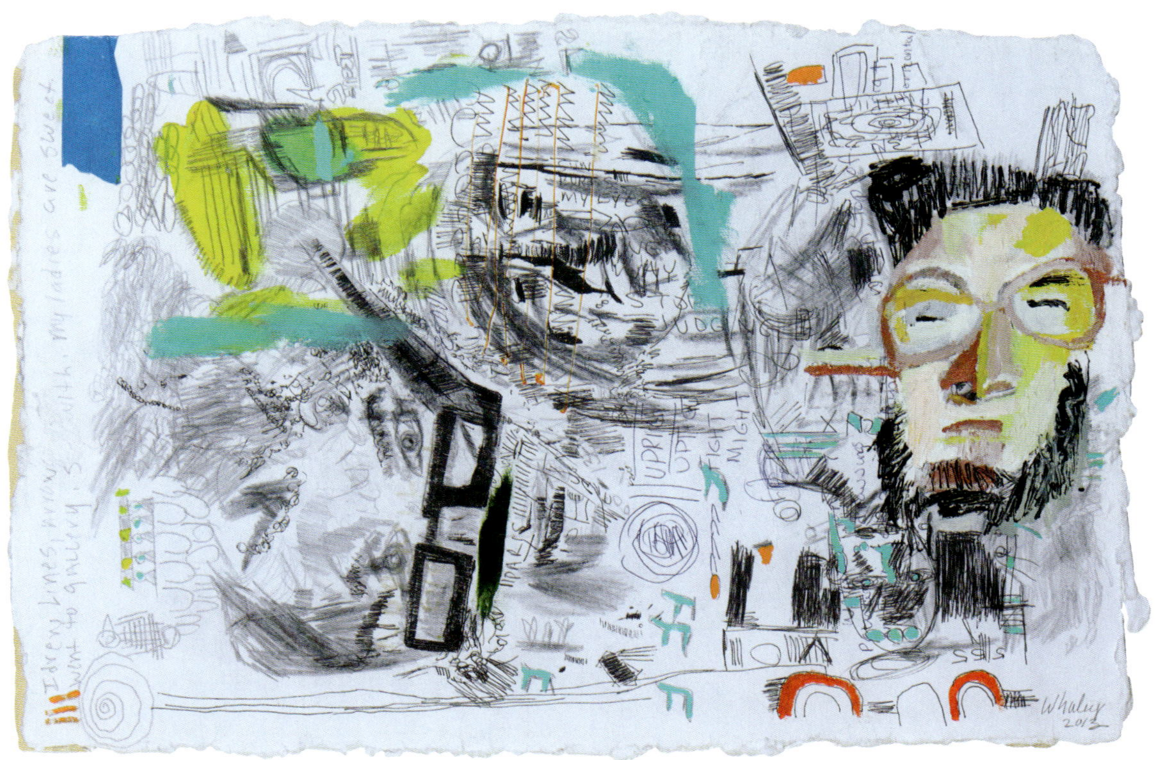

***Went to Gallery*, 2013**

"**This painting** has two primary figures, painted in an expressive manner with violent brushwork in blue hues. Their heads are shaved in the painting, to portray unification and sacrifice to the inside world they protect.

"The yellow in the second figure symbolizes both age and quarantine. Such a symbol is again shown at the bottom left, as an indicator that this change or new way of thinking is dangerous to the ways of the old world. The vomit in the painting is a form of psychic rebirth and evolution. It's shown as alchemical process of becoming whole. The colors turn from yellow to gold and then black to reach the outside world.

"The painting poses a question about the final outcome of the quarantine, and the release of the prisoner." —DW

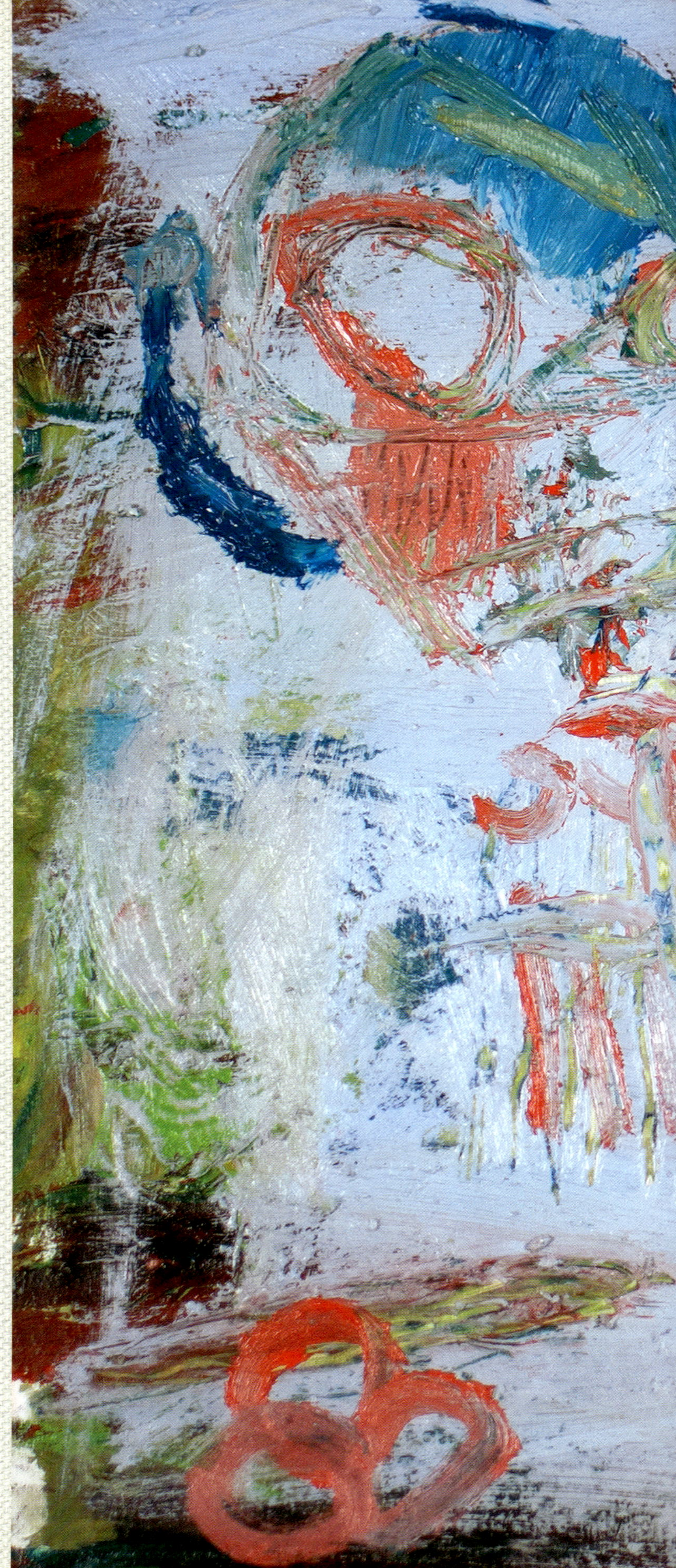

***Guardian*, 2011**

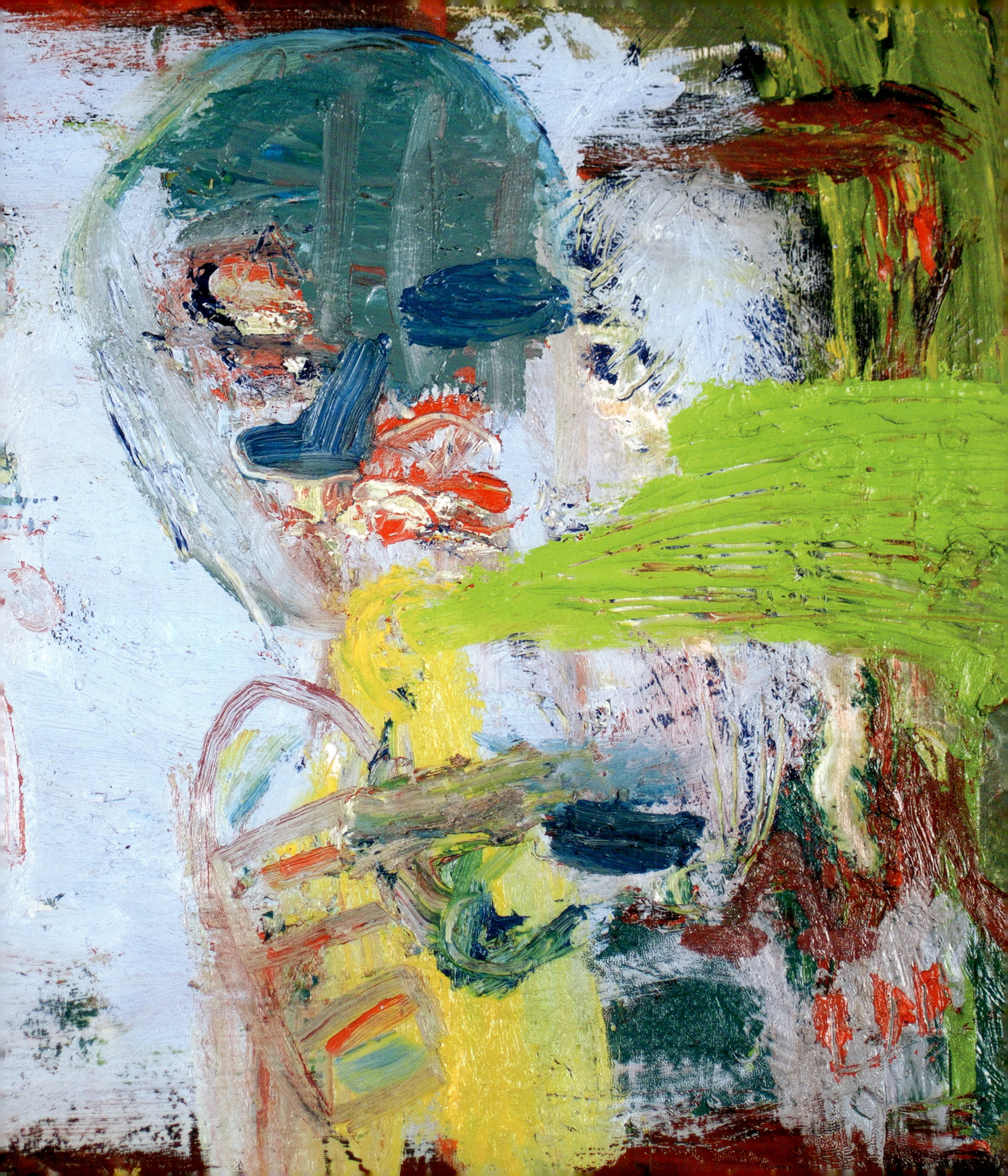

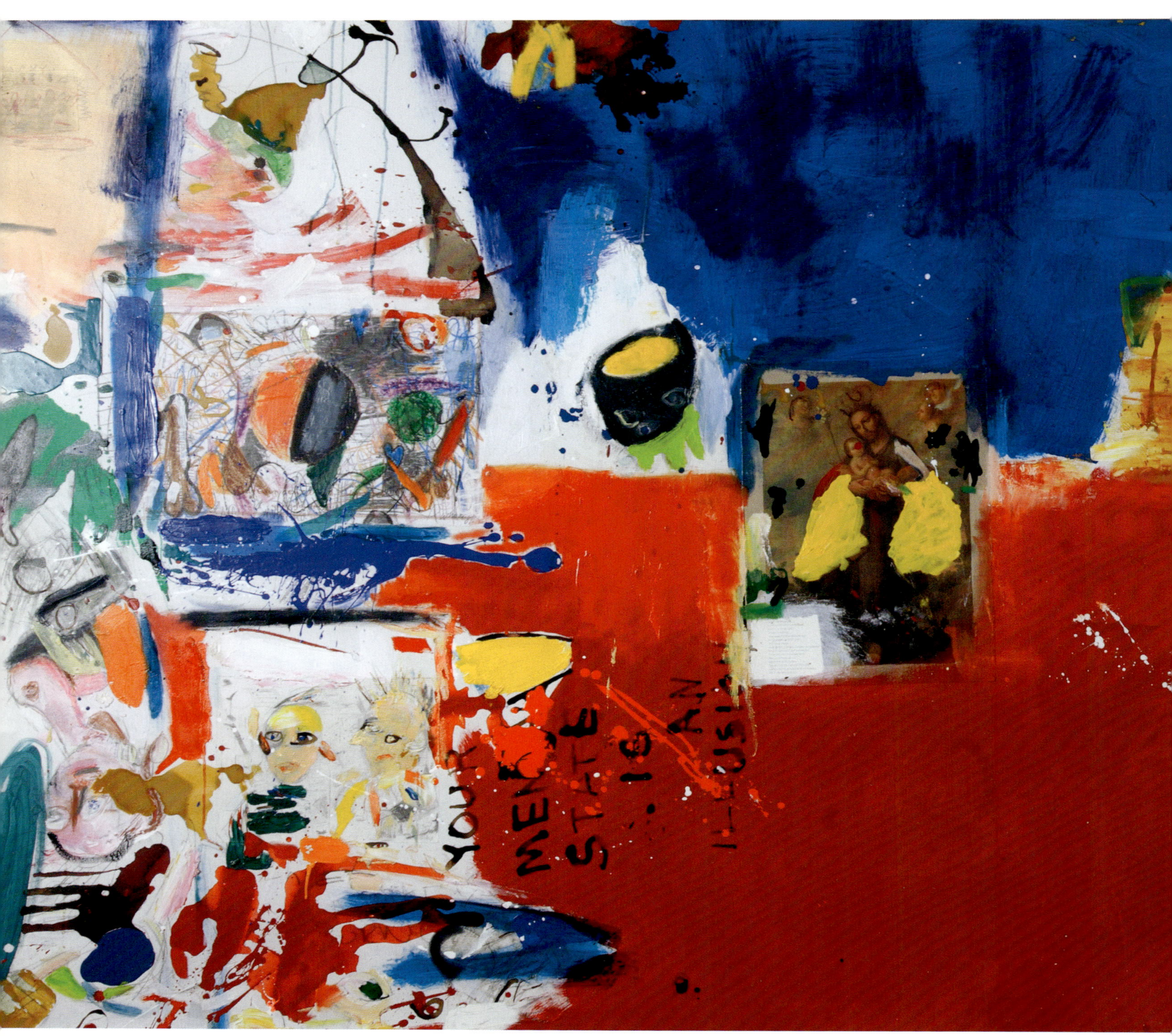
YOUR
STATE
IS AN

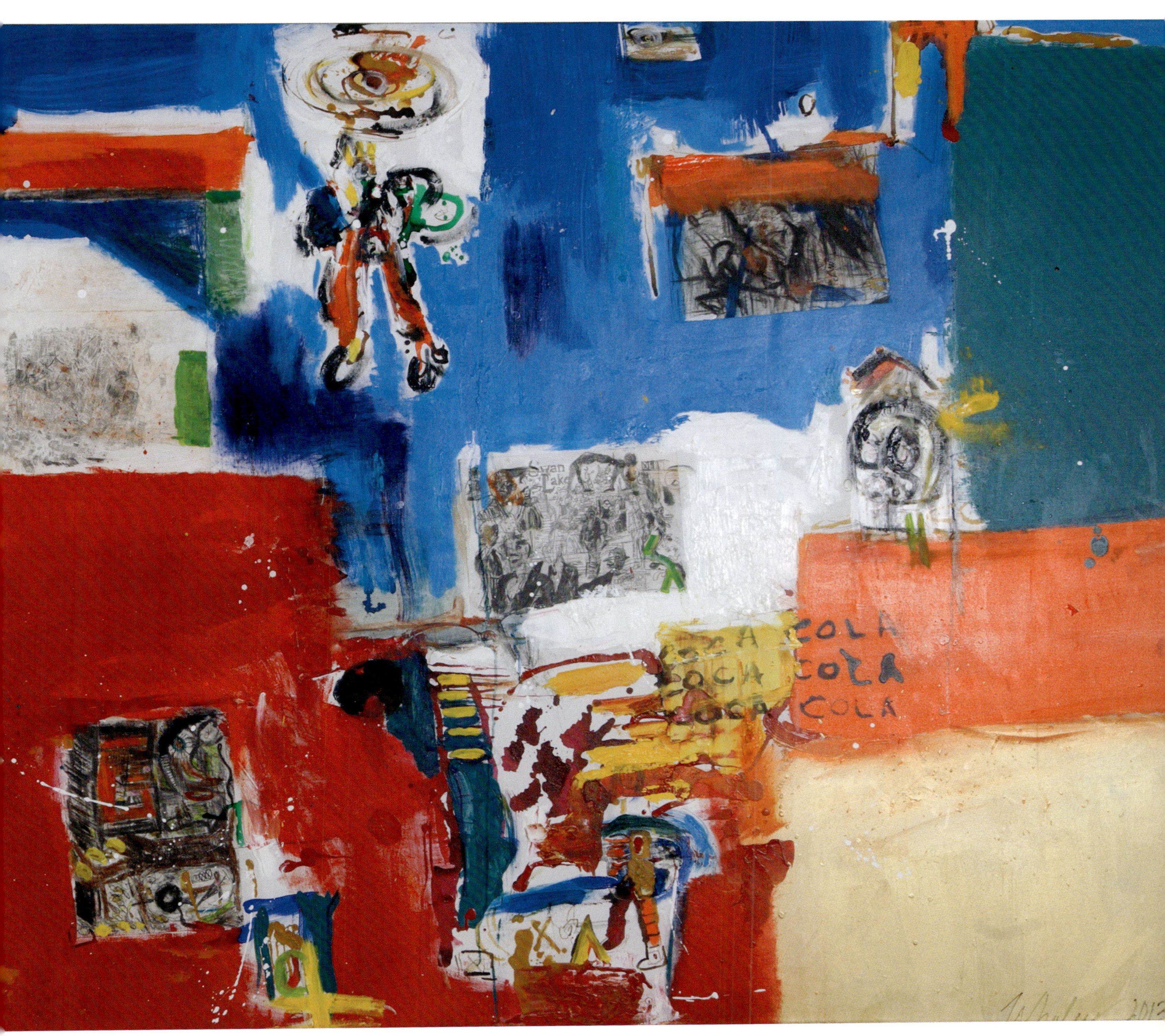

***Your Mental Illness Is an Illusion I (aka Hurricane)*, 2013**

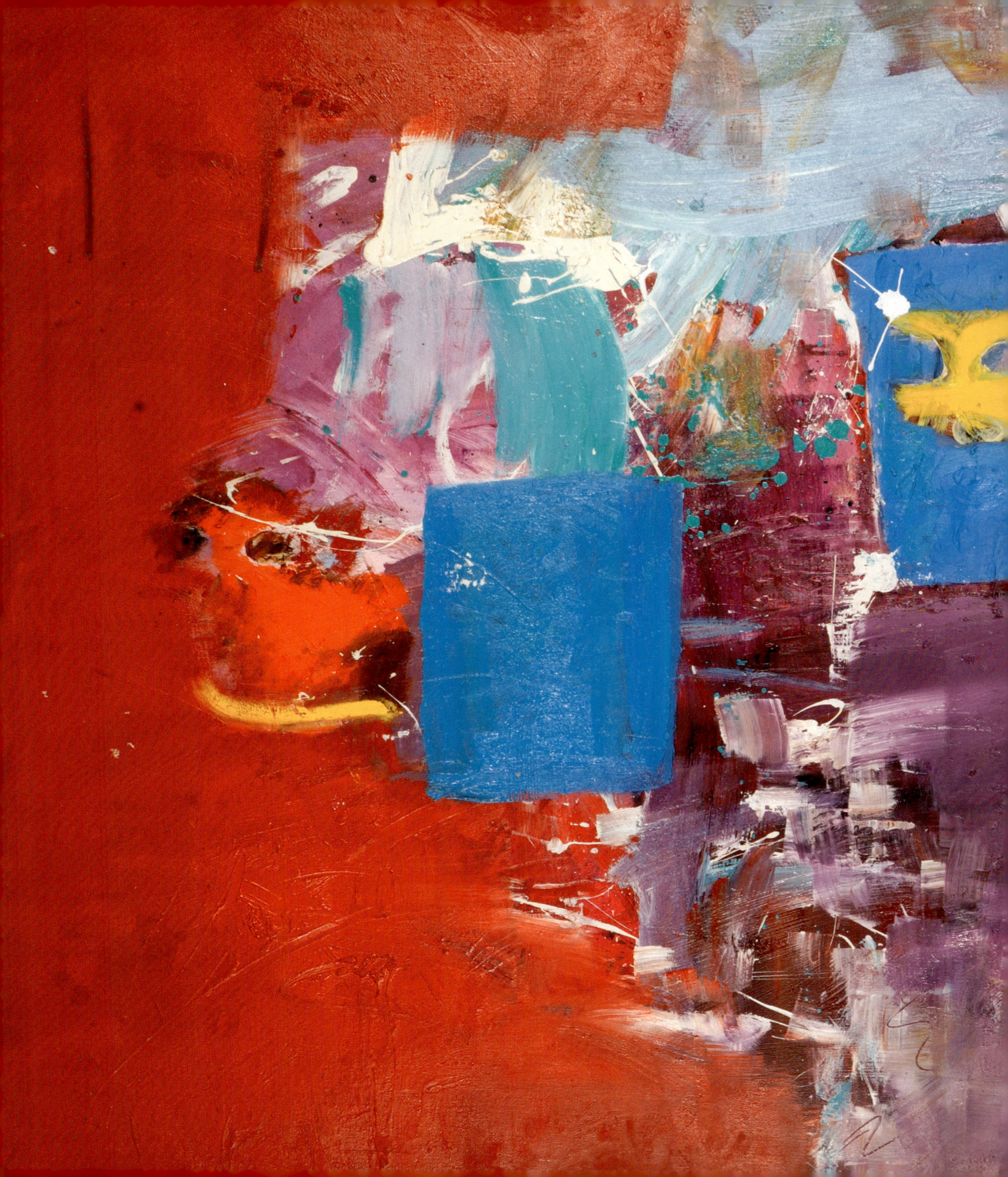

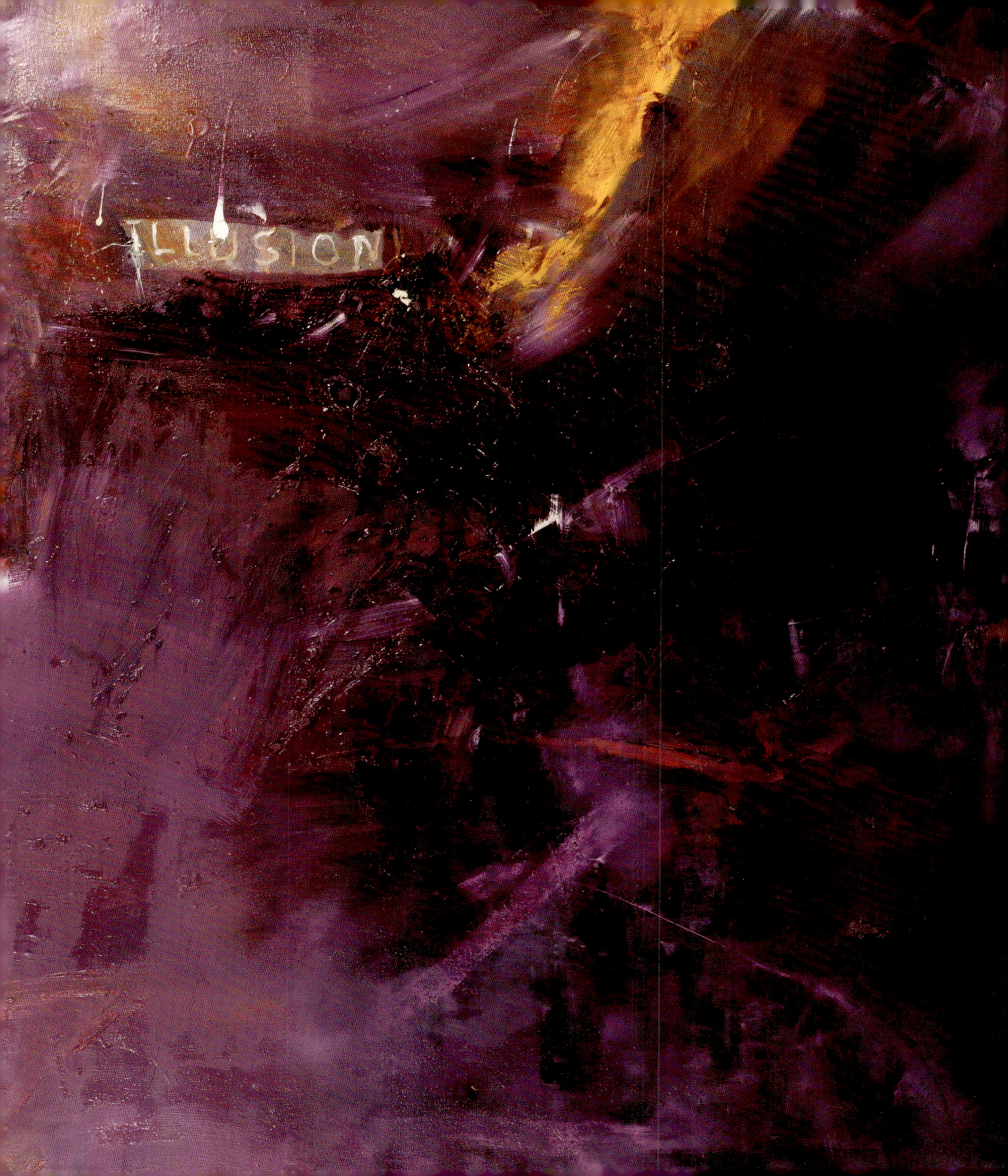
ILLUSION

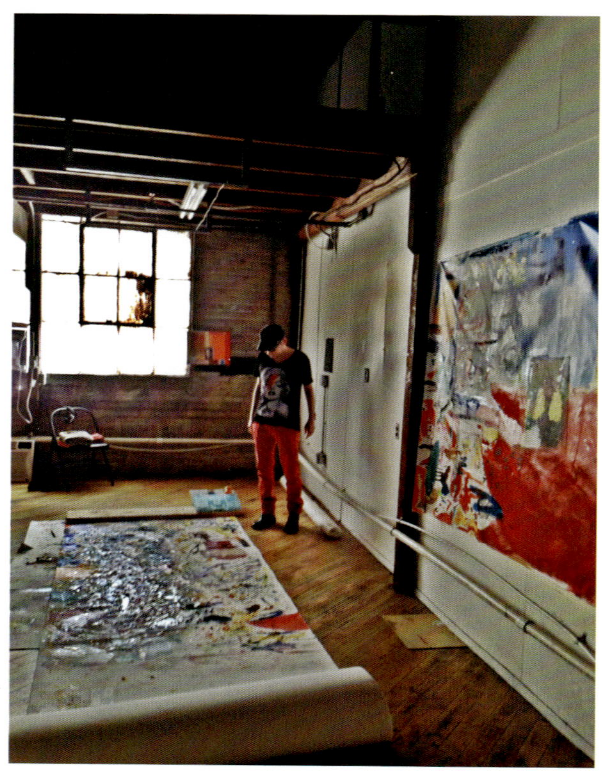
Davyd Whaley in his New Orleans studio.

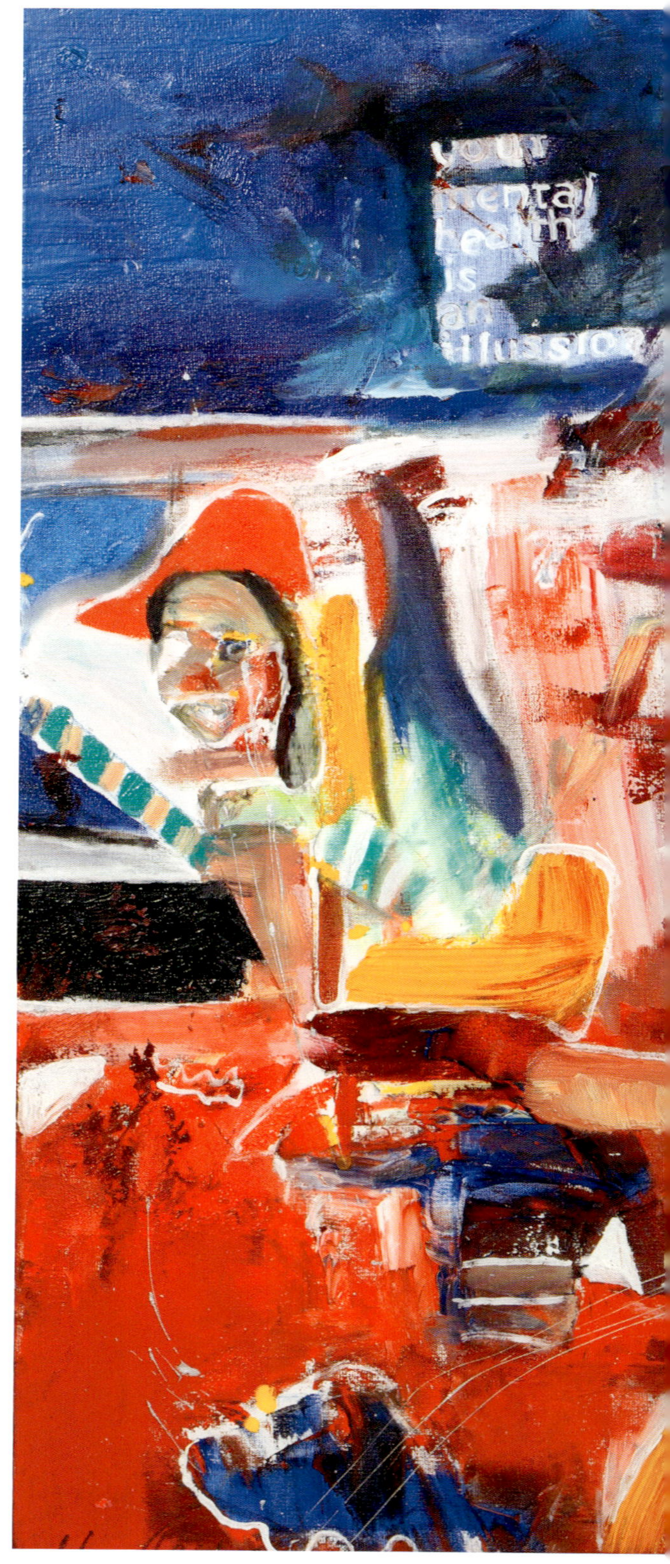

Overleaf: *Your Mental Illness Is an Illusion II*, 2013

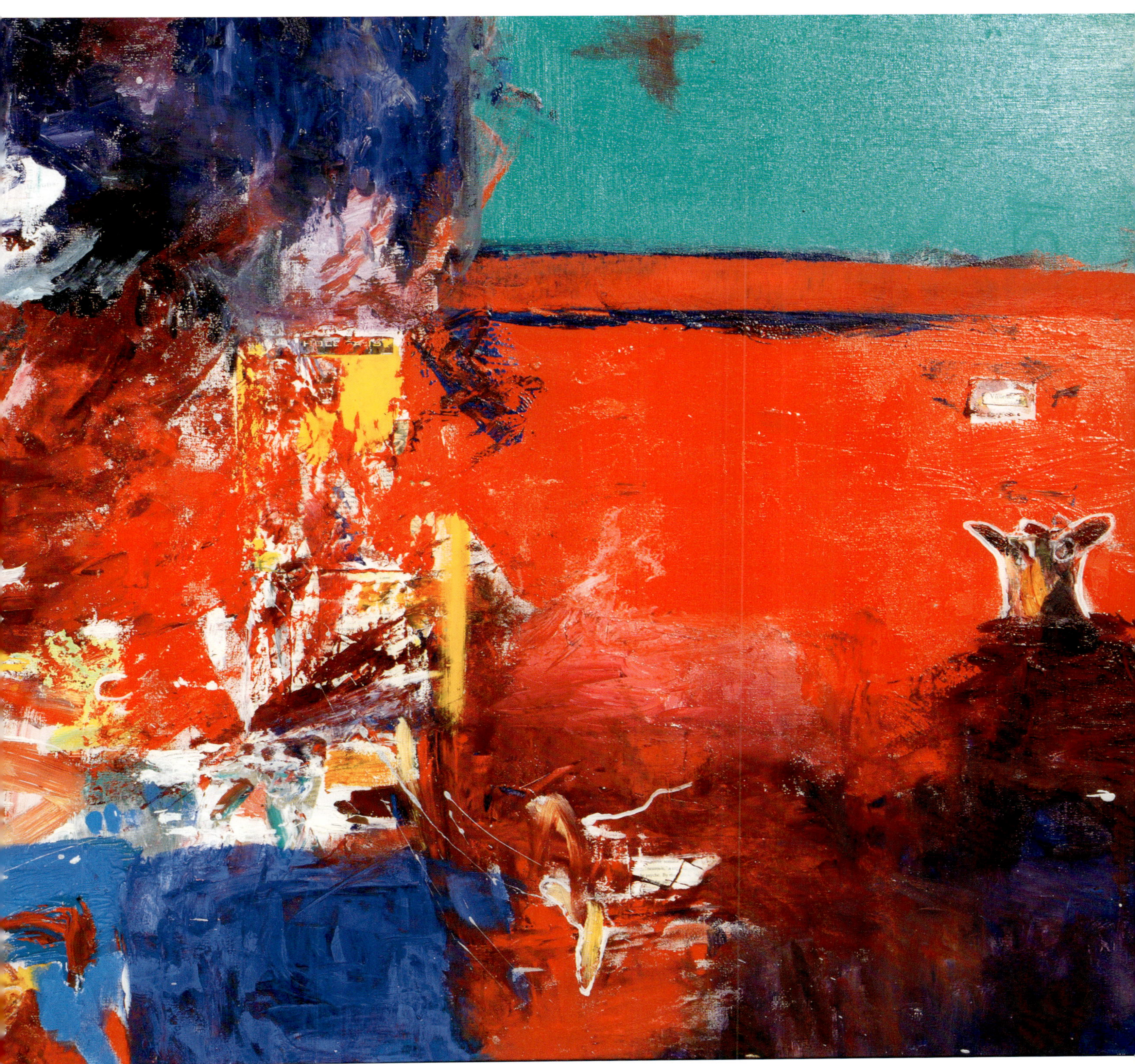

***Your Mental Illness Is an Illusion III*, 2013**

"**Provider** is a painting about the nuclear family. The mother and father are shown as prehistoric caregivers. This is meant to be ironic, in the sense that traditional families are no longer the standard. Most families are very different in today's society. In this painting the father has sacrificed a bird as the mother prepares a meal. The boy stares down at the kill, wide-eyed. The eyes of the parents appear to look upward and out in a protective manner.

"Provider evokes one of the first paintings I did at six years of age. There is a fair amount of tension in the lines of the figures as I look back at it several years later. It's dynamic, but withholds a lot of information from the viewer. I see myself as the child, not fitting in with this family. The desire to create and re-create this image is something that's important to me as an artist." —DW

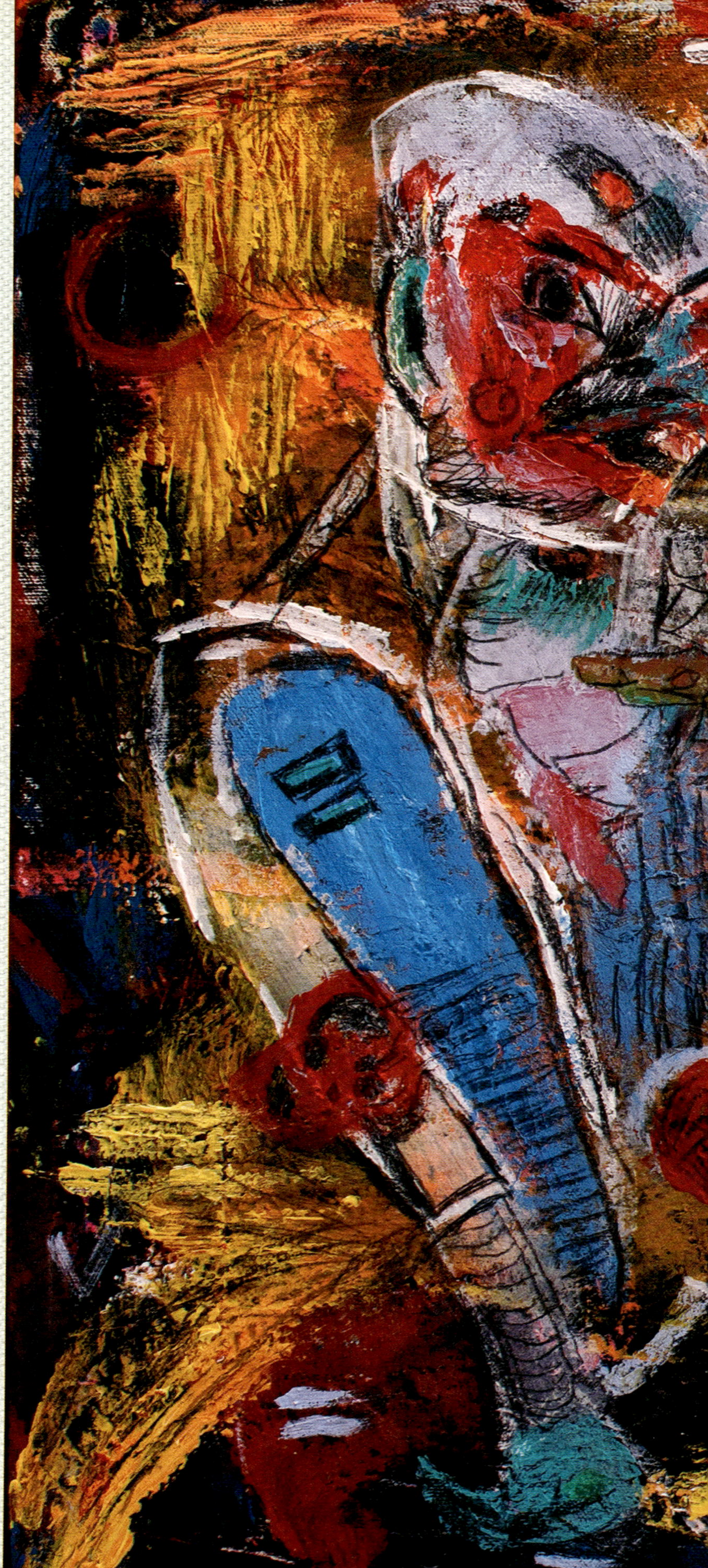

***Provider*, 2009**

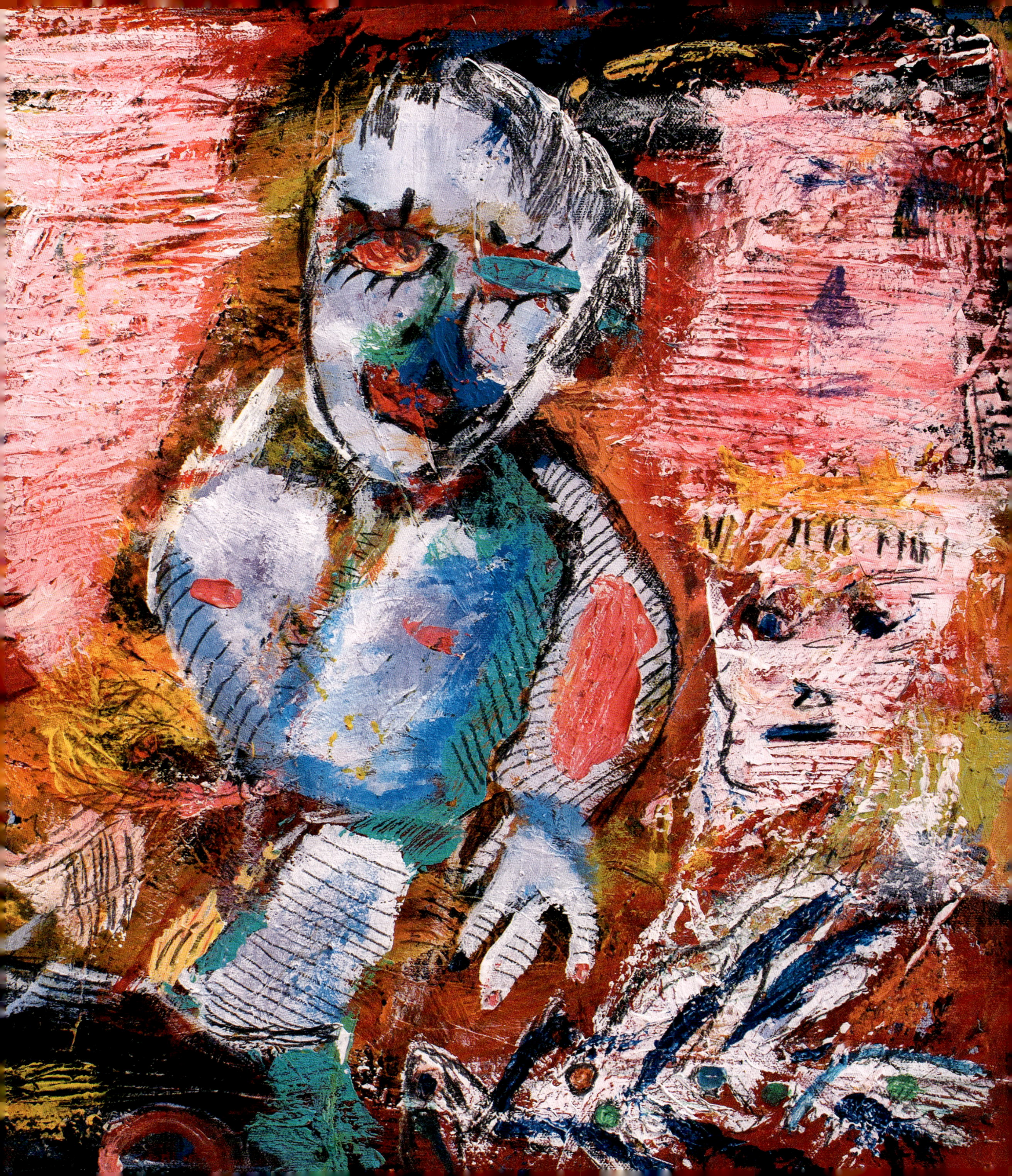

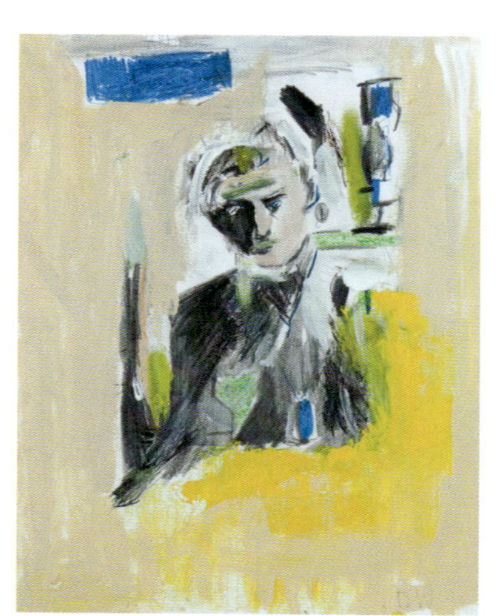

***Study for King of Pop*, 2012**

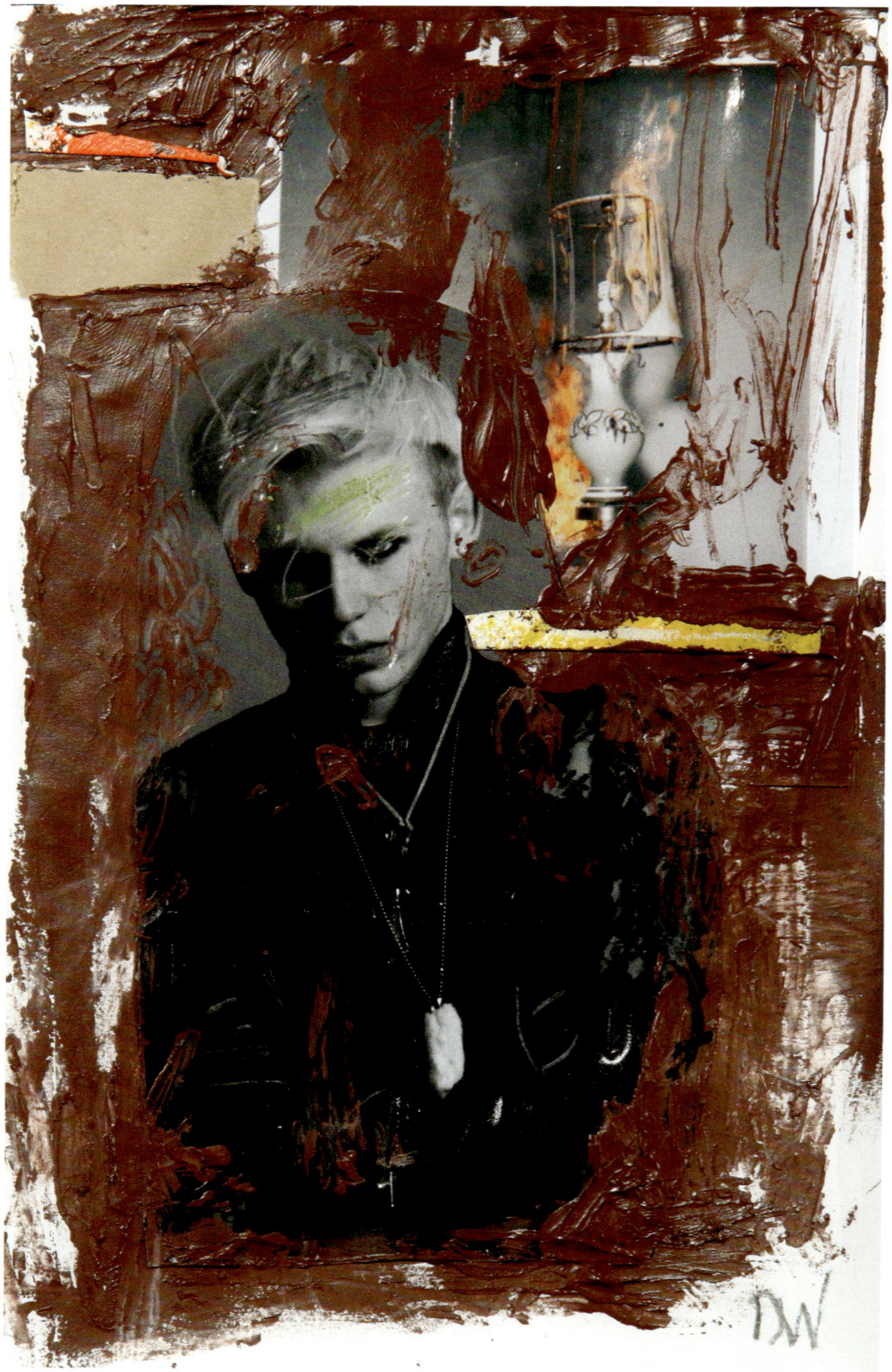

***King of Pop*, 2012**

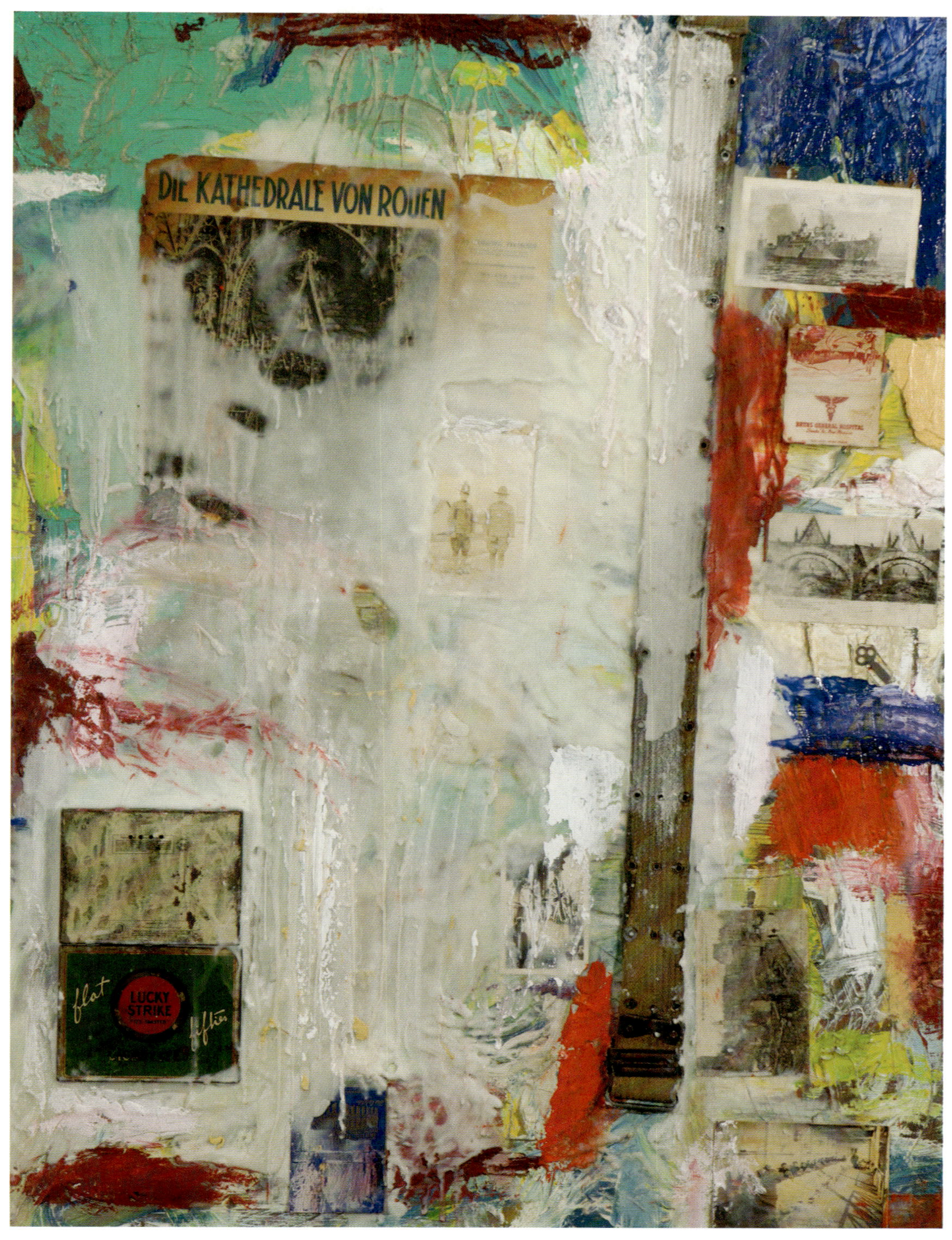

***14*, 2012**

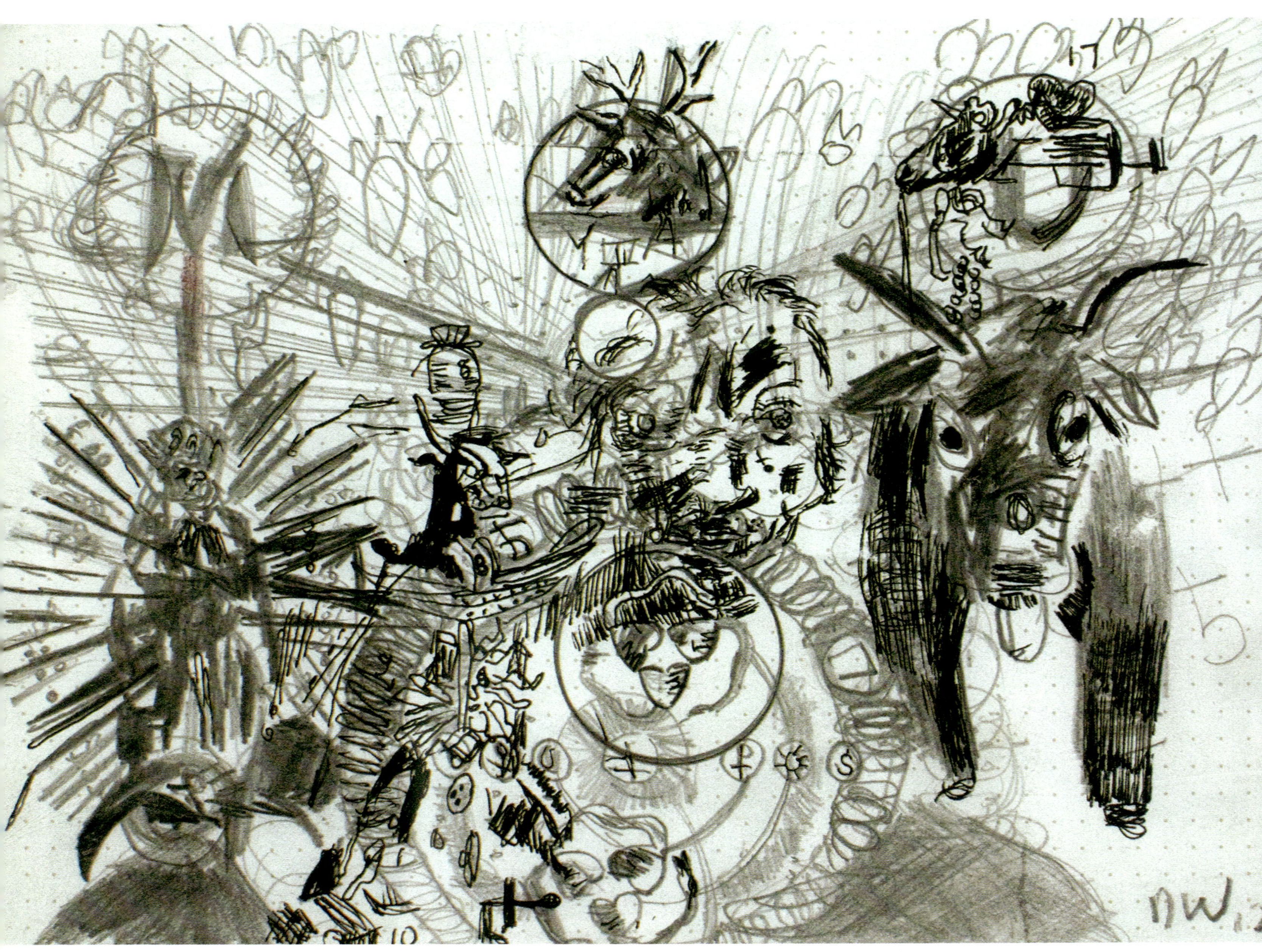

Bull and Elk, 2012

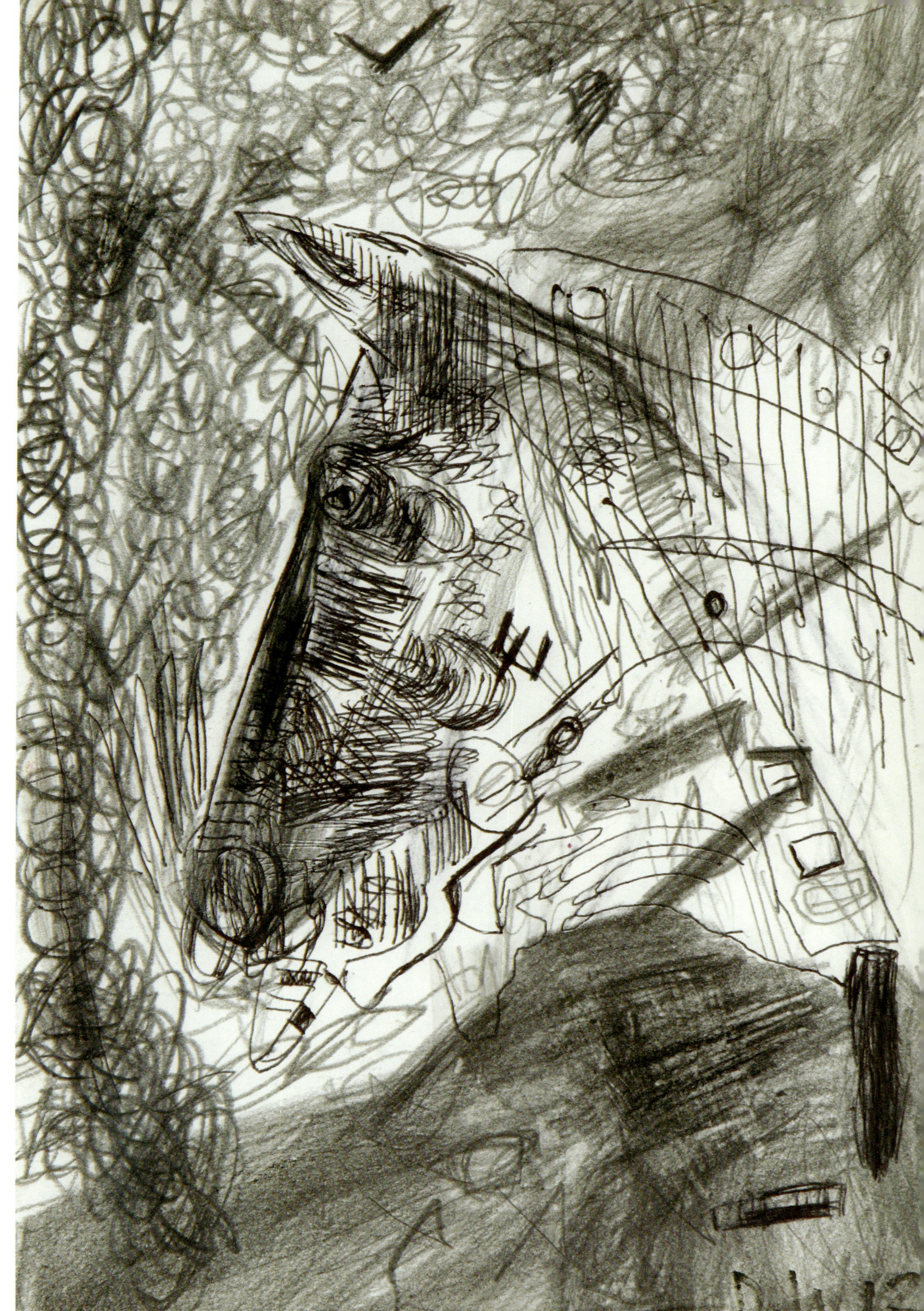

The Horse, 2012

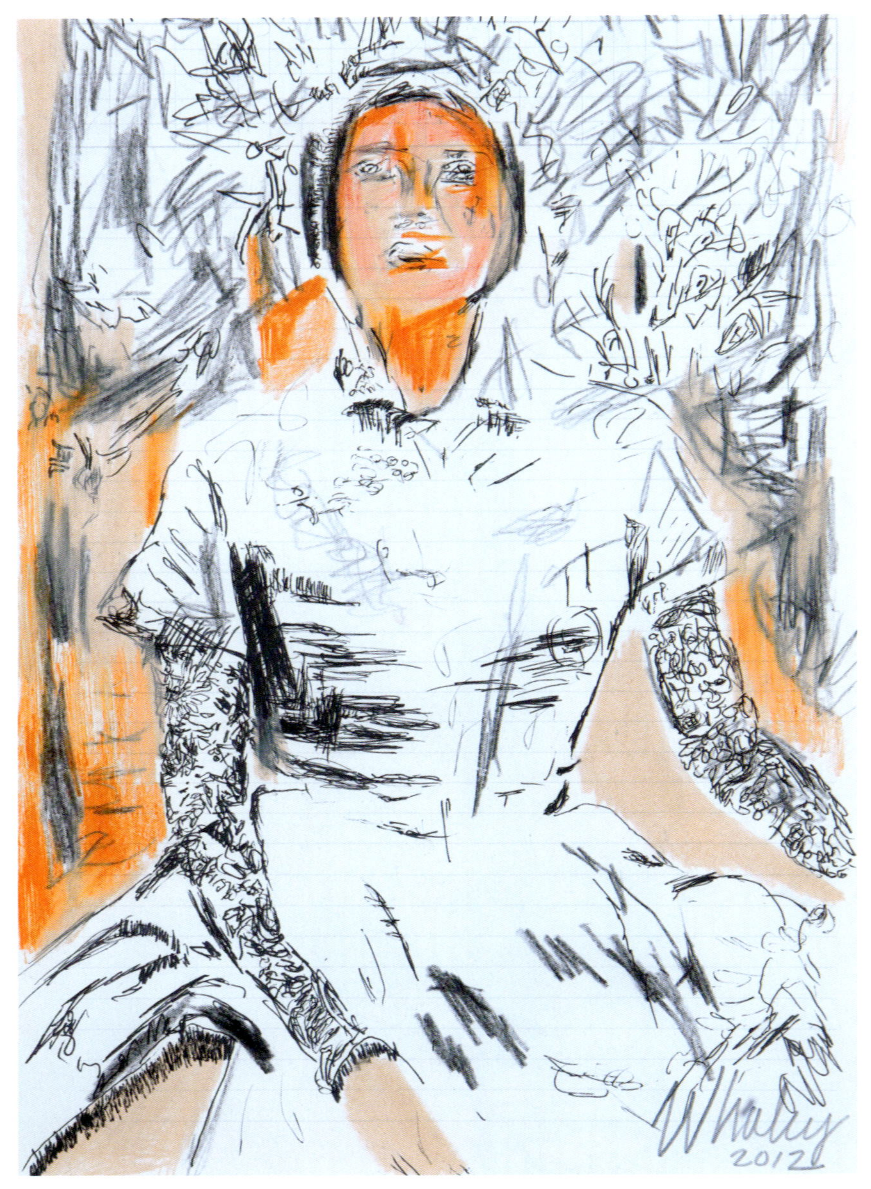

Woman in White Dress, 2012

Opposite: *Woman in Blue Dress*, 2008

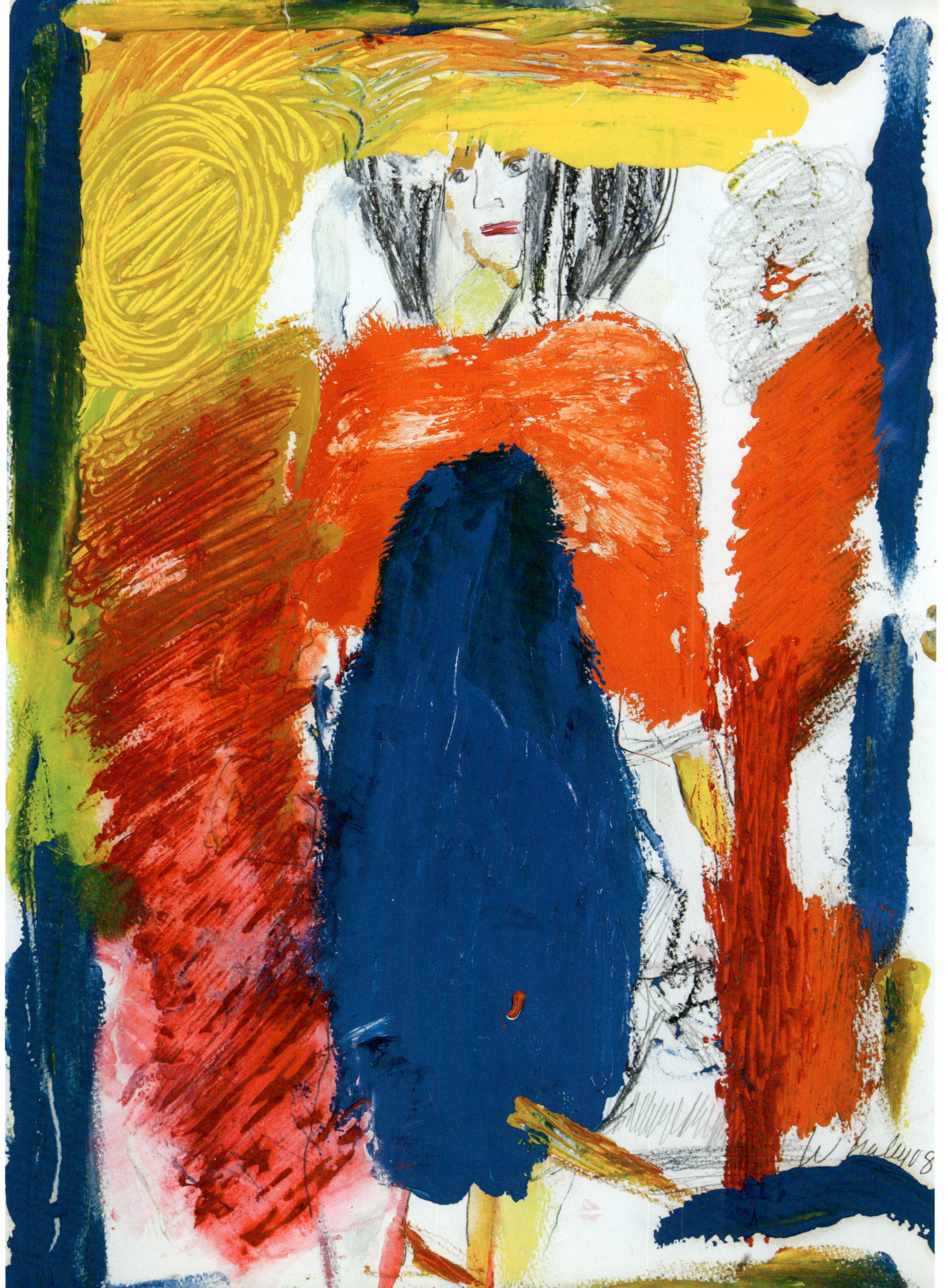

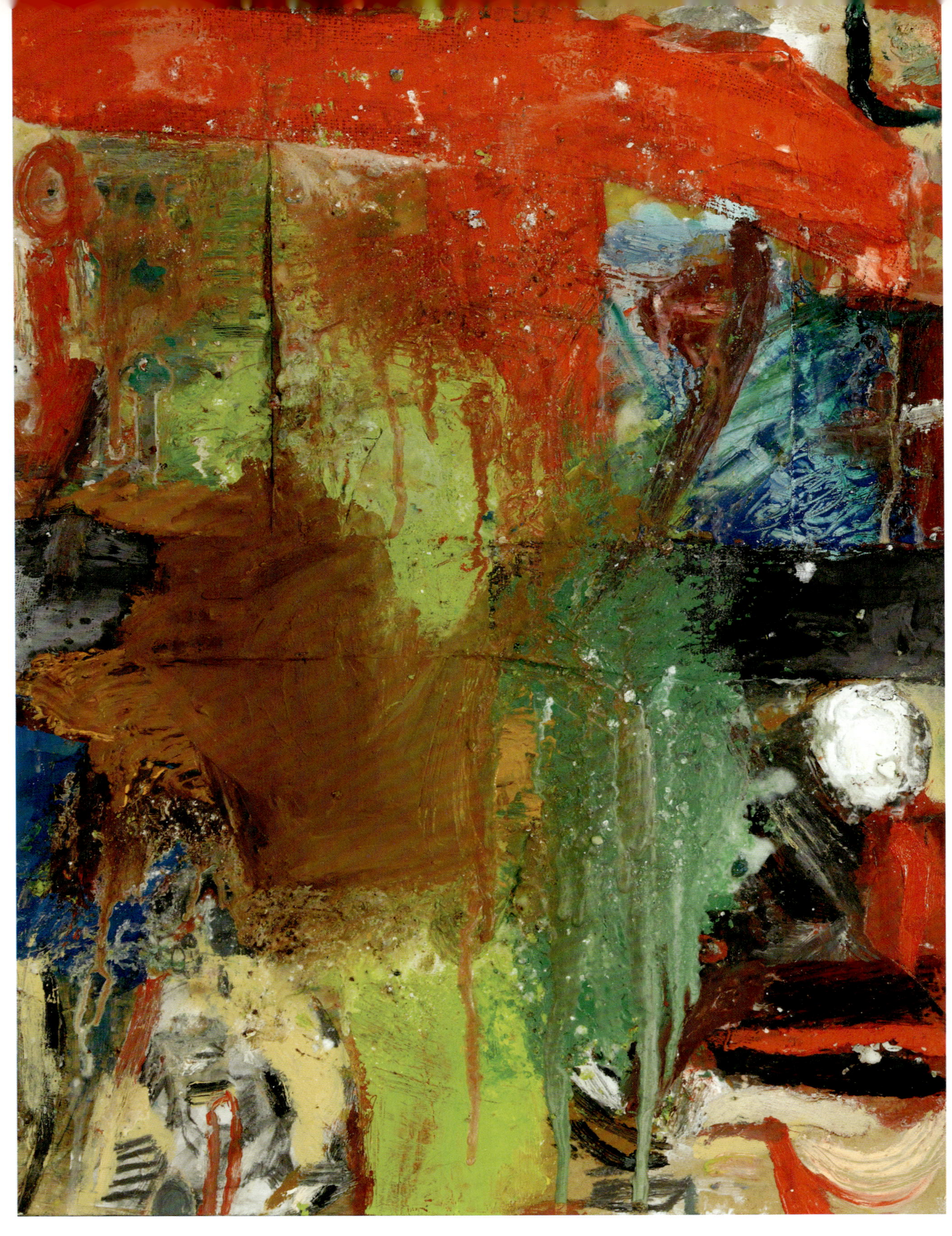

Medicine Wheel, 2012

Opposite: *My Hand Is a Violin*, 2012

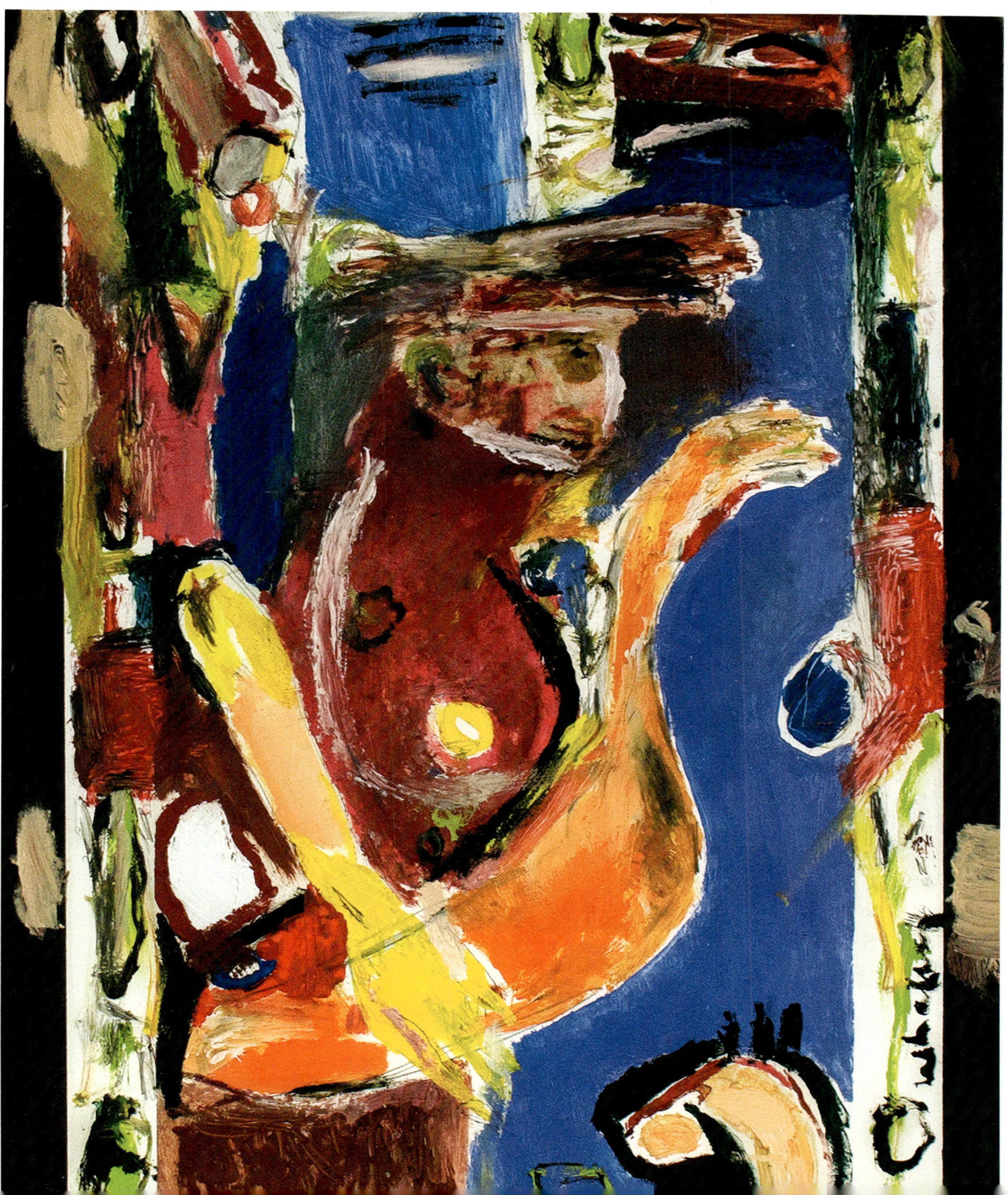

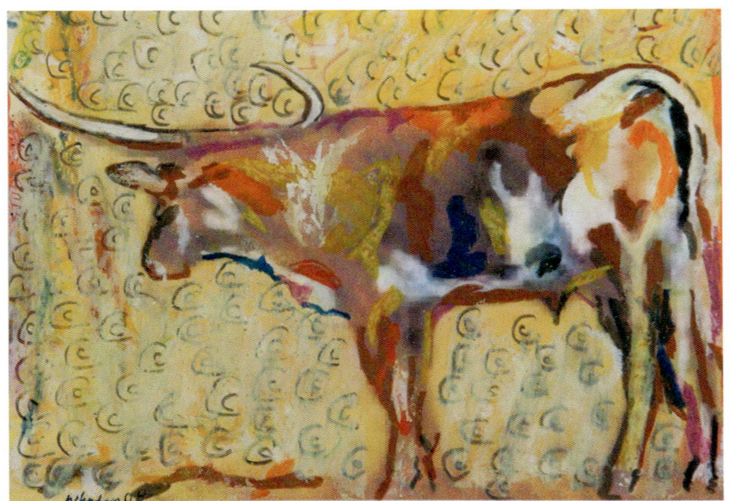

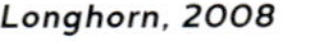

Longhorn, 2008

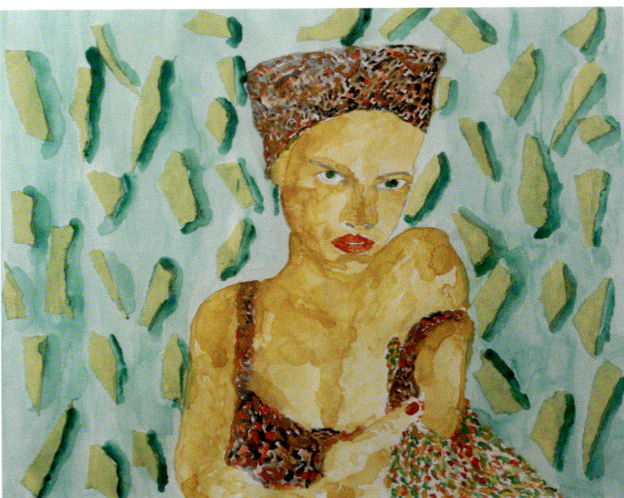

Green, 2008

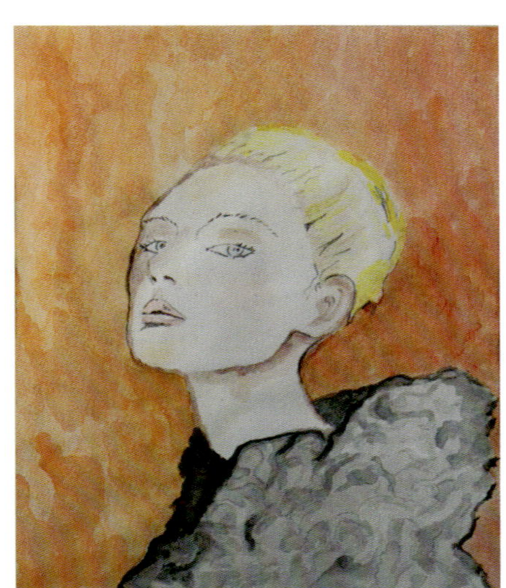

Hitchcock Blonde, 2008

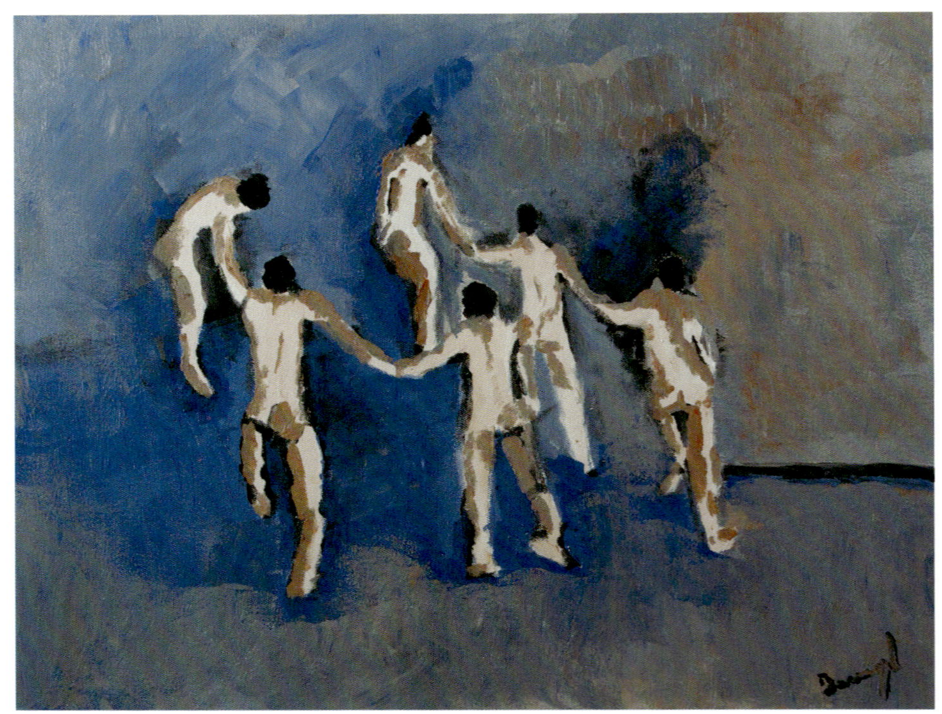

The Bathers, 2009

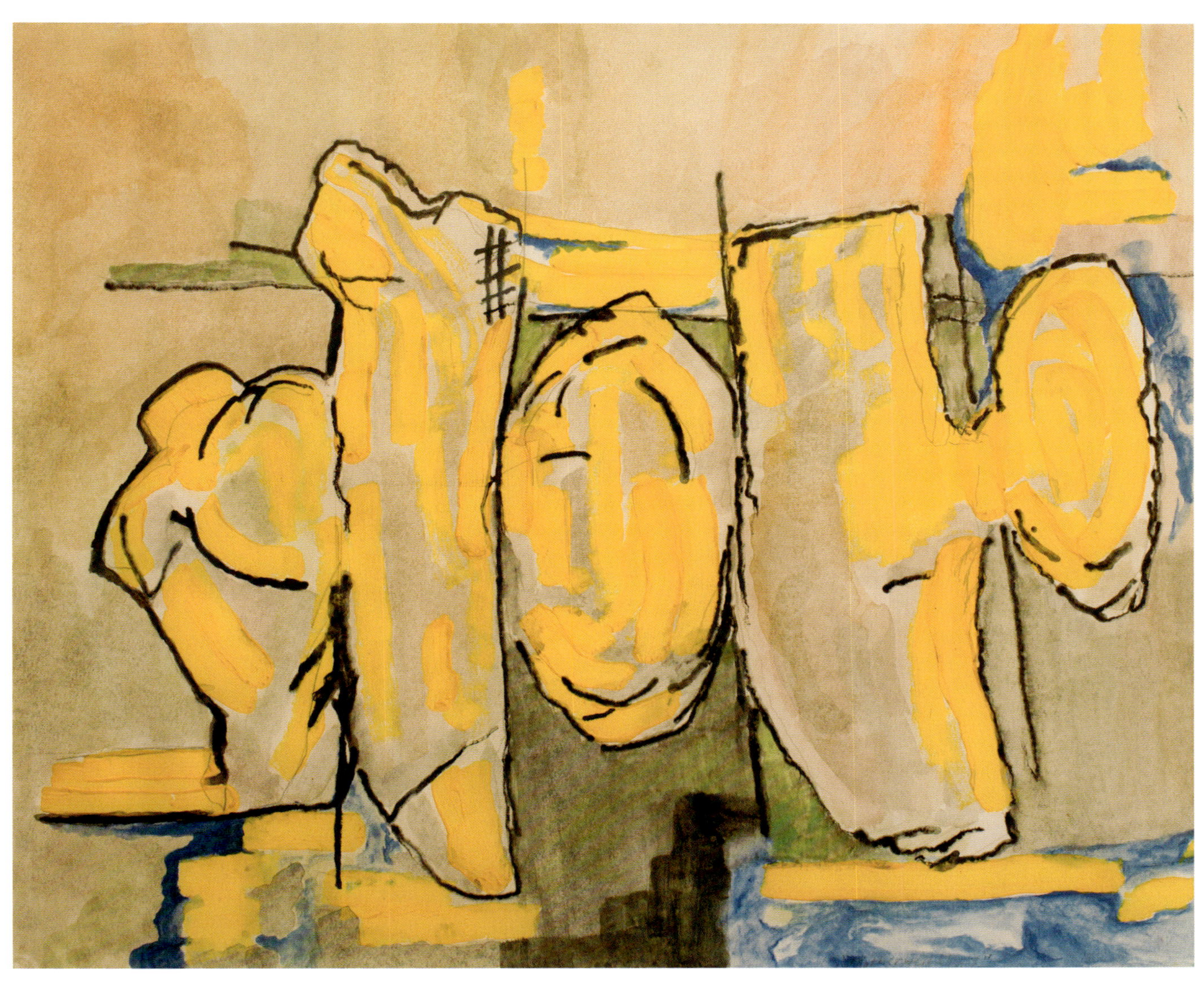

Elegy, 2008

"It's a choice to pick a scab and make it bleed."

—DW

Beauty Series

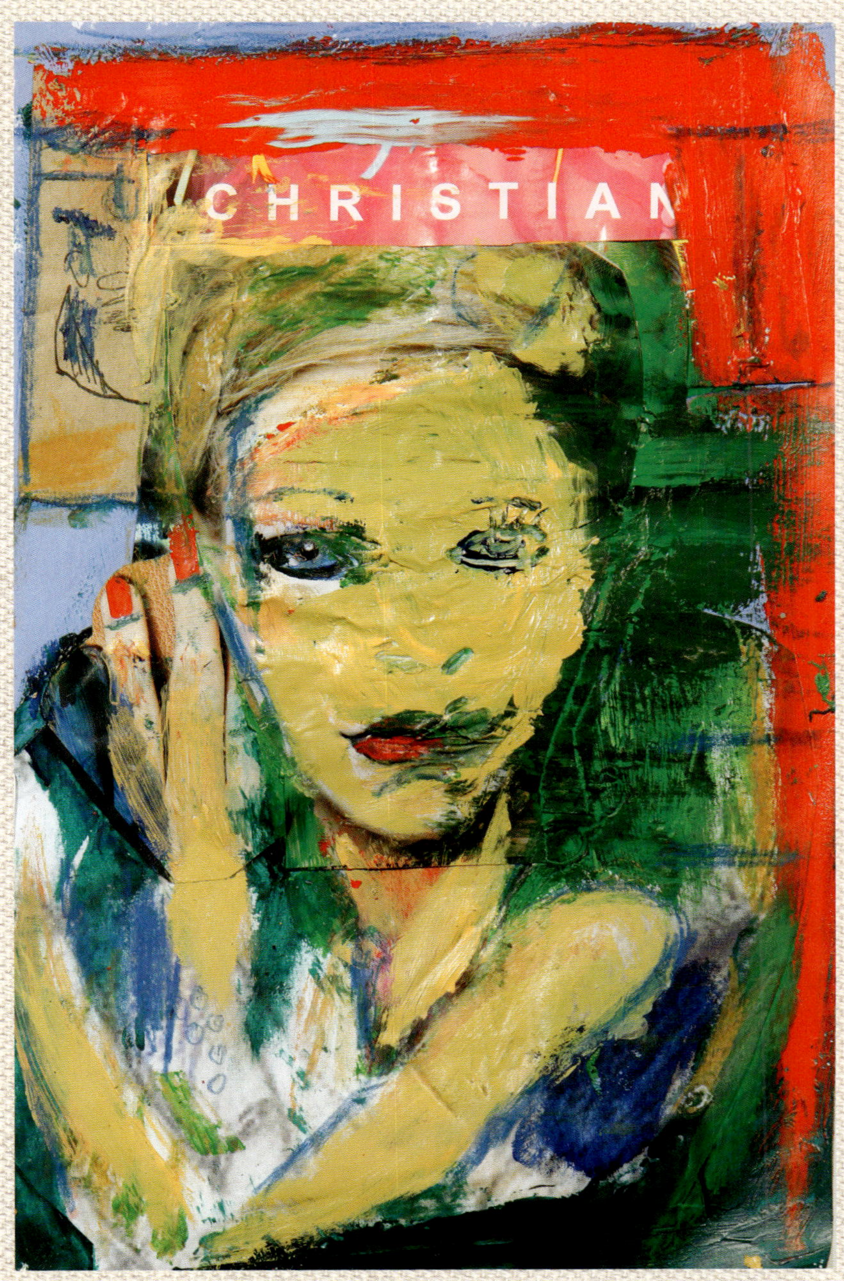

Study for Beauty, 2012

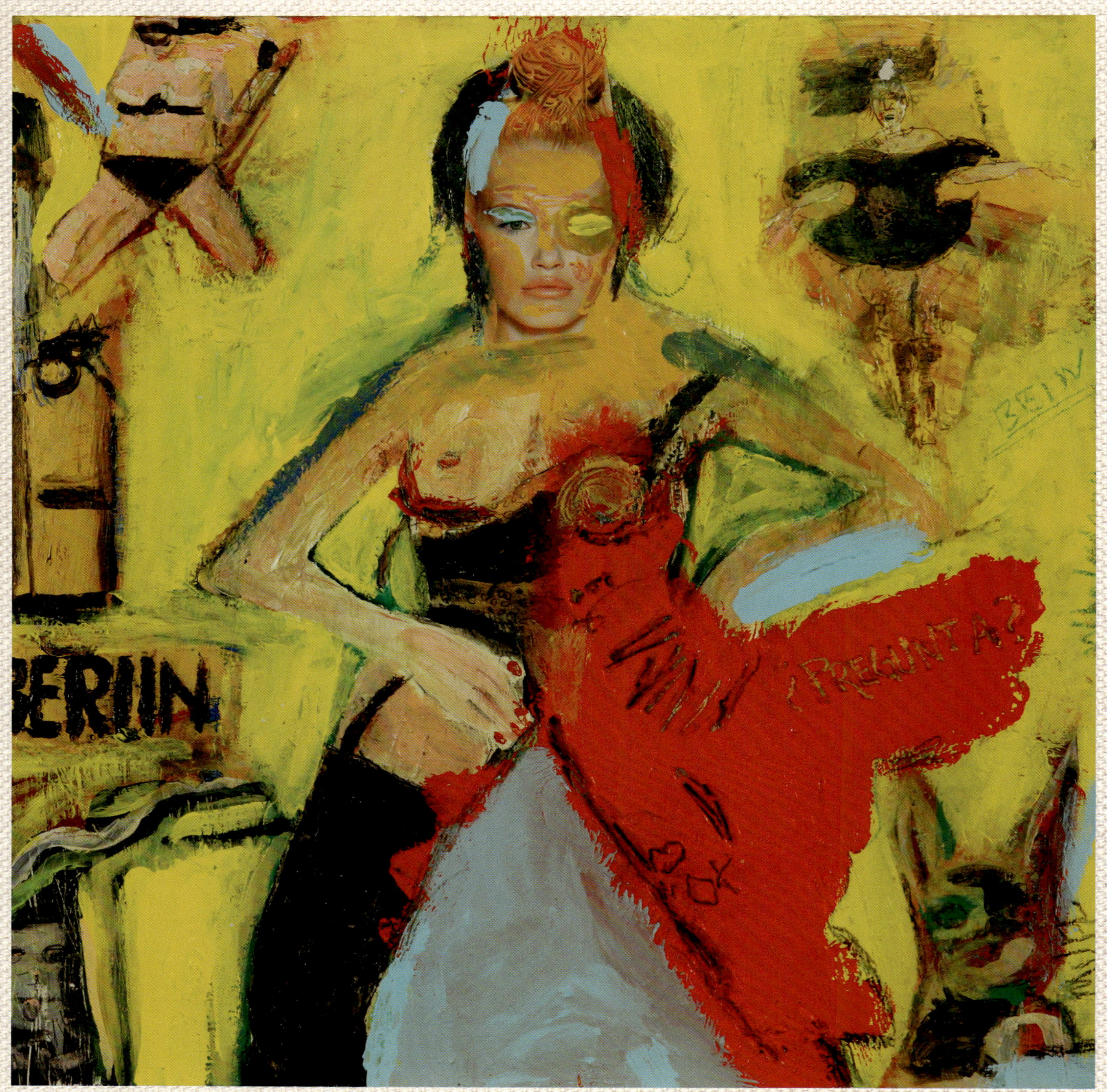

***Beauty 3*, 2012**

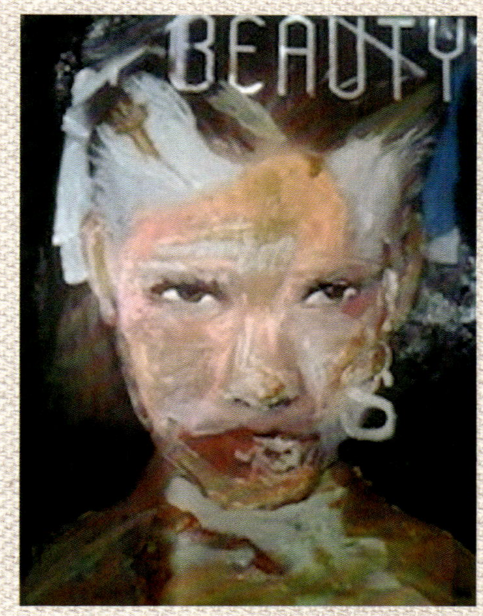

Beauty 1, 2012

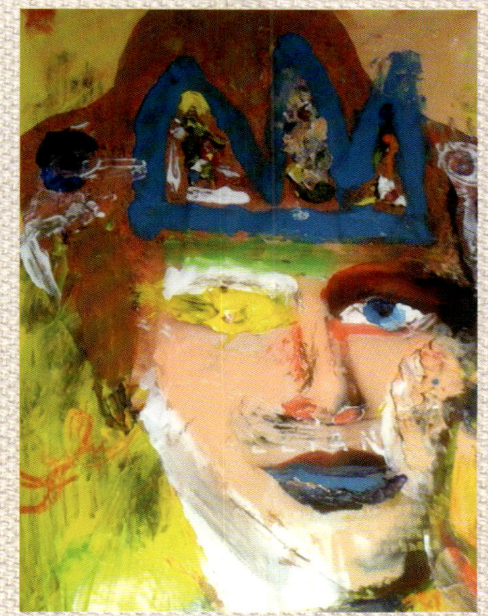

Beauty 2, 2012

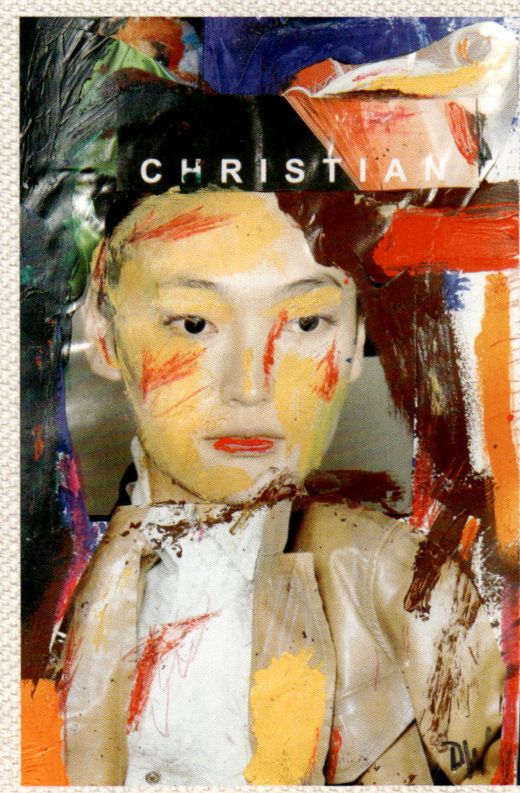

Beauty 4, 2012

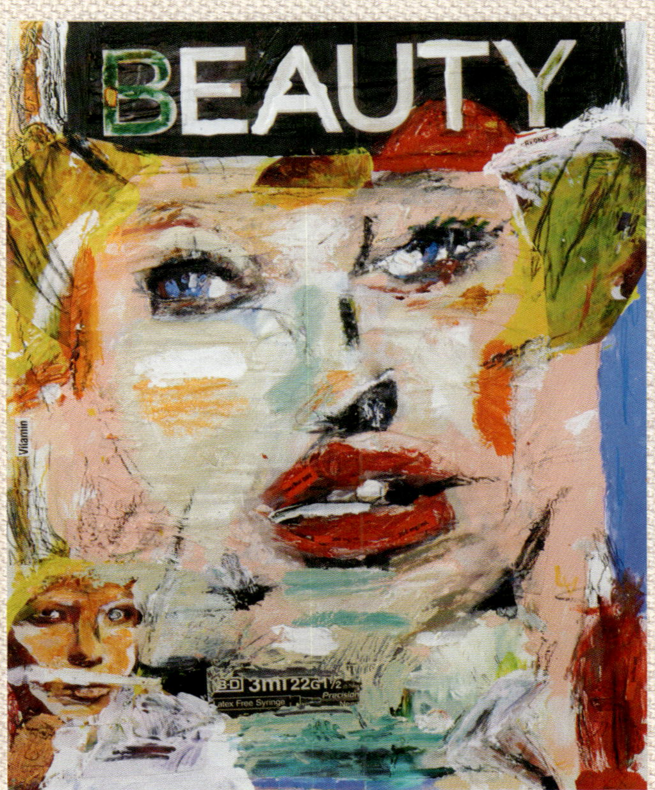

Beauty 5, 2012

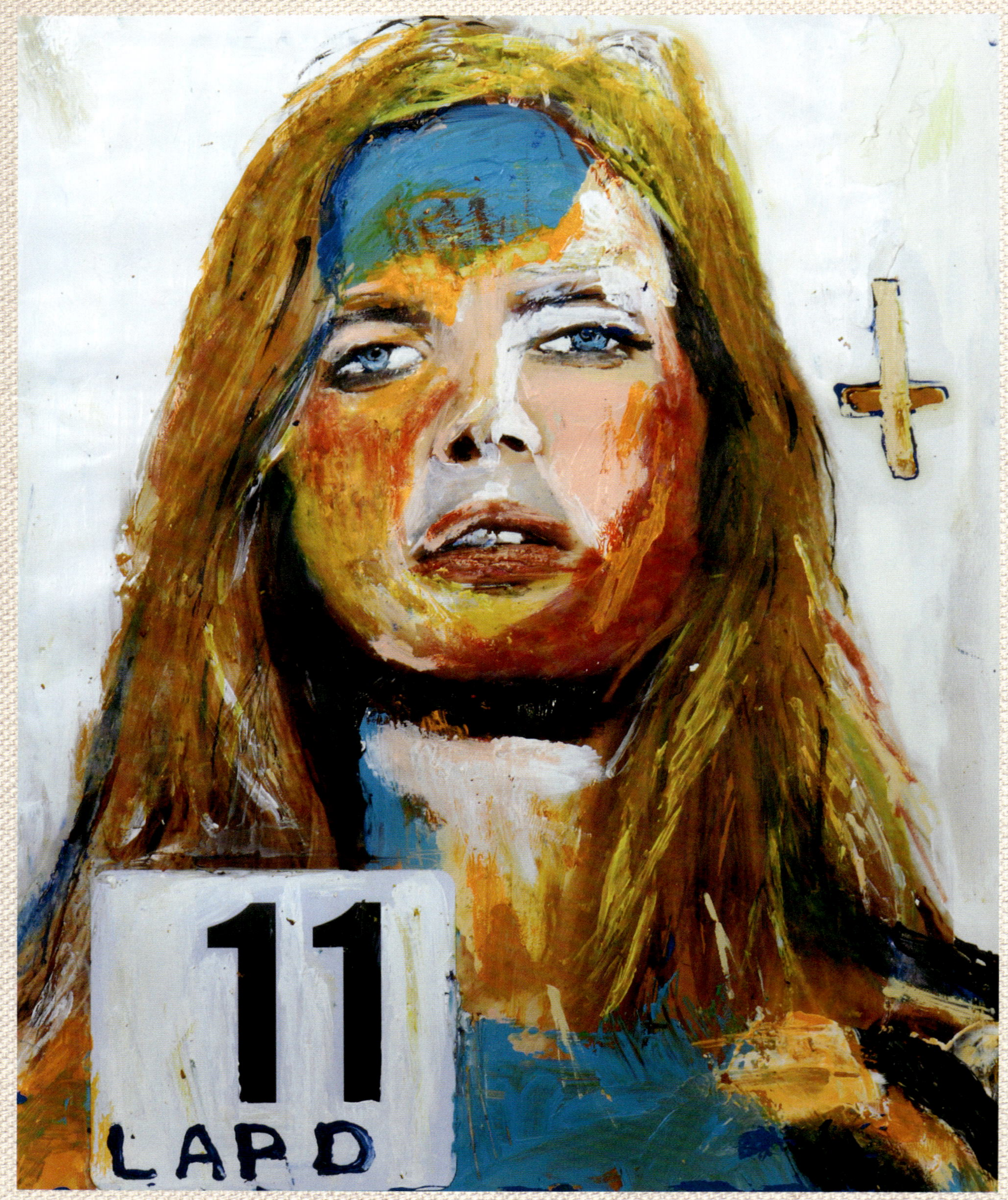

Beauty 6, 2012

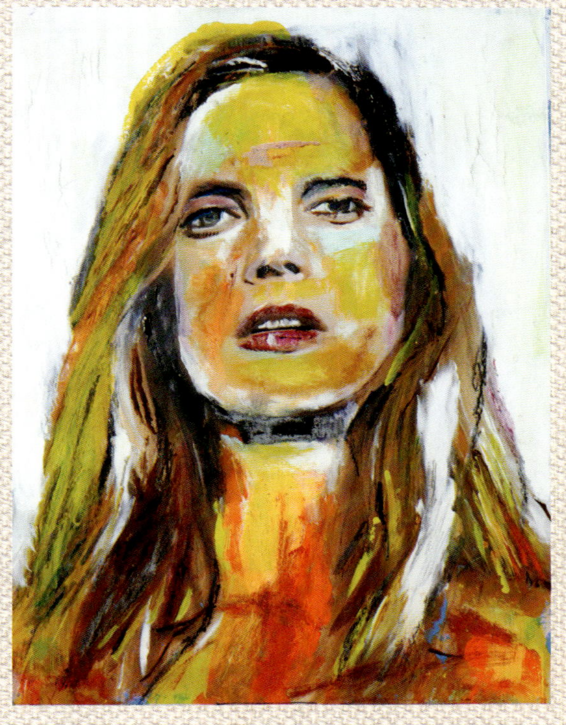

Beauty 7, 2012

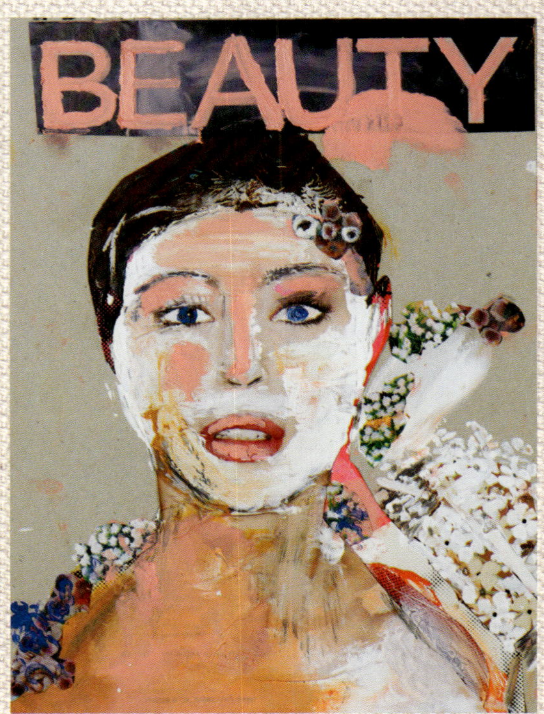

Beauty 8, 2012

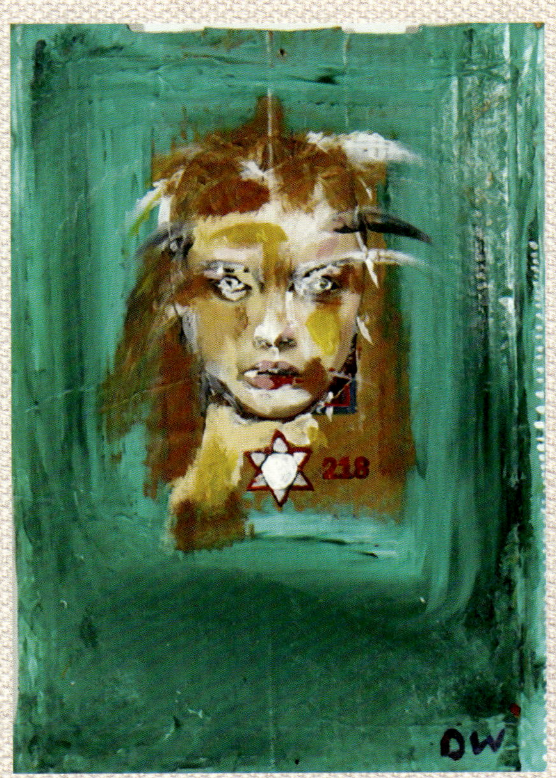

Beauty 9, 2012

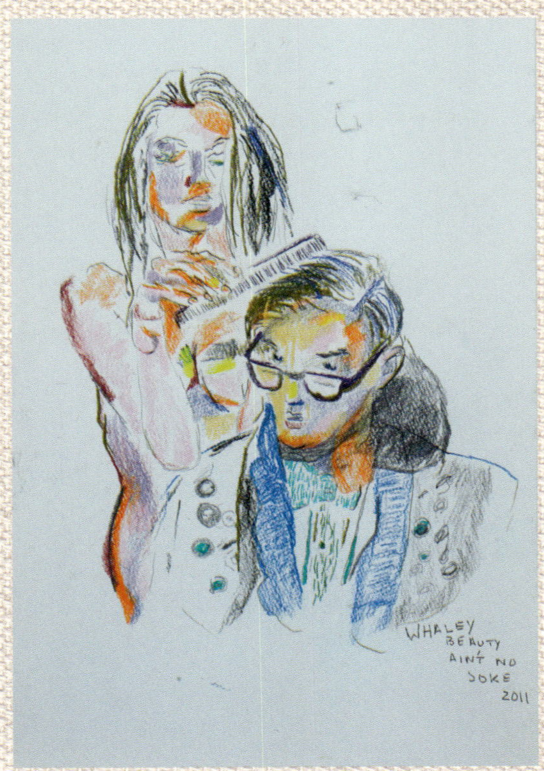

Beauty Ain't No Joke, 2011

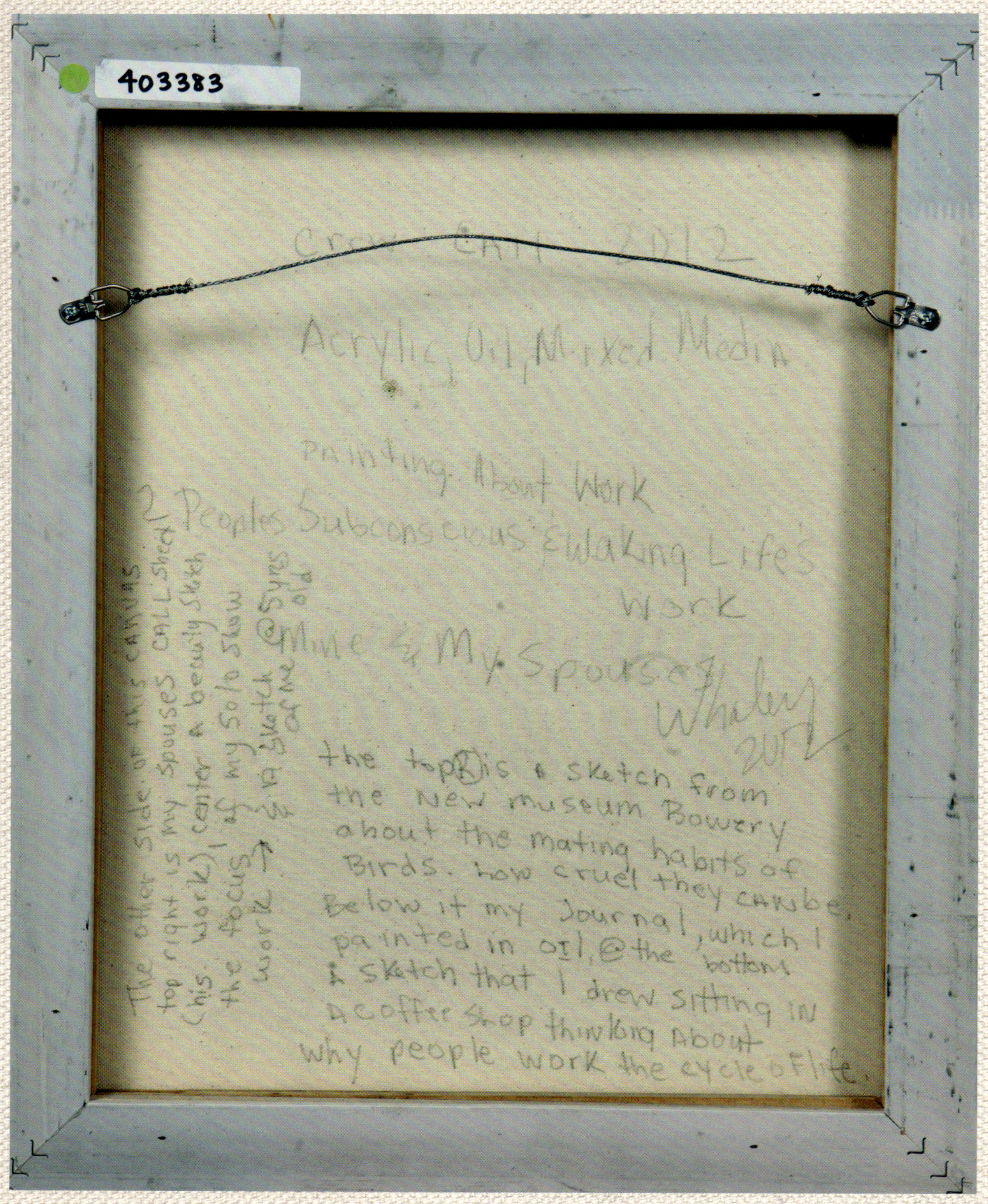

Crew Call, 2012 (verso)

Opposite: *Crew Call*, 2012

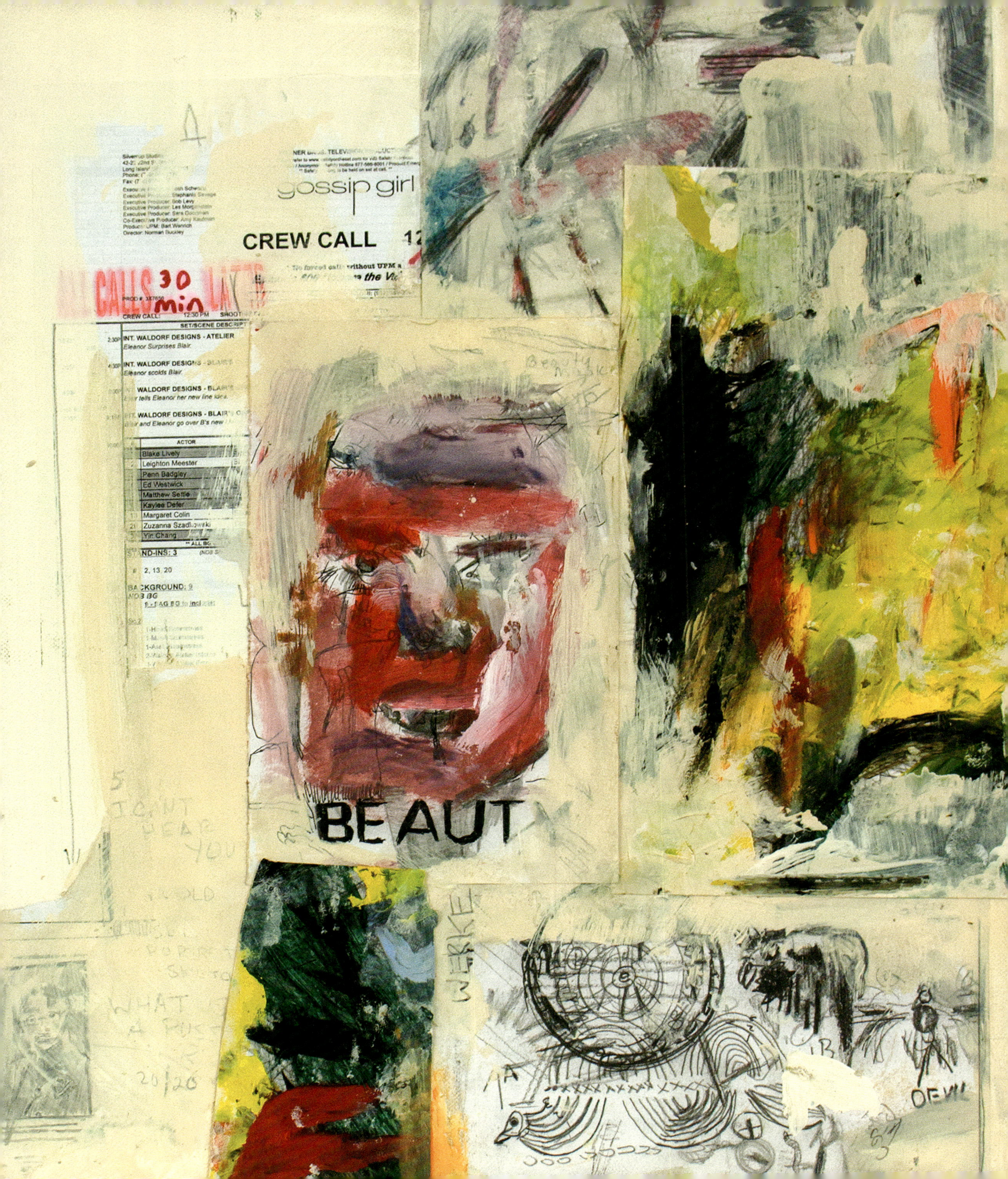

gossip girl
CREW CALL
INT. WALDORF DESIGNS - ATELIER
Eleanor Surprises Blair.
Eleanor scolds Blair.
ACTOR
Blake Lively
Leighton Meester
Penn Badgley
Ed Westwick
Matthew Settle
Kaylee Defer
Margaret Colin
Zuzanna Szadlowski
Yin Chang
BACKGROUND: 9
BEAUT
WERKE
20/20

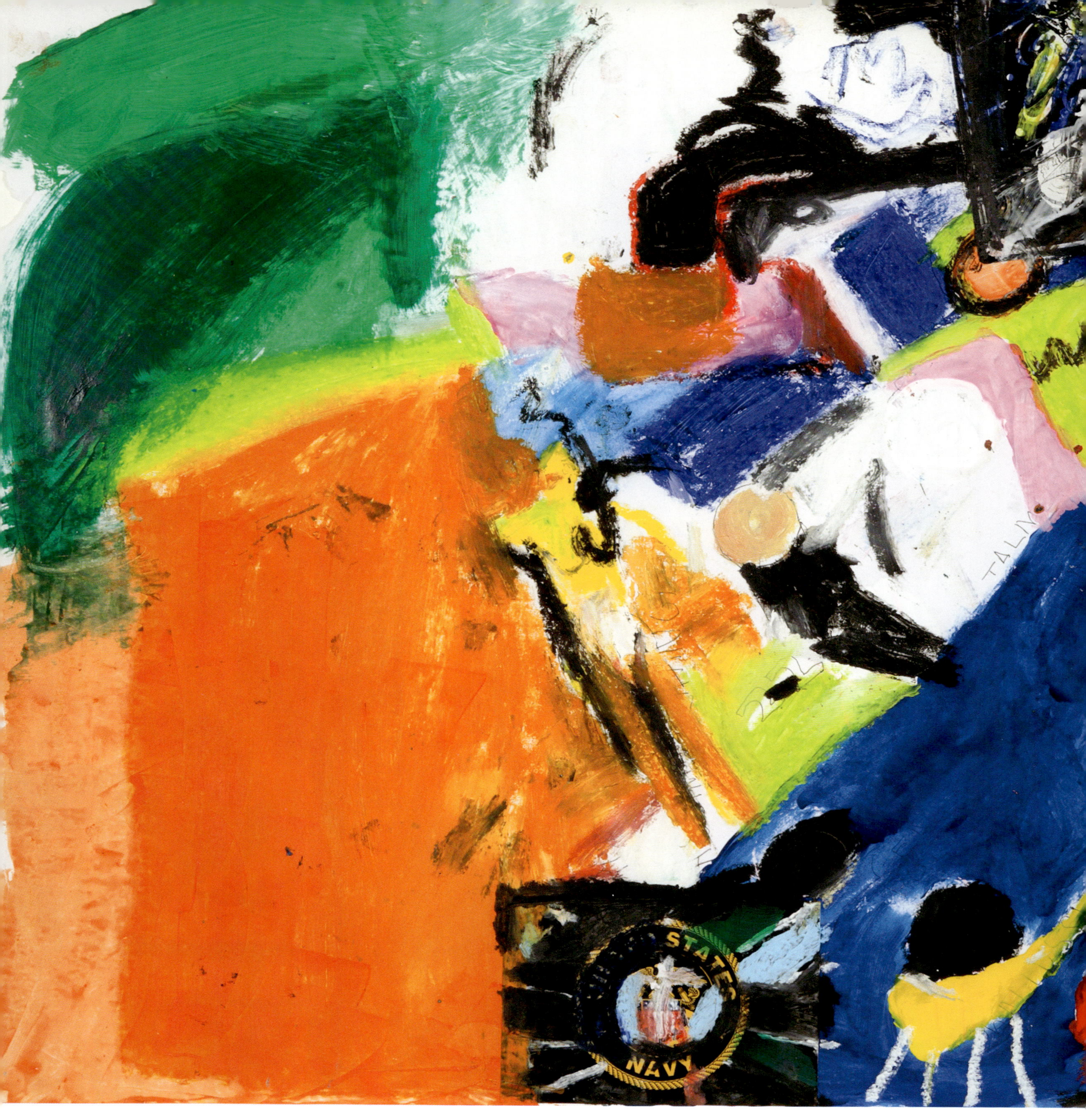
STATES
NAVY

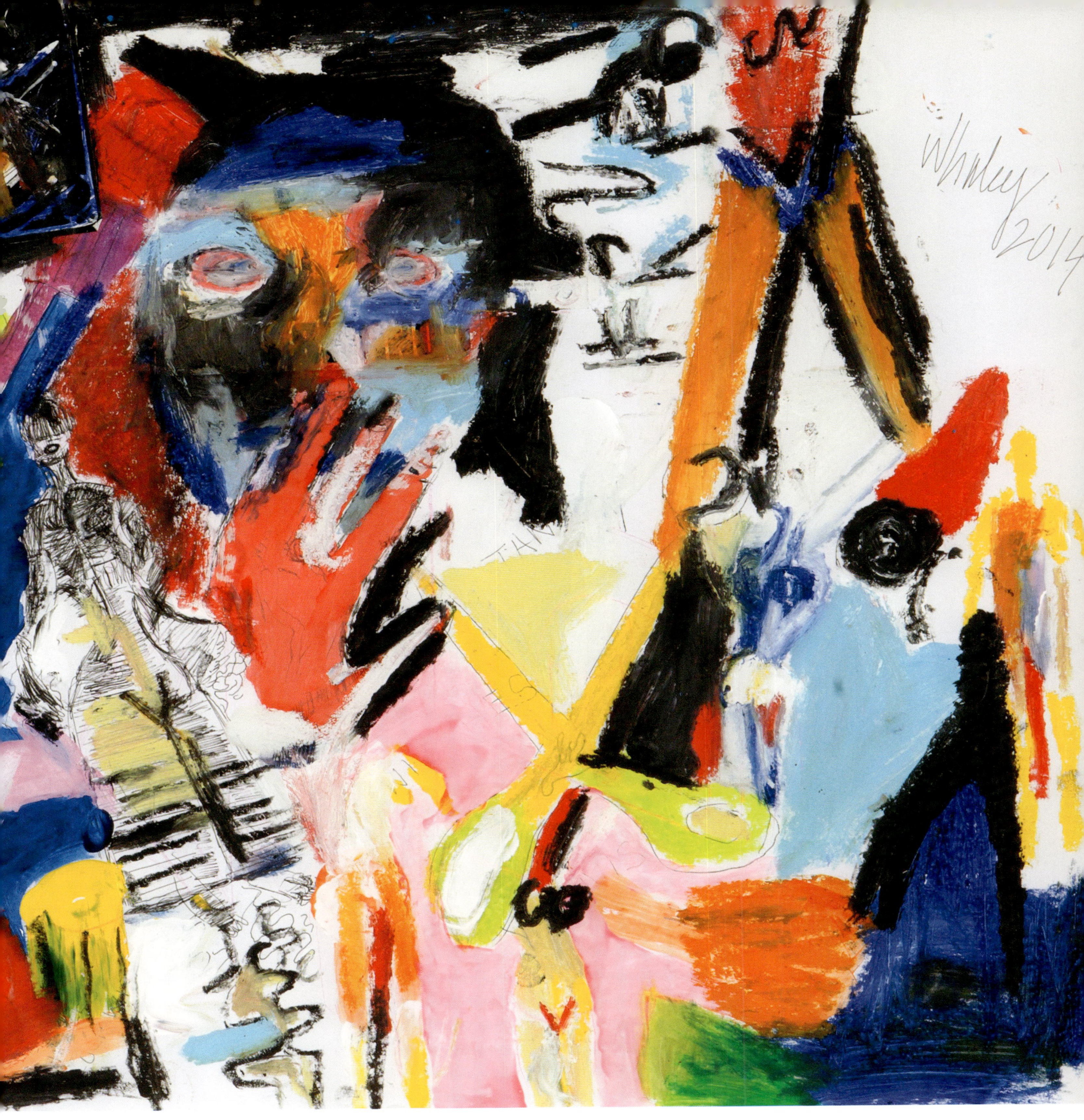

***Navy–Self Portrait*, 2014**

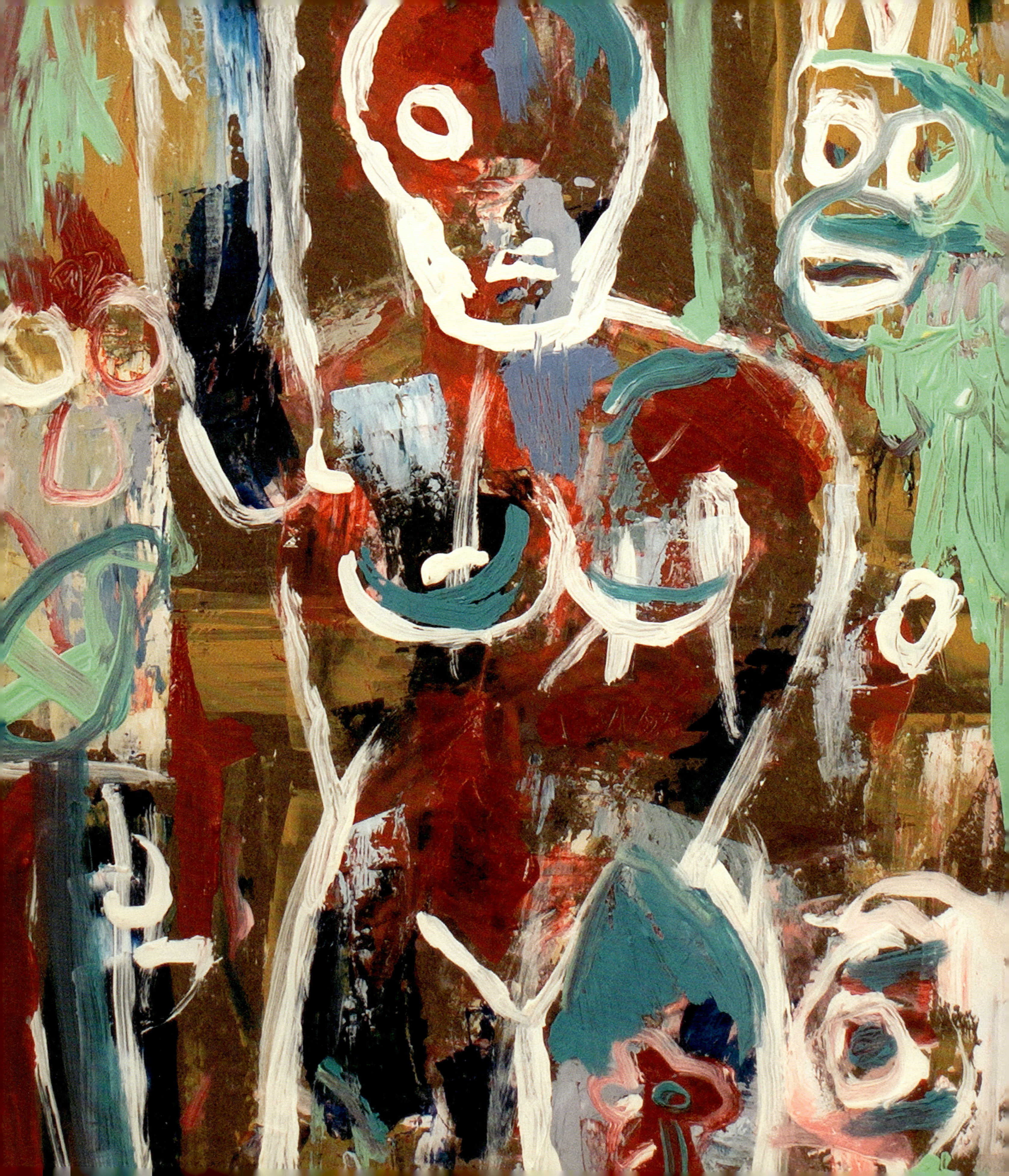

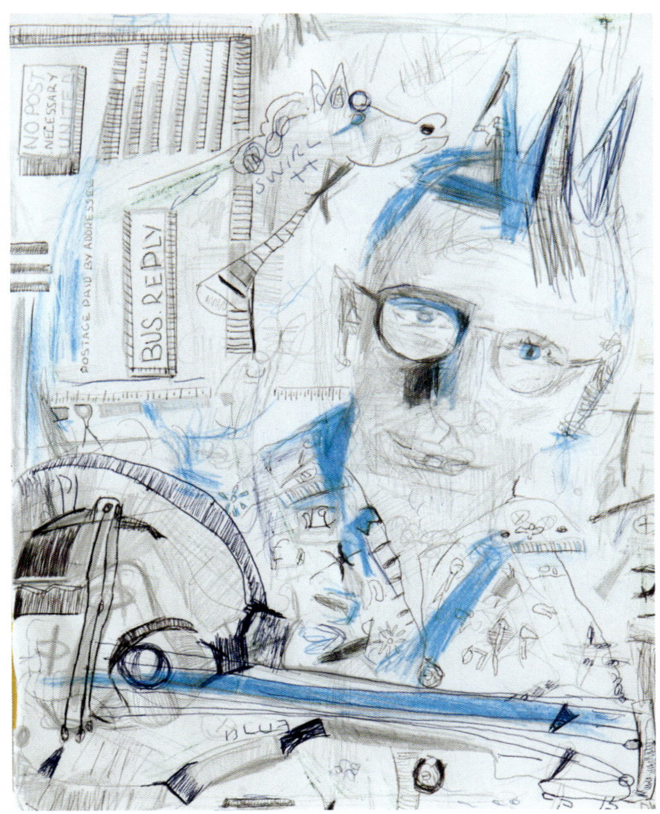

No Postage Necessary, 2011

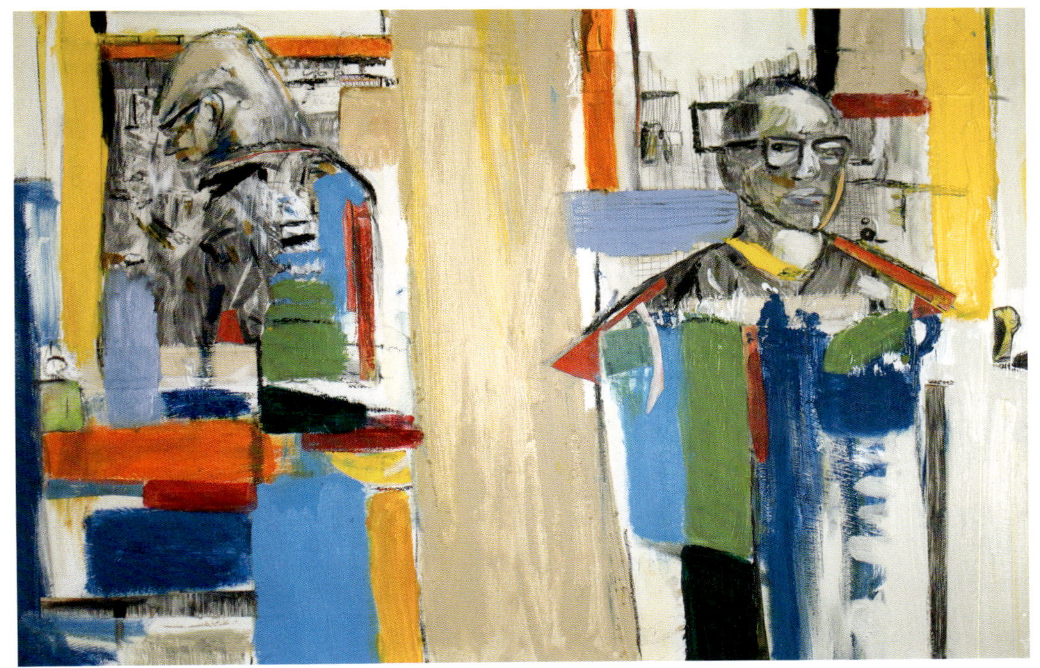

Opposite: *Monkey*, 2012

Norman at Sardis NYC and Norman at the Arclight LA, 2013

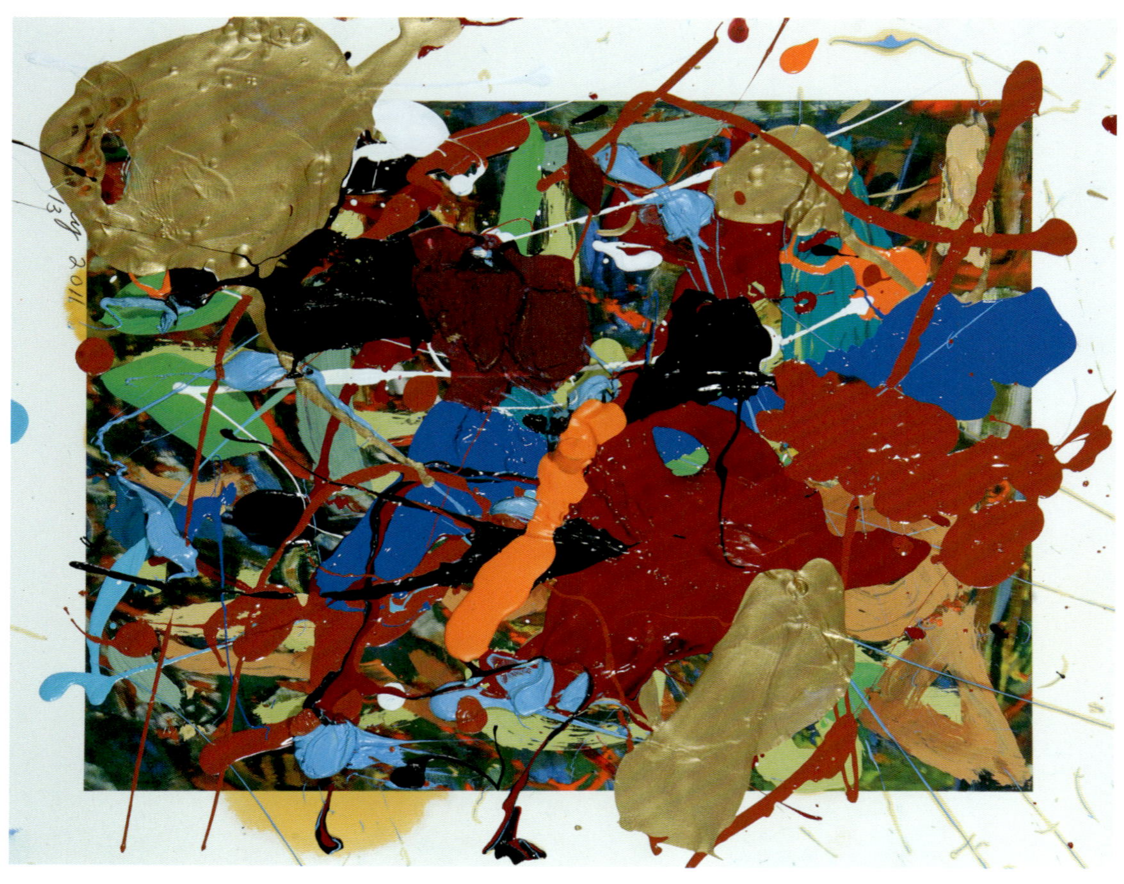

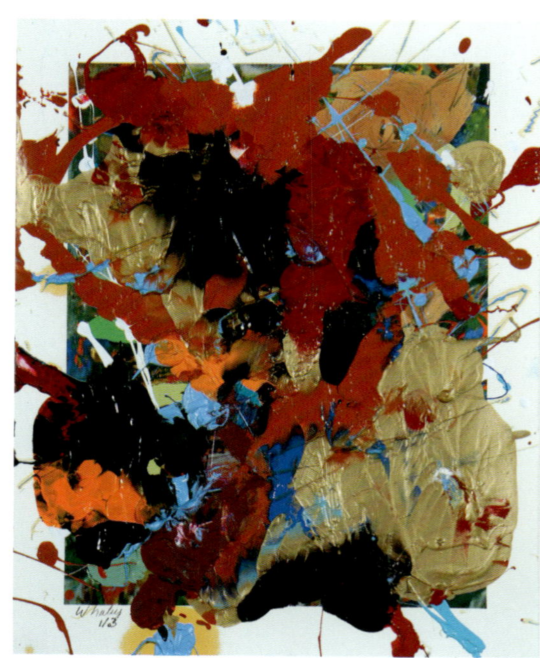

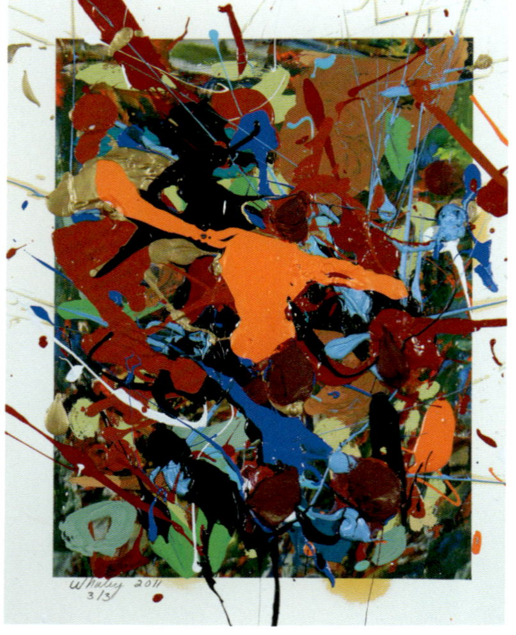

Triptych I, II, III, 2011

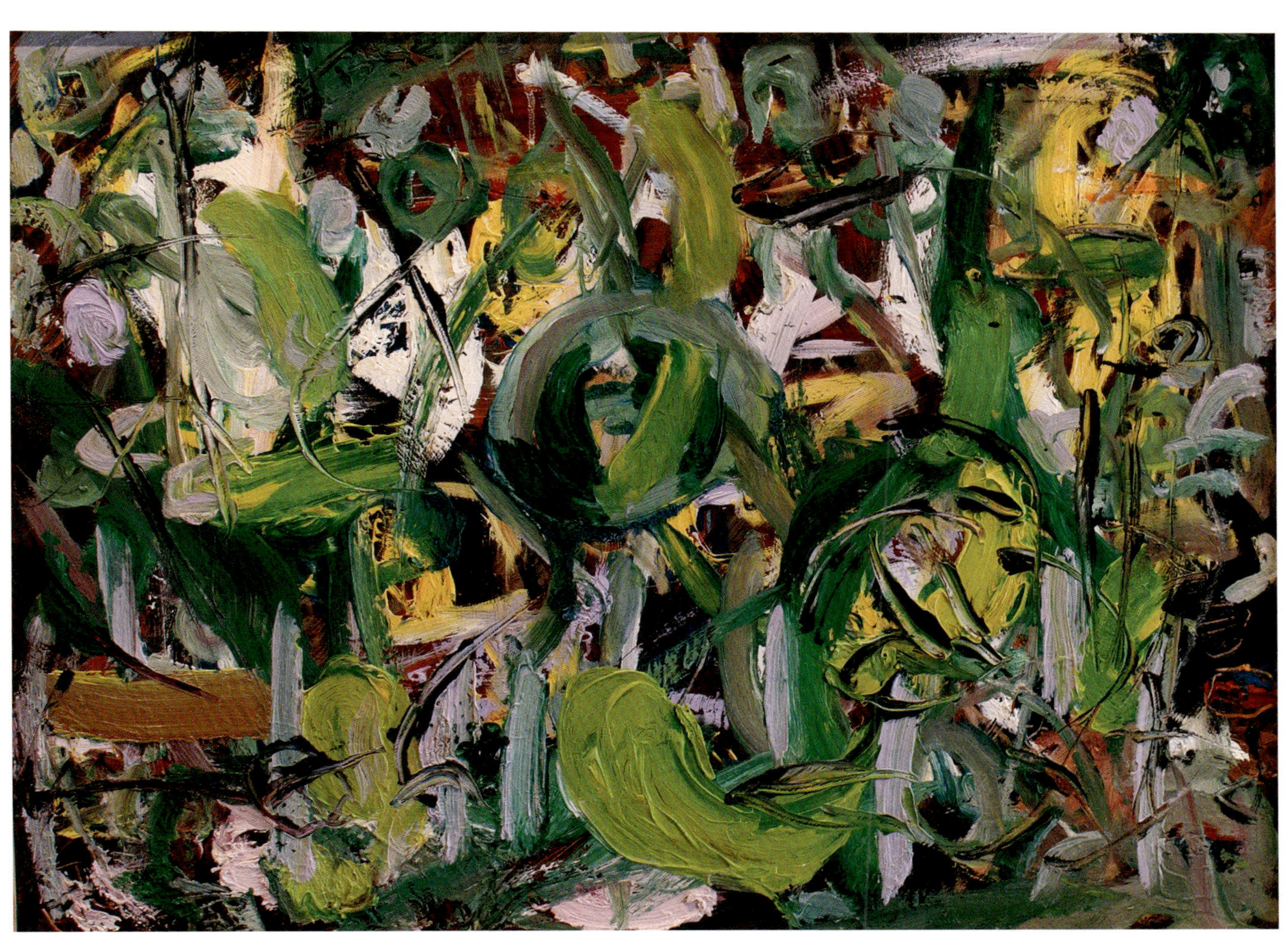

Judgment, 2010

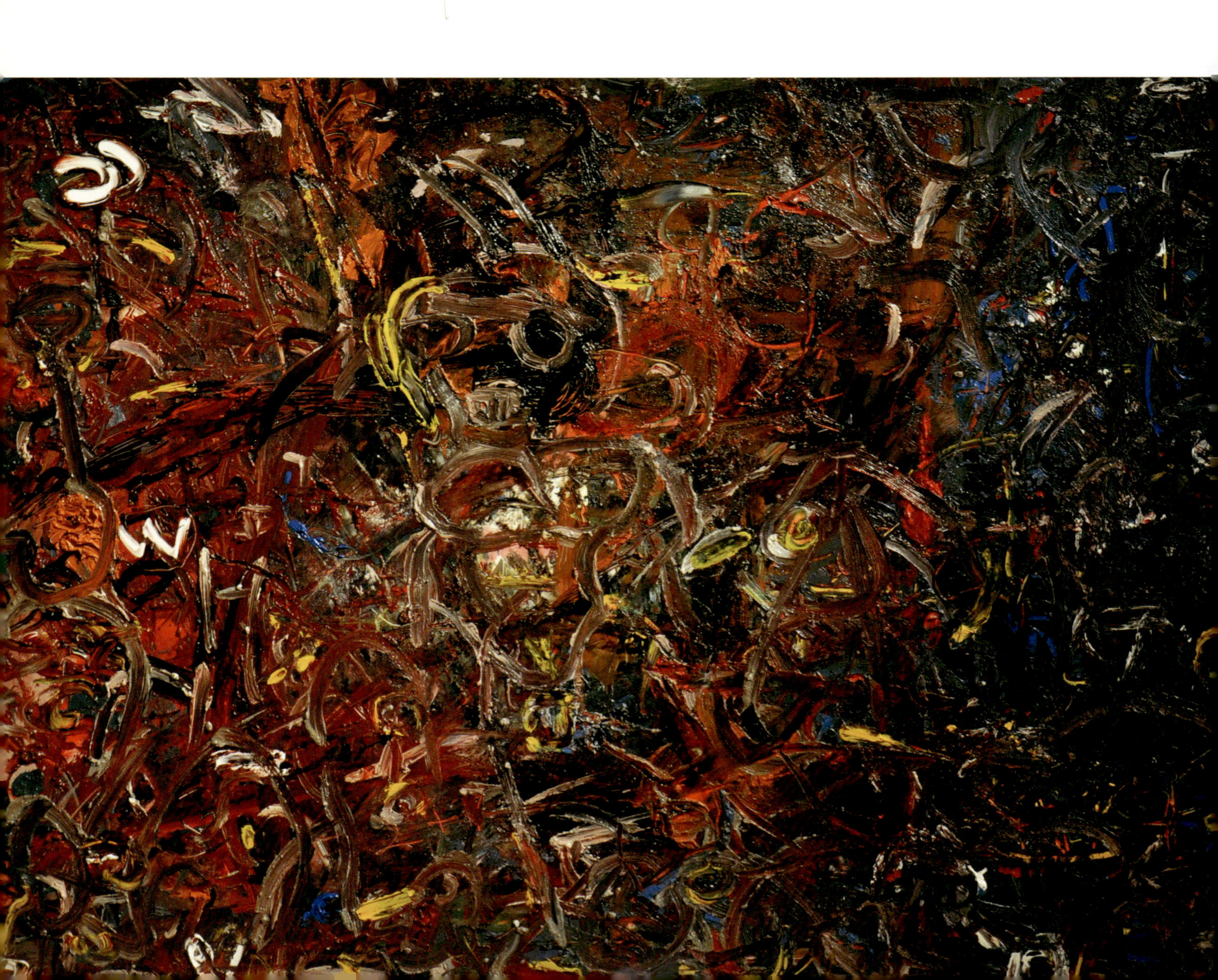

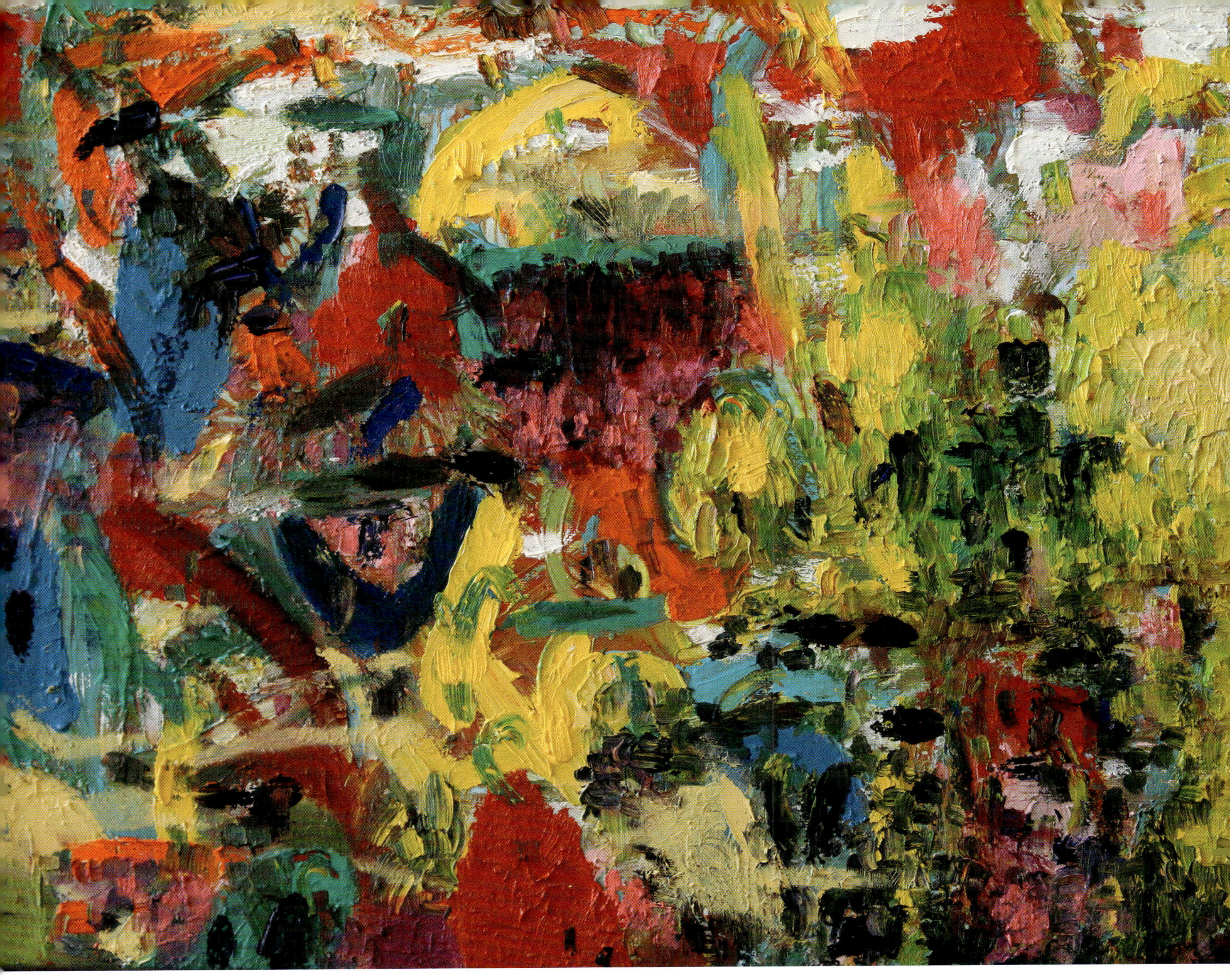

Opposite: *Shadow*, 2010

Sophia, 2010

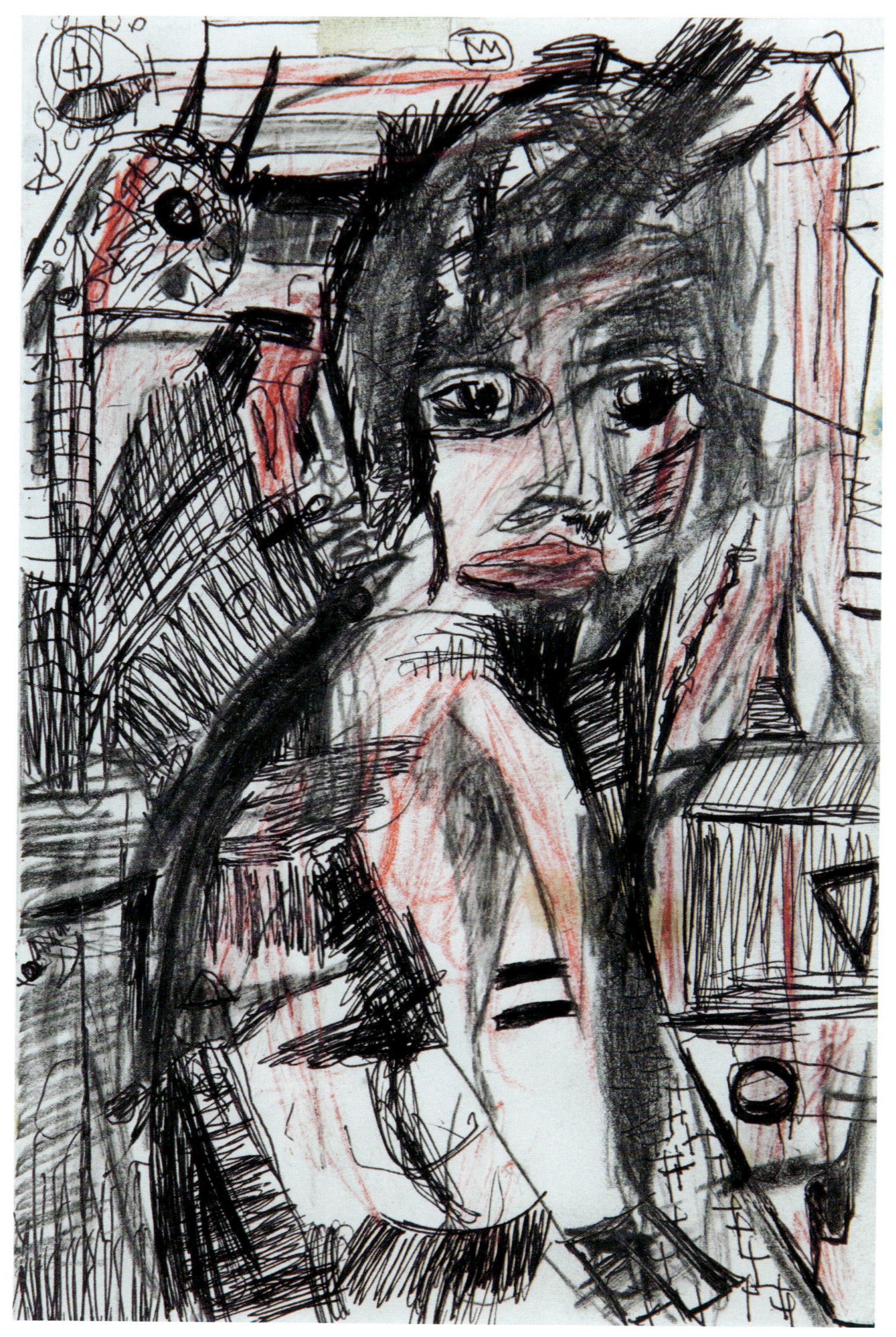

Untitled 8, 2012

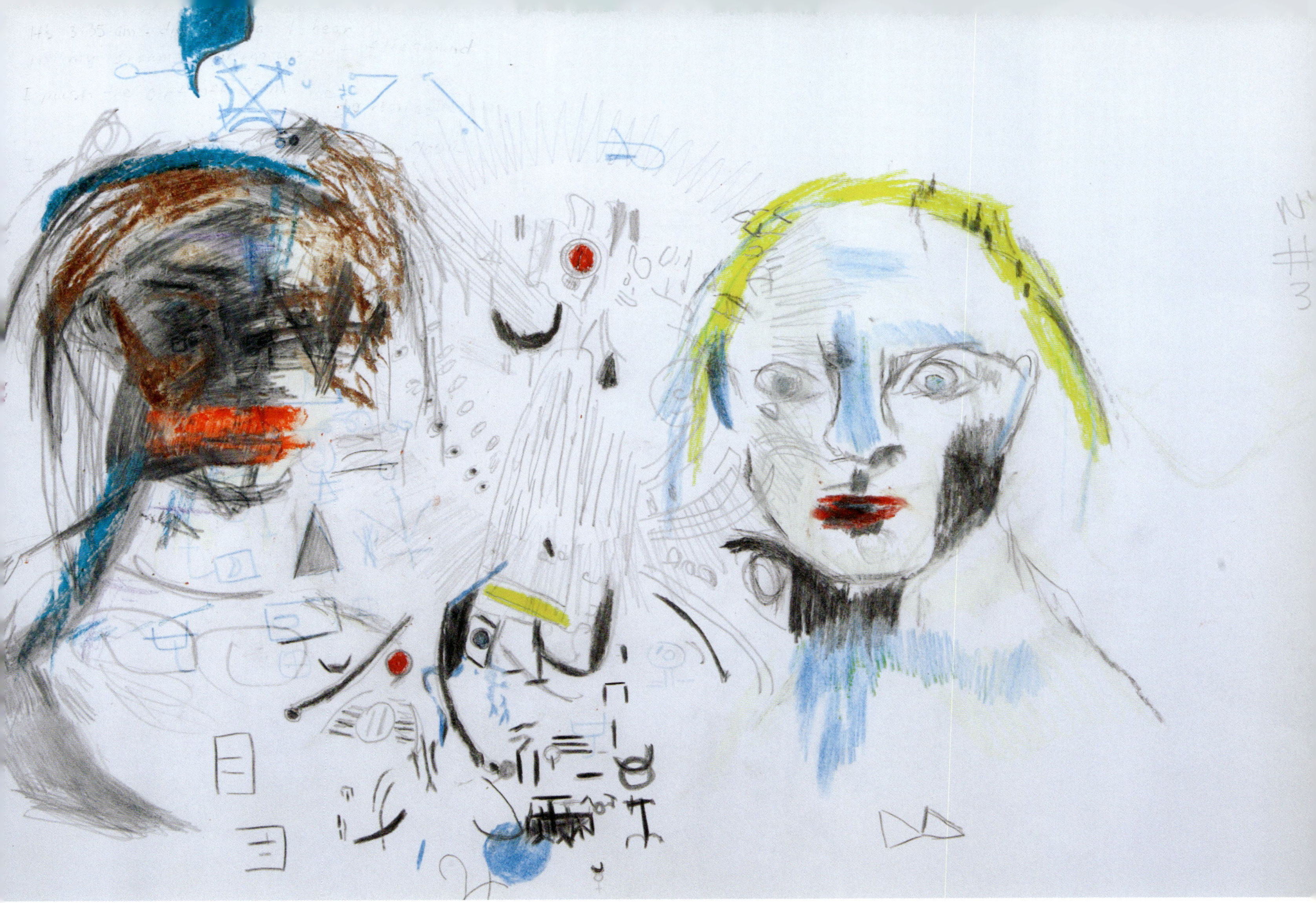

NYC 35, 2012

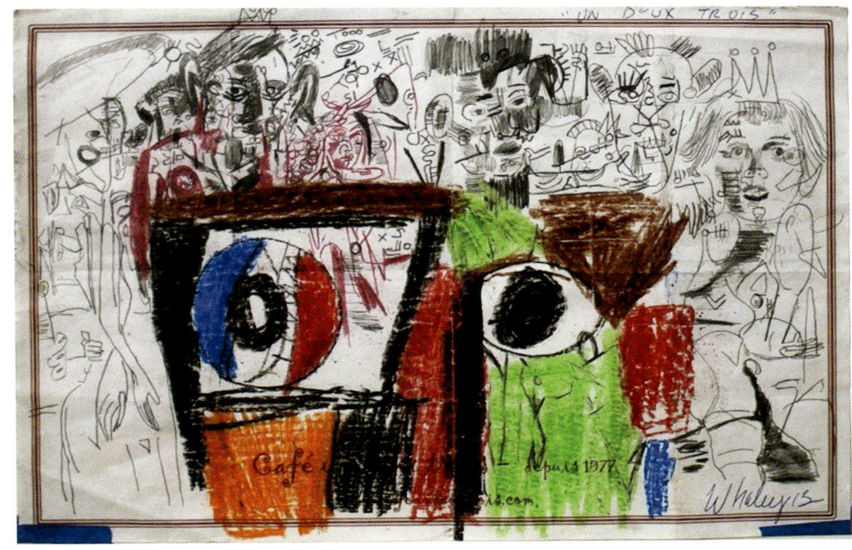

Un Deux Trois, 2013

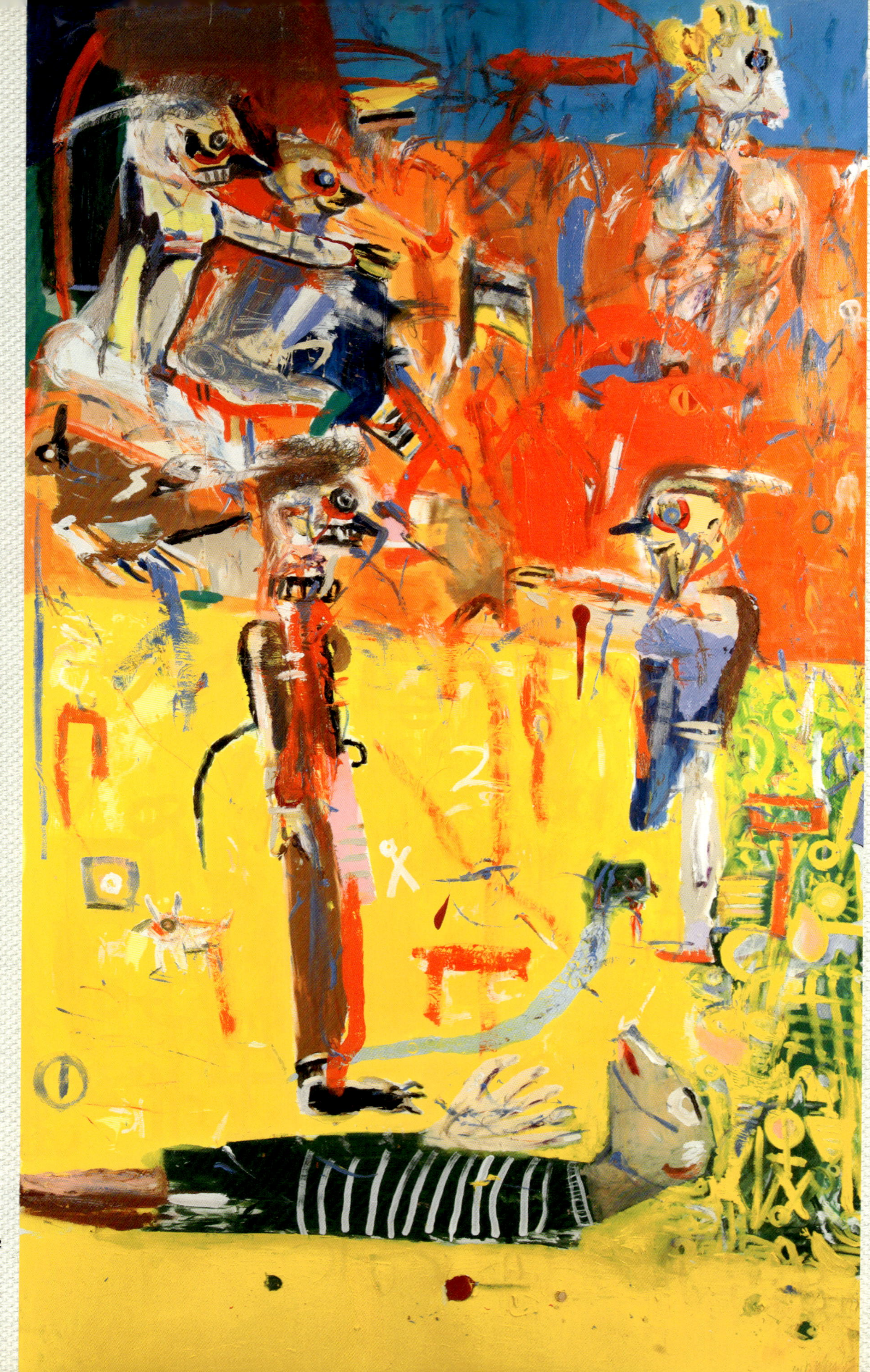

Child's Play I, 2012

"**Child's Play** is a painting which springs from my subconscious and a place of deep personal memory from early youth.

"As a boy of eight years old, I had an older teen playmate in his teen years named Bob White. He was a very peculiar and exciting creature, who lived one acre up the gravel road above our two story farmhouse—white, with black shutters and rusty orange tin roofs. I would always know he was in my yard because he would throw half-ripened green walnuts against the brick chimney and it would cause a horrible clatter and twang all the way down the roof, just like a giant gong. He would just cackle. The lady in the back kitchen would yell out a squall, telling me to 'get that boy to stop tearing down the house,' and 'don't go out and get in trouble with him. He looks strange.' She was correct on both counts. That day Bob White looked very peculiar. He was dressed proudly in his Apache Indian outfit, shirtless and wearing feathers in his hair, red circles under his eyes and two bright lines of rouge red powder under his sweaty cheeks, which matched his bare chest of four more bright red stripes. Today Bob was on the warpath, his feathers flickering against the side of his Daisy BB guns & his rubber slingshot, sticking out of his blue jeans. Bob had told me these were eagle feathers in his hair and they would give us protection today on our hunt, to keep us safe. He took the magic red powder and put red circles under both my eyes and stuck two eagle feather's in my curly brown hair. Now I was safe from the Rats. He said some spell in Indian language before giving me the Daisy BB gun and after ripping my polyester pants at the bottom. Ready to annihilate the enemies, with the fearless Apaches taking no prisoners.

"He announced, from the back-porch, that today would be an adventure. 'Davy come on we're going on the warpath,' followed by some unrecognizable Indian language. As a boy of eight years old, I wasn't analyzing the situation for what it truly could have been. At eight, do we analyze? Looking back after 30+ years and many dreams about it and with flooding memories of the scene of us two boys in that back yard, only by painting and journaling was I able to put it all together. It's so clear to see Bob White a teenager dressed shirtless, feathers in his hair and using Mrs. White's red lipstick (she had purchased from Thrifty Market to wear at Sunday church) to make marks around his eyes, in bright red circles, nipples, and bare chest. Now I realize, in some way Bob was taking on some female role, of his mother, by stealing and wearing her lipstick, that she would later be very angry with us two young cross-dressers for shooting guns and killing the neighbors' barn rats. Perhaps this was Bob's way of 'killing' his mother in this absurd Indian rat ceremony. I always thought of him as the Apache Rat King—maybe he was more likely the Oedipus King that was killing the Rat Mother. I think the figures work interchangeable with the mythology.

"On to the battle. Two warriors sat anxiously and watched the rats run across the rafter of Mr. Hick's Hog barn, high above the warm slop where the pigs rolled and pushed the milk and bread in and out of their mouths and waded thigh-high in their own waste, underneath in the sludge. Two little Indians waited, surrounding the cheese wagons, above the sows, below the squeaking targets. The smell of summer outside was of tall green grass and chiggers—if you were lucky enough maybe mulberry or honeysuckle would blow through the cracks in the barn, but always walnut. I tried thinking about the smell of walnuts and noticed the red eyes of the pigs looking at us. They seemed clever for not taking the cheese, but always annoyed by these games. The rats always came for the cheese, just like Bob said. We giggled at the naïve rats momentarily. Then with his call we pulled our blasters and fired; bam-bam-bam. Three went down.

"Suddenly I felt grief and guilt. I have guilt for killing Mrs. White and wearing her lipstick and Bob pulls his hand free from his Daisy bee bee gun and pulls out hair from his head and chews on it and sucks it in his mouth and laughs. Ha-ha-ha ha-ha—it turns in to a mumble and he gets very compulsive about pulling out his hair. I look away from him and look out the door of the barn for a minute. He started shooting again. Bam-Bam-Bam. The overwhelming smell of hay and manure came into my nostrils and I didn't want to play.

"I believed in him, that Bob was an Apache warrior and he was speaking in languages to the great gods. I needed a hero. I bought into the fact that he was wearing eagle feathers and magic paints to protect us. When he put an arm around me, I felt I was brought into the myth of this secret land." —DW

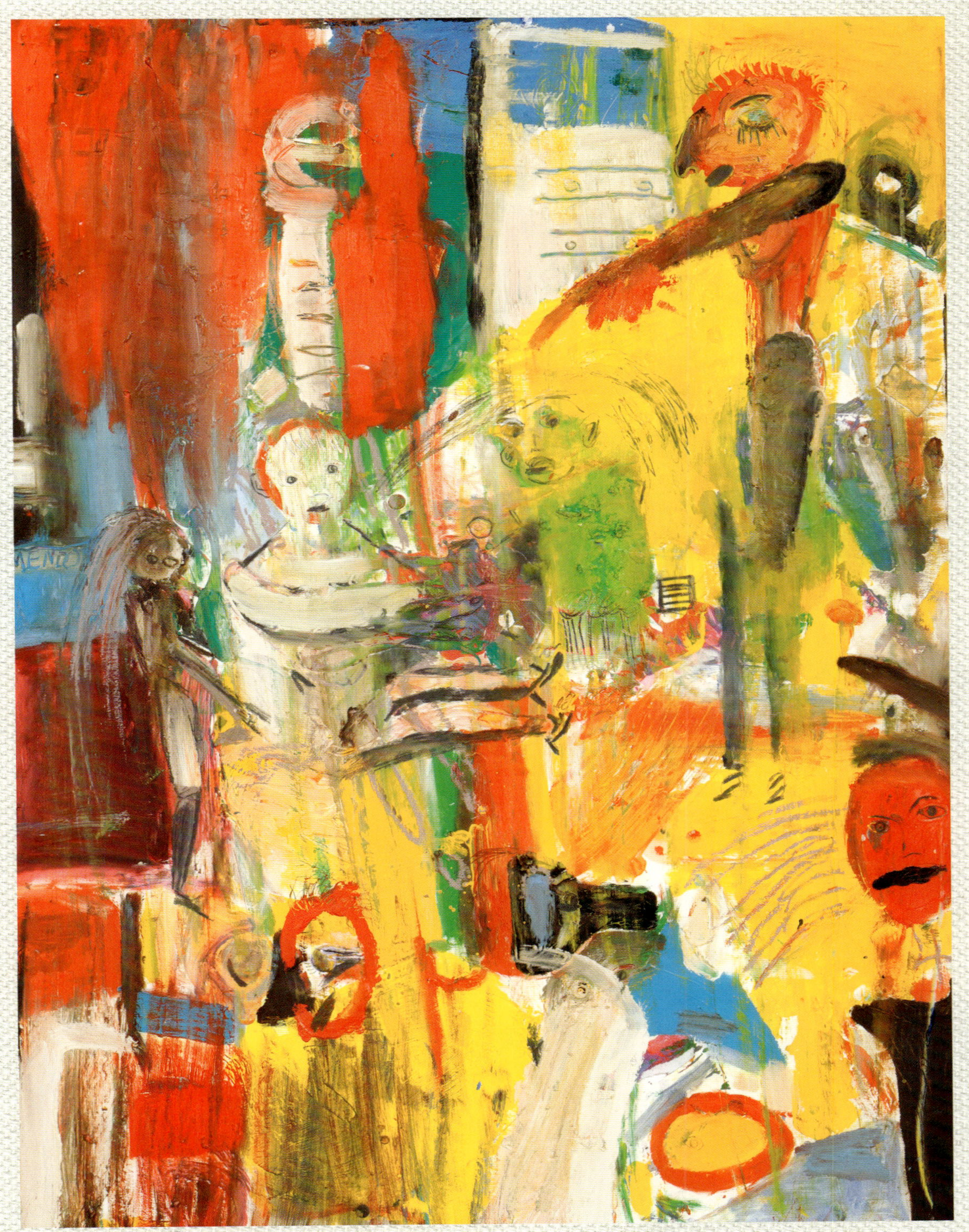

Child's Play II, 2012

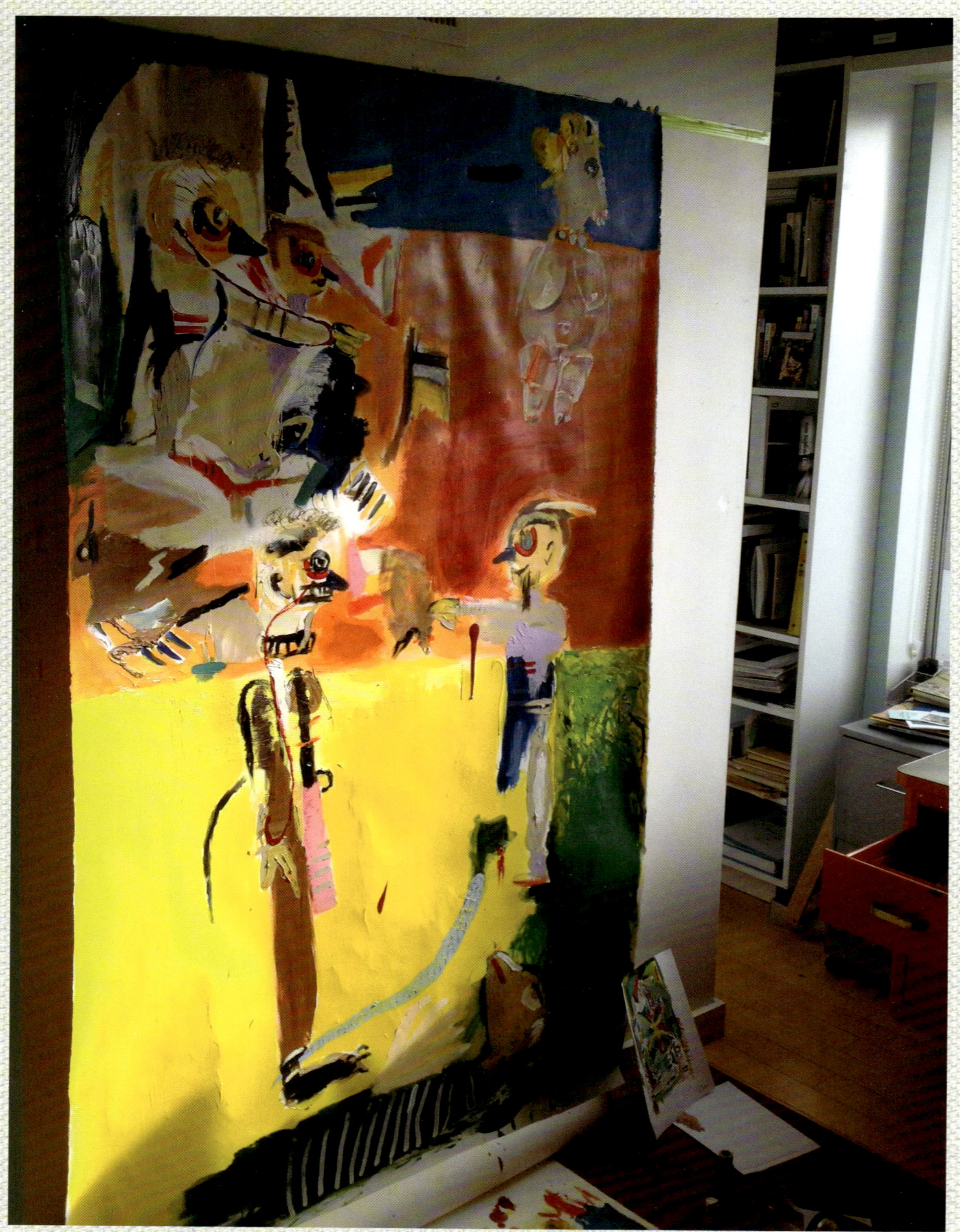

From Davyd Whaley's Journal

October 18, 2012

"I painted 13 hours on *Child's Play.* Began abstracting painting, symbols, lines—dots—throwing, slashing, painting yellows, blues, reds, flake whites. Added legs to sitting figures at the top left portion of the painting and covering the female figure with blues and red geometric and alchemical symbols throughout the painting. Not satisfied with the painting. At rest it's an action painting and more so becoming a color field painting—energy and emotion-based—something I have to get out.

"I no longer cry when I work on this painting. I'm beginning to move beyond the attachment I had when it first began, and the memories started coming back of being a young man of 8 or 10 years old. Getting dressed up as an Indian and playing games. I'm now more focused on the technical details of making a painting; using the right materials, steeping the paint to ensure the oil base will set and adhere firmly to the acrylic underbase, selecting the proper filbert brush, to weave in detailed, intricate highlights, which will give the painting a luminosity and beauty. This is important to me. I want this work to show such complexity and masterful beauty. This is why I spend 12 hours painting, it takes around 3 hours to detail a small 6-inch square.

"Painting from part memory and part dream is also very difficult when working on this level of detail. I imagine using a photograph, instead of imaged ideas/scenes and using perhaps people instead of almost cartoon-looking characters. May have been easier. However I'm trying to stay true to my imagination as a child of 8–10 years old to create this image in the likeness of what I saw in my mind at the time, versus cheating and copying from books, magazines or online for ideas.

"This is about me and for me as it is the most personal thing thus far I've chosen to share as an artist to date. I plan on sharing more and documenting the process through writing, Jungian analysis and painting.

"These are the tools which help me as an artist understand where I've come from, what has happened to me in my my life, and also serve as a guide to where I'm going. We create by creating and dealing with conflict in life.

"Although I have no desire to reconnect with much of my past, by that I mean the persons in it which were harmful or things which may have caused harm—I do have a willingness to embrace the conflict and pain and put down the story of the conflict.

"My conflict is allowed as long as it crosses no boundary for me or my loved ones. I'm allowed to use this in my art making process."

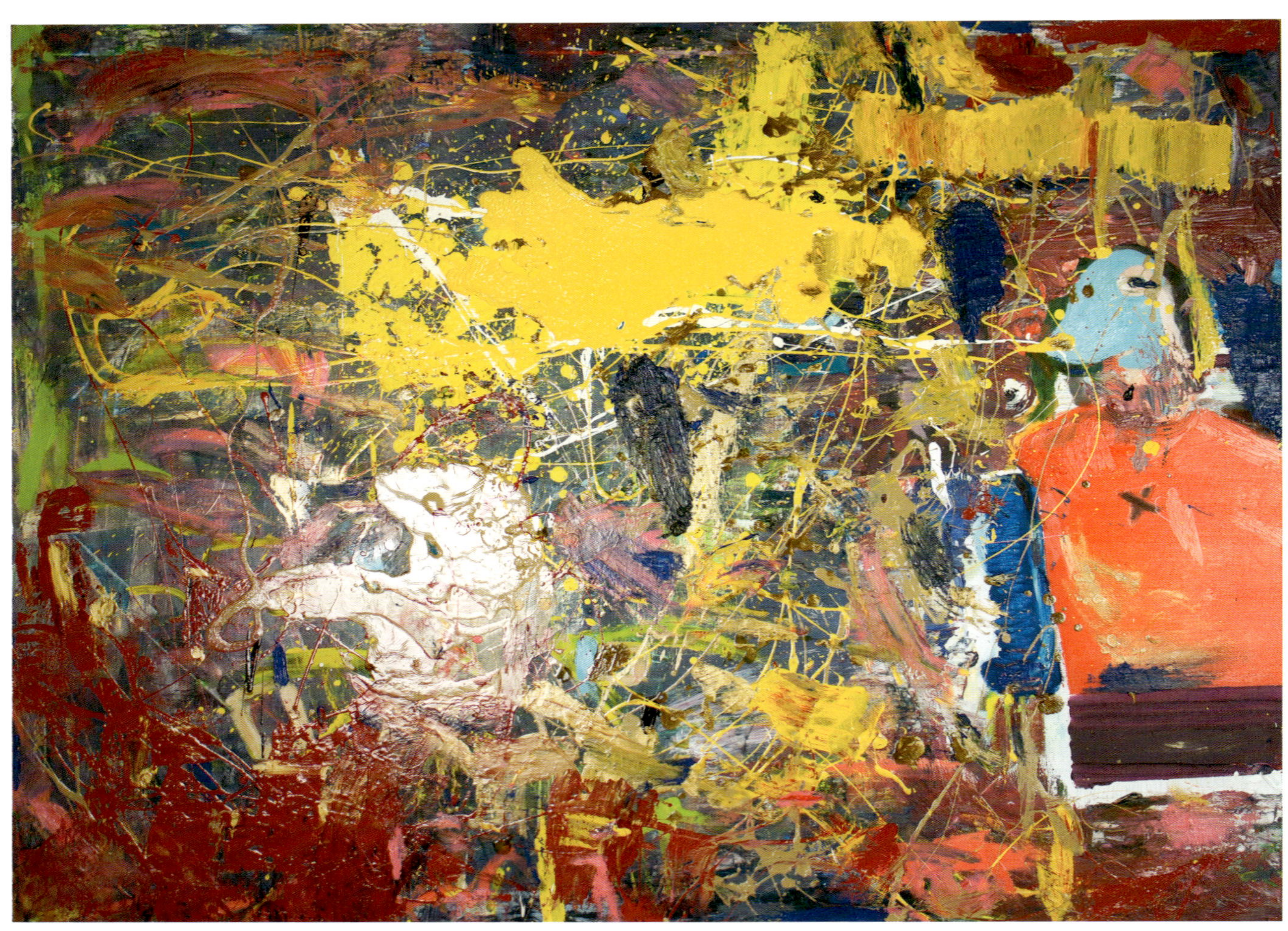

Circumvented, 2013

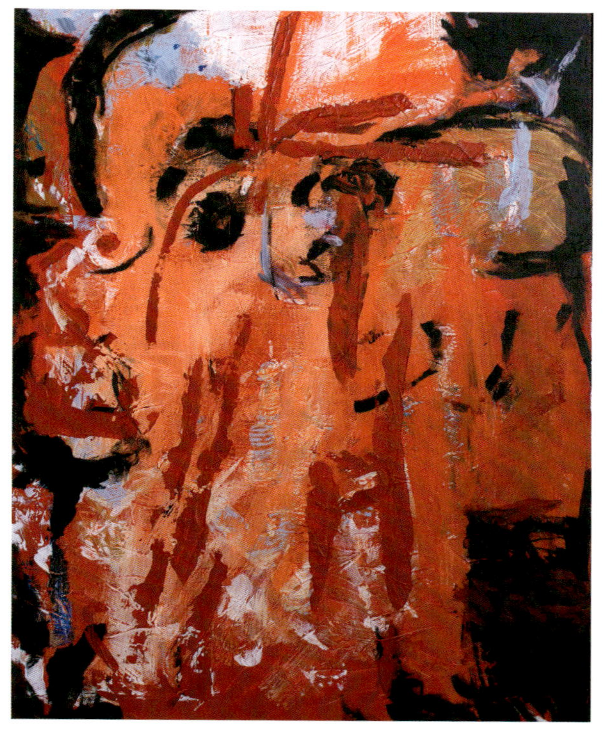

Retrograde, 2009

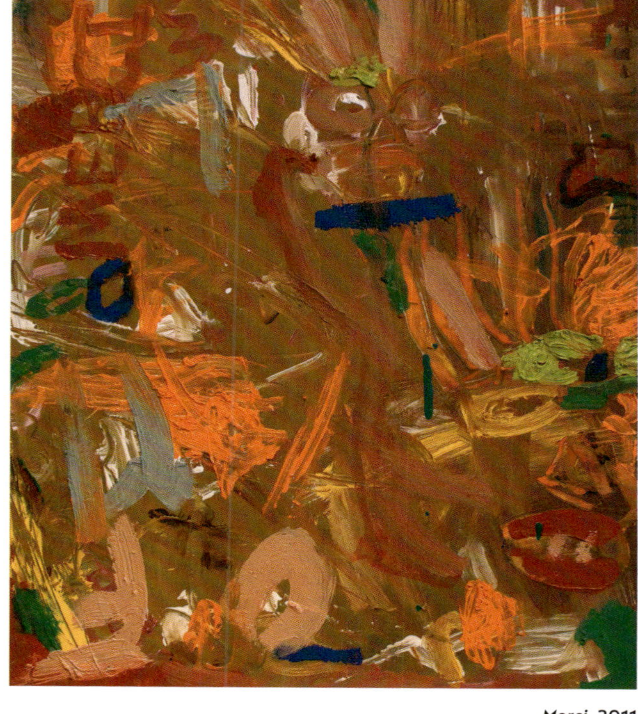

Merci, 2011

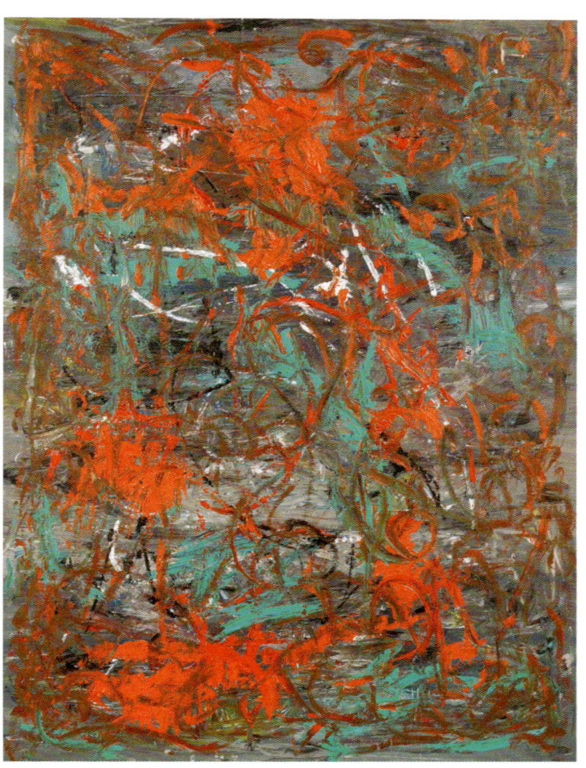

Six, 2010

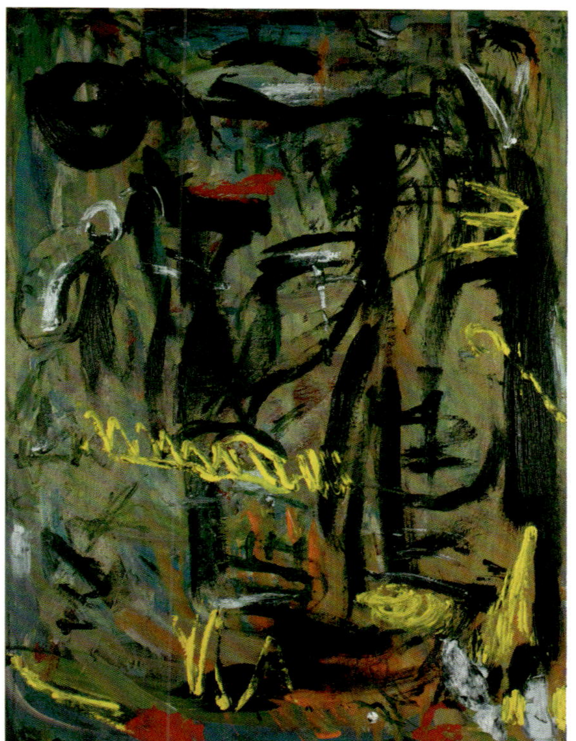

Journey, 2011

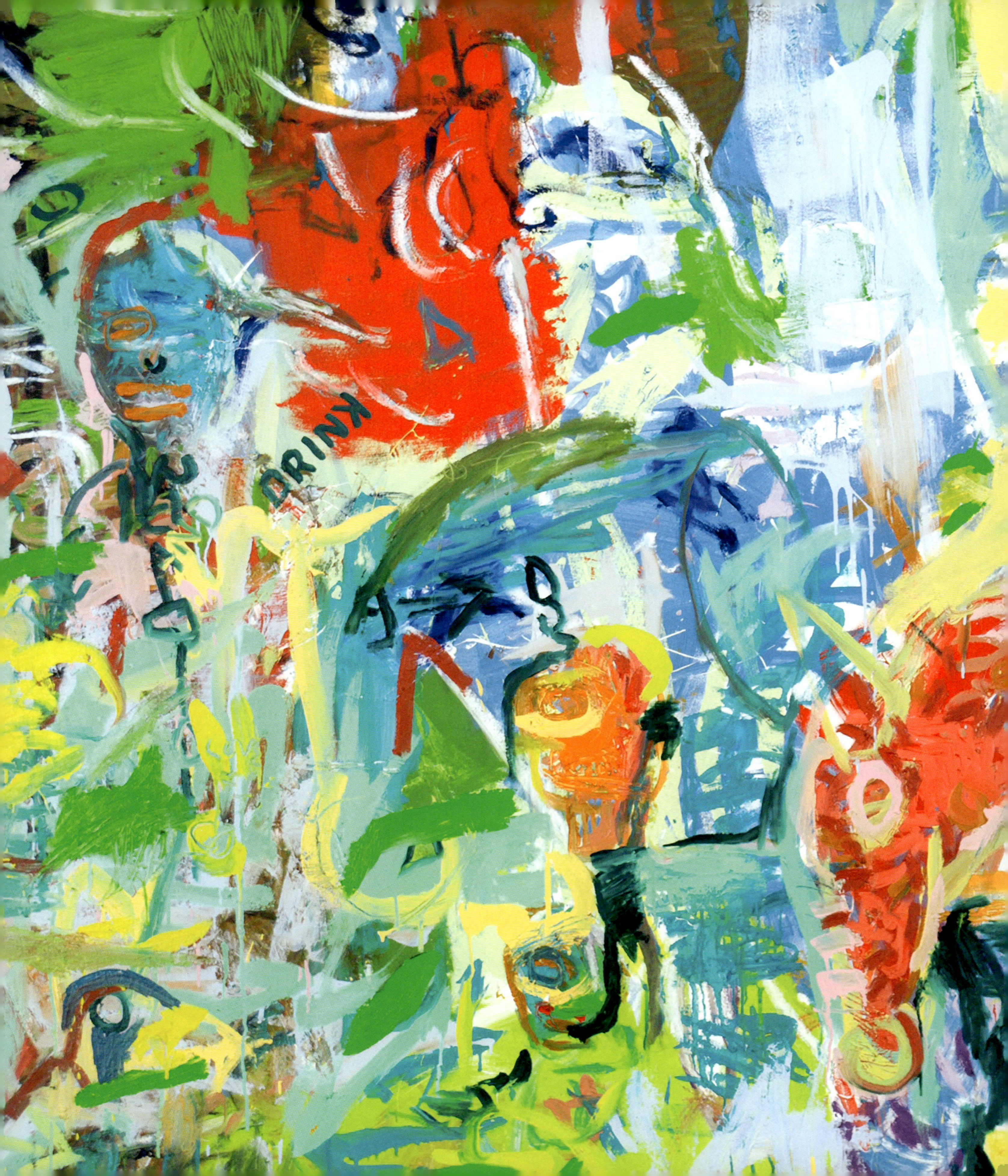
DRINK

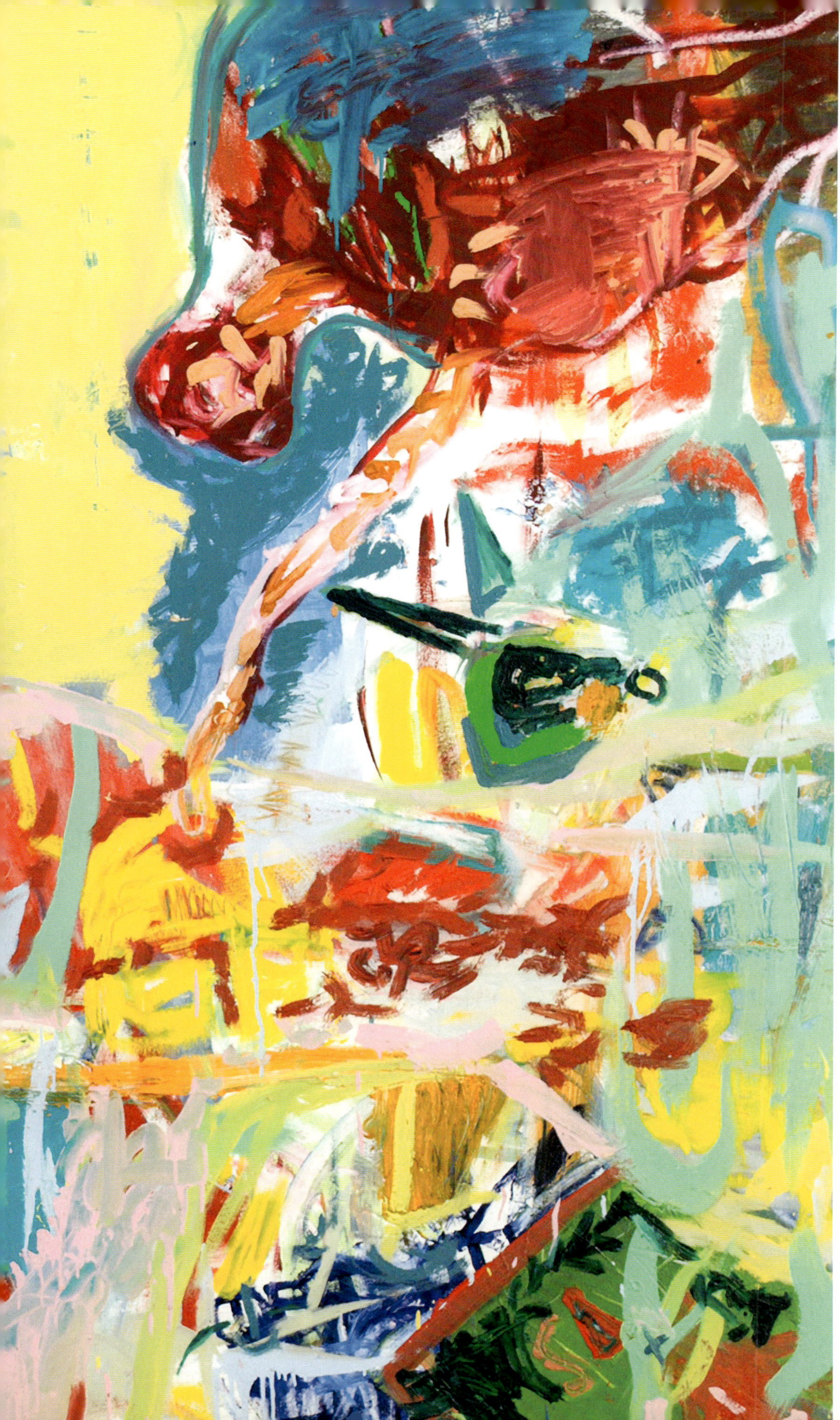

Angels and Horses, 2010

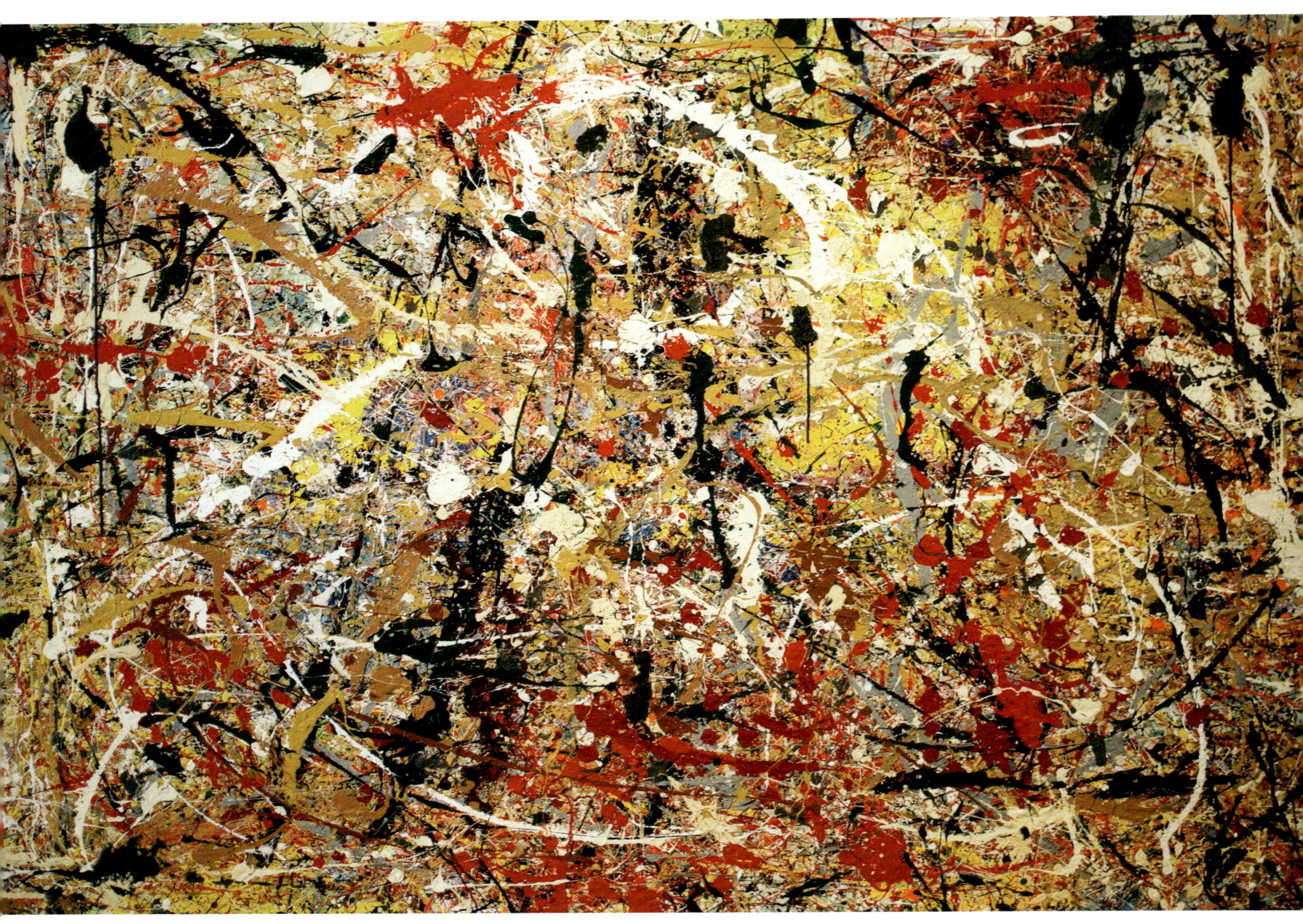

Come Back to Me, 2013

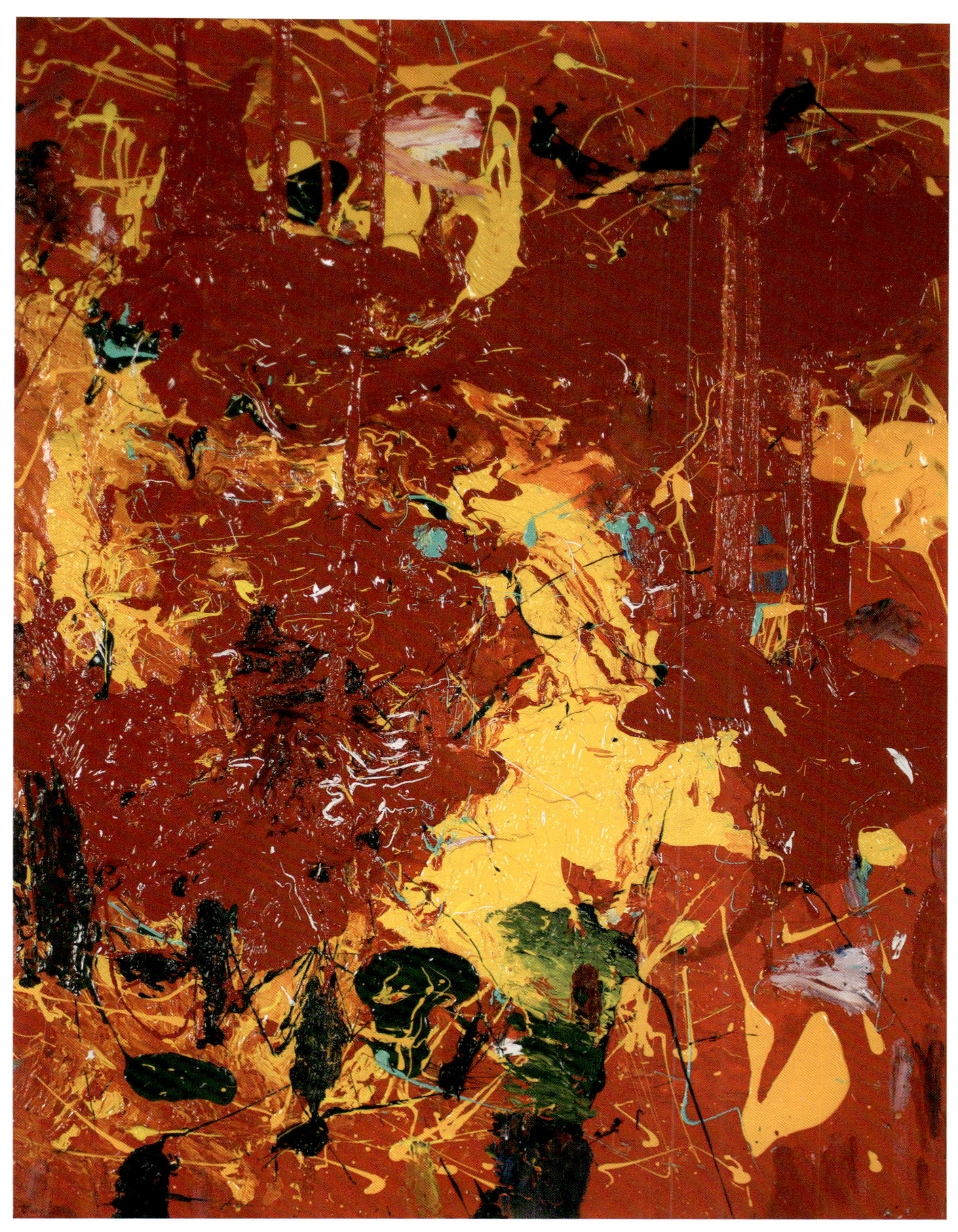

***Insistent Rhythm*, 2013**

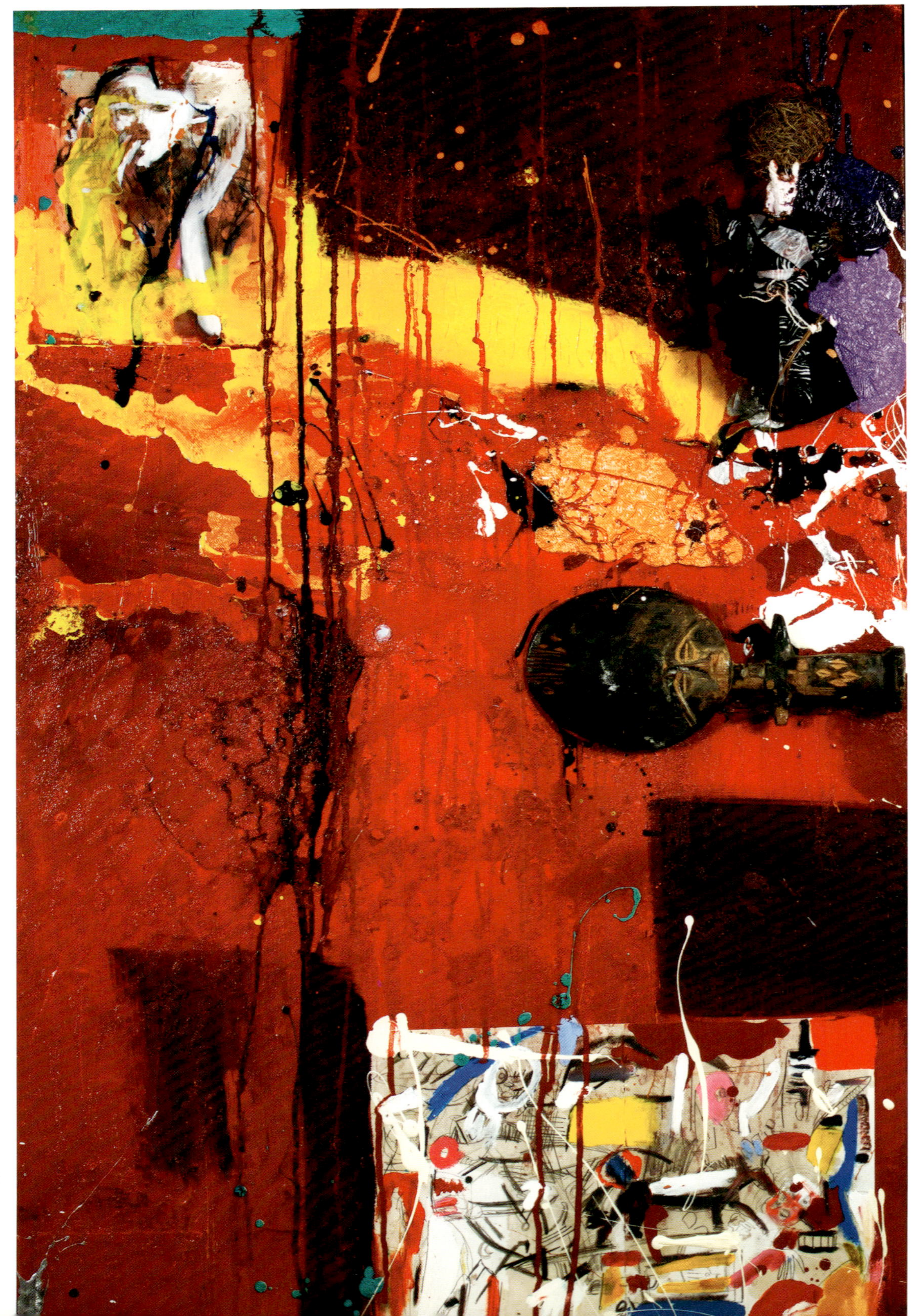

Fertile Instinct, 2013

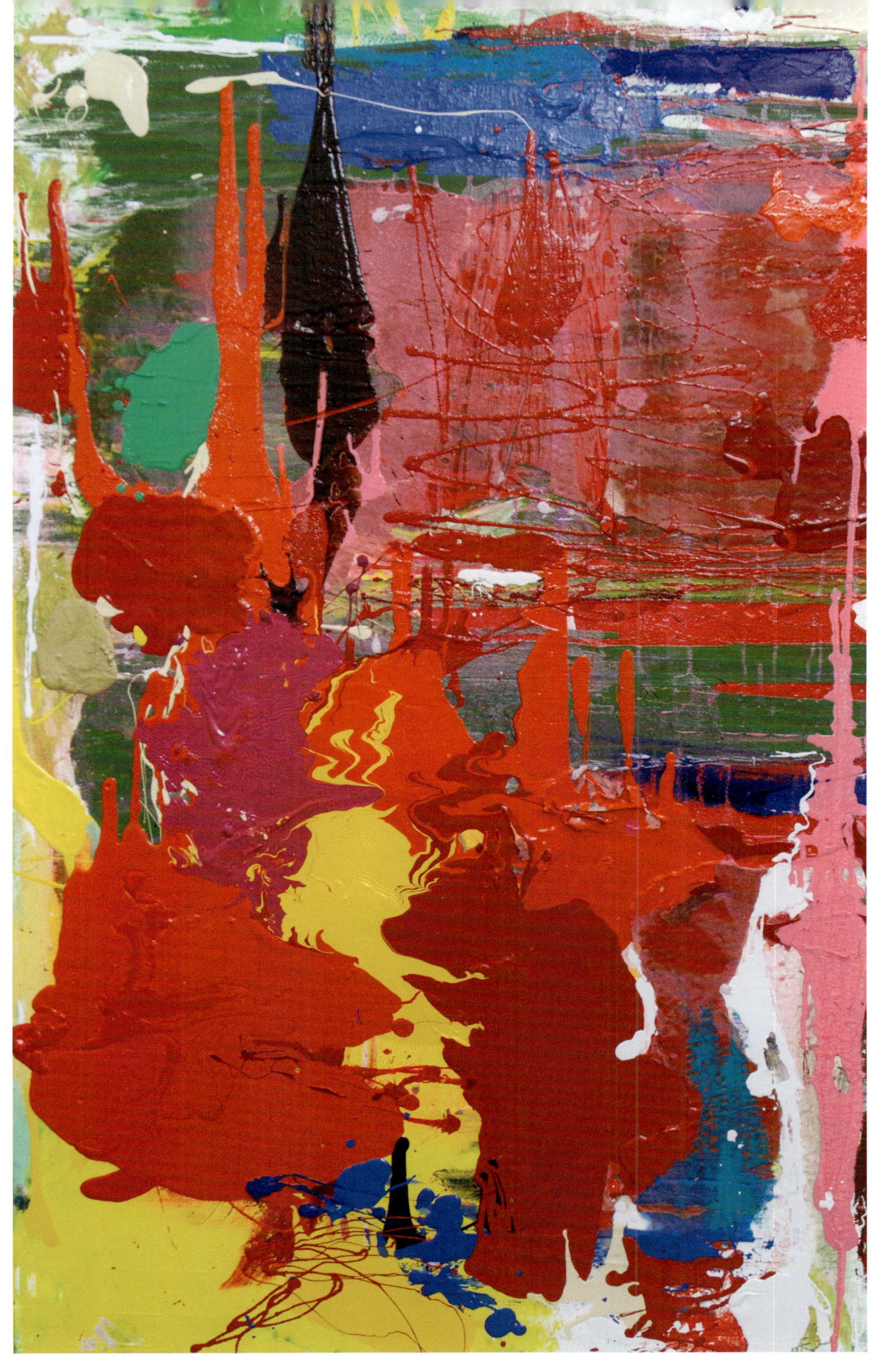

Swing, 2013

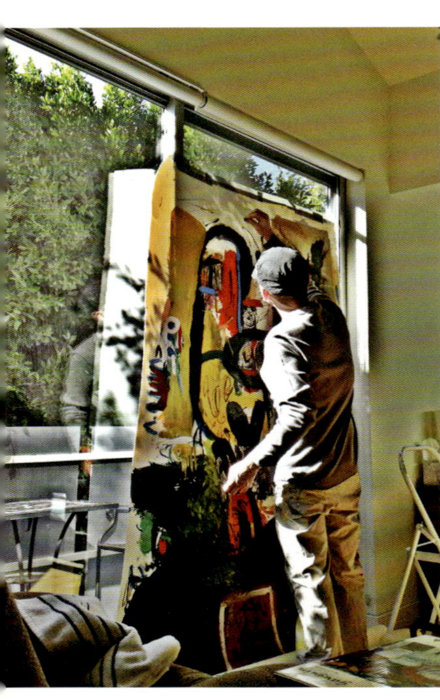

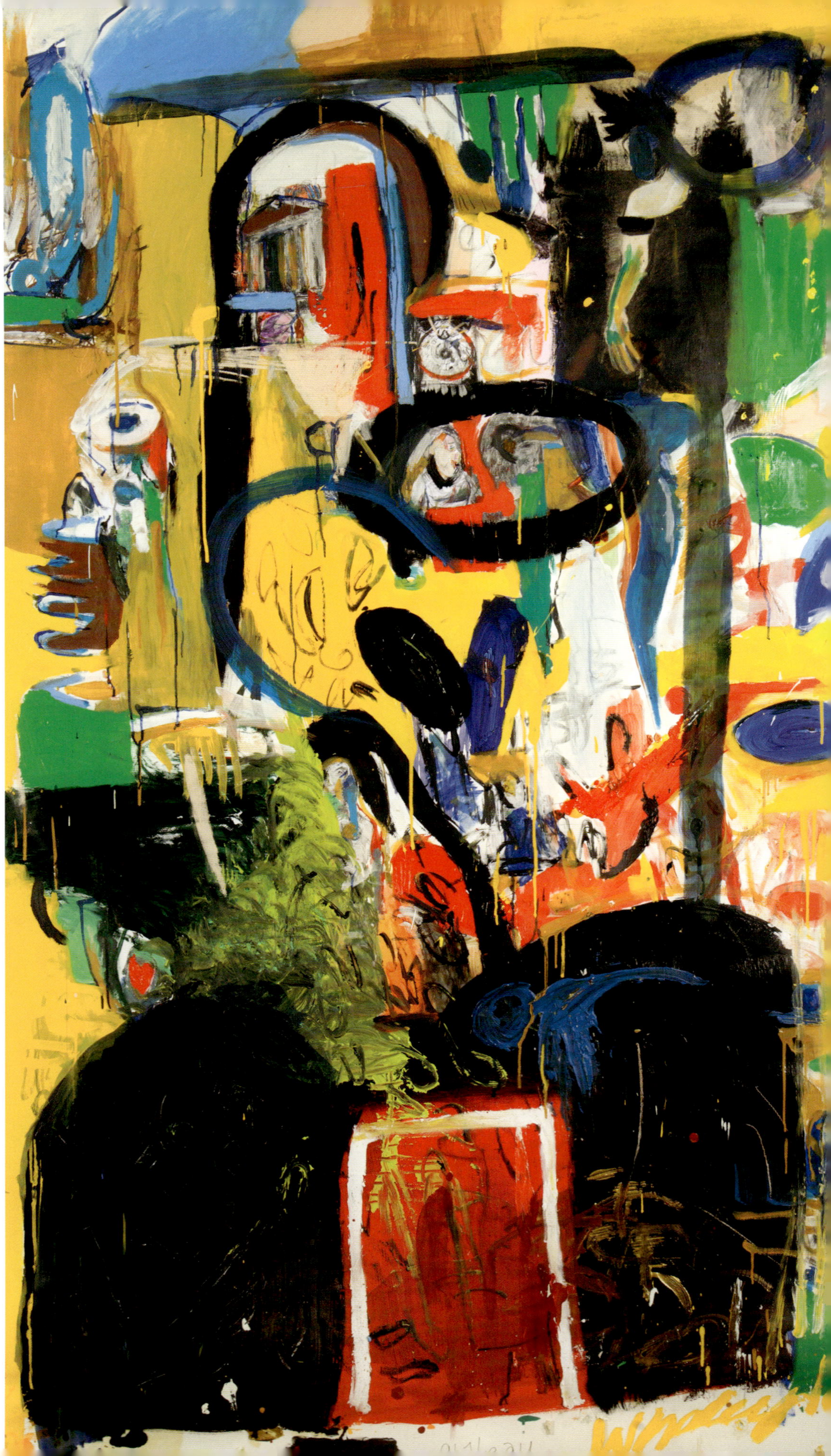

Chateau, 2012

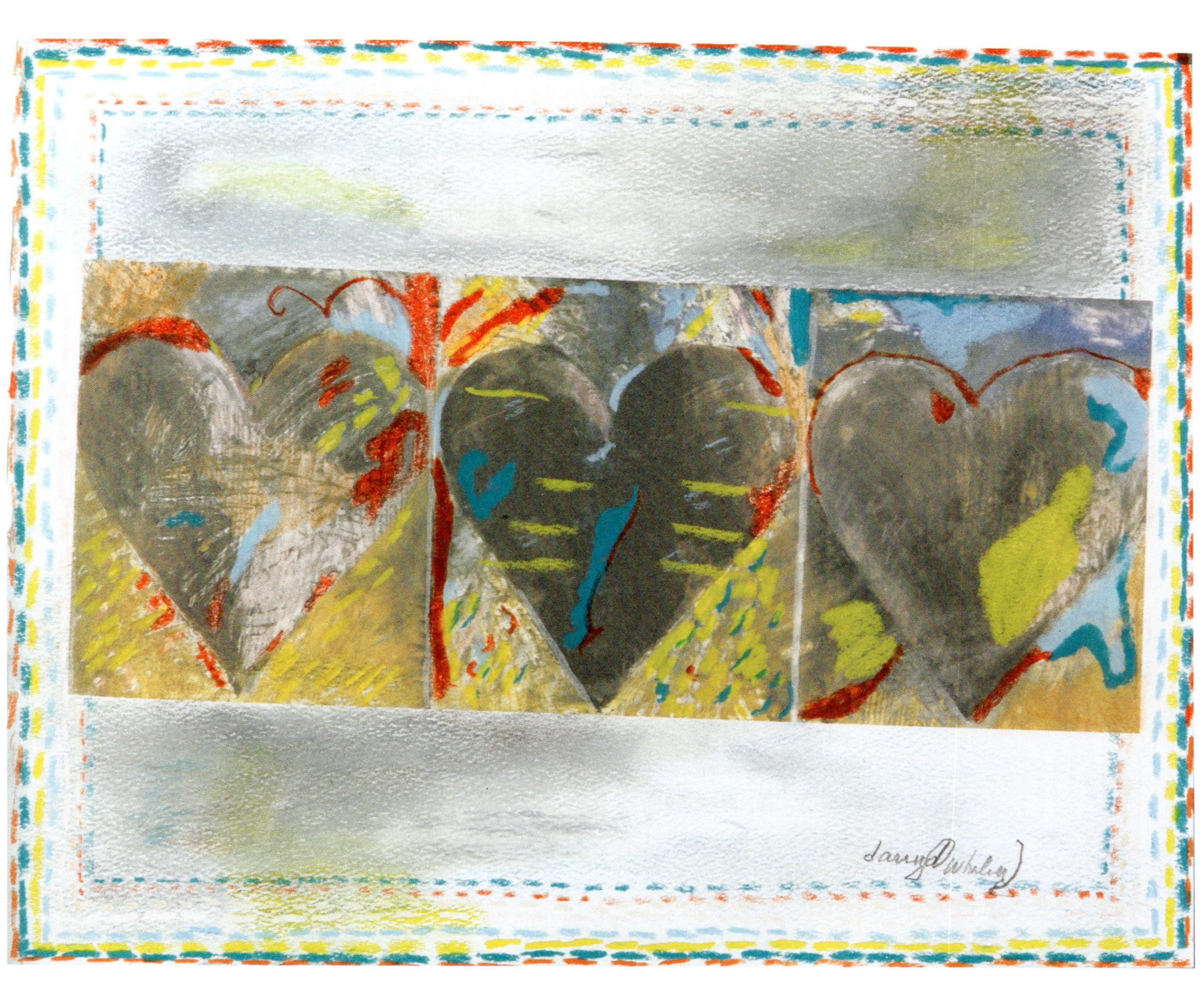

Three Heart Chakra, 2009

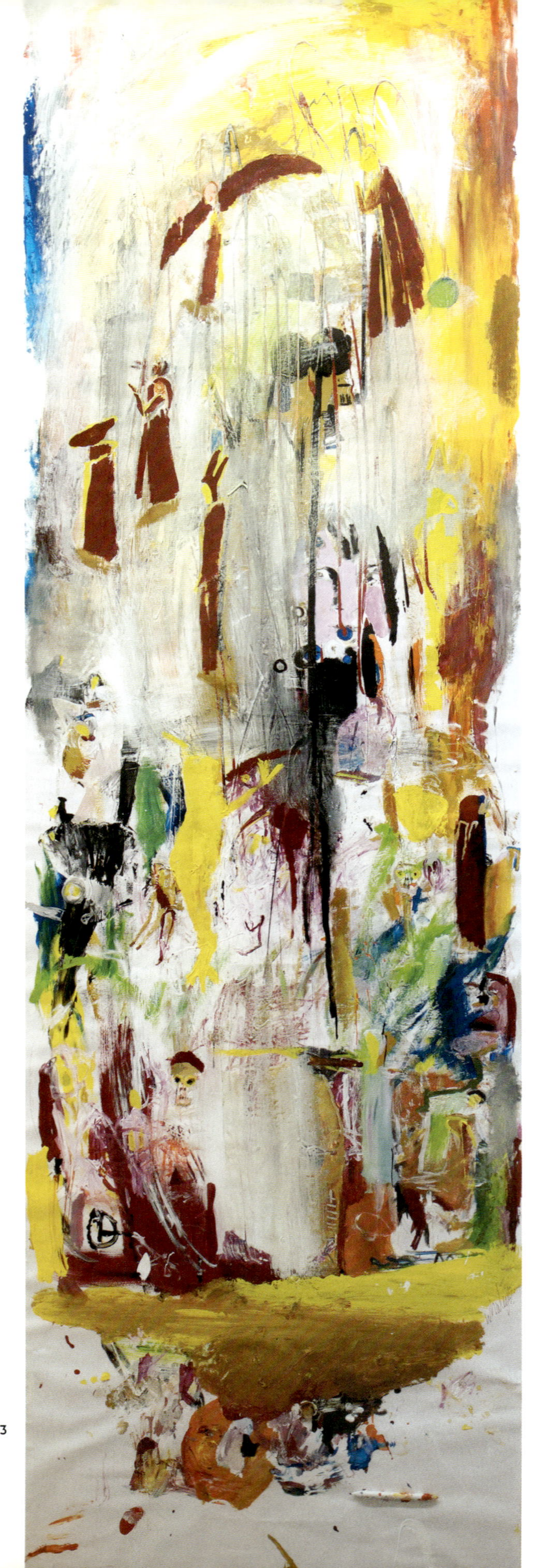

Loki, 2013

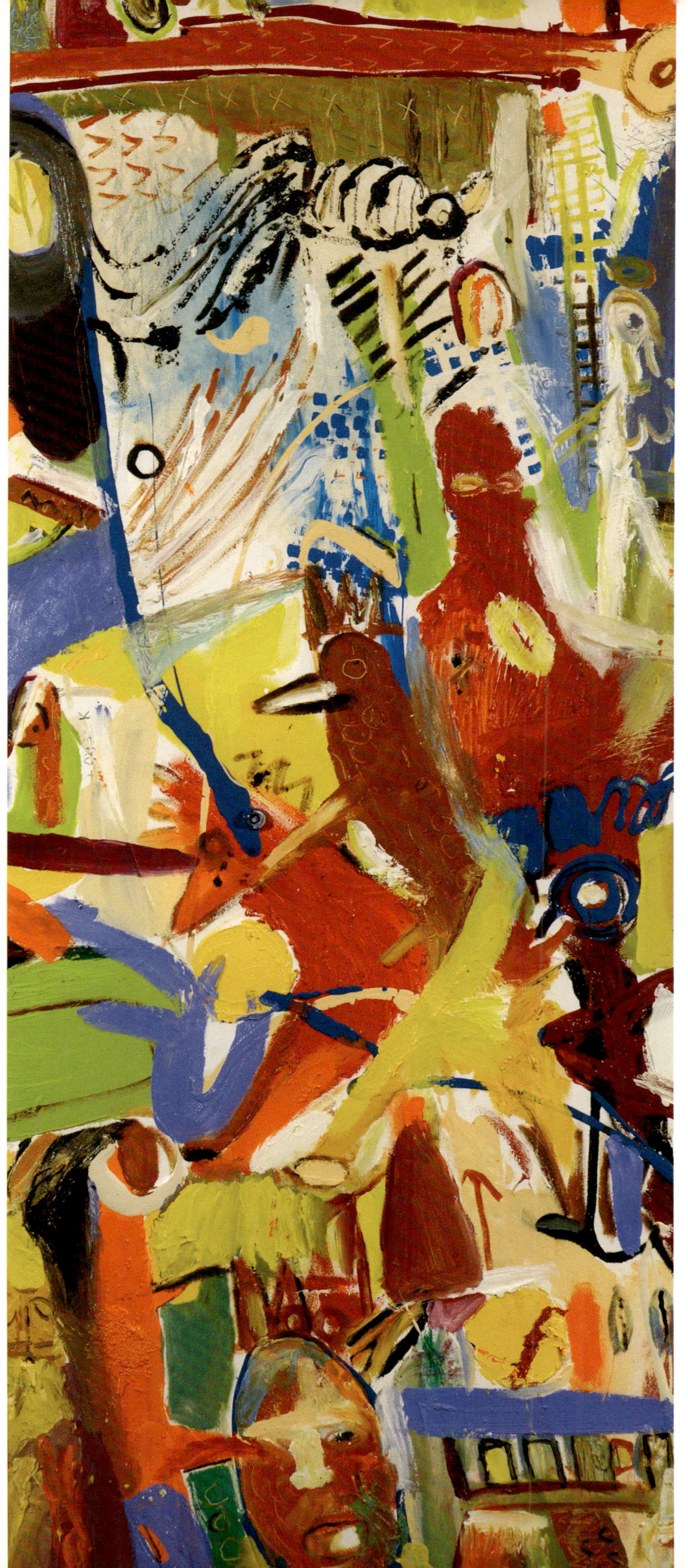

7 Doors, 2012

Pages 126–127: *Hoo Doo*, 2013

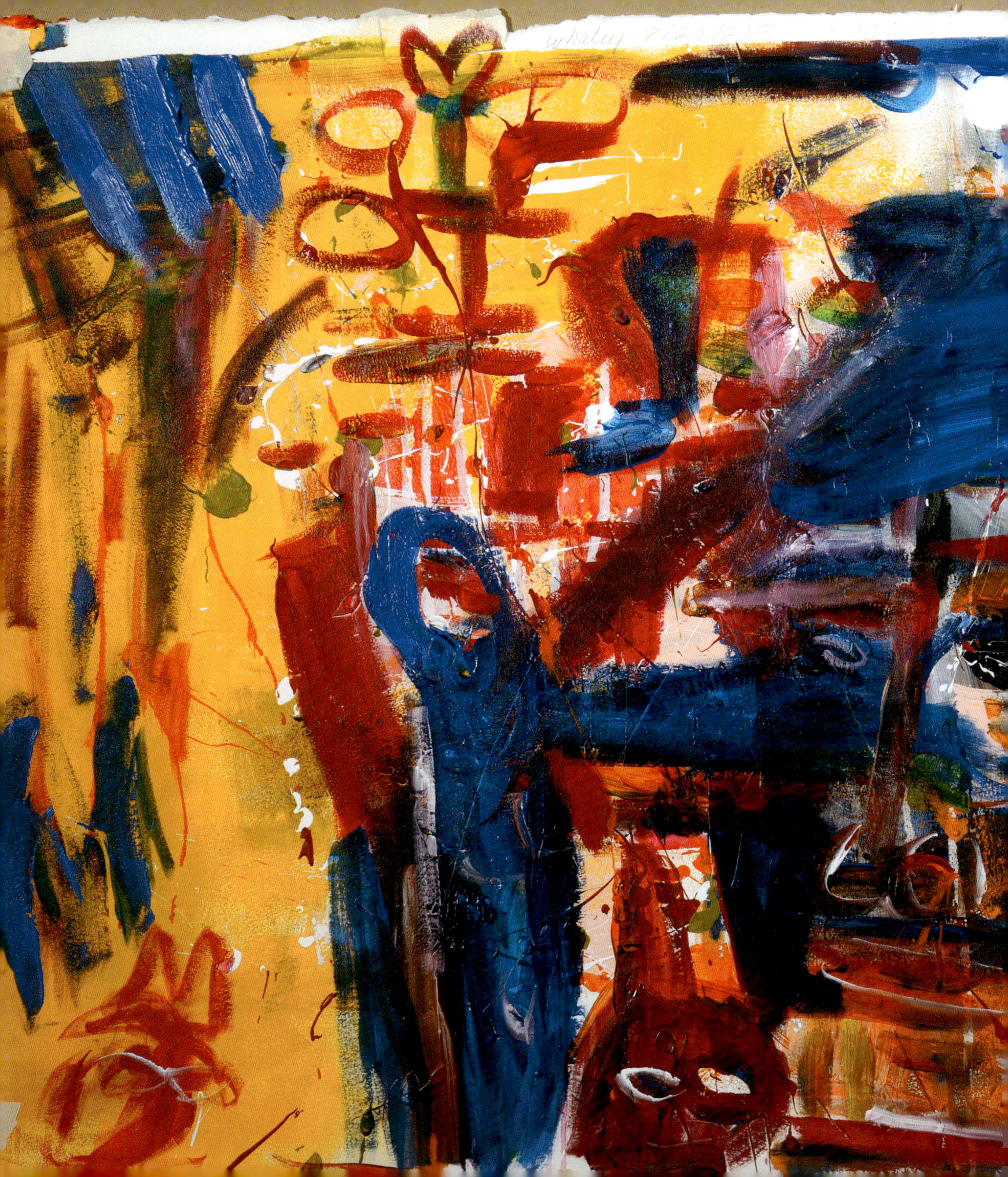

whaley

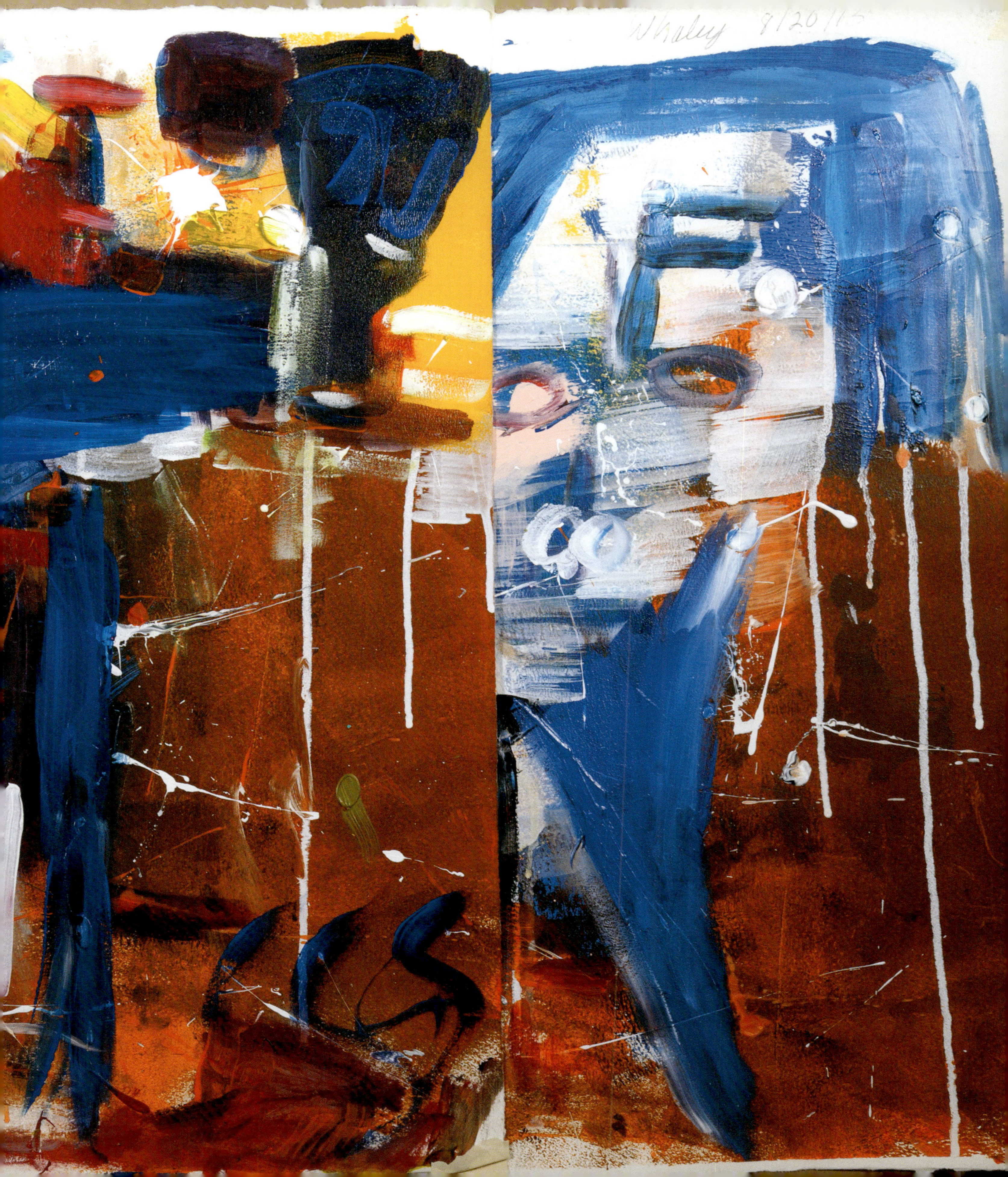
Whaley 8/20/15

"Life gives you change.
It's your job to take the pain, recycle the parts that work better than before,
and find grace and beauty among the chaos."

—DW

Hero Series

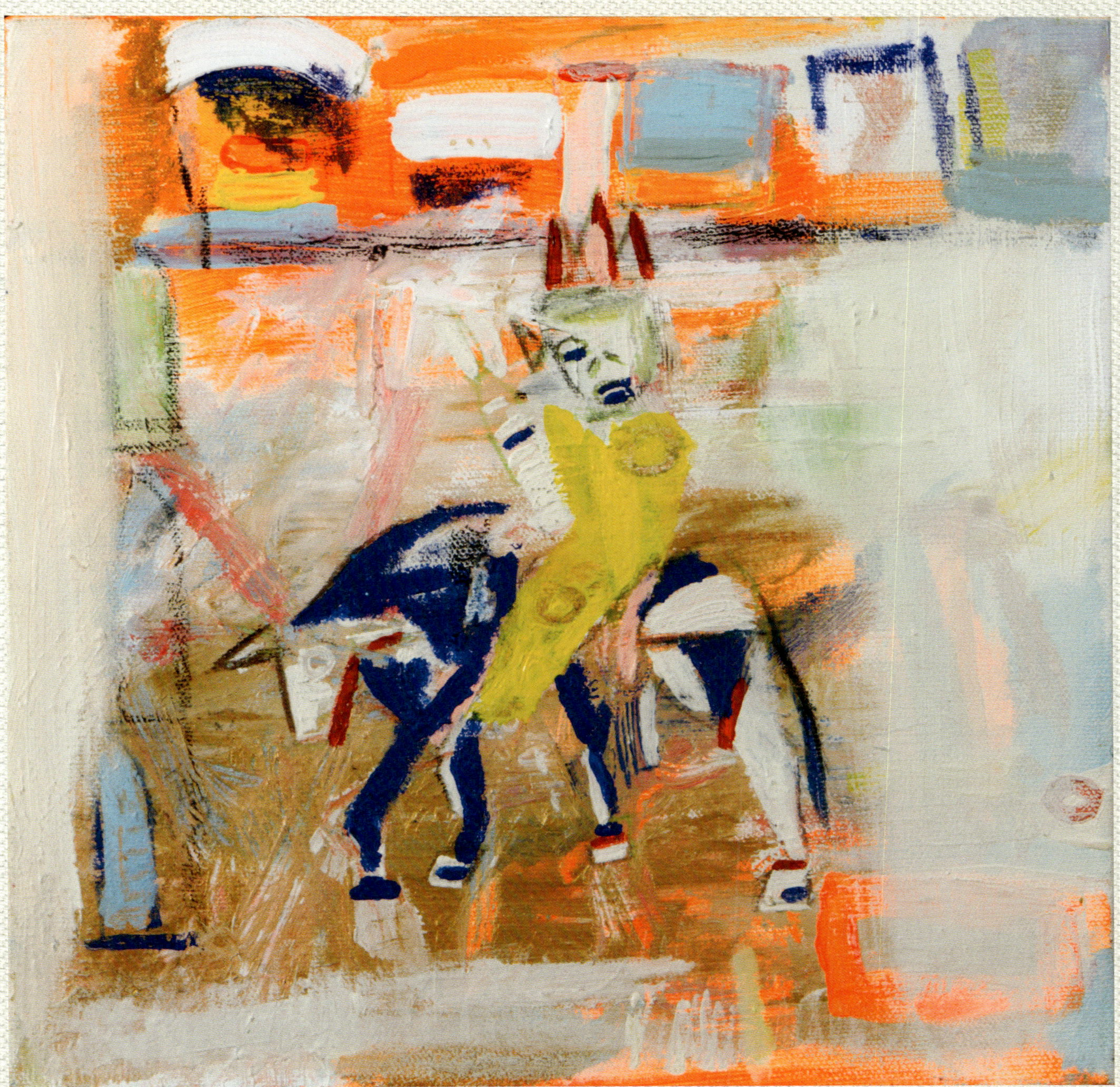

Hero, The Fool, 2011

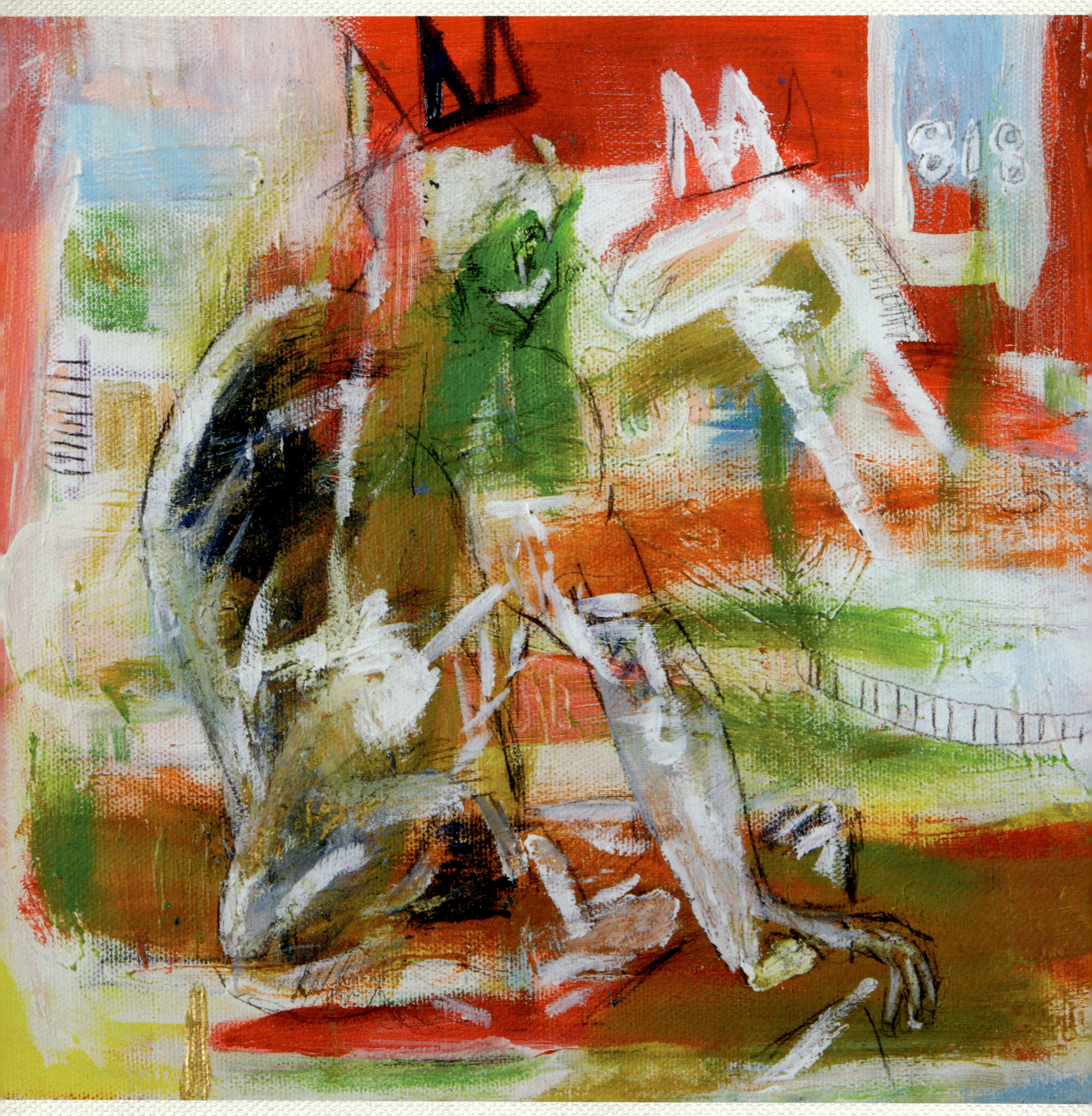
818

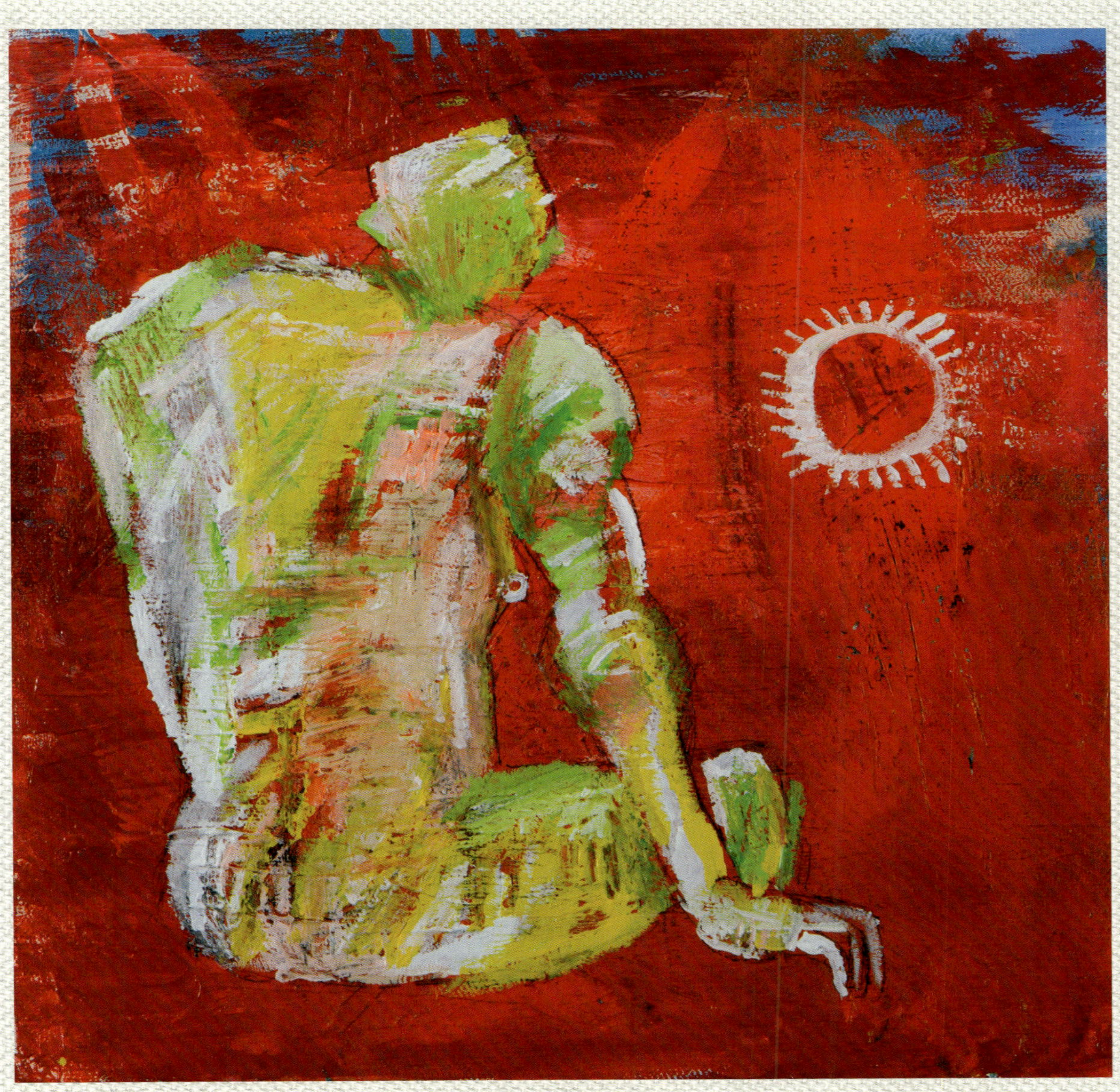

Opposite: *Hero I*, 2011

Hero II, 2011

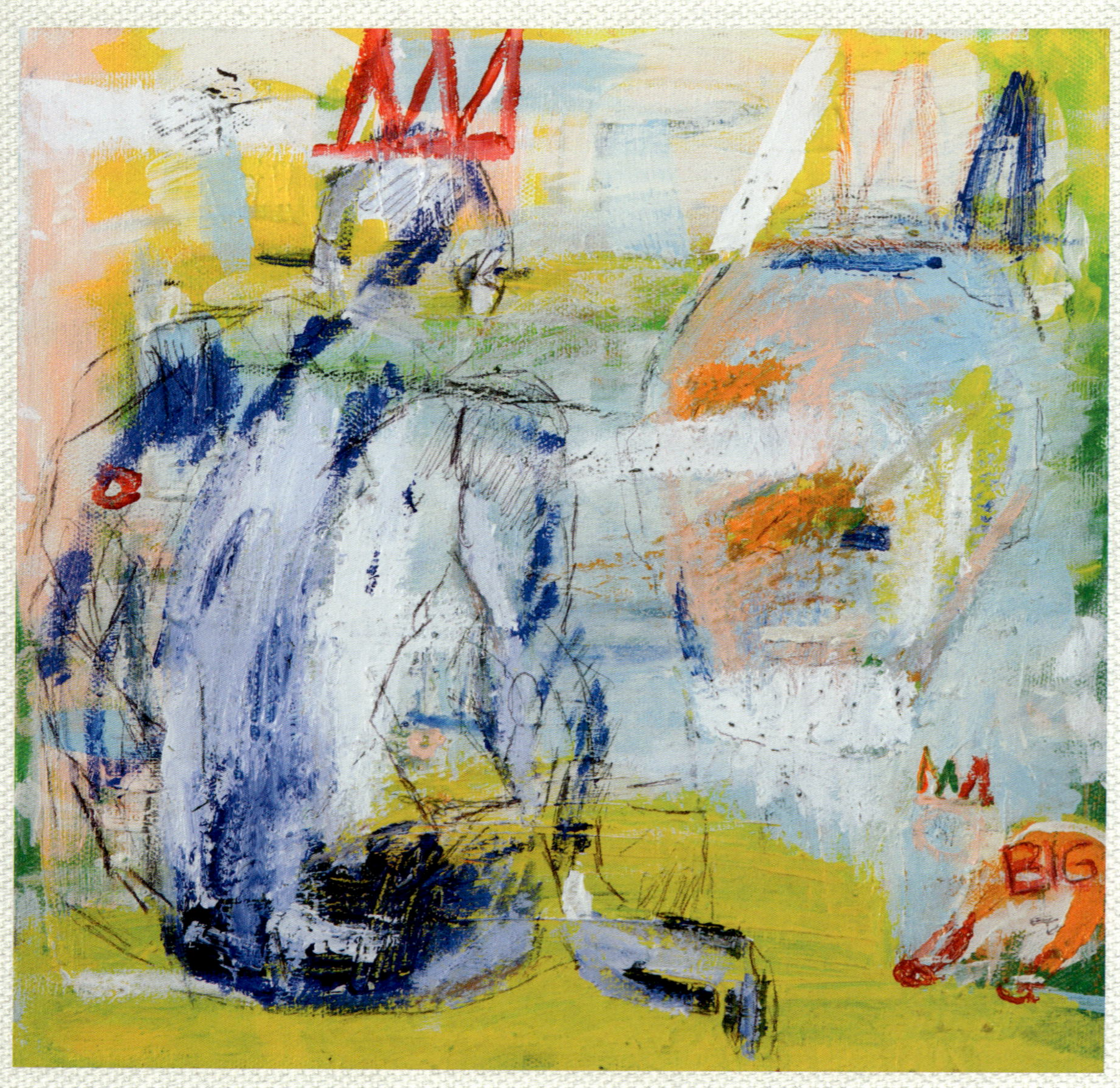

***Hero III*, 2011**

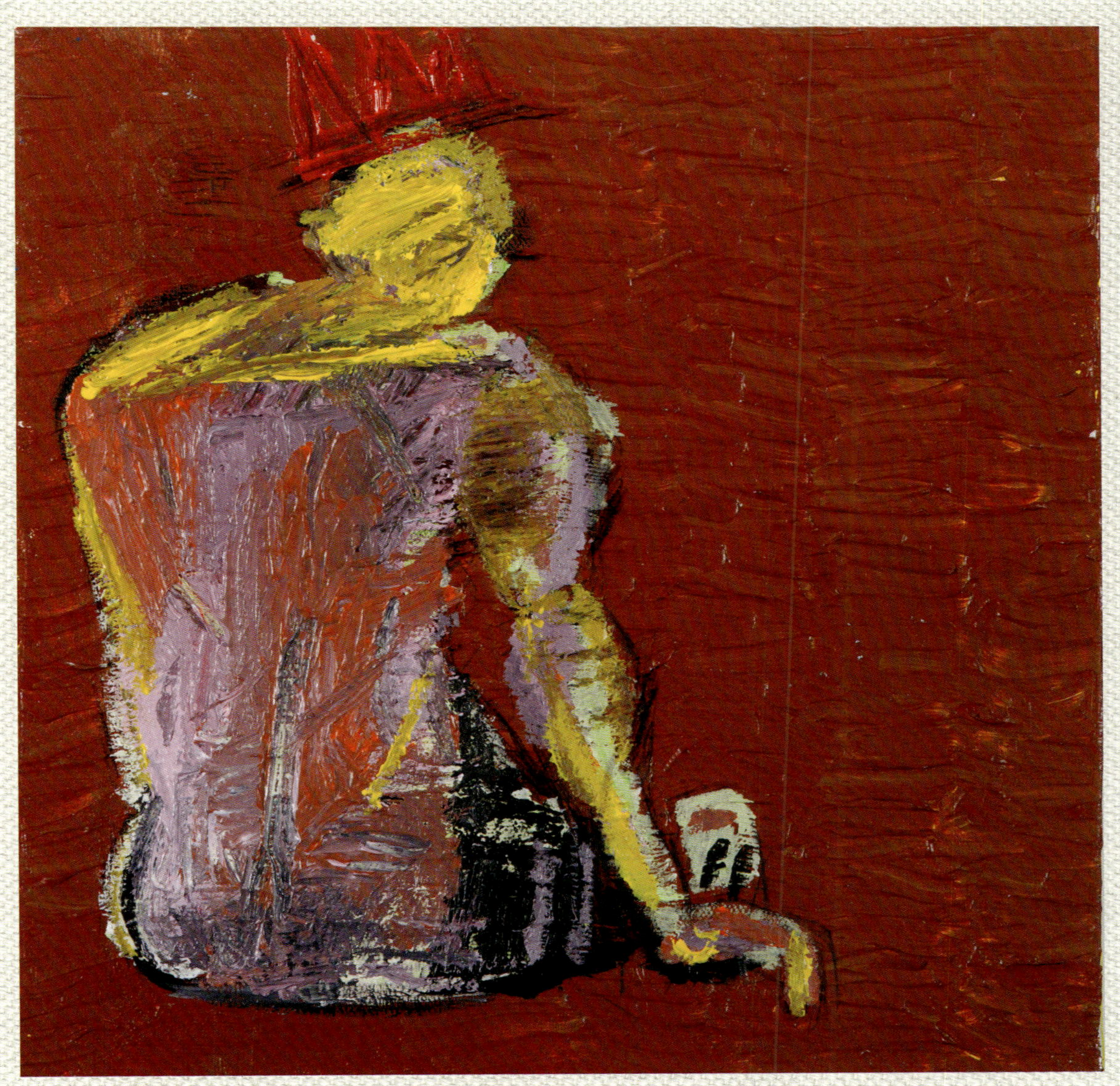

Hero IV, 2011

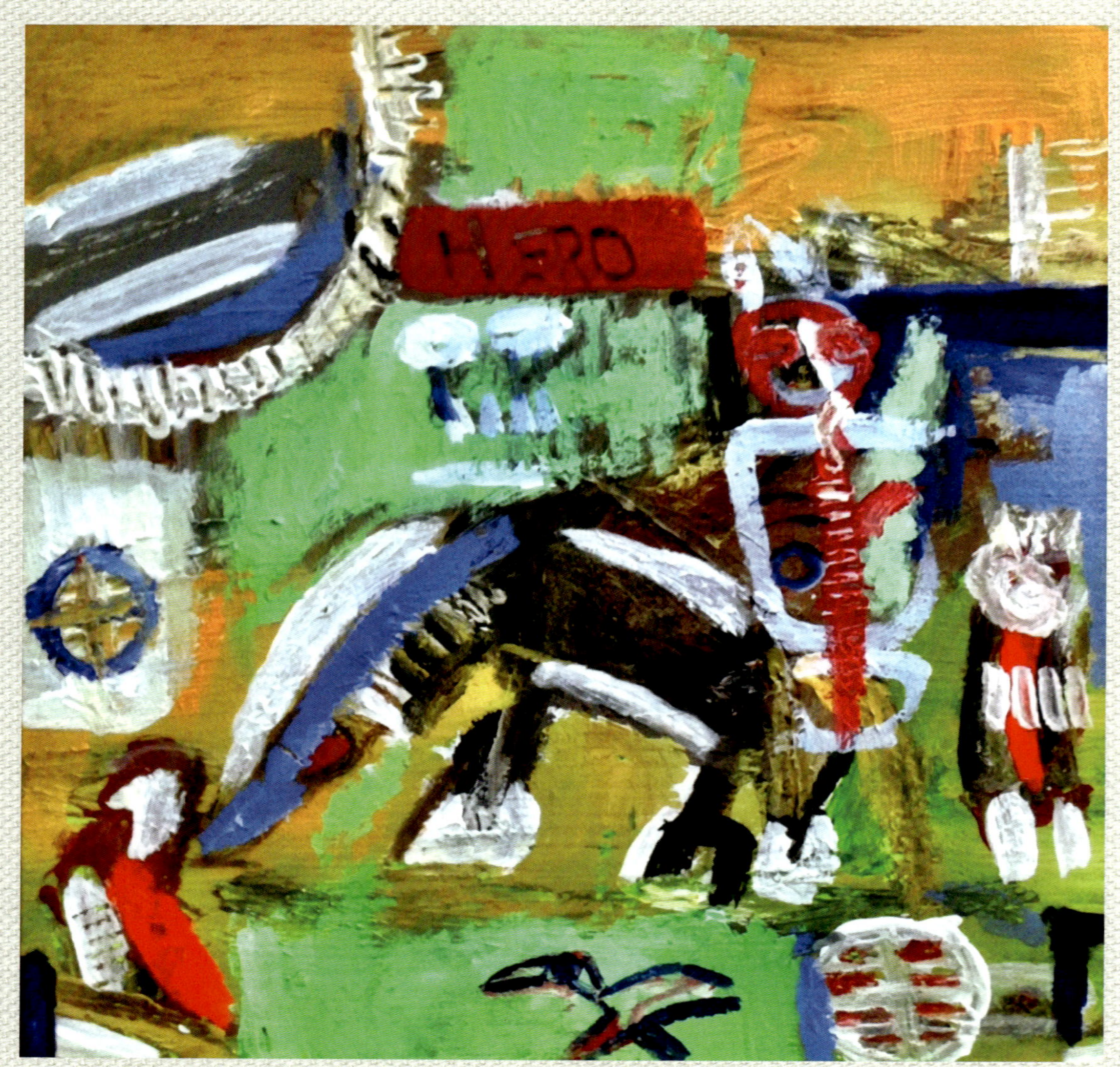

Hero V, 2011

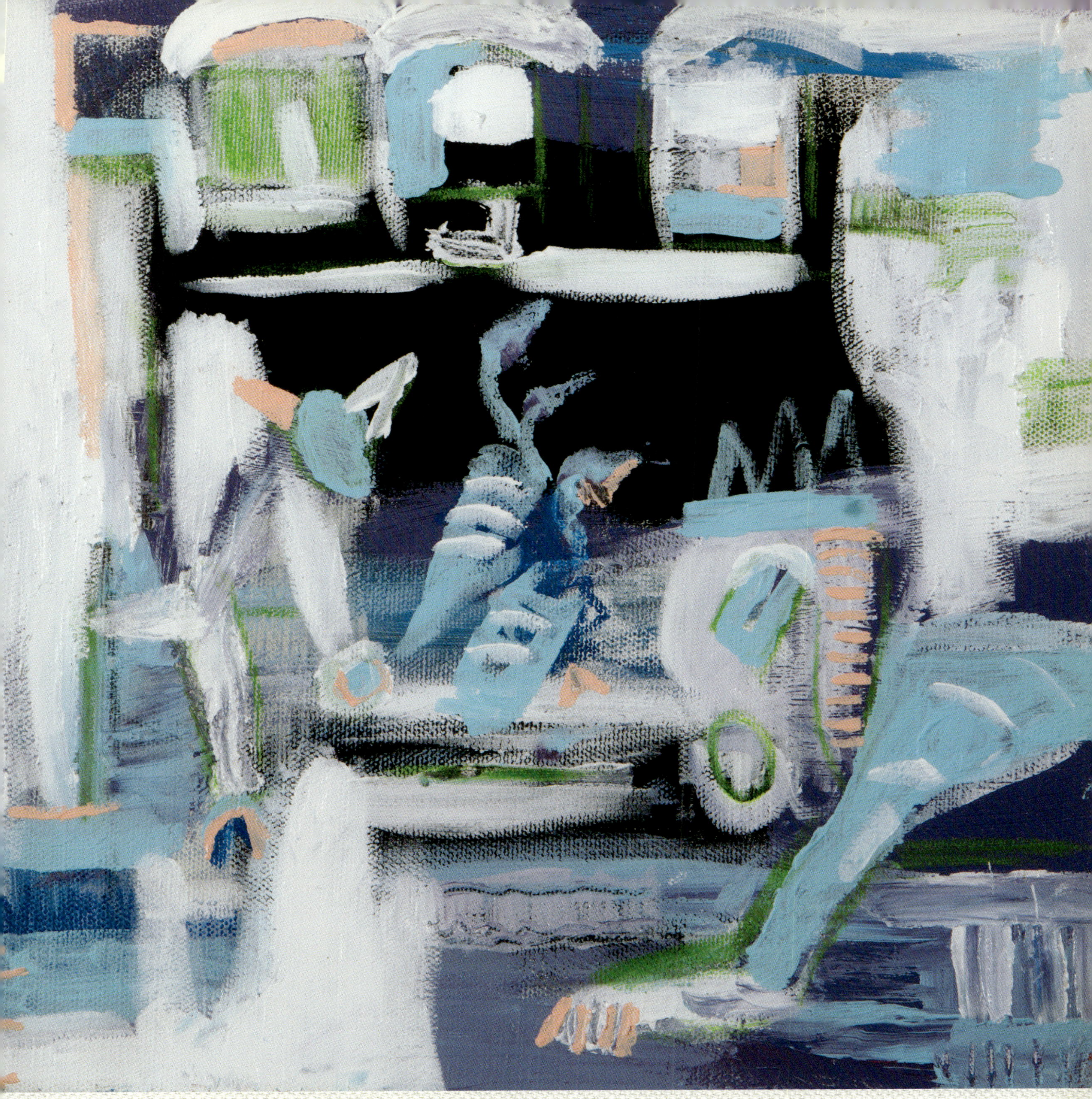

Hero, Enki, 2011

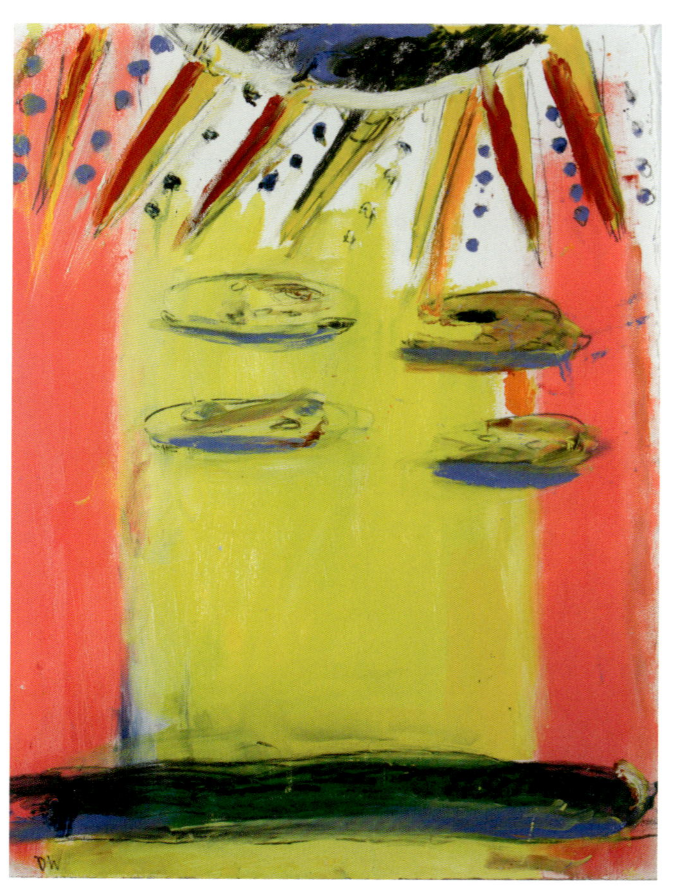

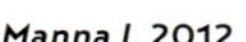

***Manna I*, 2012**

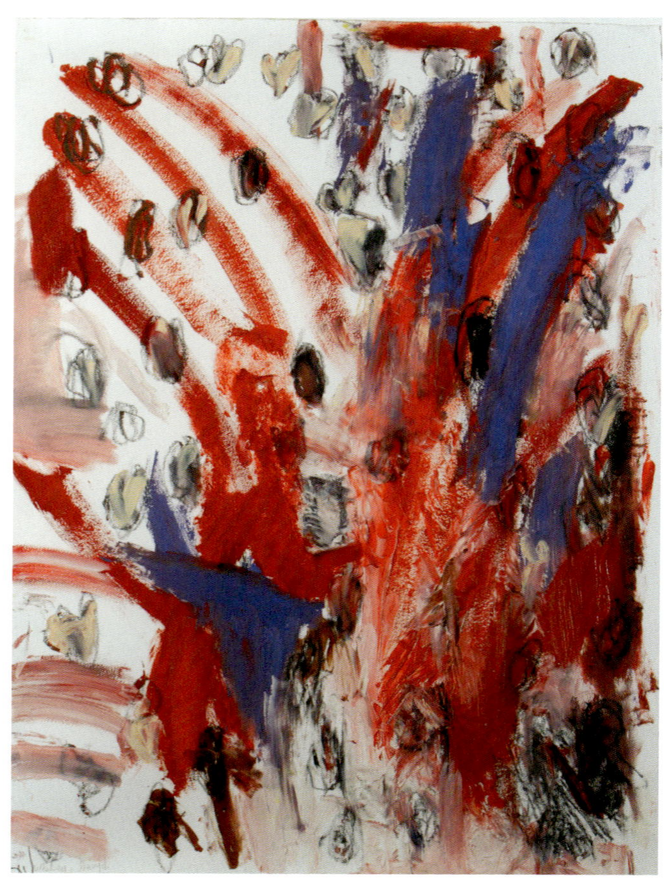

***Manna II*, 2012**

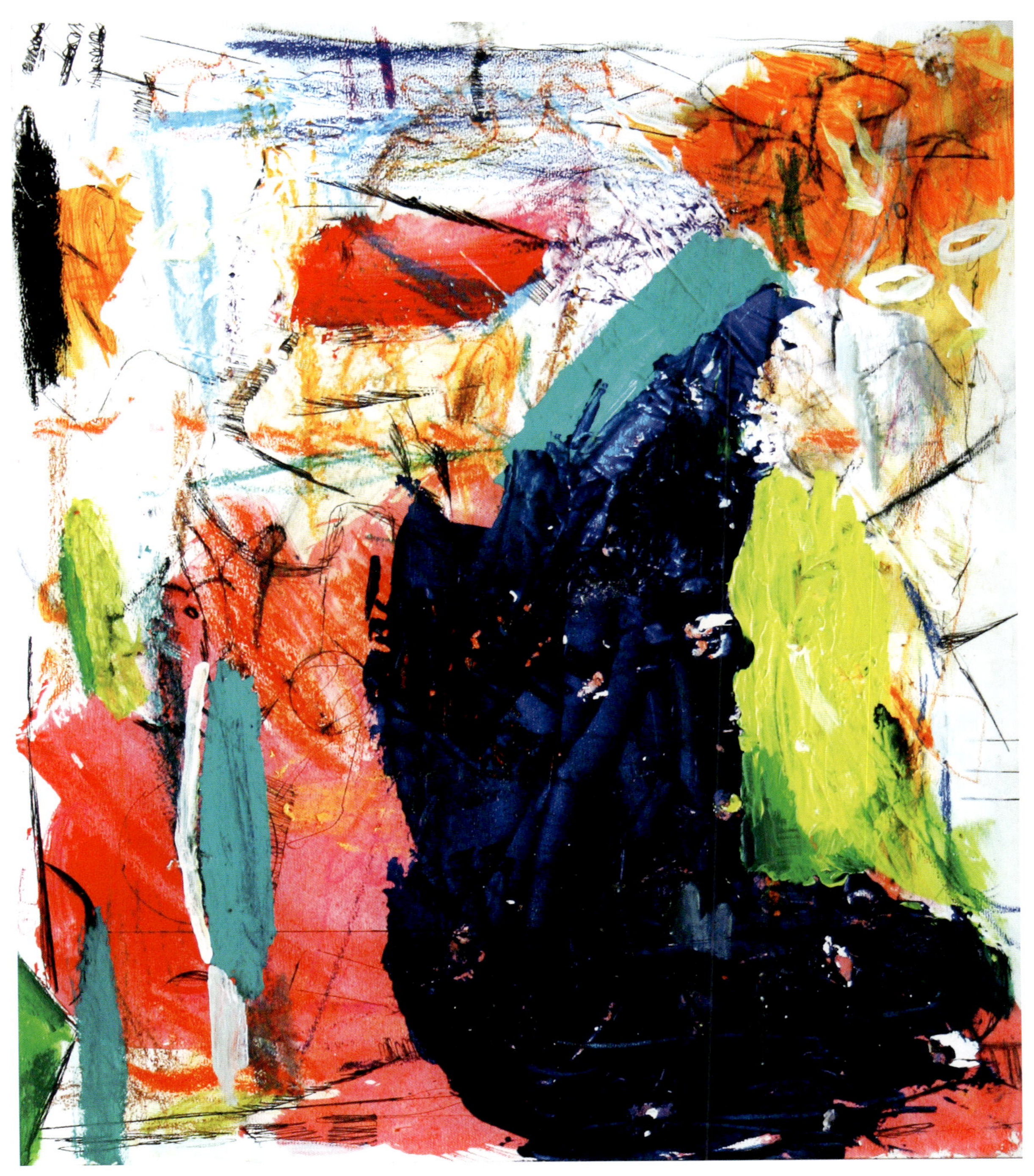

***False Fjord*, 2012**

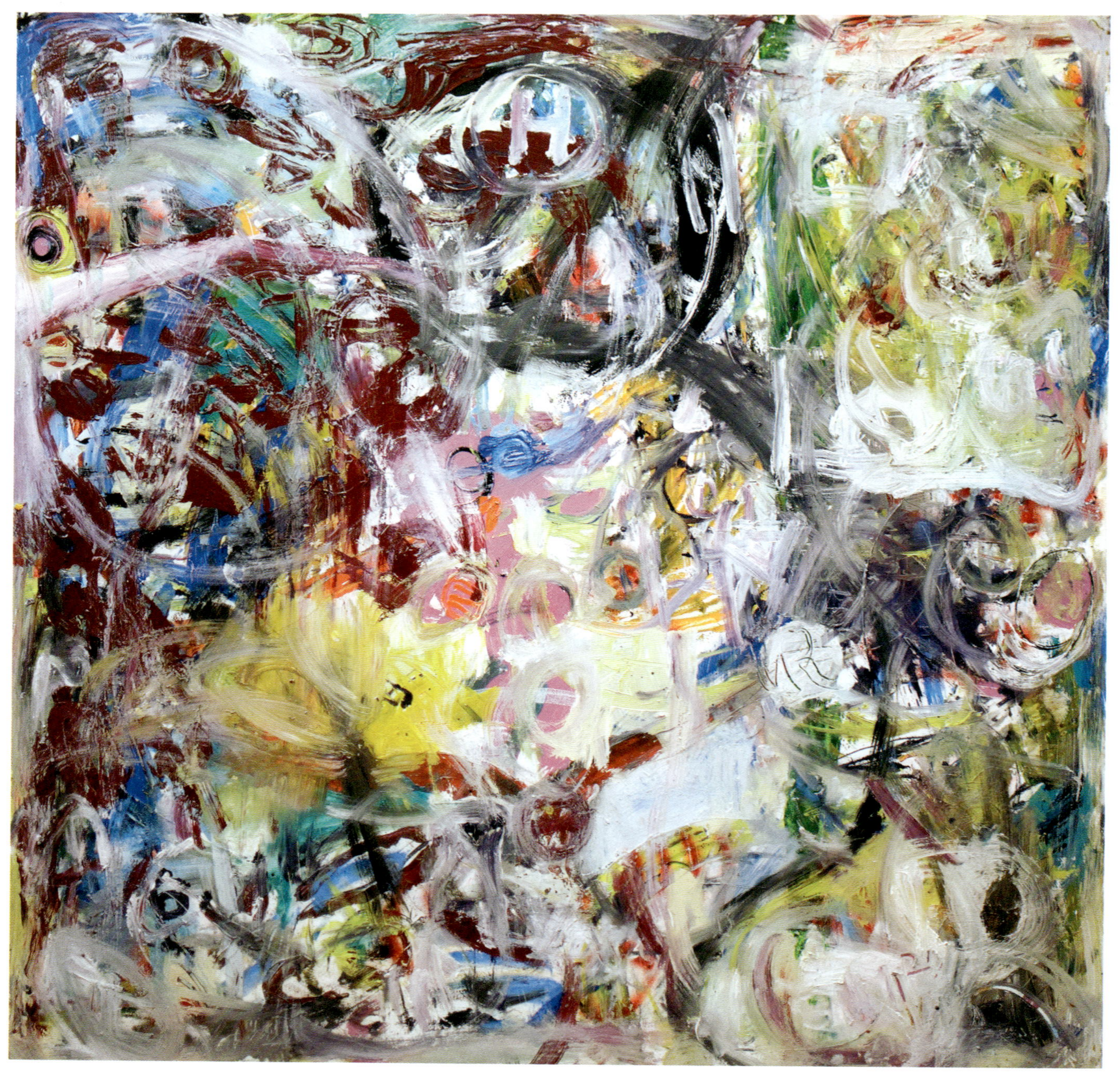

***Defeat of Chaos*, 2010**

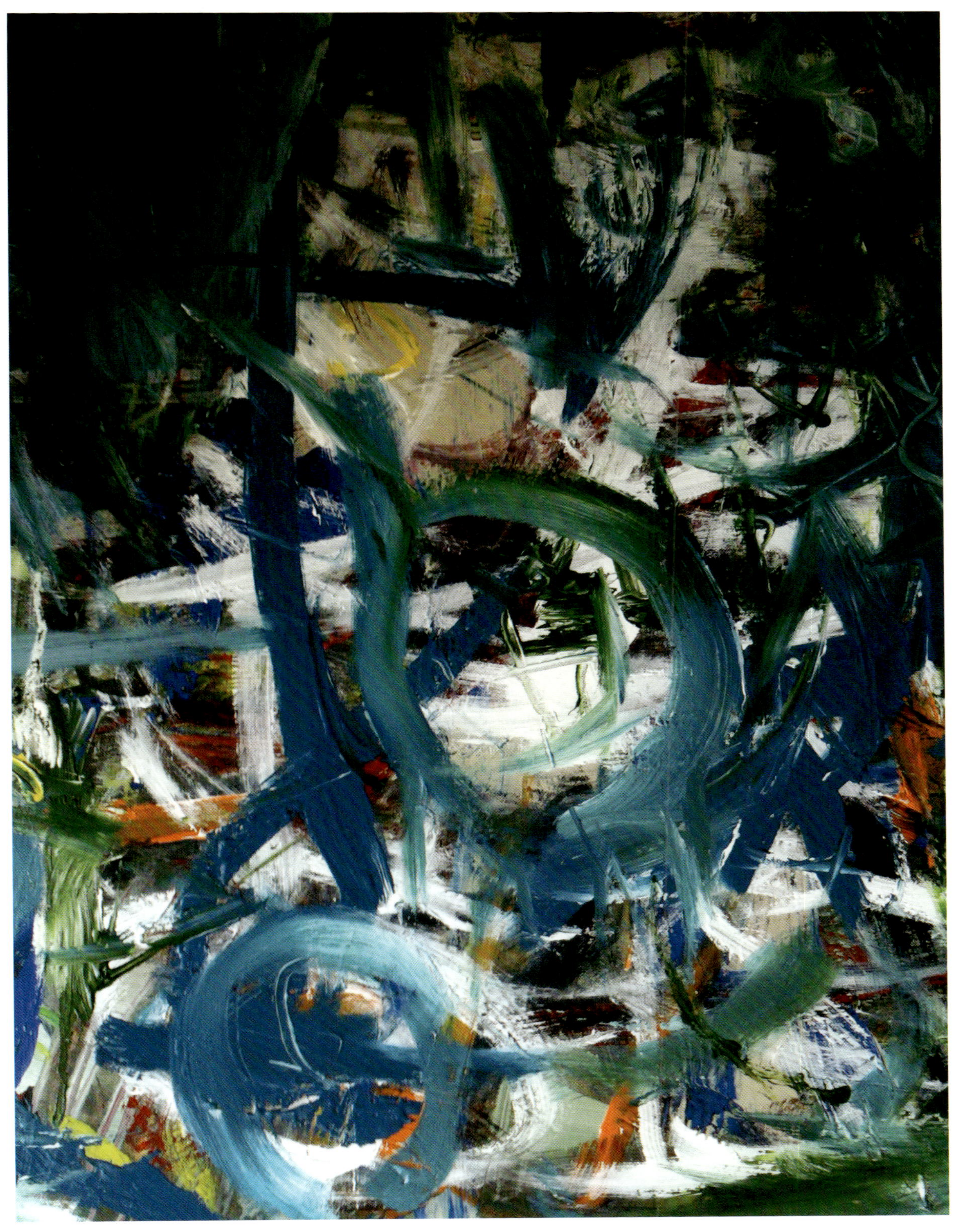

***Ceylon*, 2010**

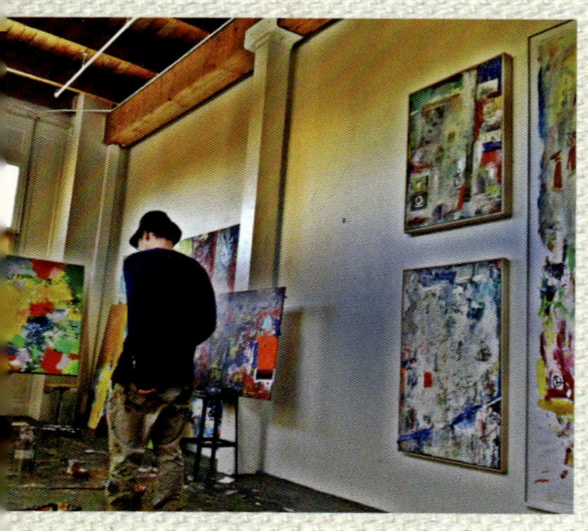

"This is a portrait of my past, mummified in wax done as a project while attending UCLA 'Destroy the Picture, Painting the Void'—UCLA Extension, Fall Semester 2012.

"I created the painting as a 3 dimensional mixed media over a period of six weeks, using letters, personal objects, paint, sculpture and wax.

"Underneath graffiti, a shiny saw blade cuts its way from the inside out, exposing the formative years of my life as an artist. Peeking through the surface are letters, written to my best friend from me, during my time as a sailor, away from home.

"A twisted yellow hospital card, mangled and melted, came from my time studying nursing. It was my entry to the ICU. Fog covers the face of a wristwatch and the band has turned green by the heat and melting wax. I once used the watch, to check the pulse of patients in emergency rooms, coming face to face with life and death. Now it just sits on the left hand side of this weathered painting, its purpose to remind me of another time.

"The smell and gauzy feel represent my feelings of the past.

"There are two appendages to the painting; they show the irony of the support I hoped to provide in my past occupations. One of the elements is more stable than the other, intentionally. Having worked two support professions in my life, prior to becoming an artist, one profession had greater significance and was of greater stability.

"To create a sense of the destruction of the past, I used a combination of heat, water, blunt force, cutting, throwing, sawing, drilling, chopping and various other methods of deconstruction.

"The white represents emptiness, and a type of death, when considering the past. However the one tiny red square represents life and vitality." —DW

Opposite: ***Surrender*****, 2012**

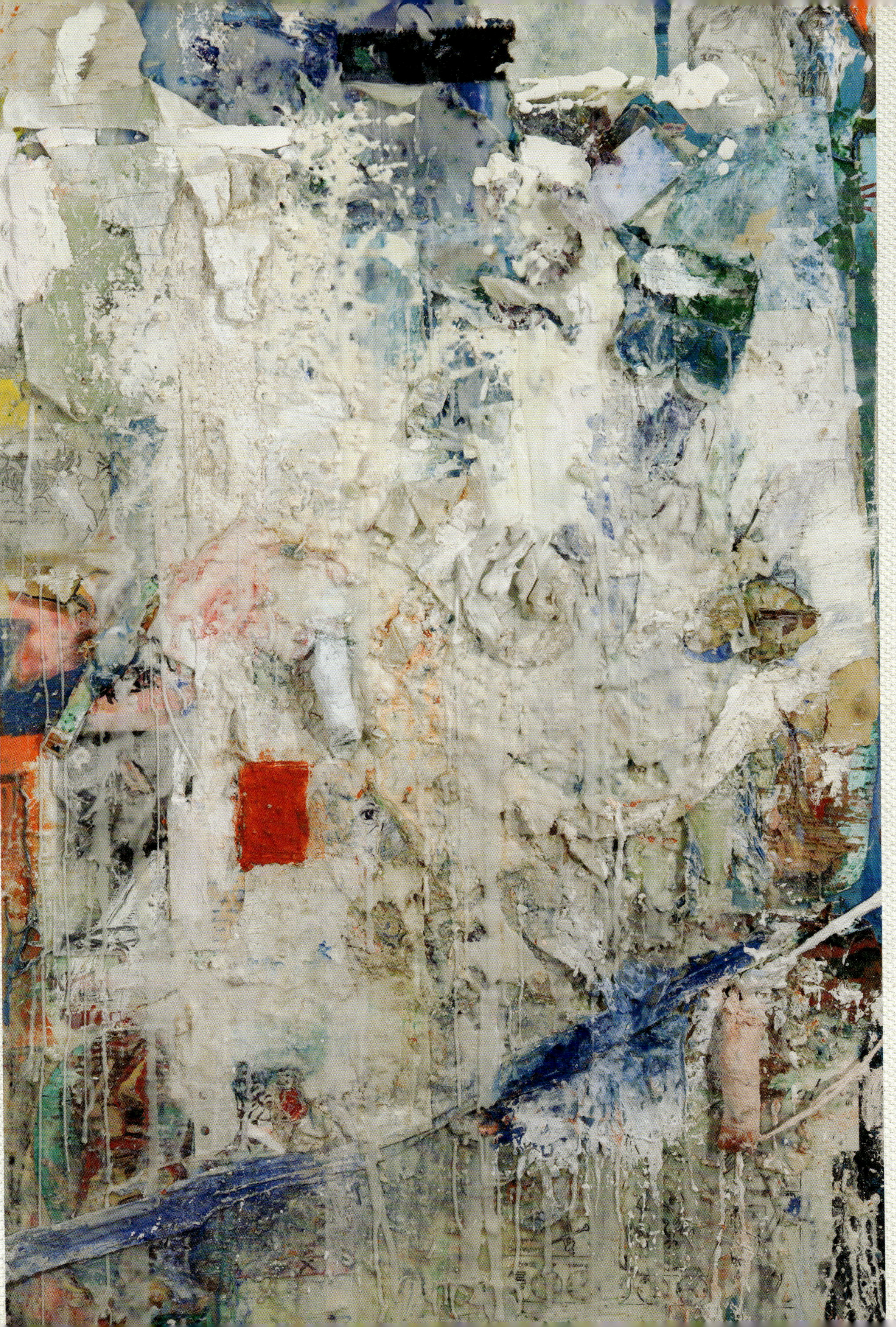

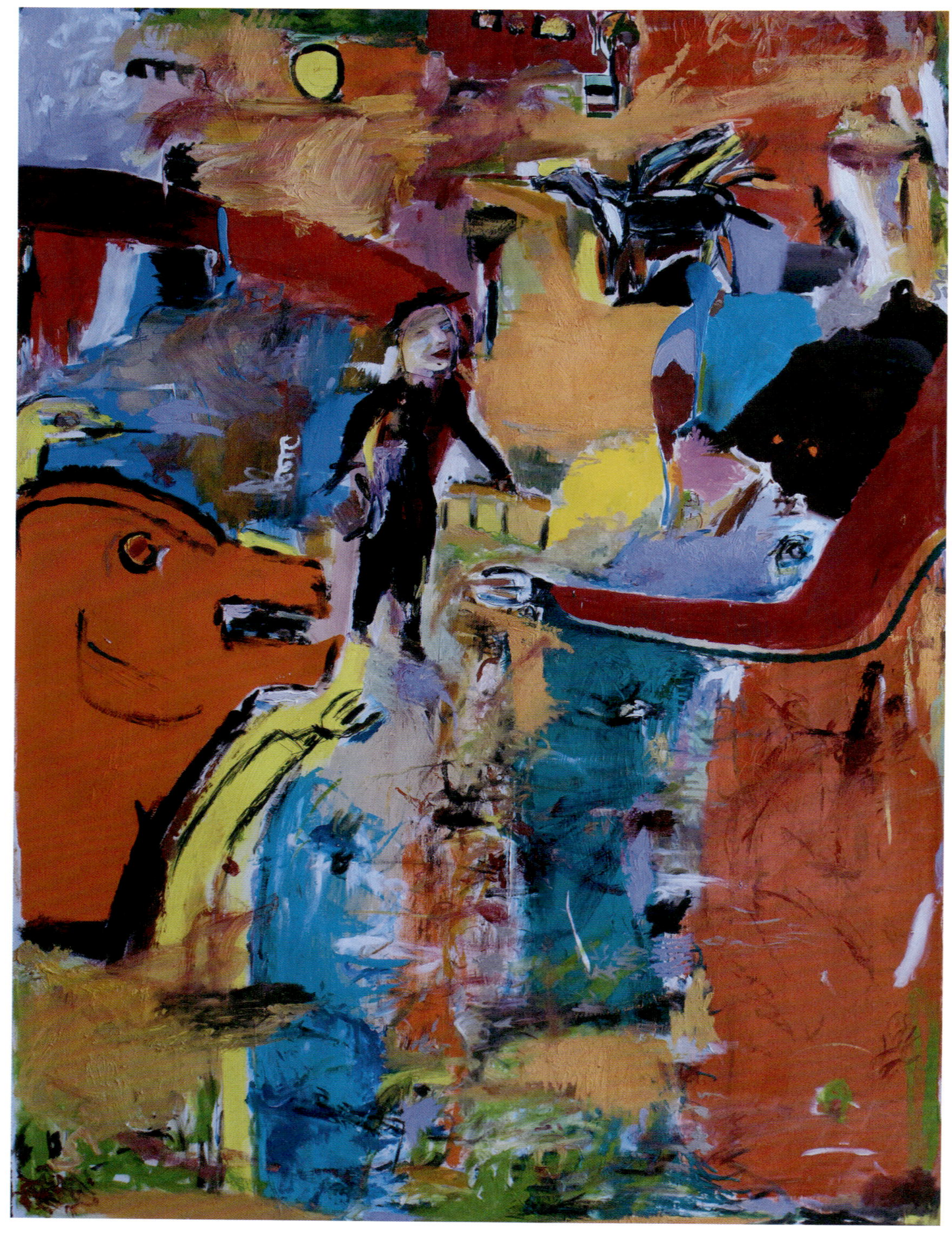

Loyal Beast, 2012

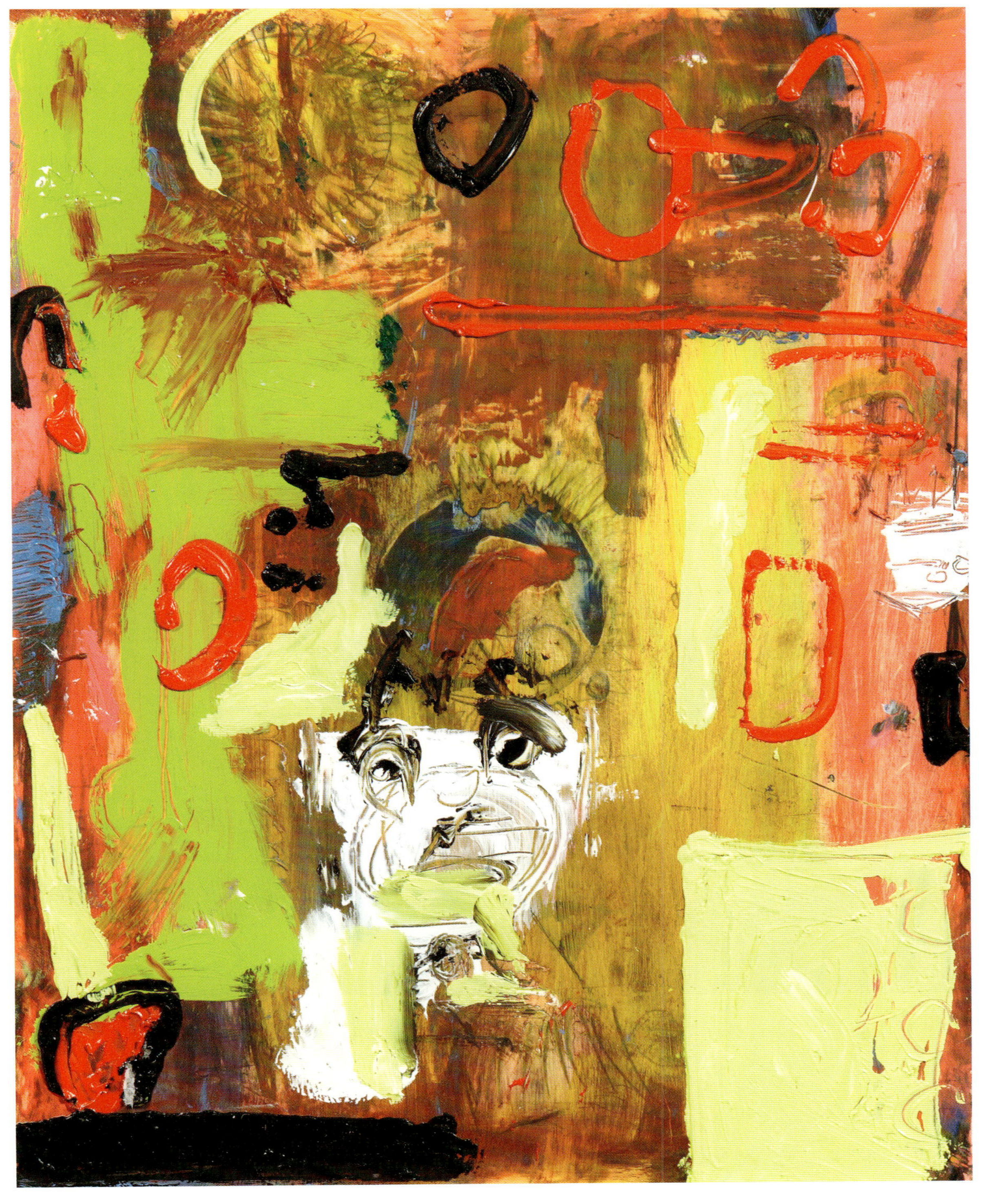

***Resurrection*, 2012**

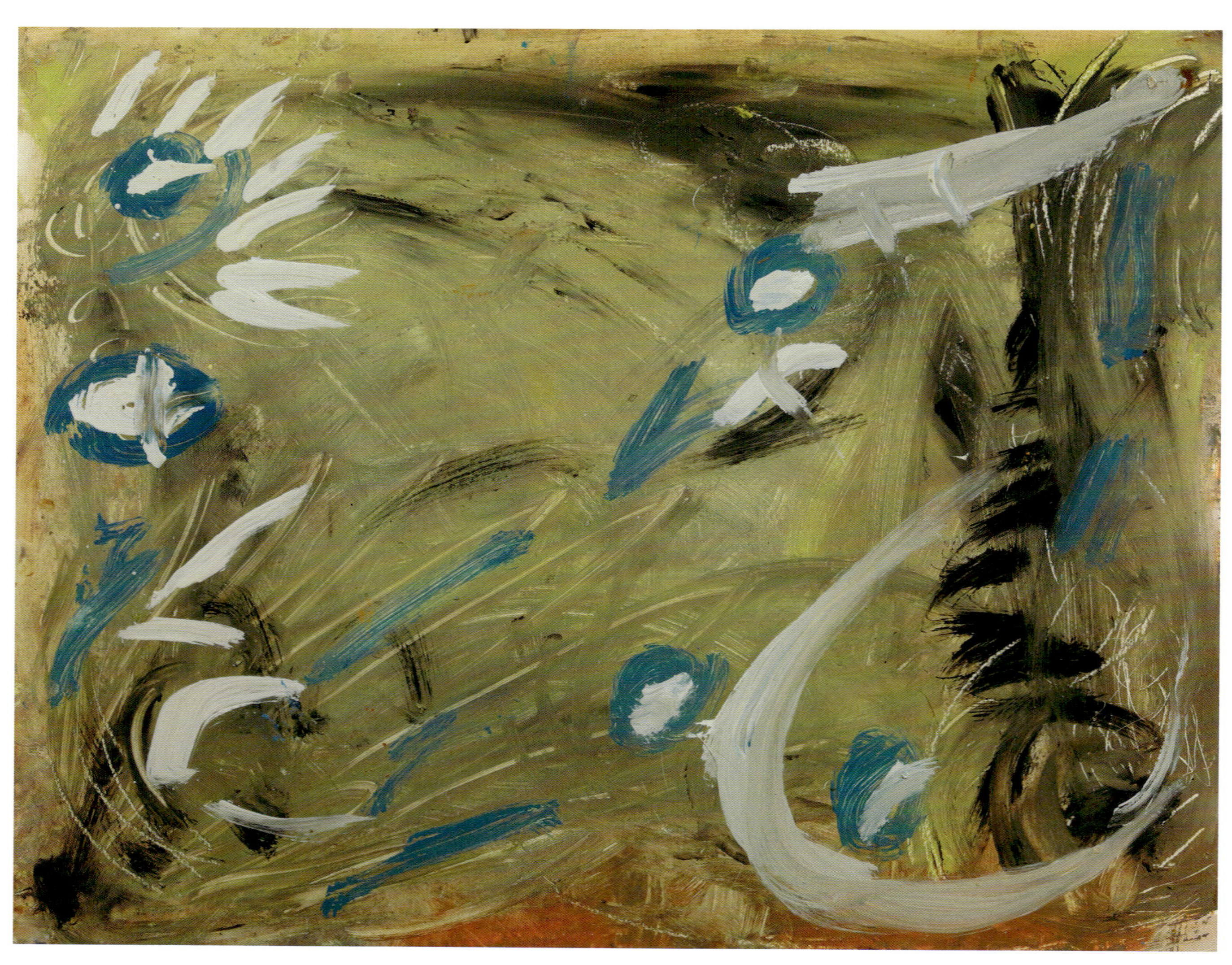

Tiamat, 2010

Opposite: *Sunflower*, 2012

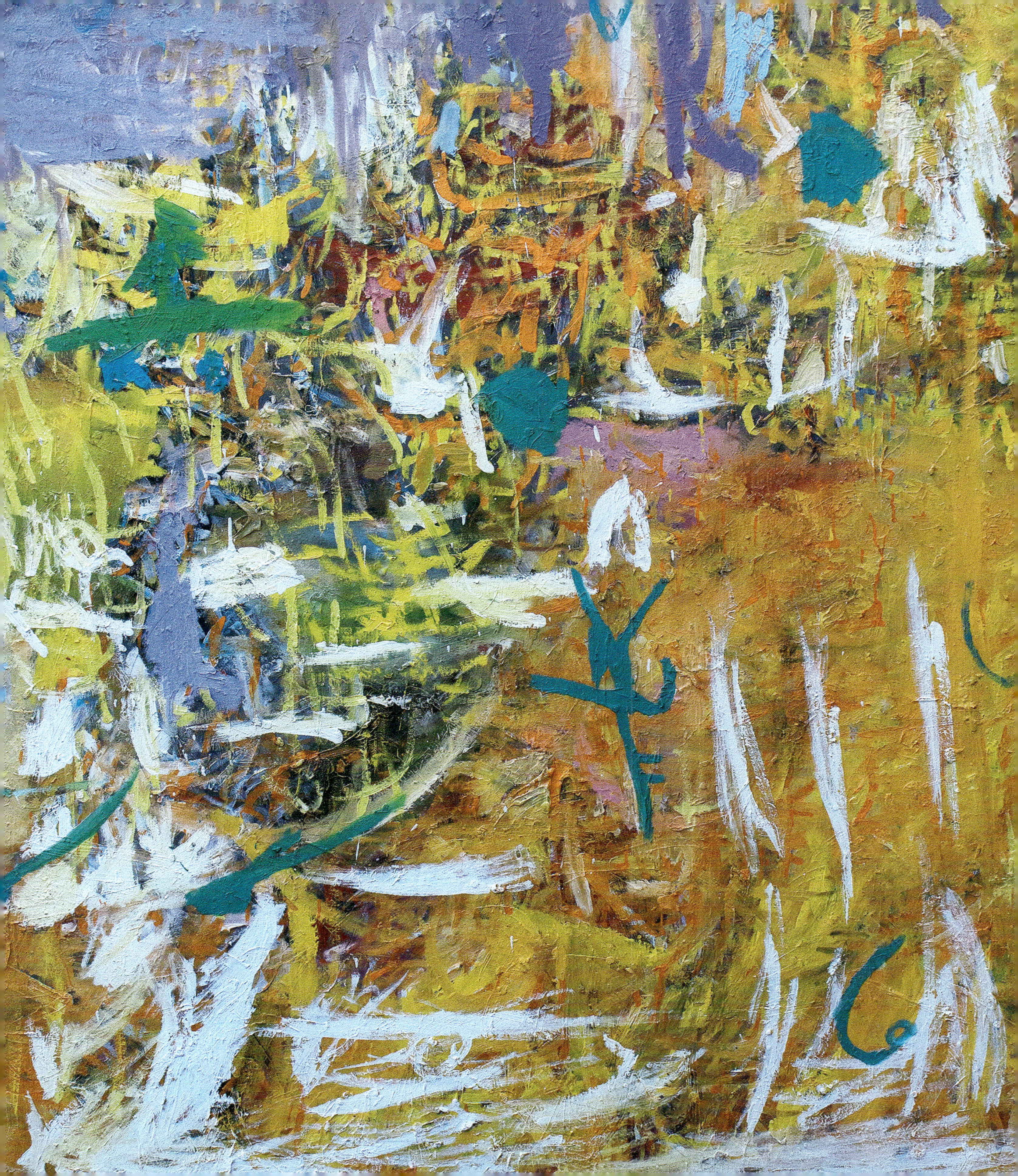

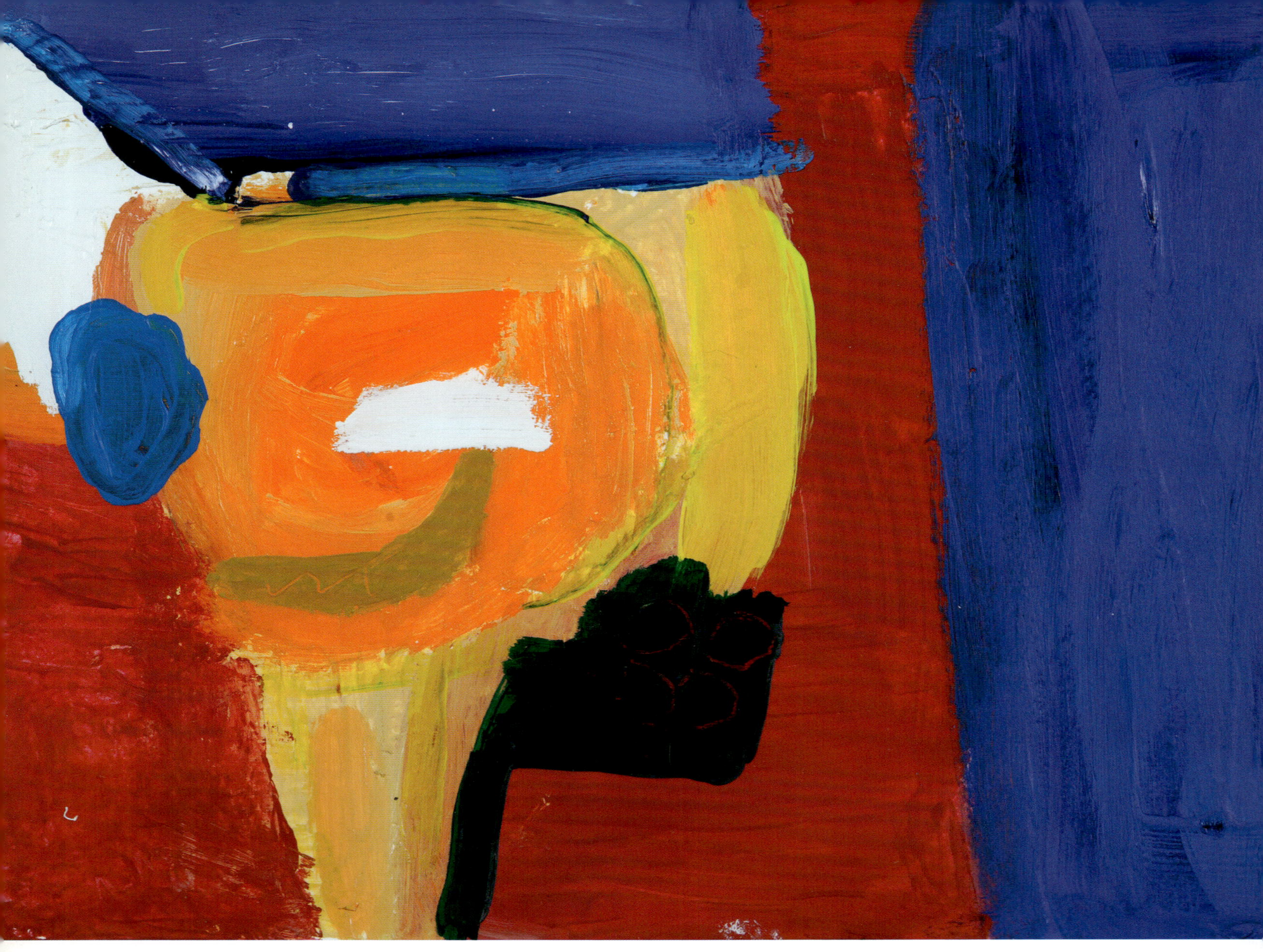

Blue Hat, 2013

Opposite: *Color Studies in Blue & Yellow 2*, 2014

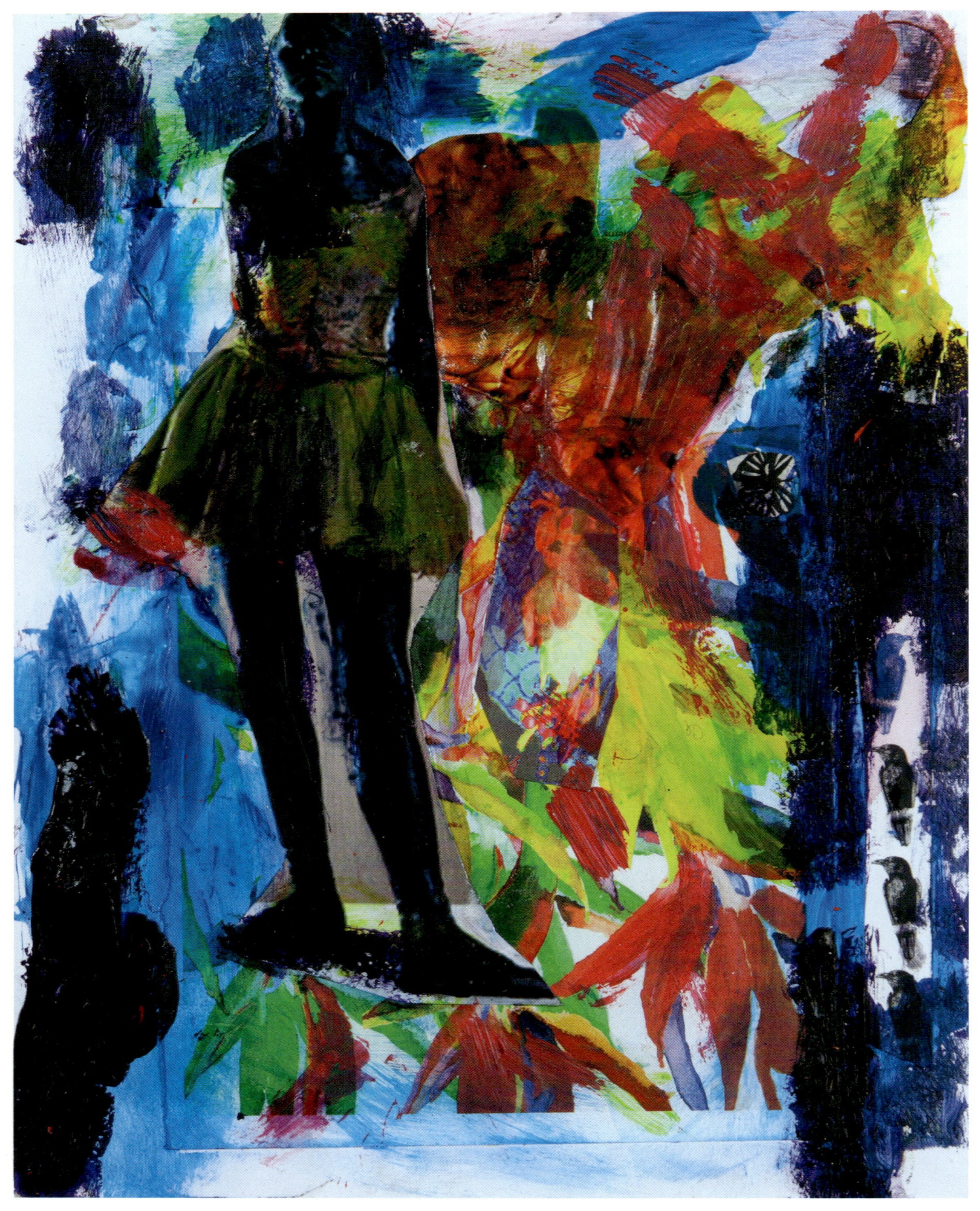

***Degas Dancer*, 2011**

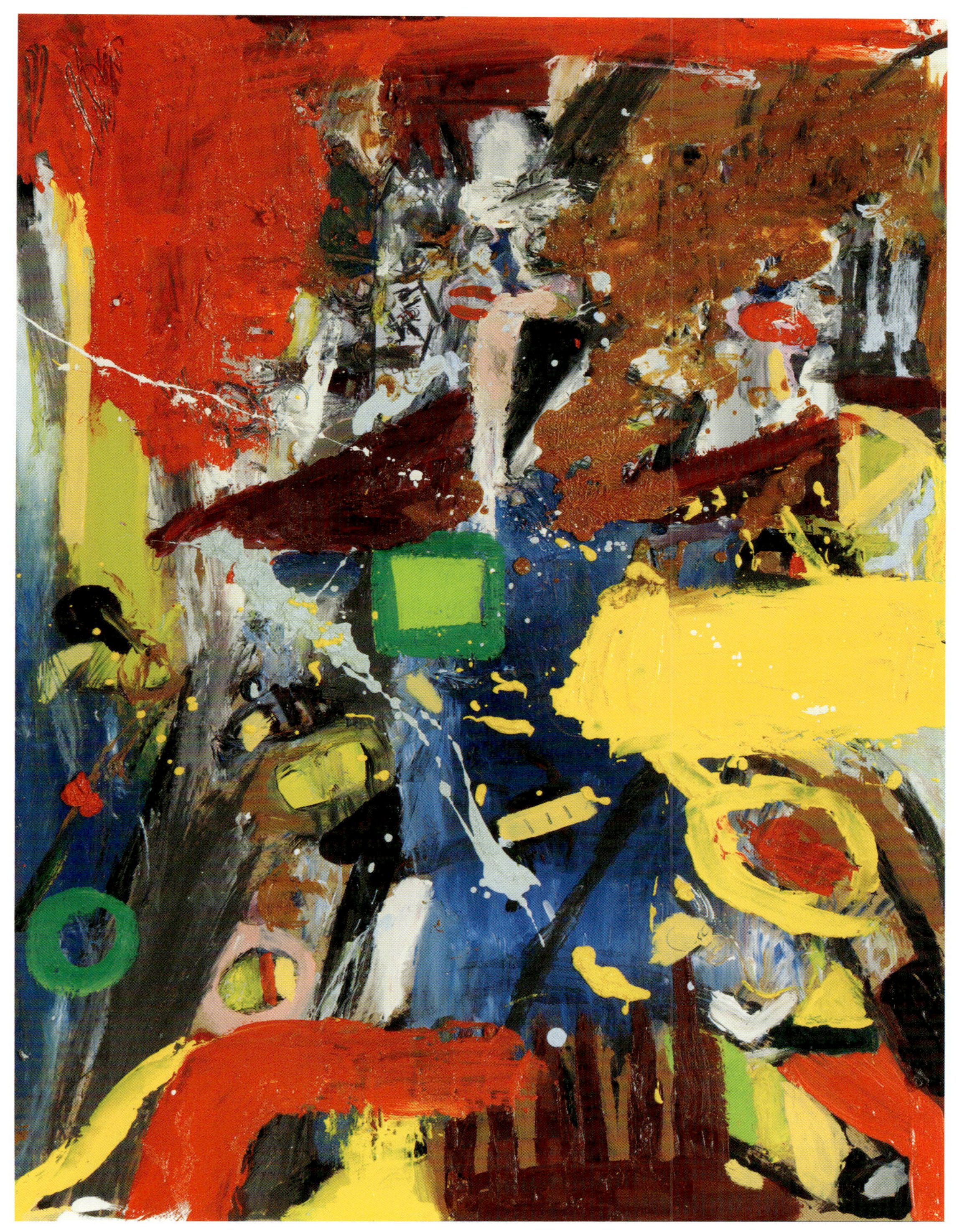

***Wishbone*, 2012**

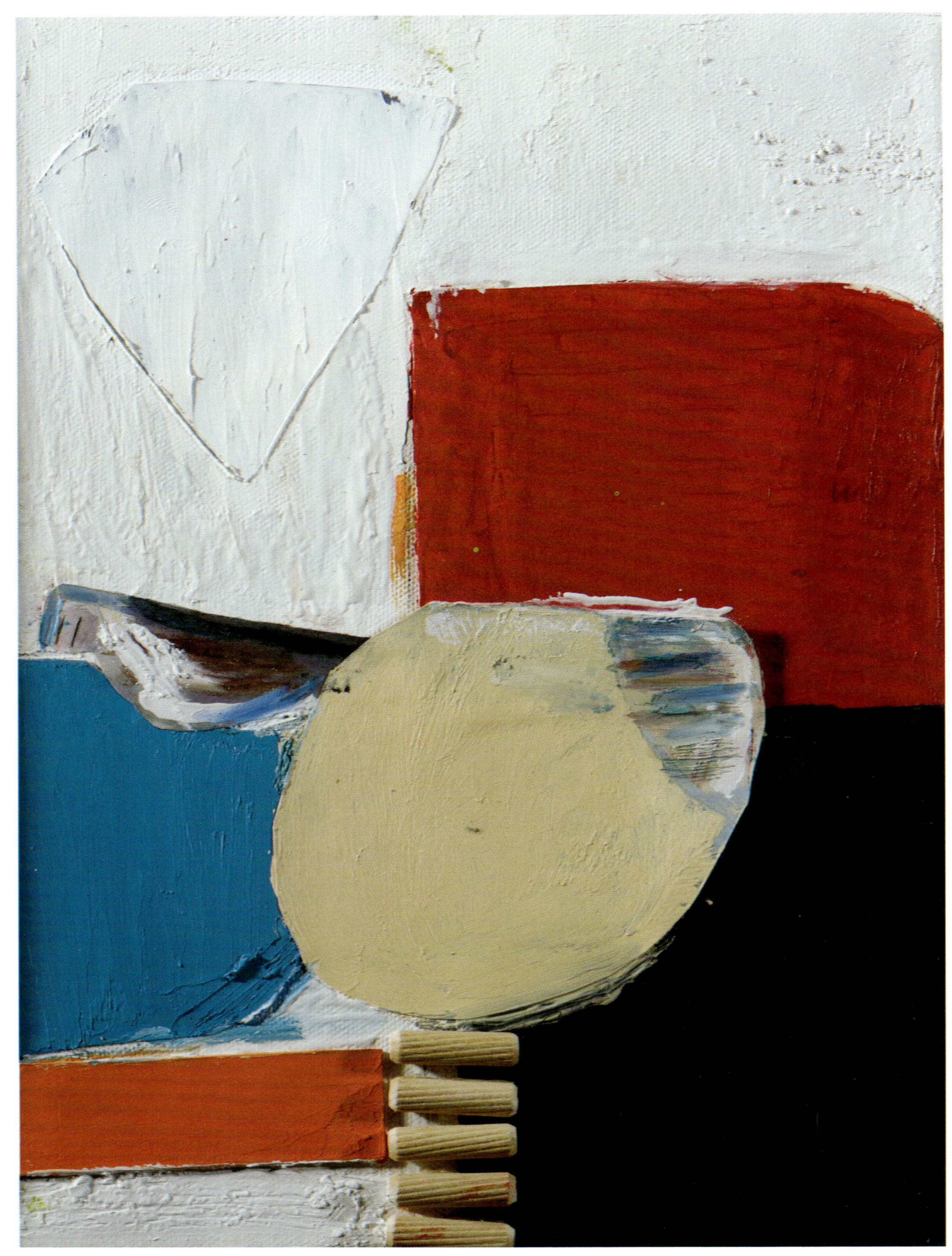

***Nest Series 1*, 2011**

"Small amounts of risk taking, for great amounts of freedom and long term joy are worth the risk."

—DW

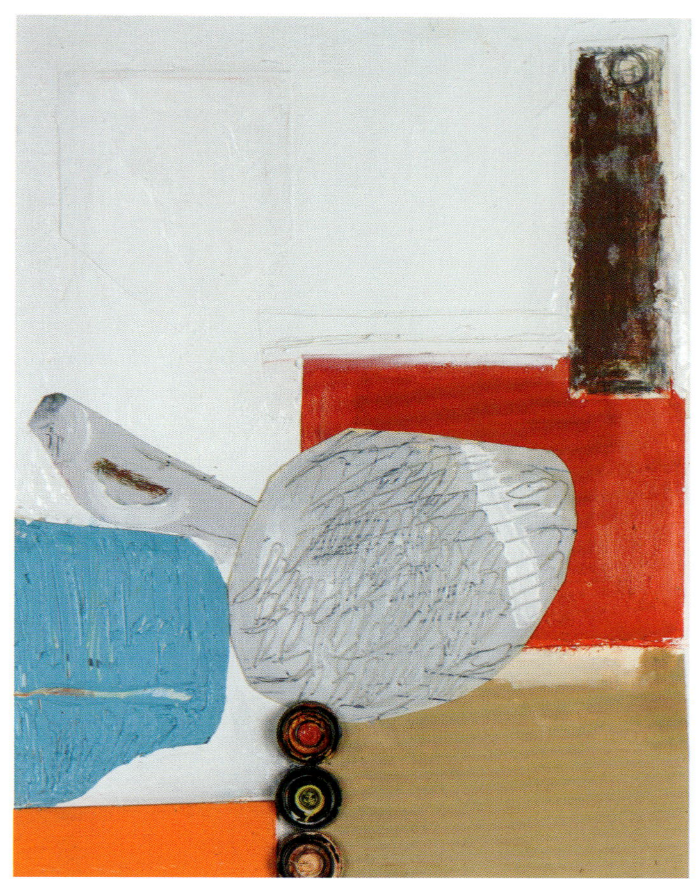

***Nest Series 2*, 2011**

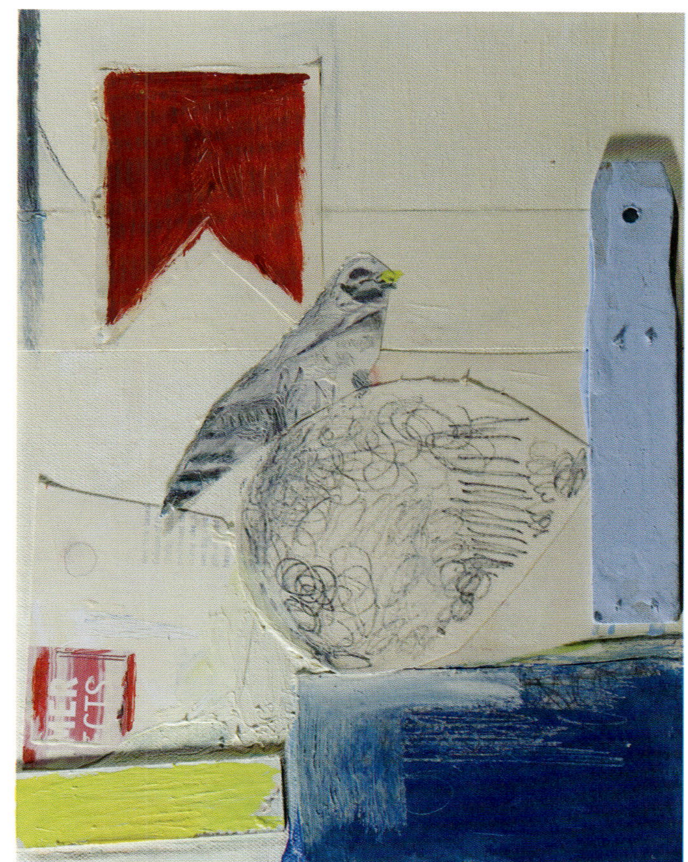

***Nest Series 3*, 2011**

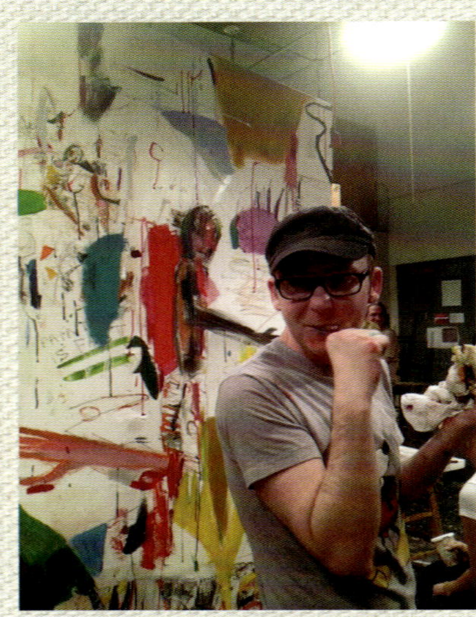

Davyd at the Art Students League, 2013.

"This is my last work completed at the Art Students League of New York City, while studying with Larry Poons. The title of my painting comes from his quote 'Color is your only weapon.' It has a dull white wash of color over the mid-section to calm and cool the palate.

"I studied under Larry for several years. His message was always very consistent and very forceful. The text used in the painting 'copy of a copy' reflects another of his teachings. He told us to stop copying what we saw as artists and create our own visions of what we felt. In the painting, a change of direction has happened for the lower figure in the middle of the painting, a break with the past. This idea is represented by the pink arm of the lower figure, which is reversed from the shadowy figure above him in the painting. The two figures are separating, as I was separating from my teacher and finding my own vision.

"The work combines four graphite and chalk studies from notebooks and four gestural figures. The main focus of the painting is color, using around 29 different oils to make geometric shapes and lines. Each time Larry gave me feedback, not always positive by the way, I would scribble his comments onto my canvas, knowing this would be the last time our paths would cross as teacher and student." —DW

Opposite: ***Color Is Your Only Weapon*, 2013**

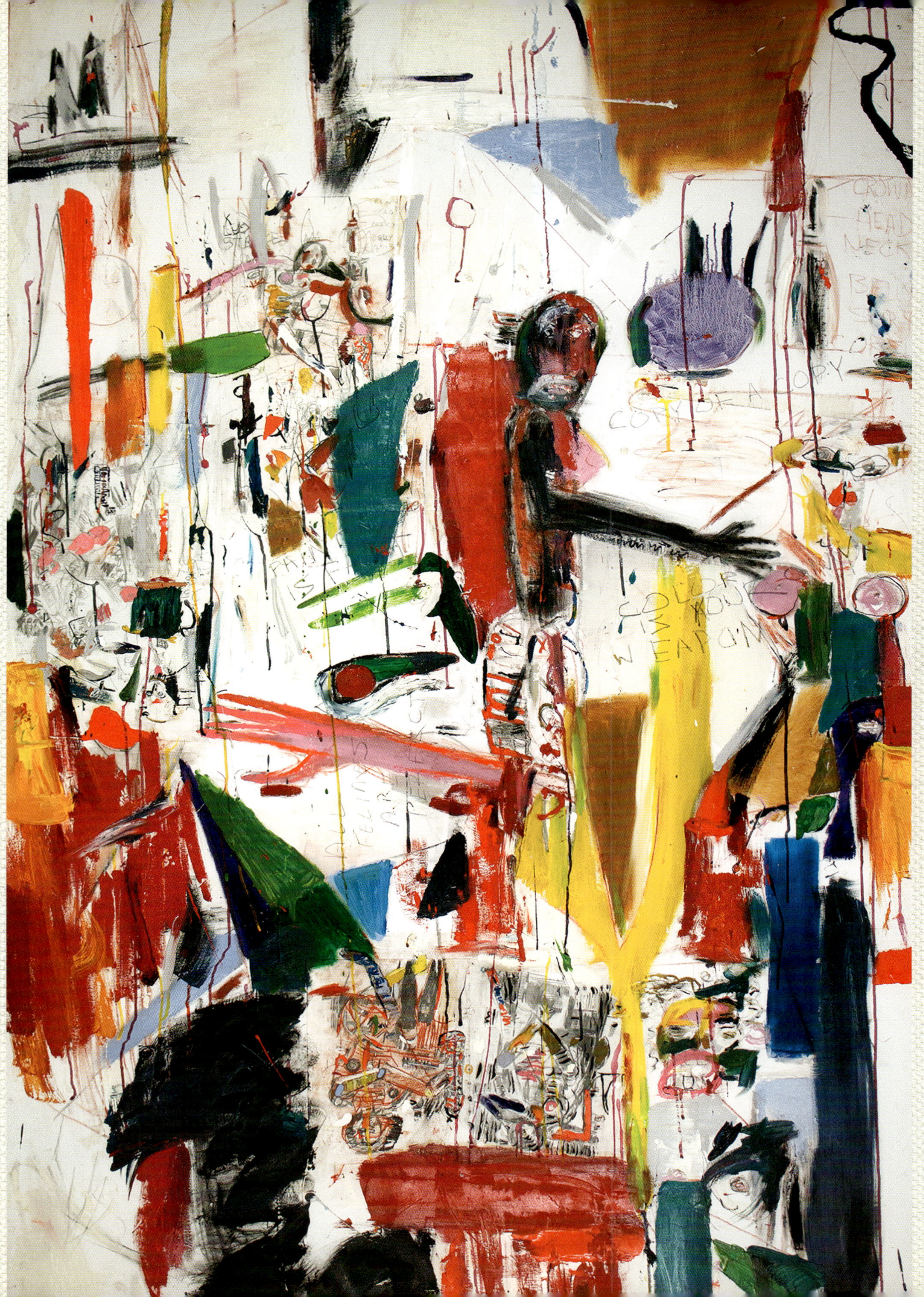
CROWN
HEAD
NECK
COPY OF A COPY
COLOR
YOUR
WEAPON

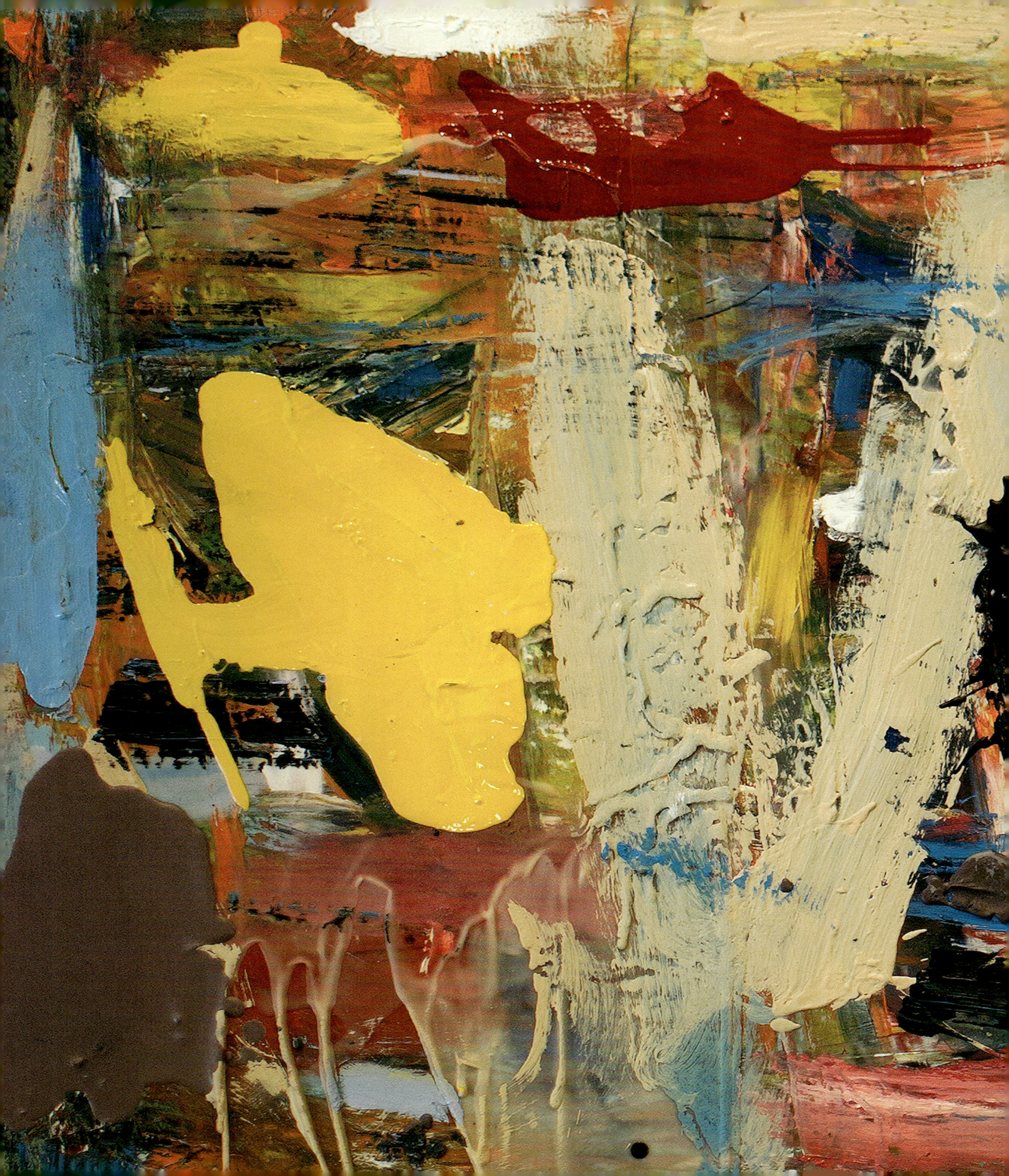

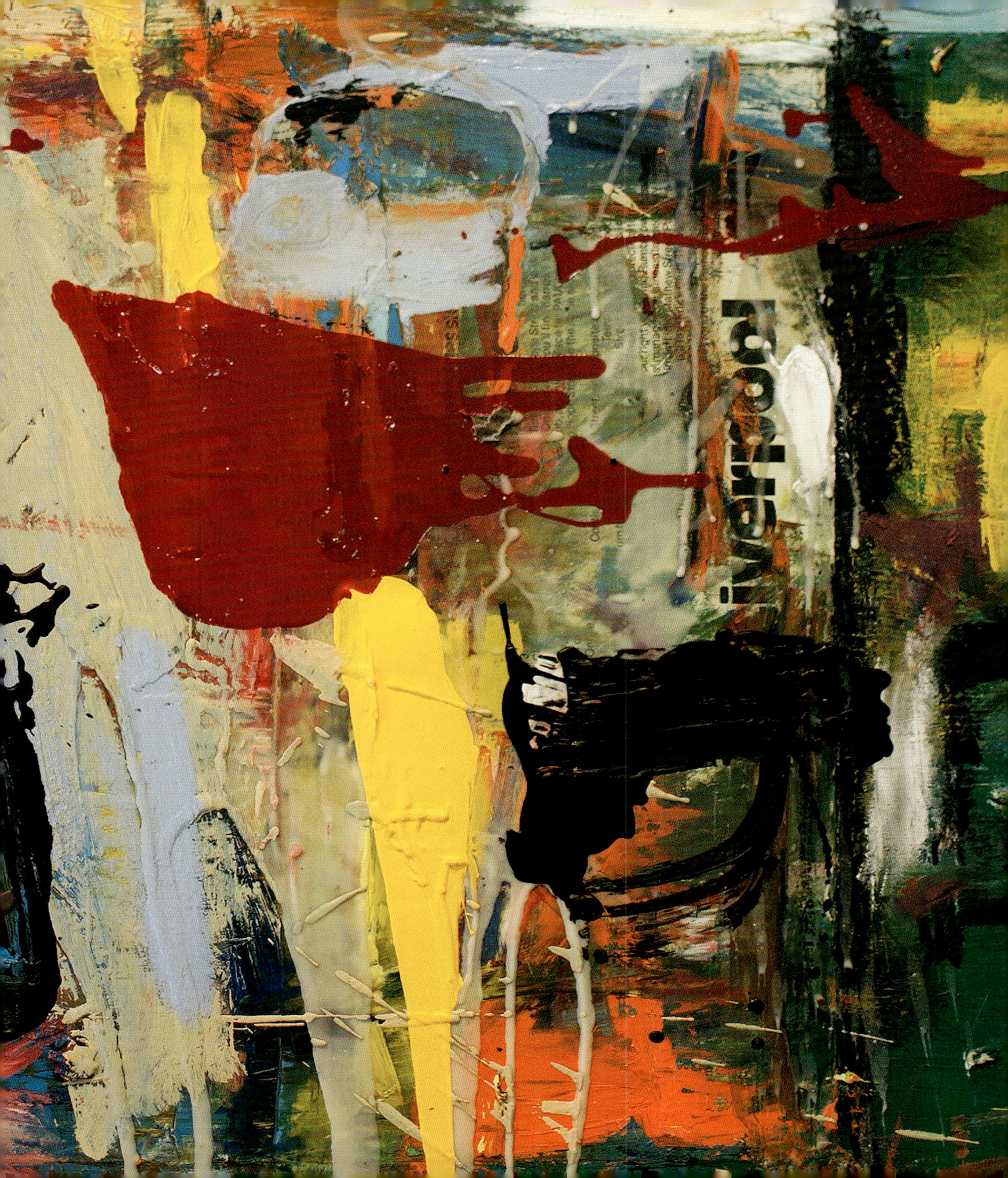

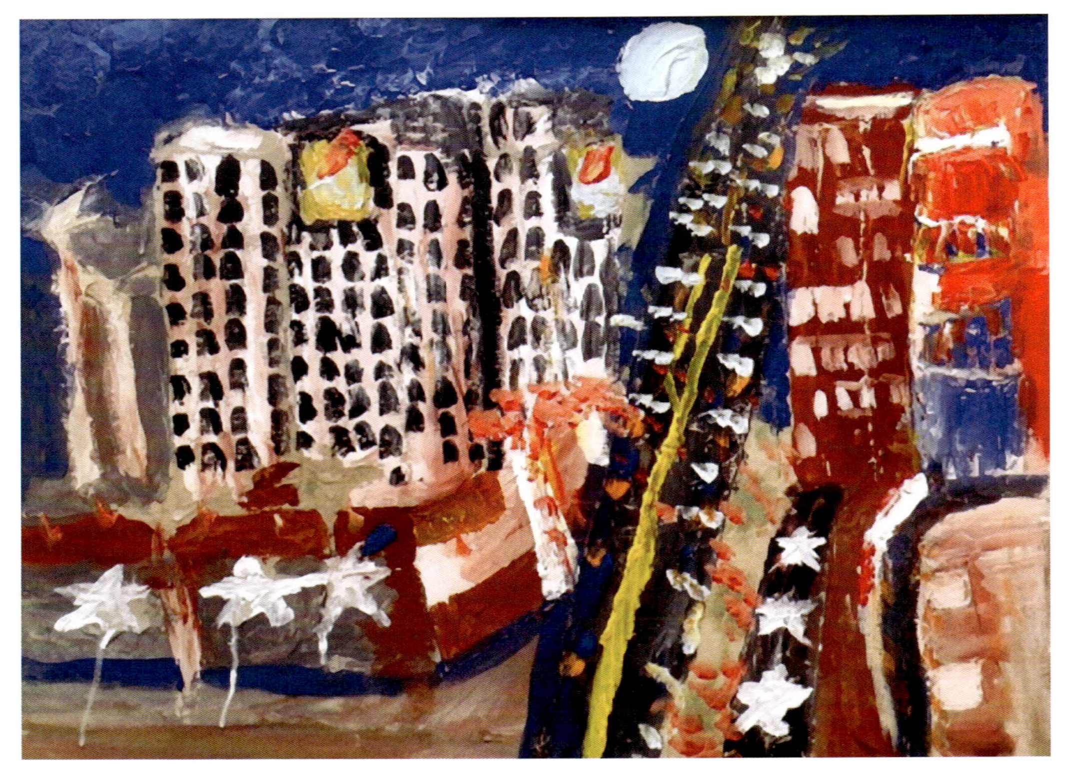

Sunset and Vine, 2007

Overleaf: *Liverpool*, 2013

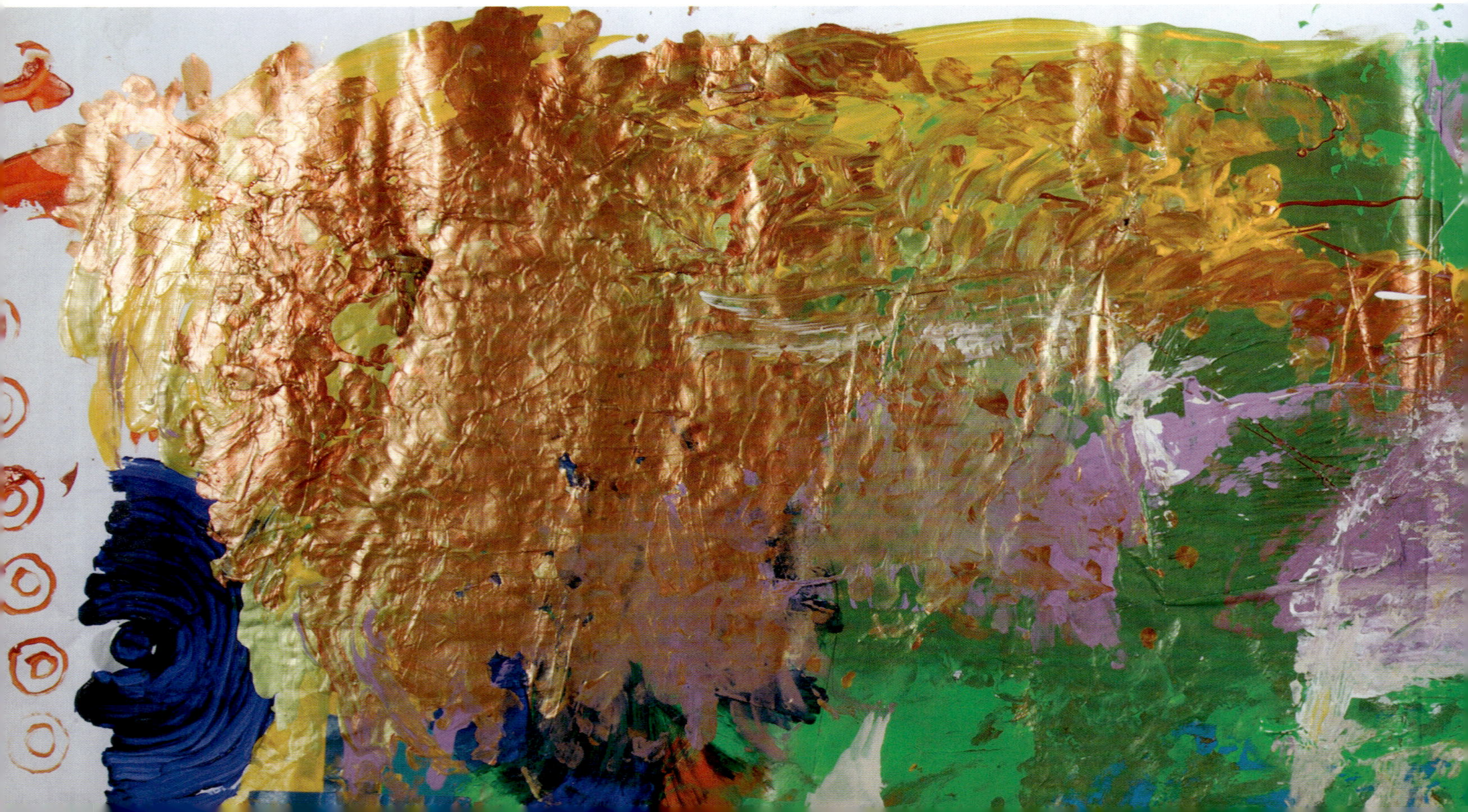

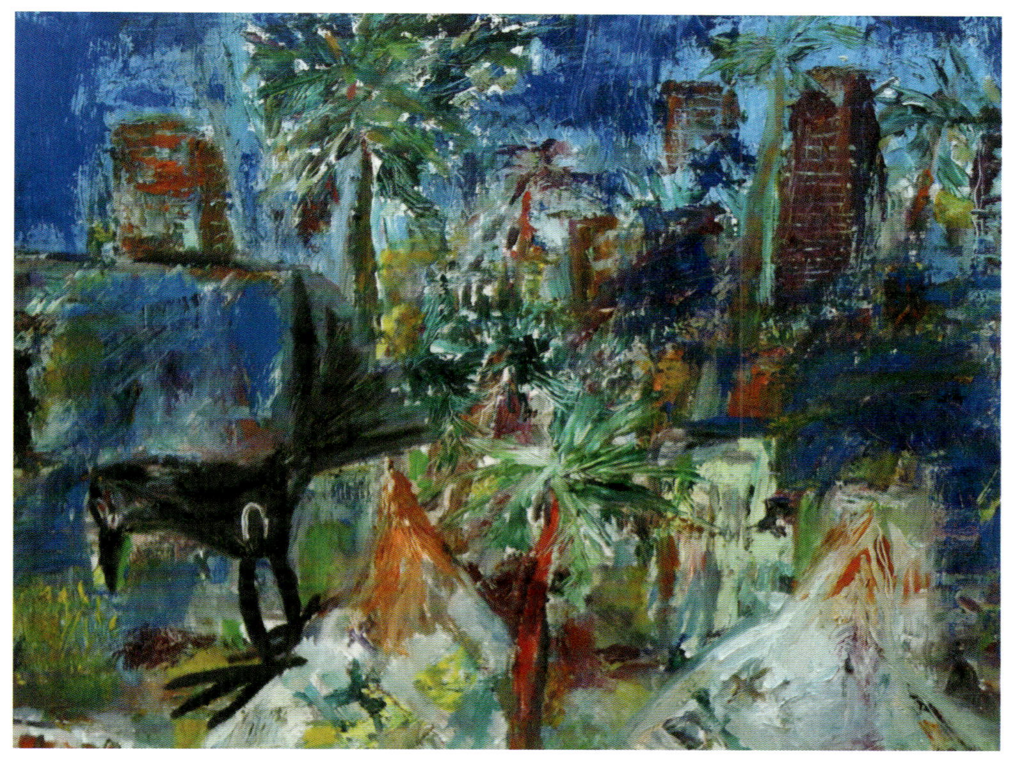

Curson, 2010

Below: *Scroll 32*, 2012

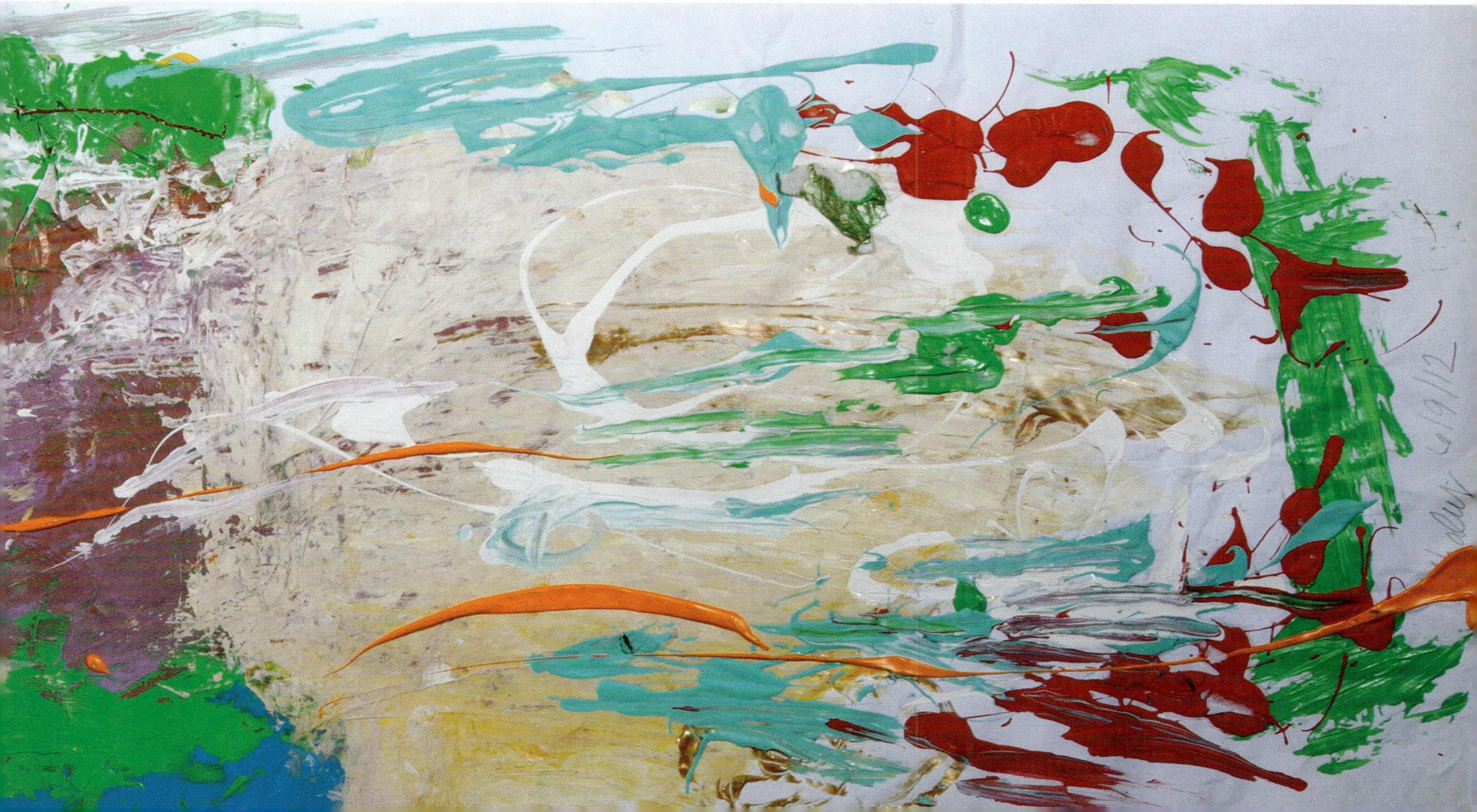

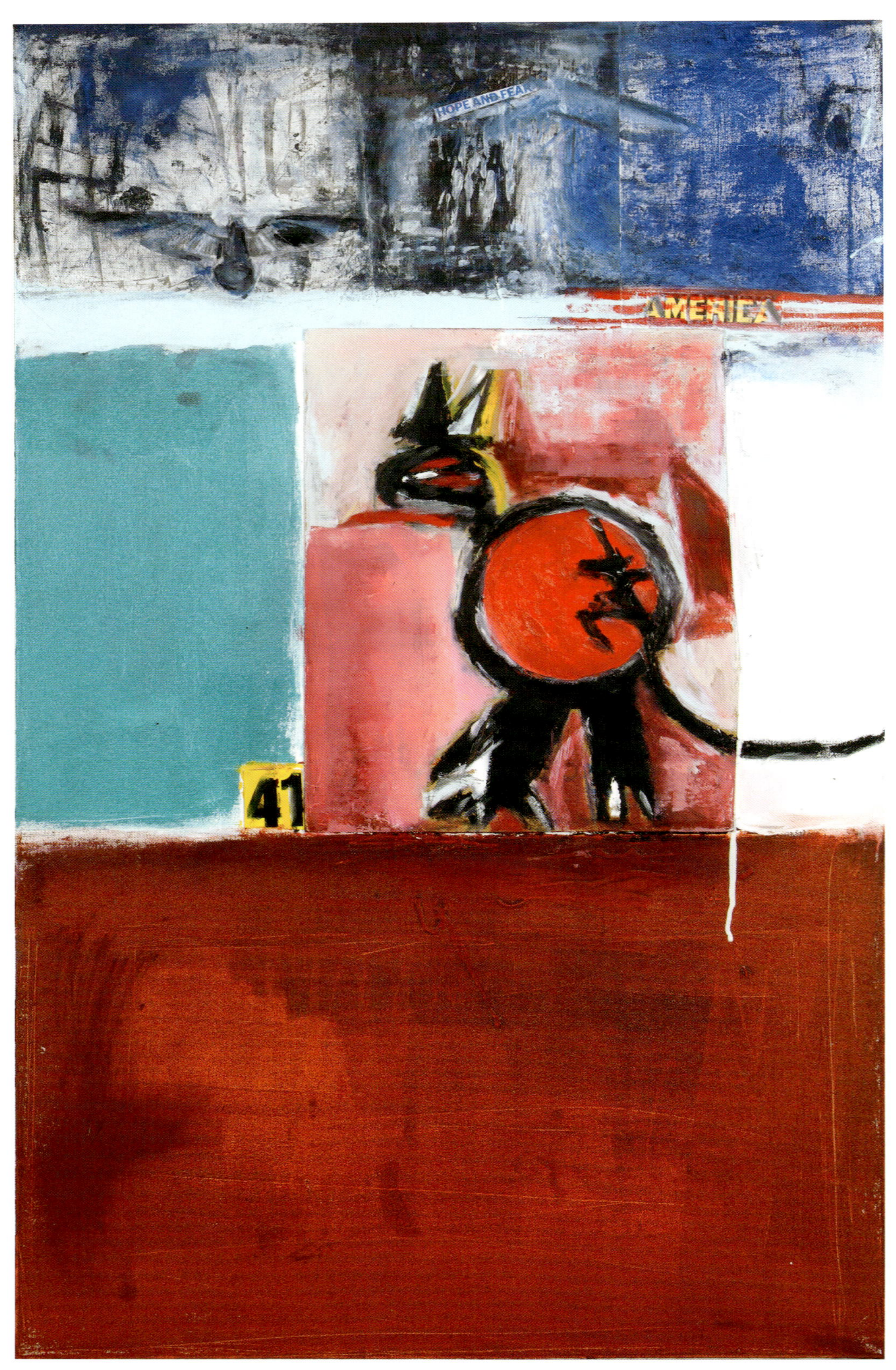

Hope and Fear. 2014

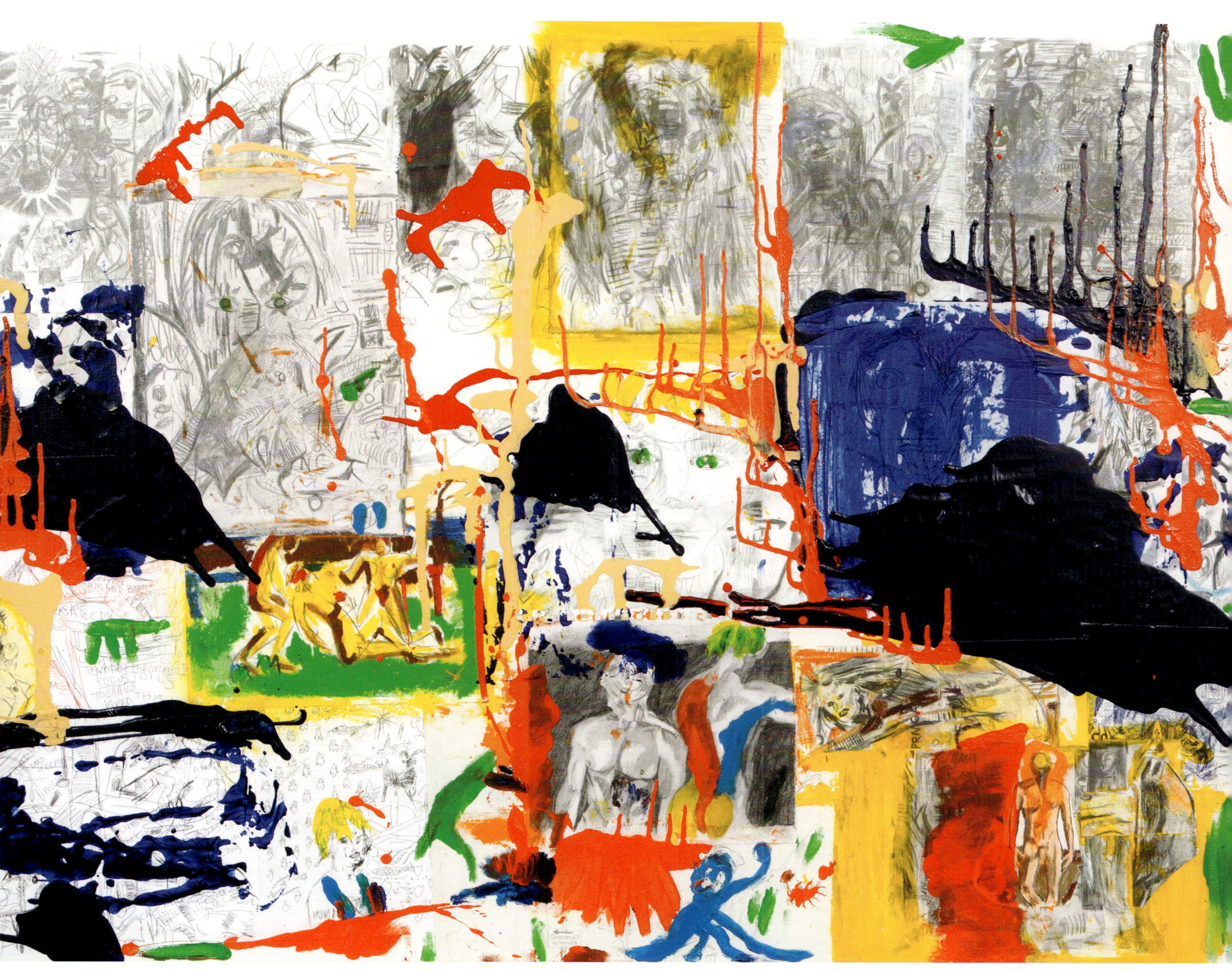

***Be Devil*, 2014**

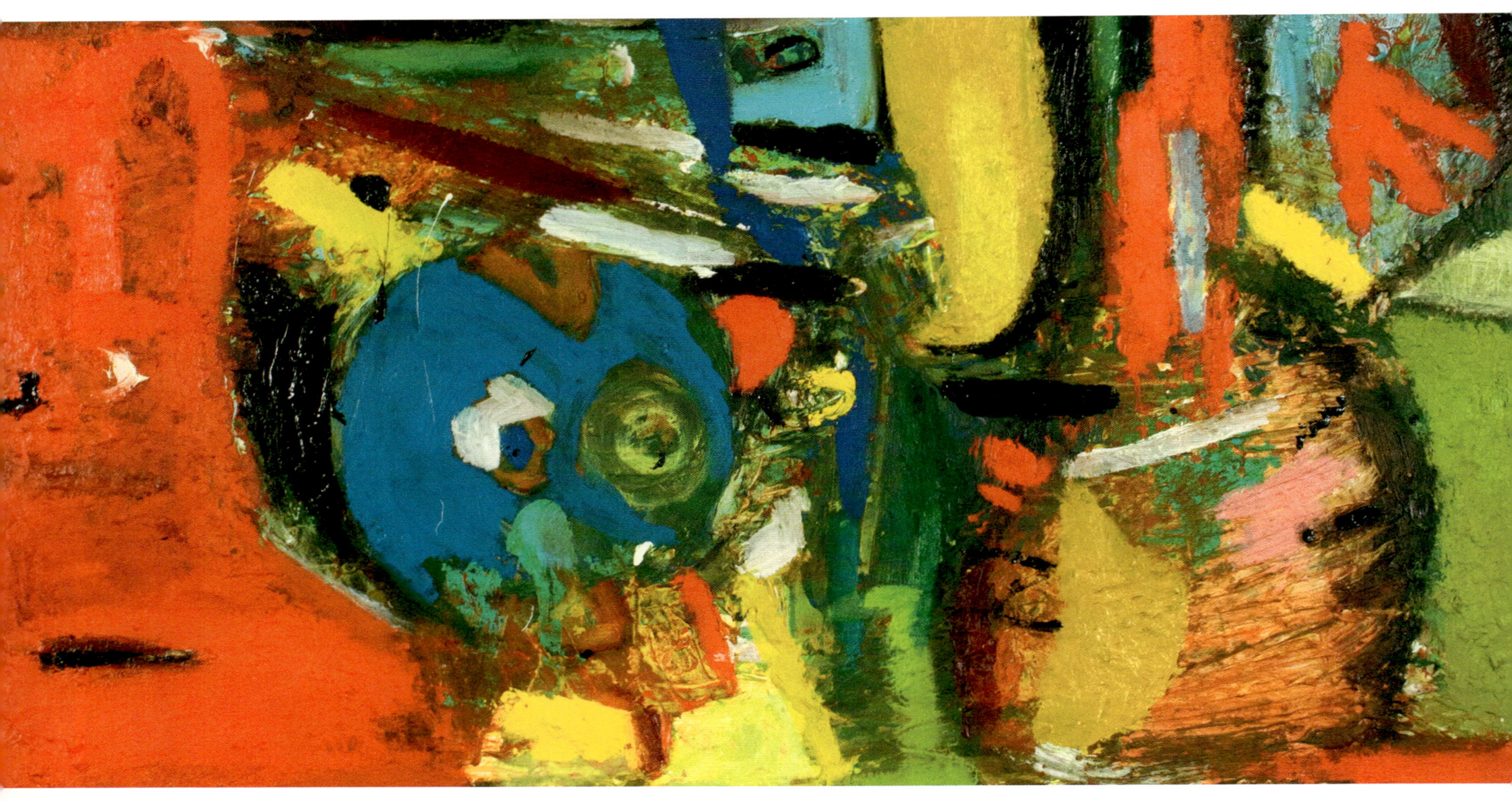

The Giver, 2013

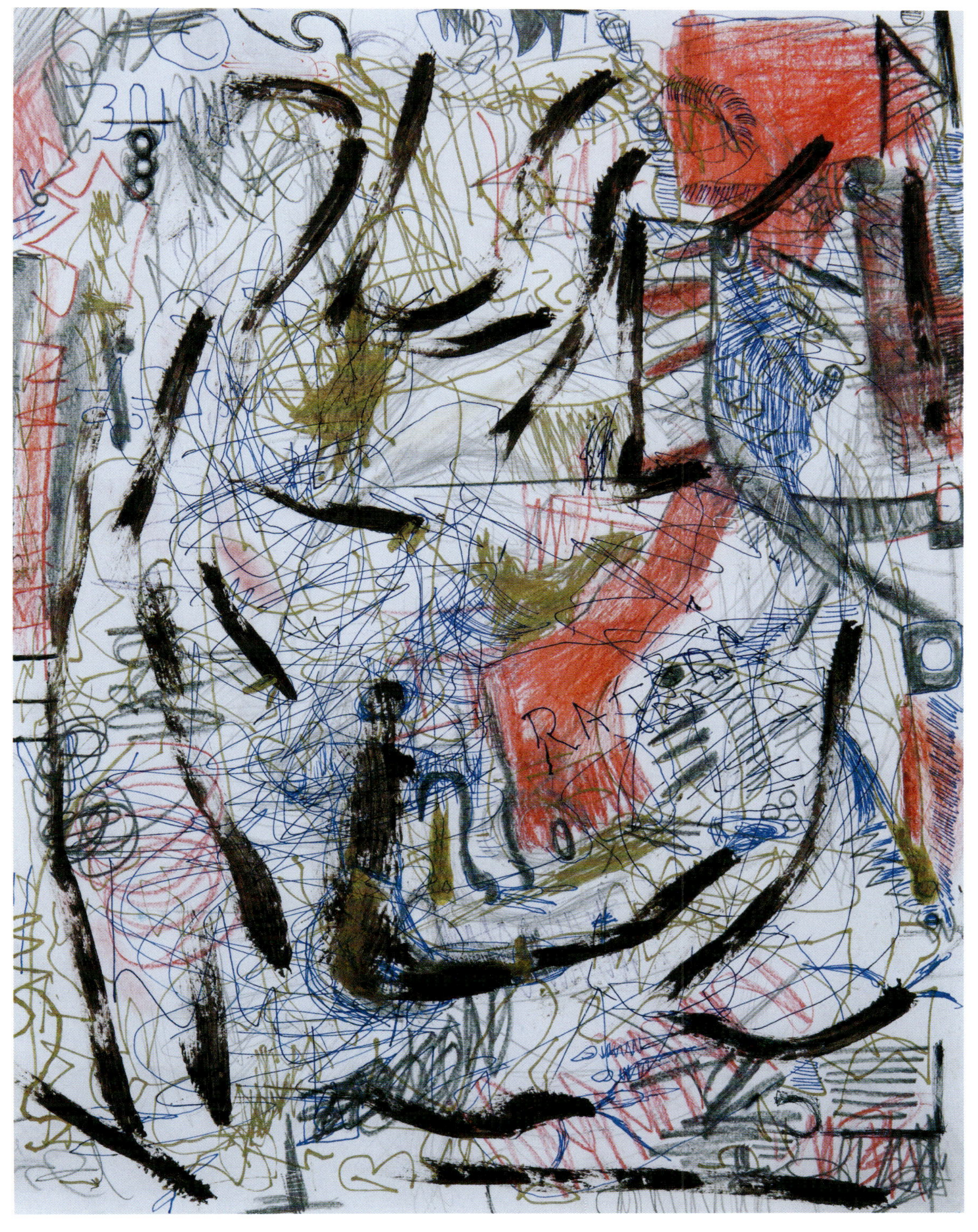

***Rat*, 2013**

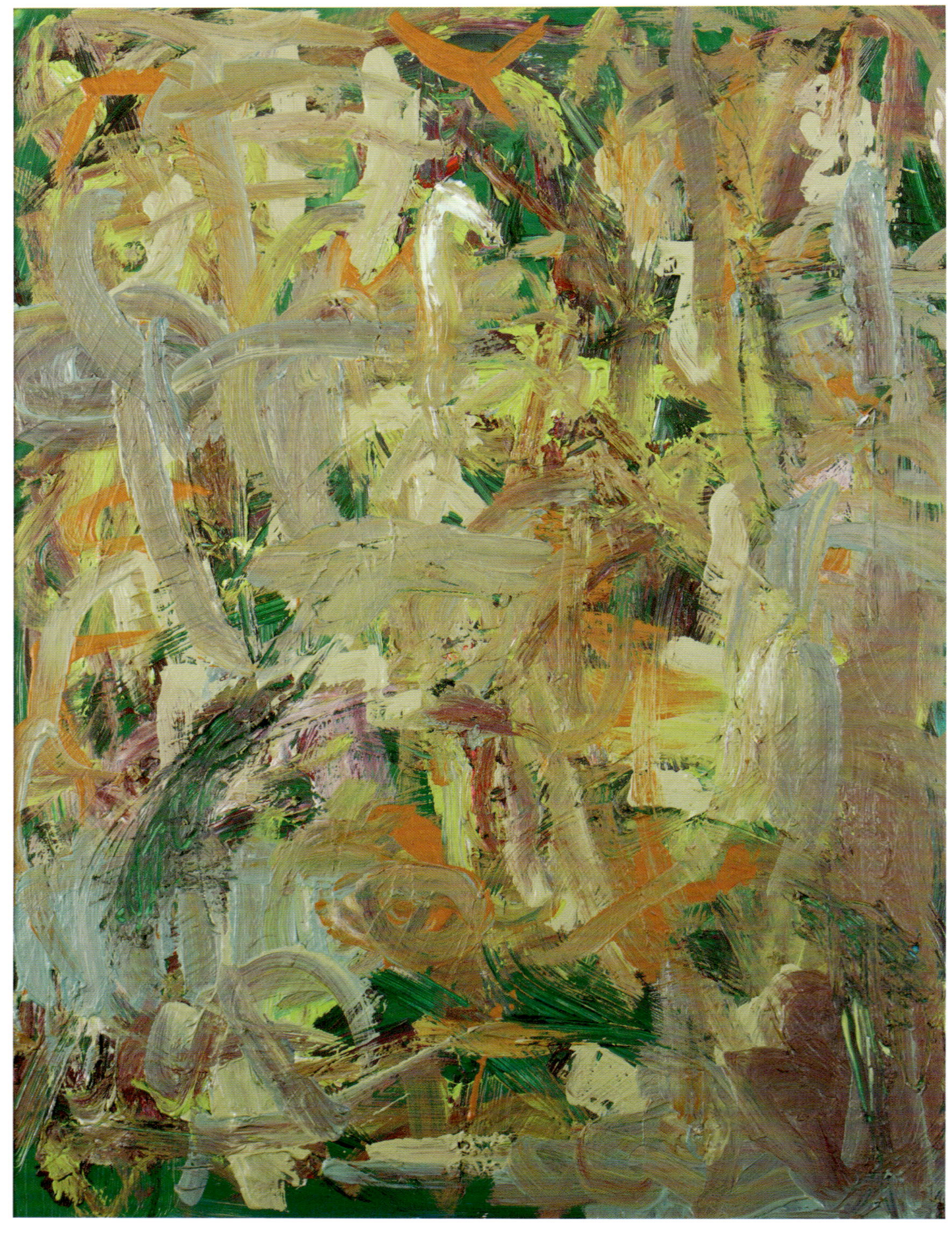

***Meditation*, 2010**

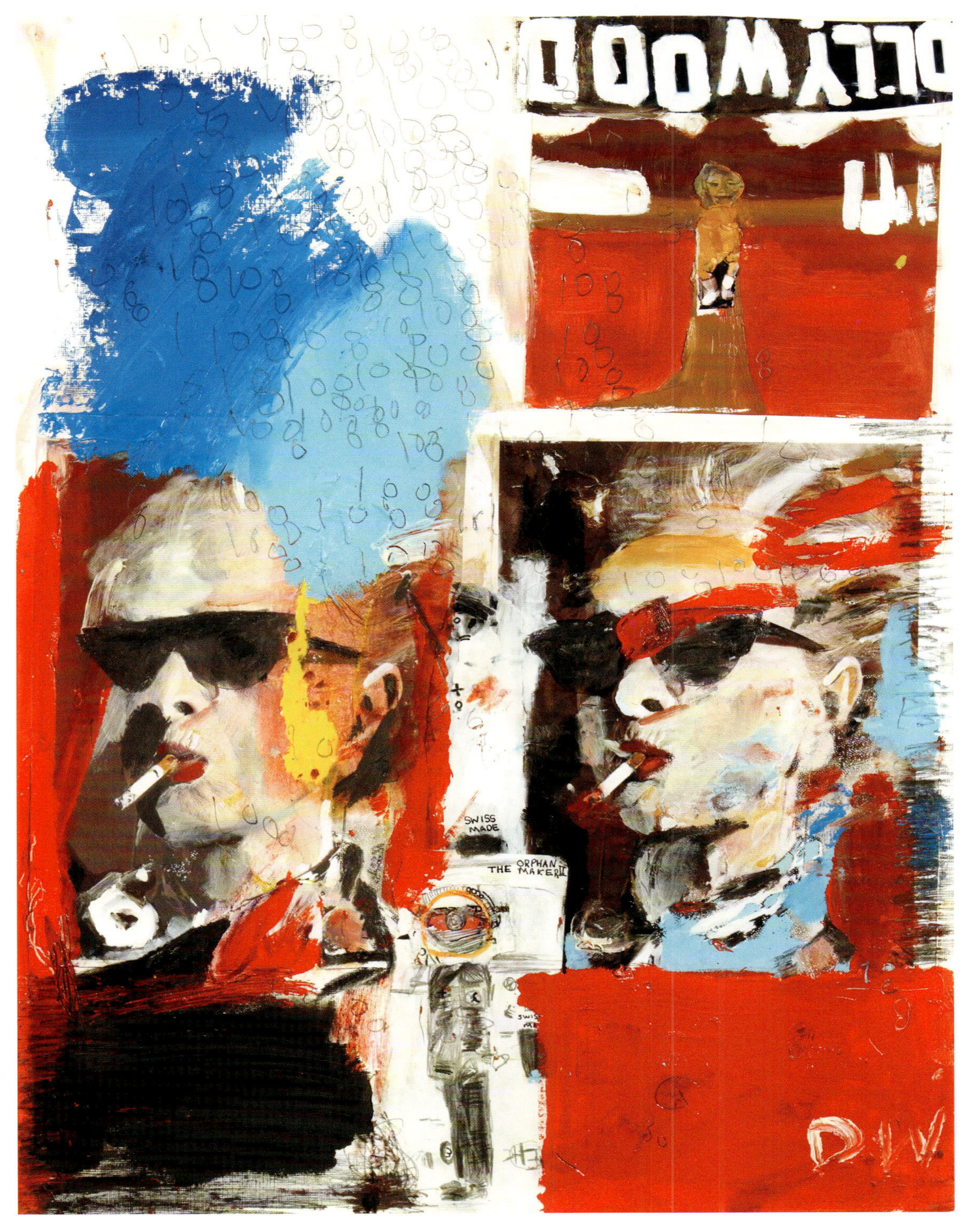

Orphan Maker, 2012

"Painting manifests an alternate universe in which our subconscious world becomes a reality."

—DW

Santa Monica Series

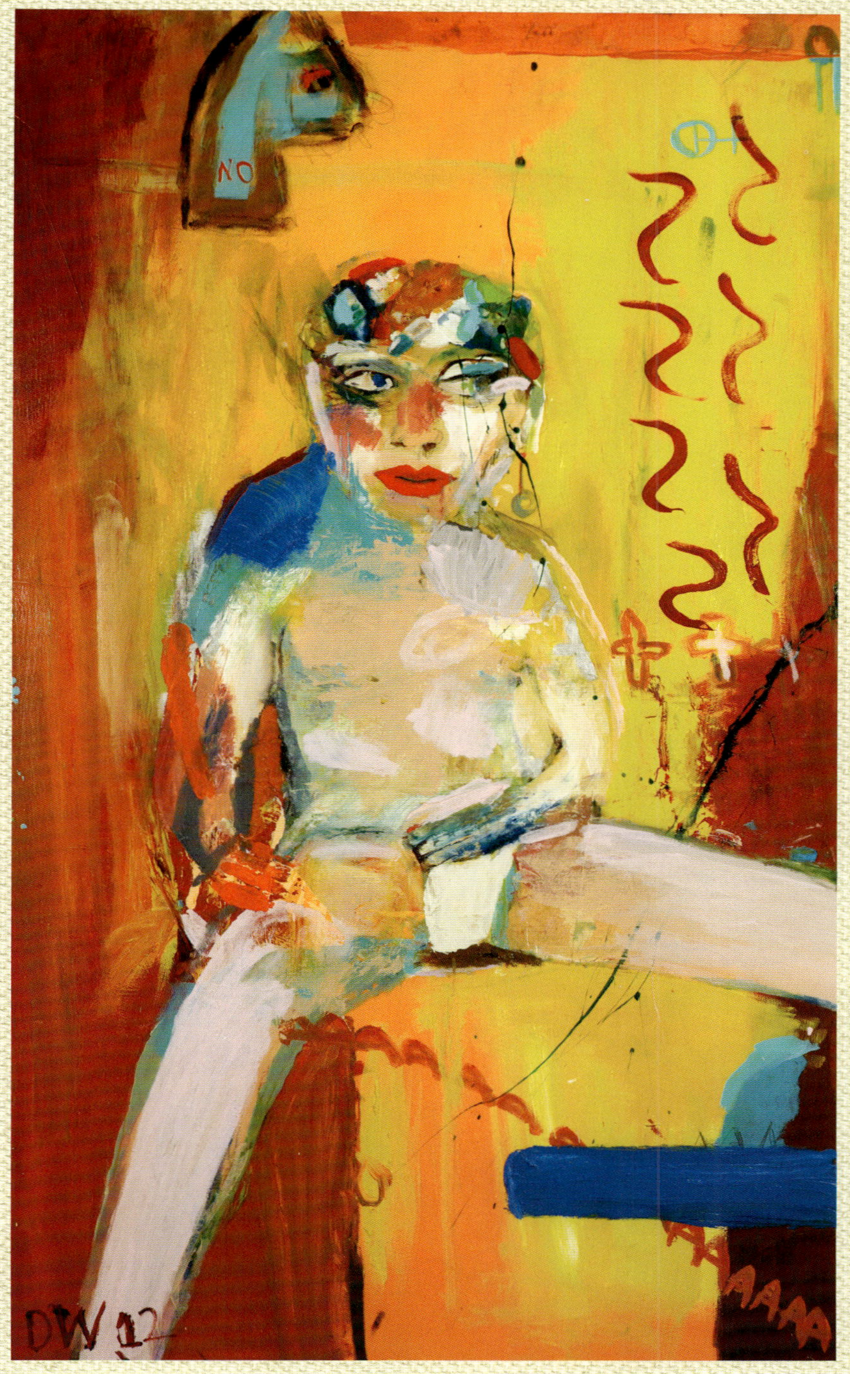

Santa Monica IV, 2012

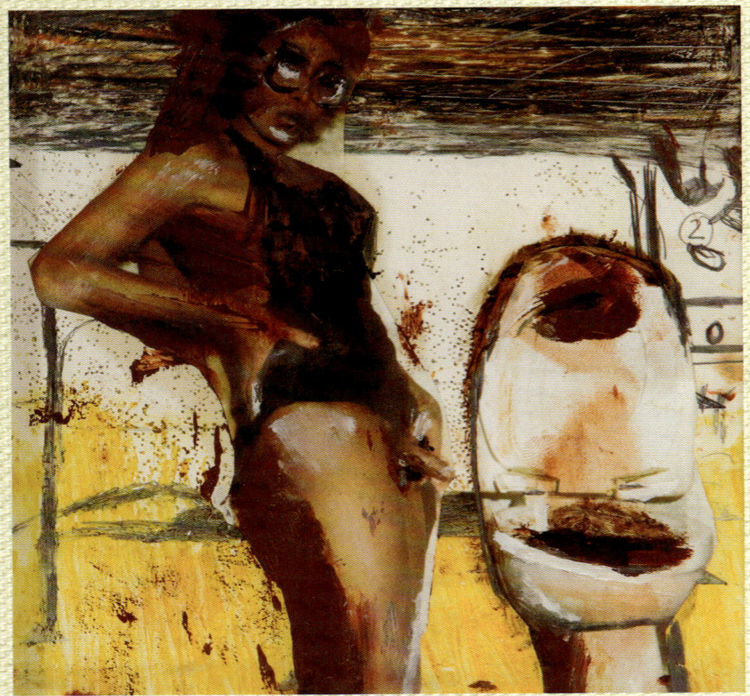

Santa Monica I, 2012

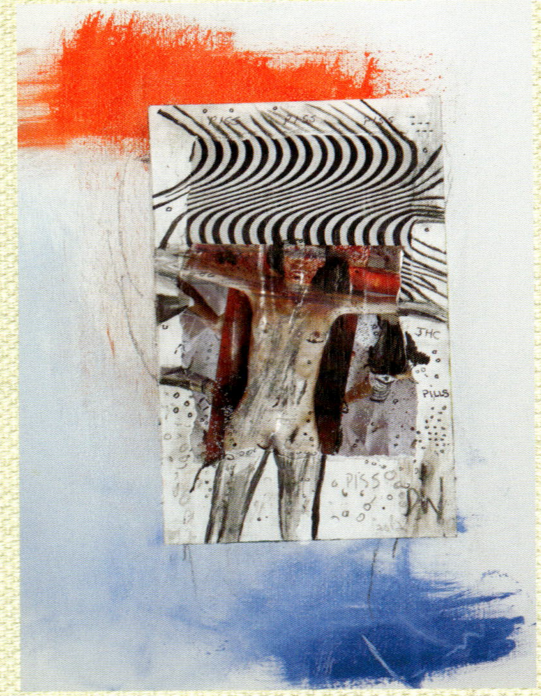

Santa Monica II, Piss Man, 2012

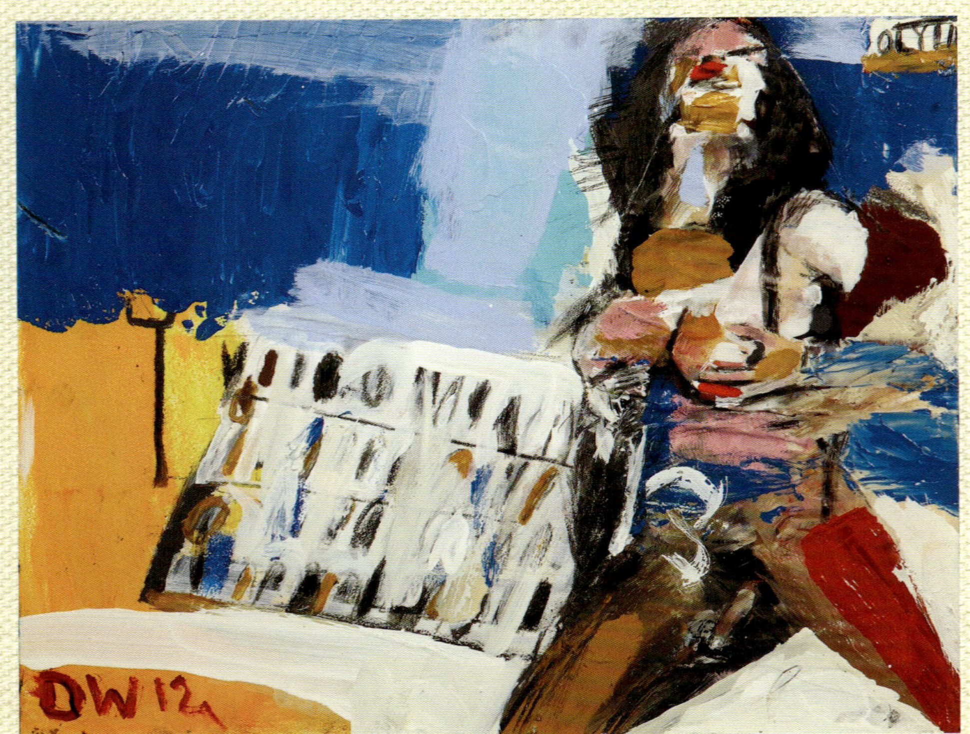

Santa Monica III, Arena, 2012

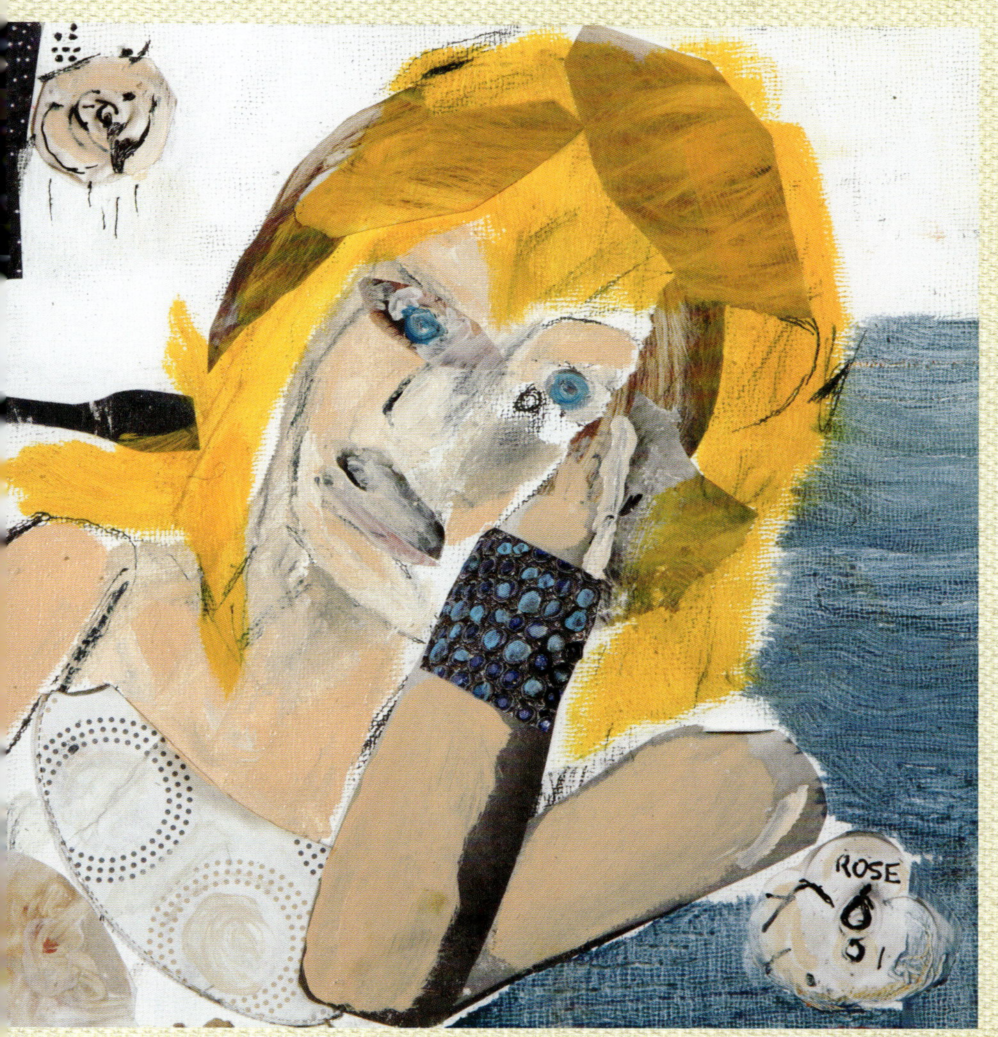

Santa Monica V, Rose, 2012

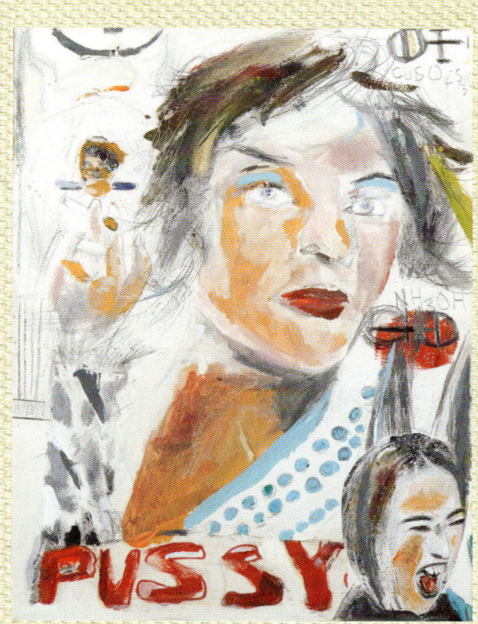

Santa Monica VI, Pussy Riot, 2012

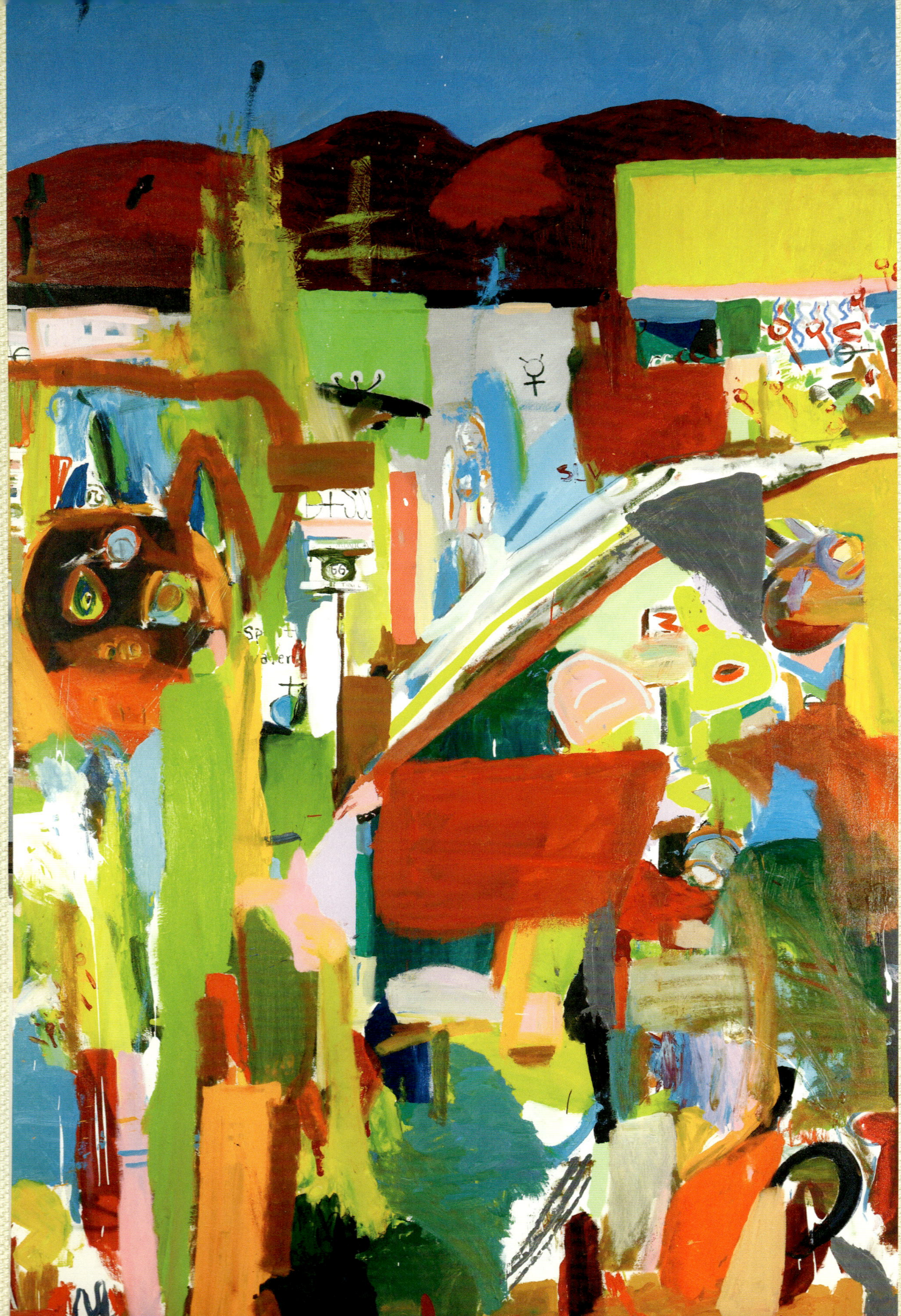

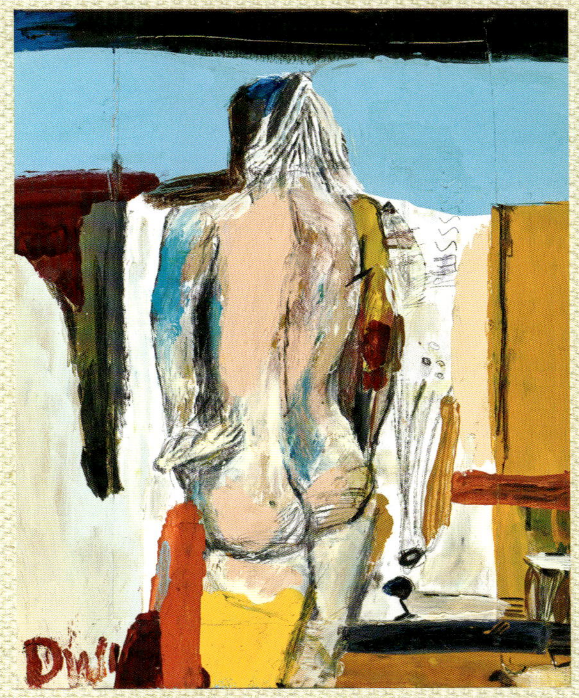

***Santa Monica VIII*, 2012**

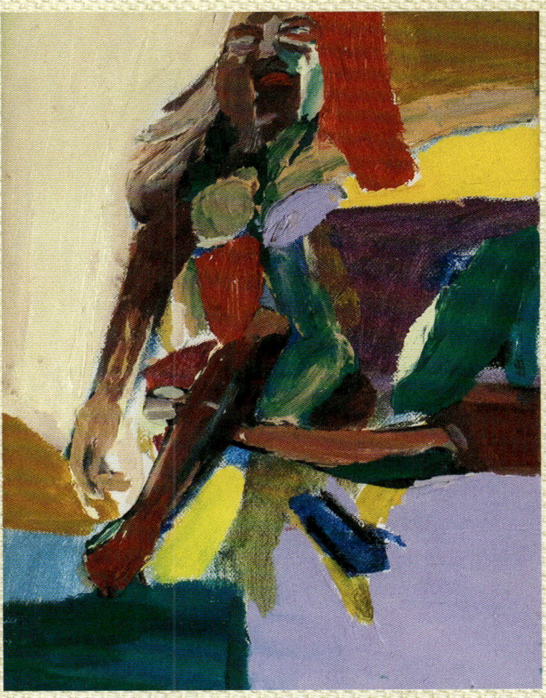

***Santa Monica IX*, 2012**

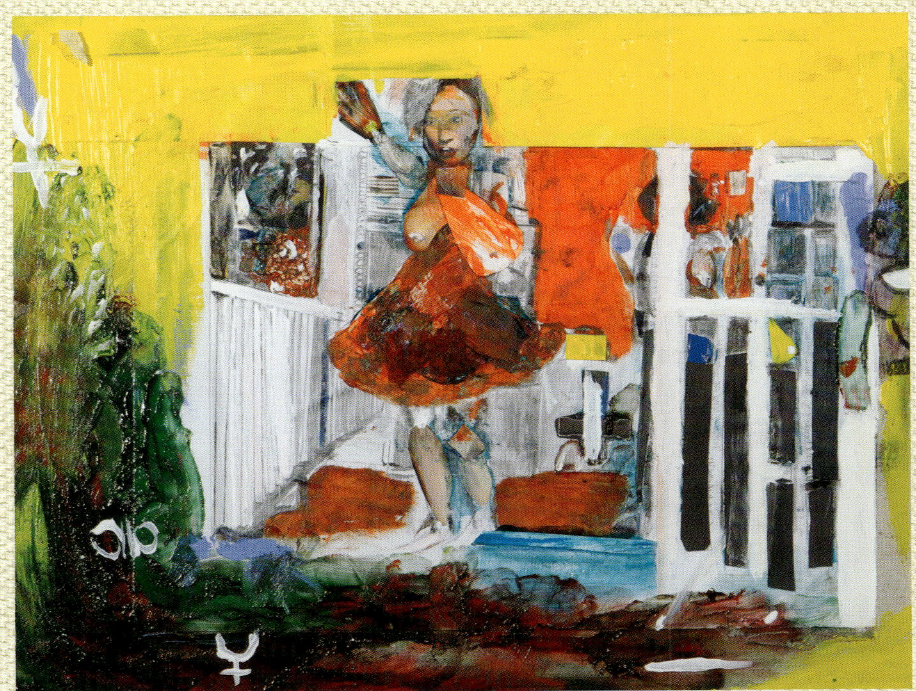

Opposite: *Santa Monica VII, Route 66*, 2012

***Santa Monica X*, 2012**

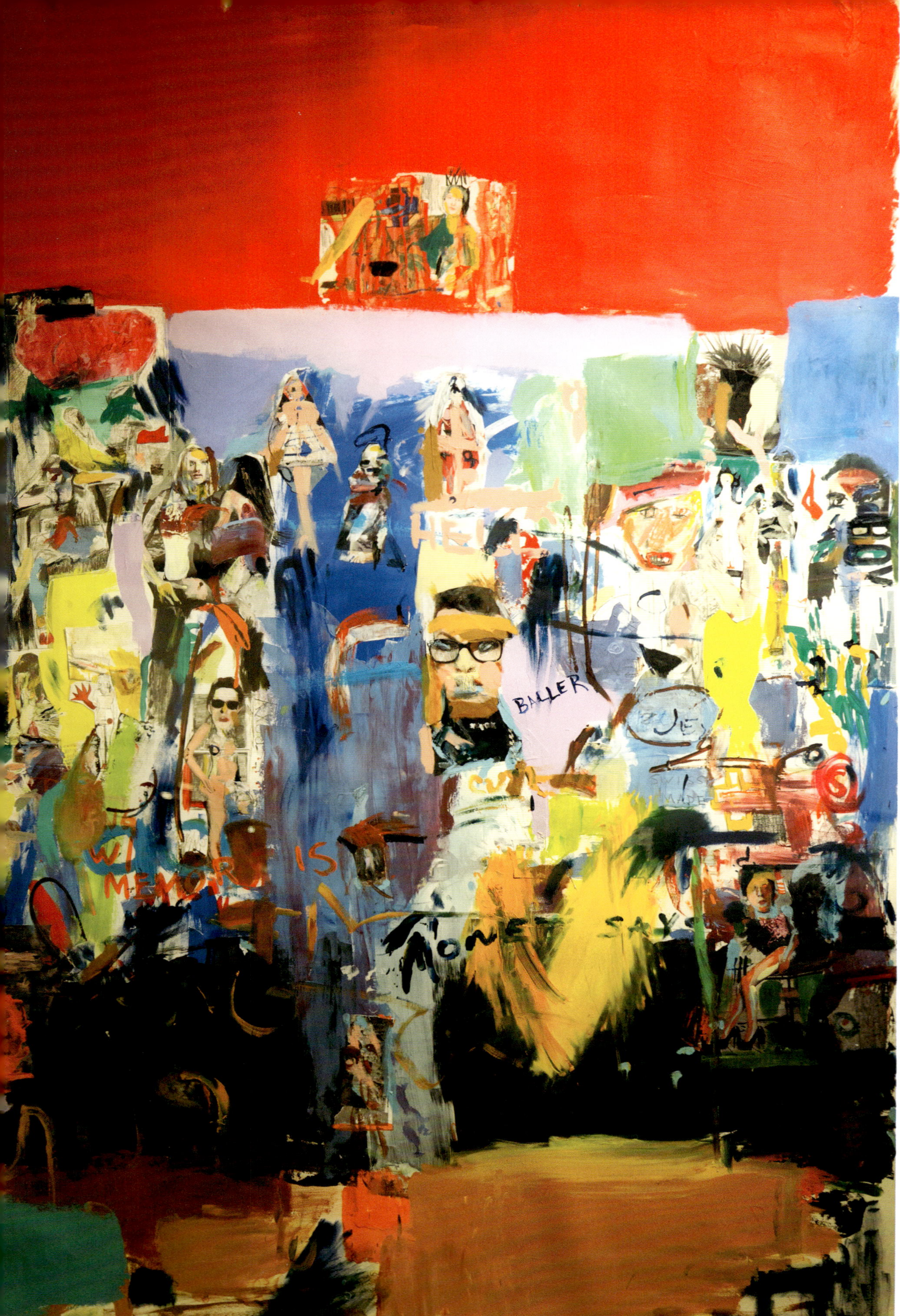

Heaven and Hell, 2012

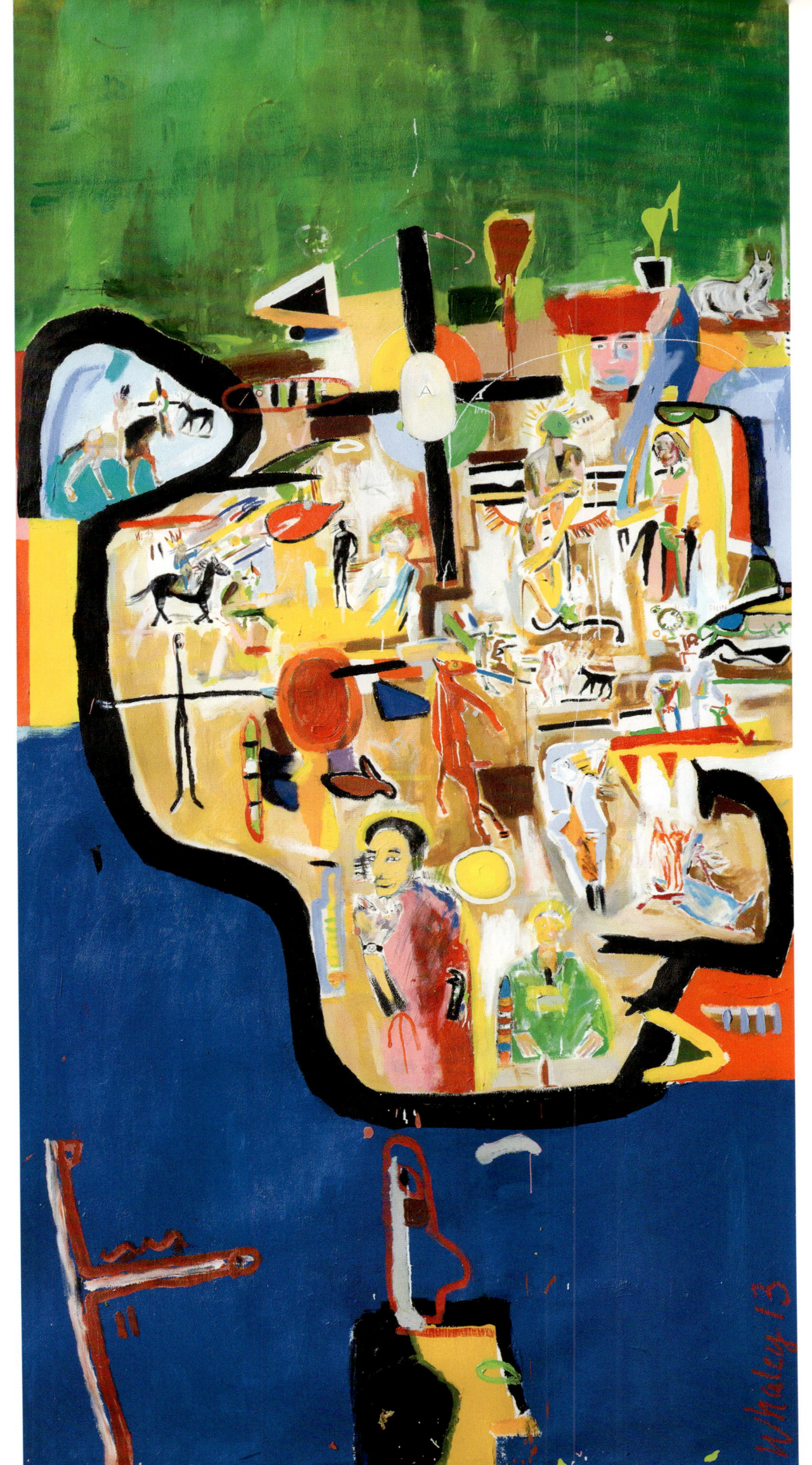

Revelations, 2013
Selected for
2013 Florence Biennale

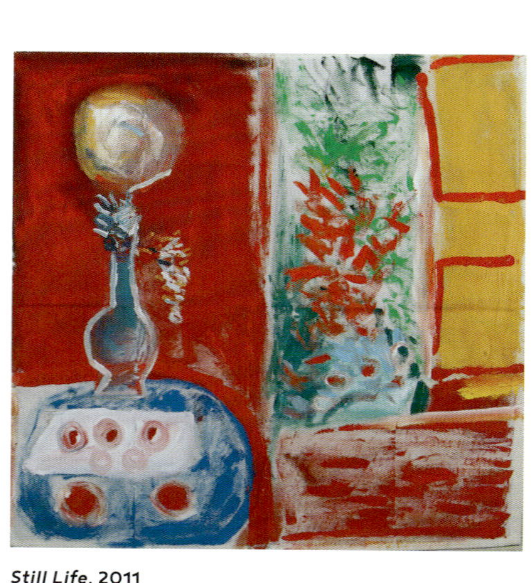

Still Life, 2011

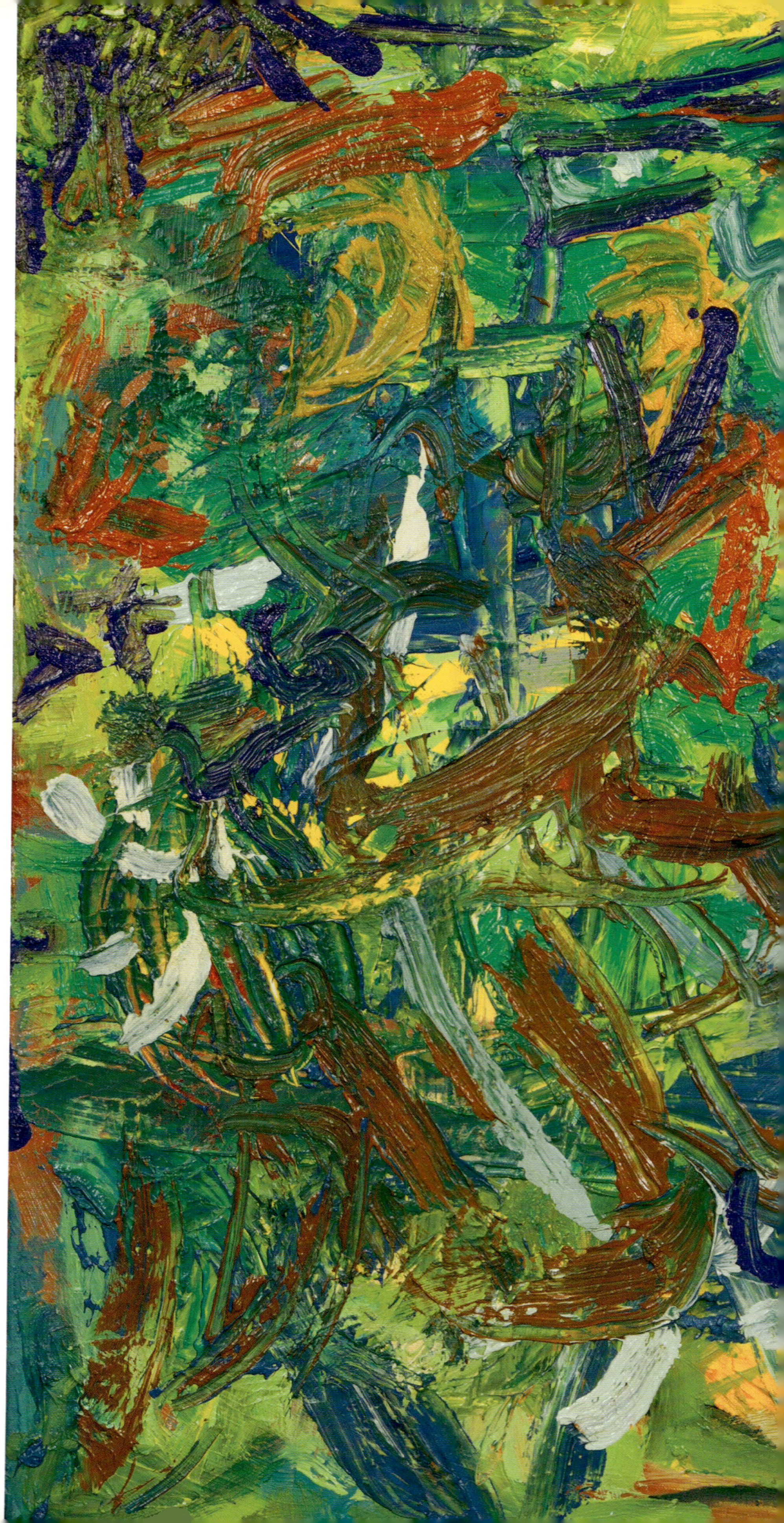

Fire and Water, 2011

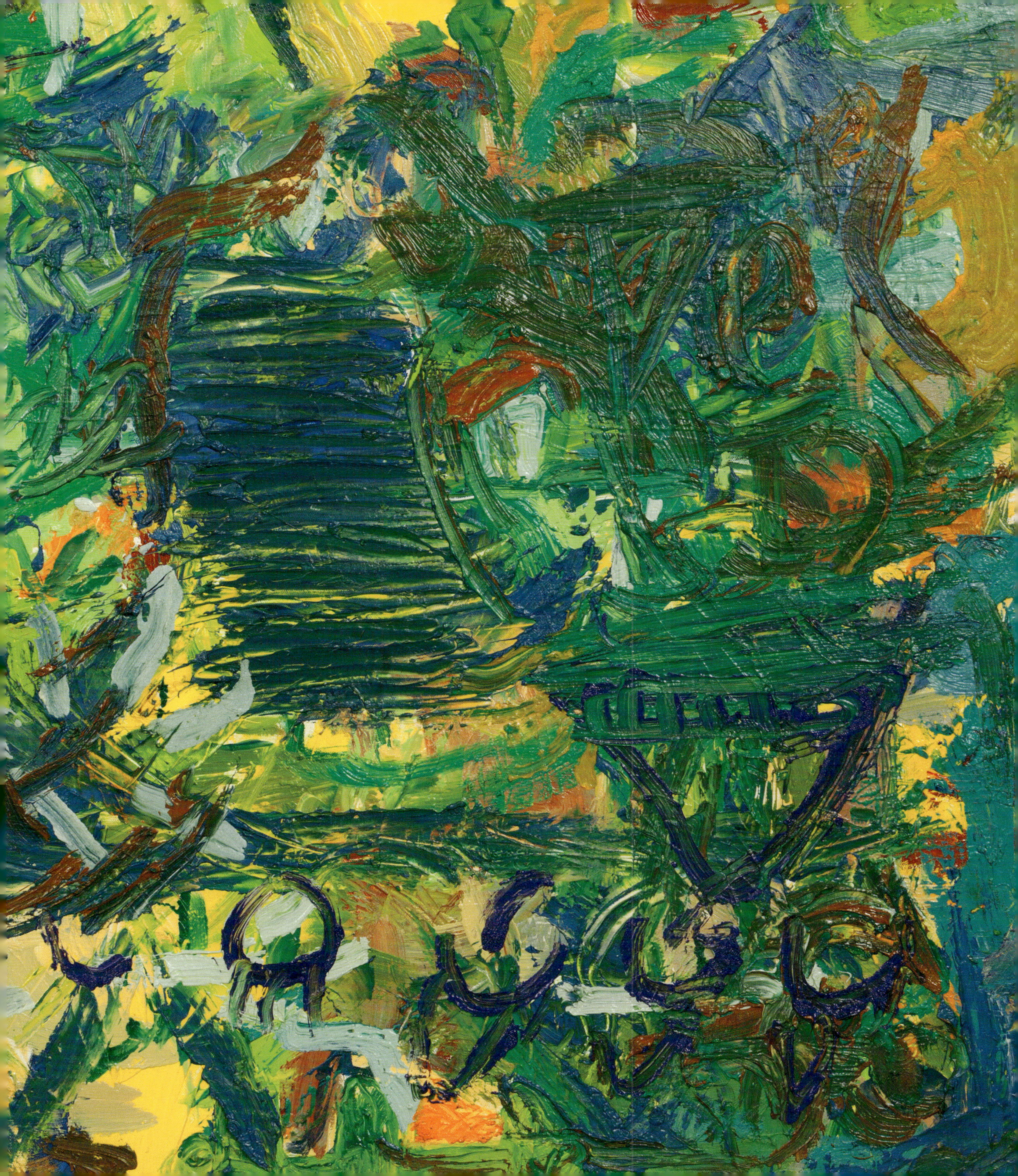

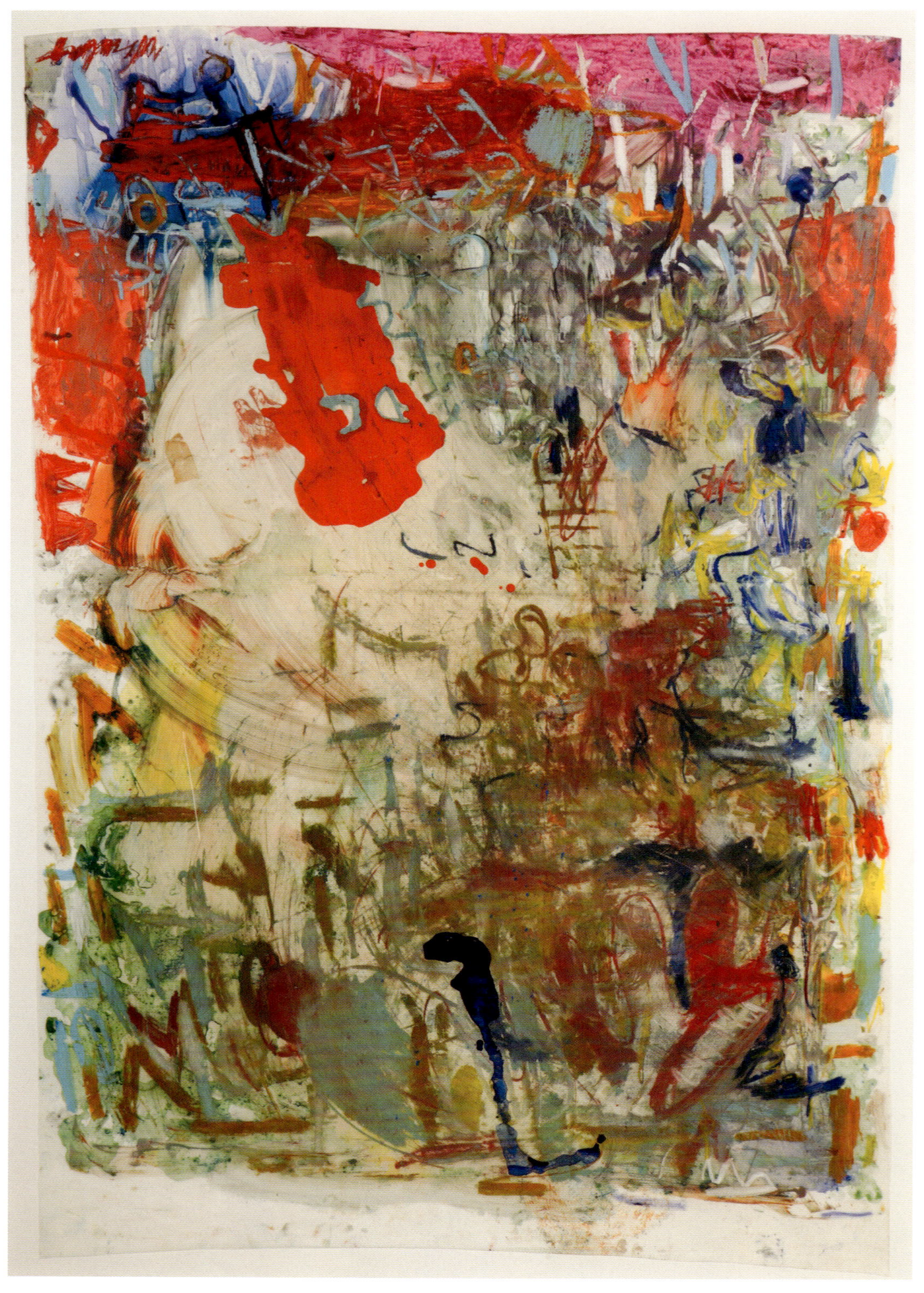

***A Colorful Mind*, 2014**

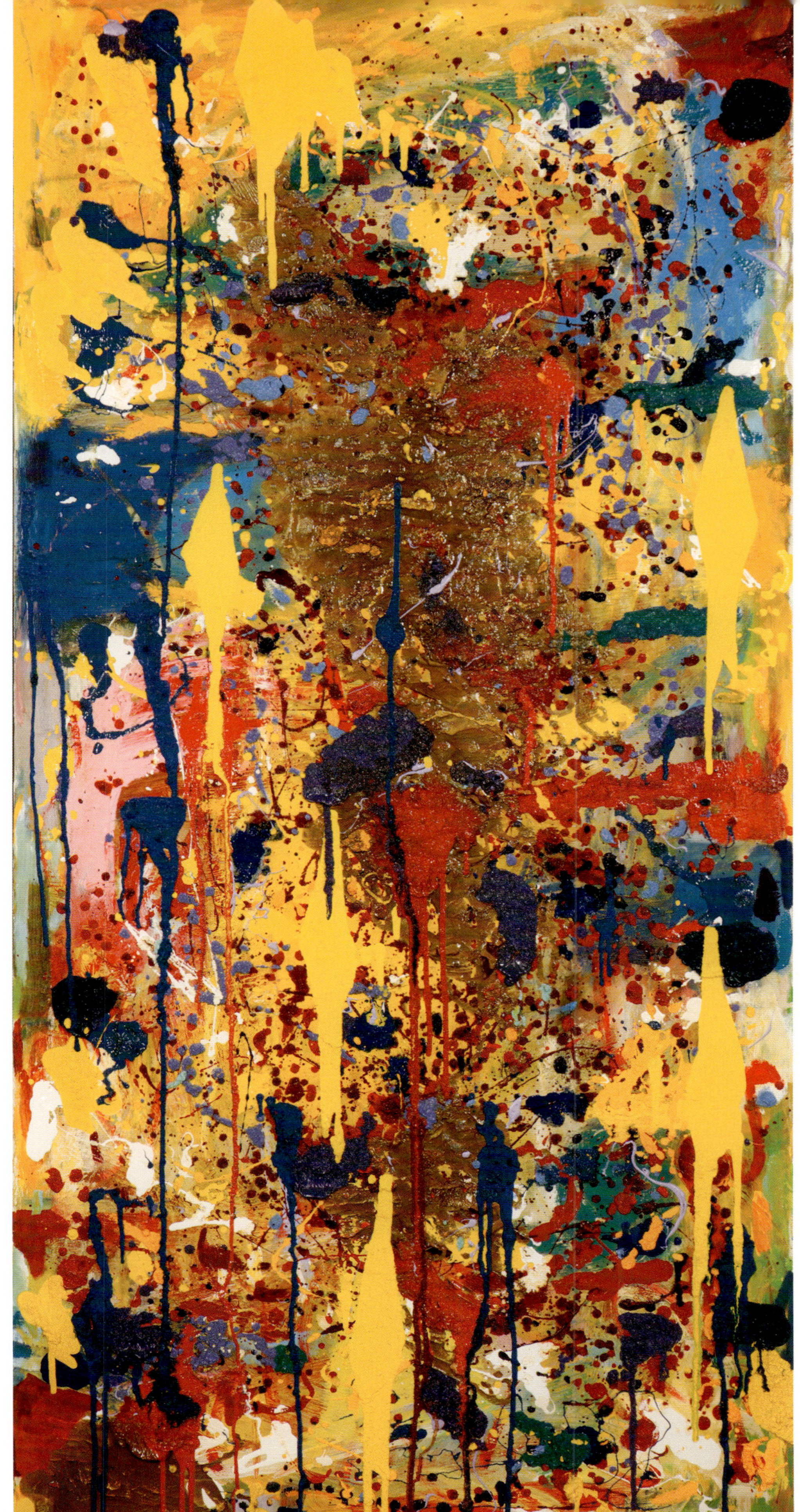

Le Soleil, 2014

"What makes a painting good is light.
Light is essential to any good painting. You can't have a good painting without light.
You can paint anything you want as long as it has light."

—DW

Sky Series

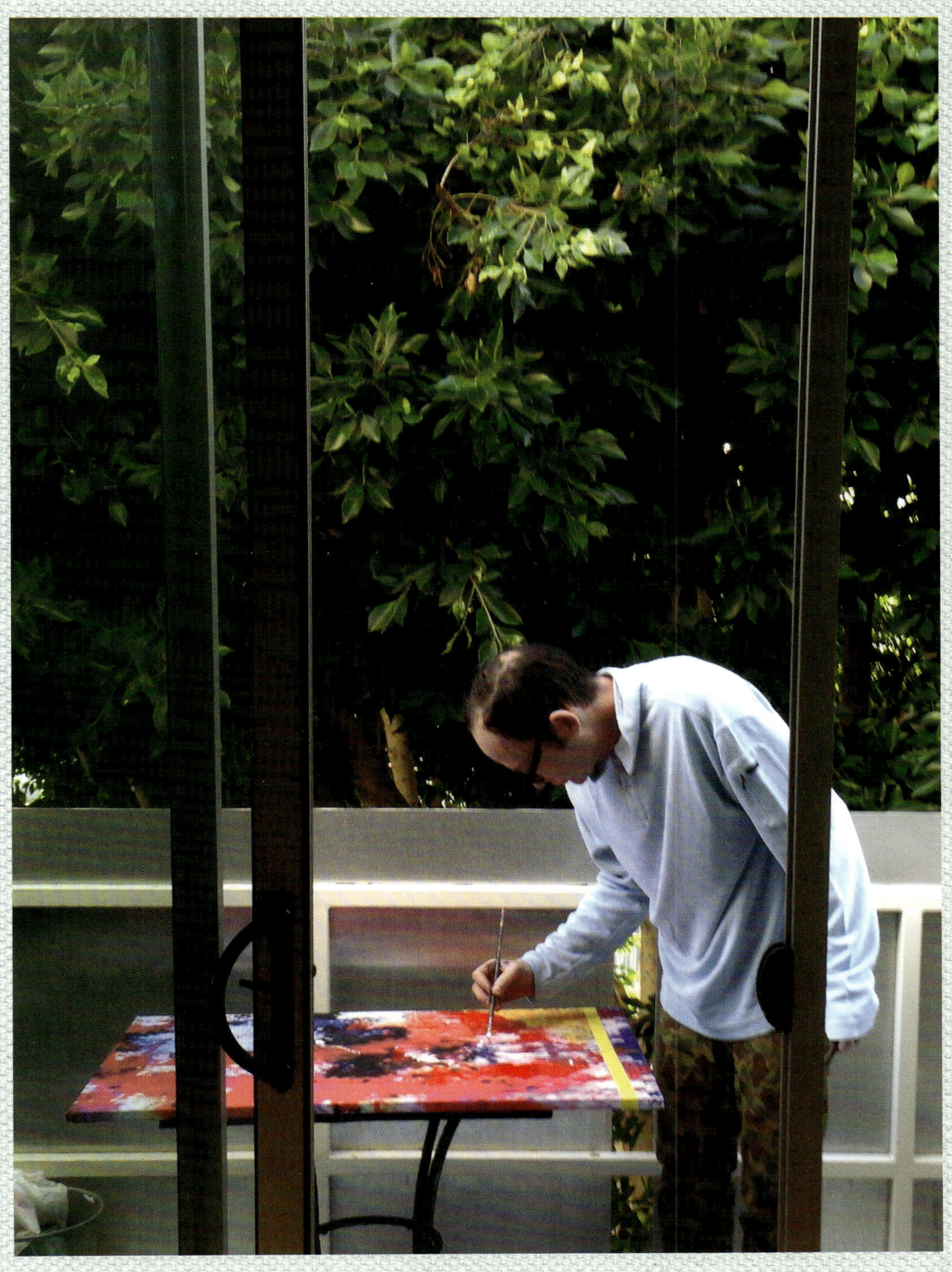

"Light scattering is defined as the dispersal of a beam of particles or of radiation into a range of directions as a result of physical interactions."

Opposite: ***Reinventing En Plein Air*** **(aka** ***Scattering of Light*****), 2014**

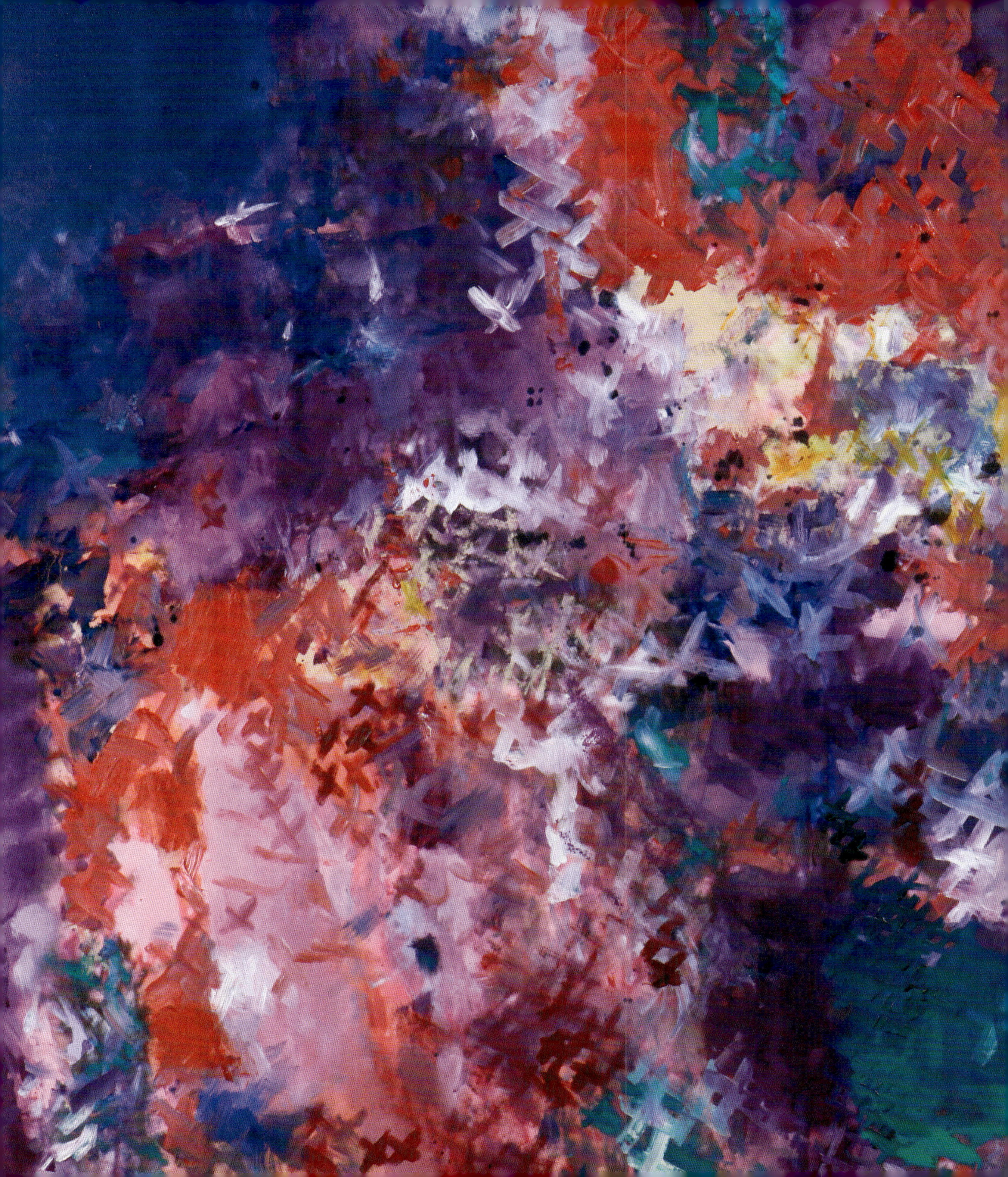

"The material in a white dwarf no longer undergoes fusion reactions, so the star has no source of energy. As a result, it cannot support itself by the heat generated by fusion against gravitational collapse, but is supported only by electron degeneracy pressure, causing it to be extremely dense."

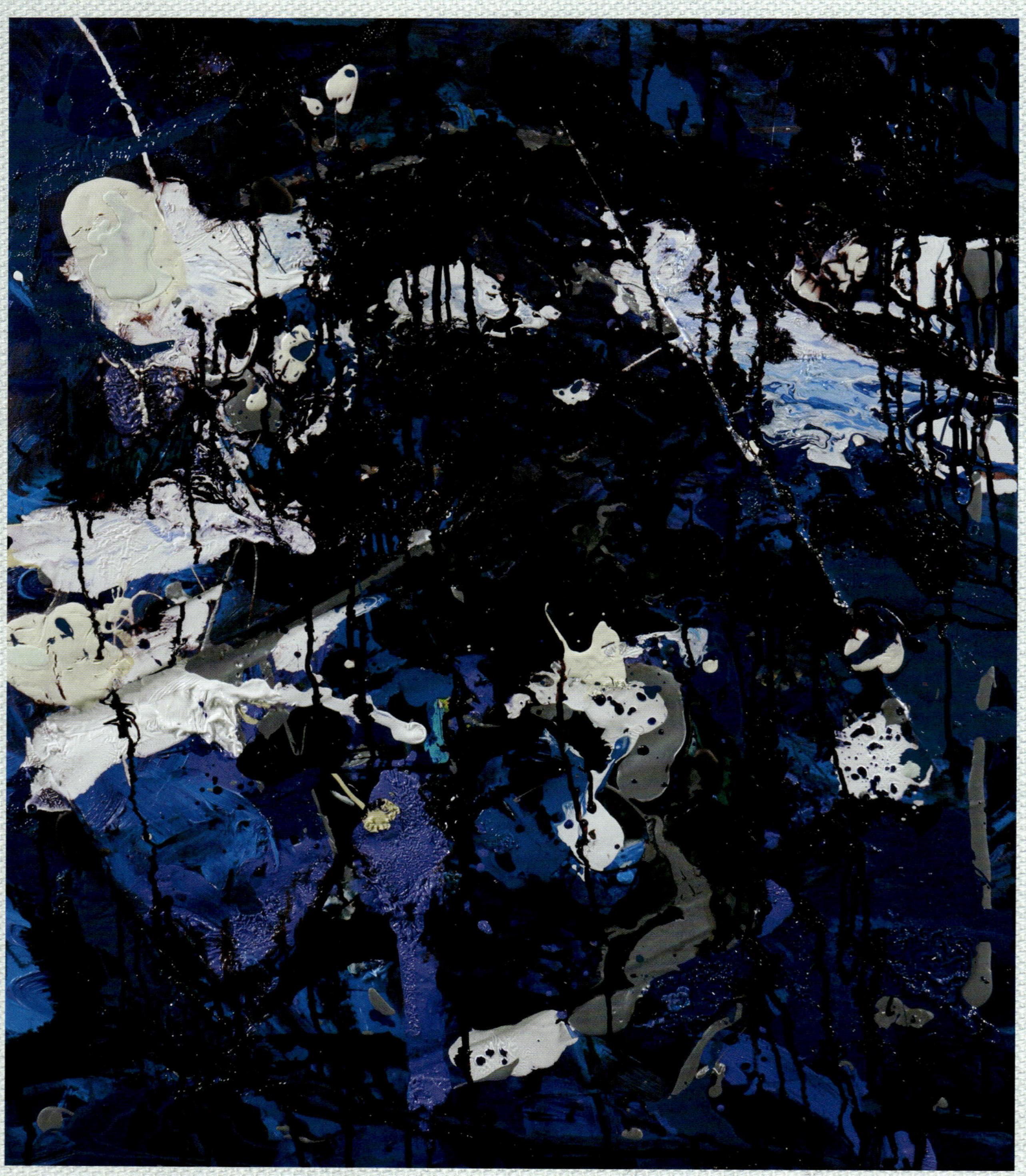

***White Dwarf*, 2014**

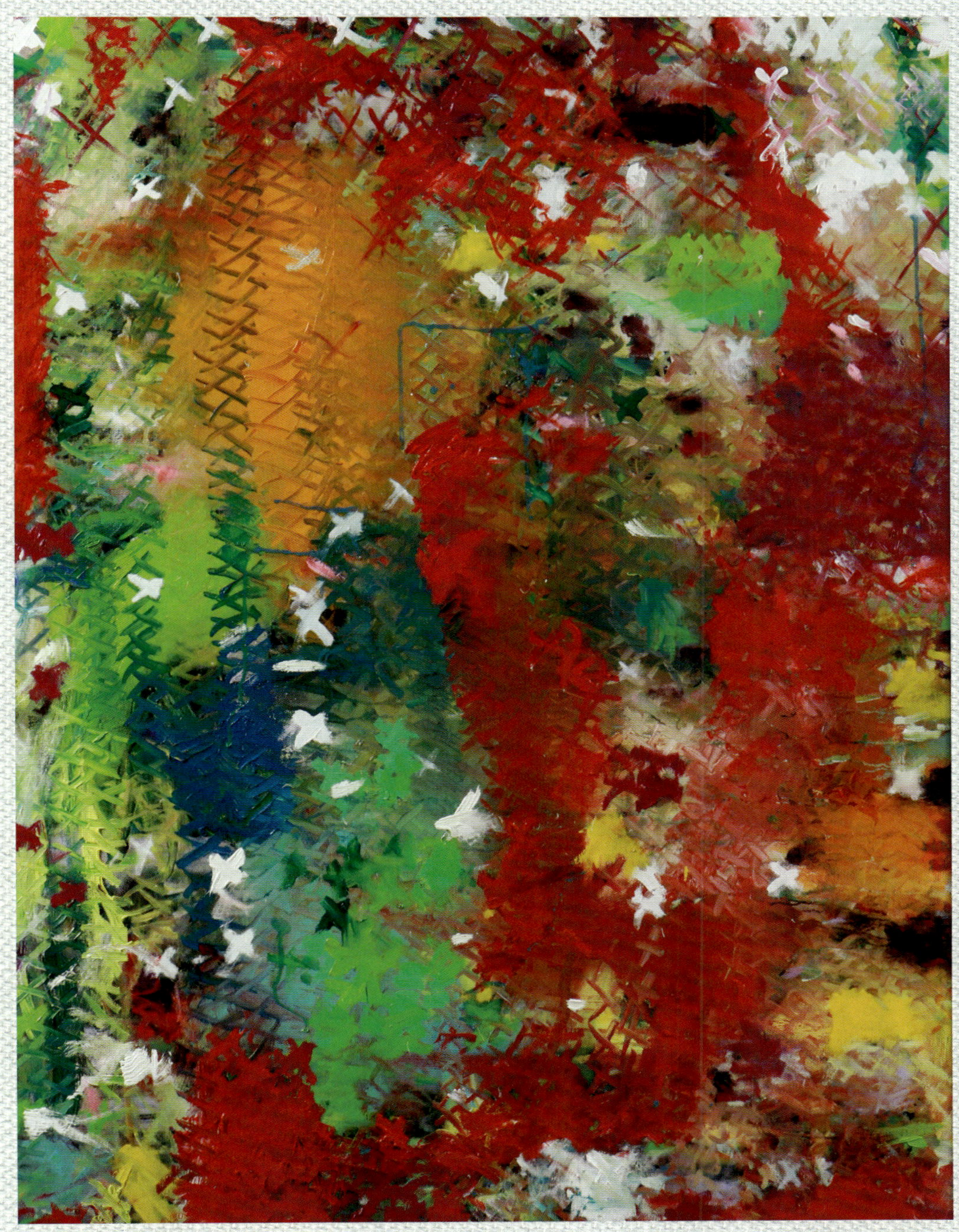

Wave Length, 2014

"In physics, the wavelength of a sinusoidal wave is the spatial period of the wave—the distance over which the wave's shape repeats, and the inverse of the spatial frequency. The range of wavelengths or frequencies for wave phenomena is called a spectrum. The name originated with the visible light spectrum but now can be applied to the entire electromagnetic spectrum as well as to a sound spectrum or vibration spectrum."

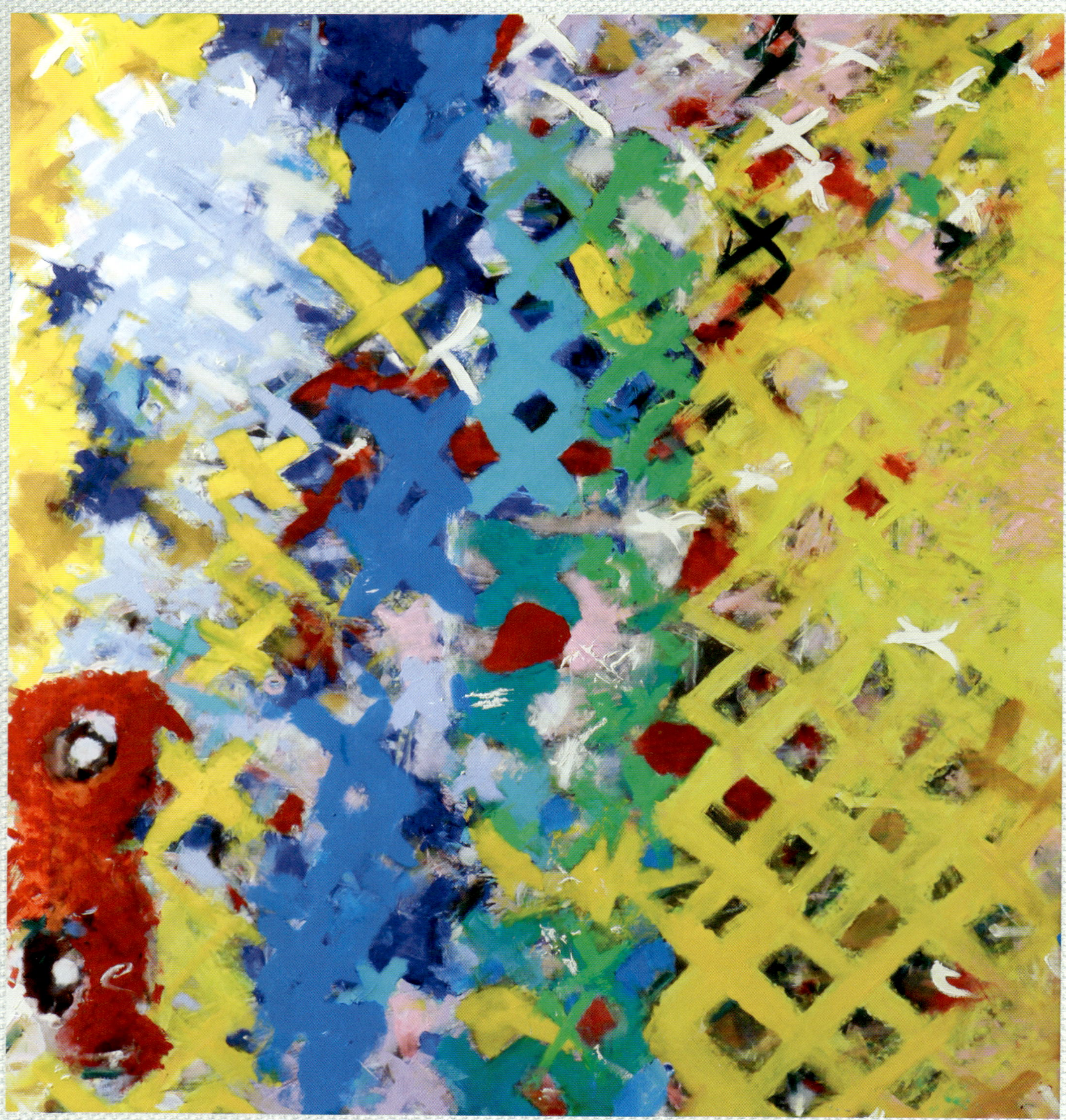

***Horizon*, 2014**

"In general relativity, an event horizon is a boundary in space-time beyond which events cannot affect an outside observer. In layman's terms it's defined as 'the point of no return,' the point at which the gravitational pull becomes so great as to make escape impossible. An event horizon is most commonly associated with black holes. Light emitted from inside the event horizon can never reach the outside observer."

"Red giants are stars that have exhausted the supply of hydrogen in their cores and switched to thermonuclear fusion of hydrogen in a shell surrounding the core. However, their outer envelope is lower in temperature, giving them a reddish-orange hue. Despite the lower energy density of their envelope, red giants are many times more luminous than the Sun because of their great size."

Opposite: ***Interior Red*, 2014**

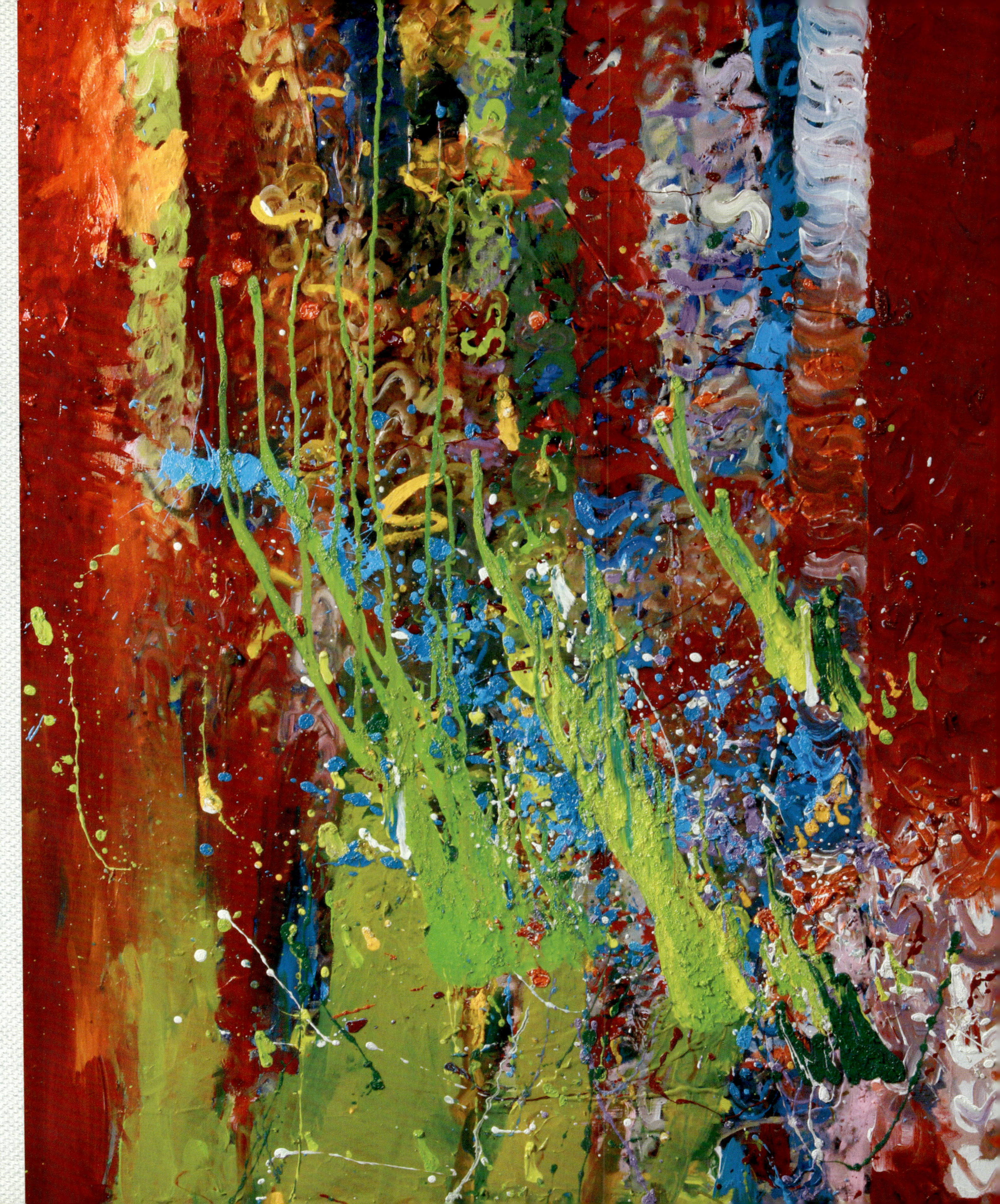

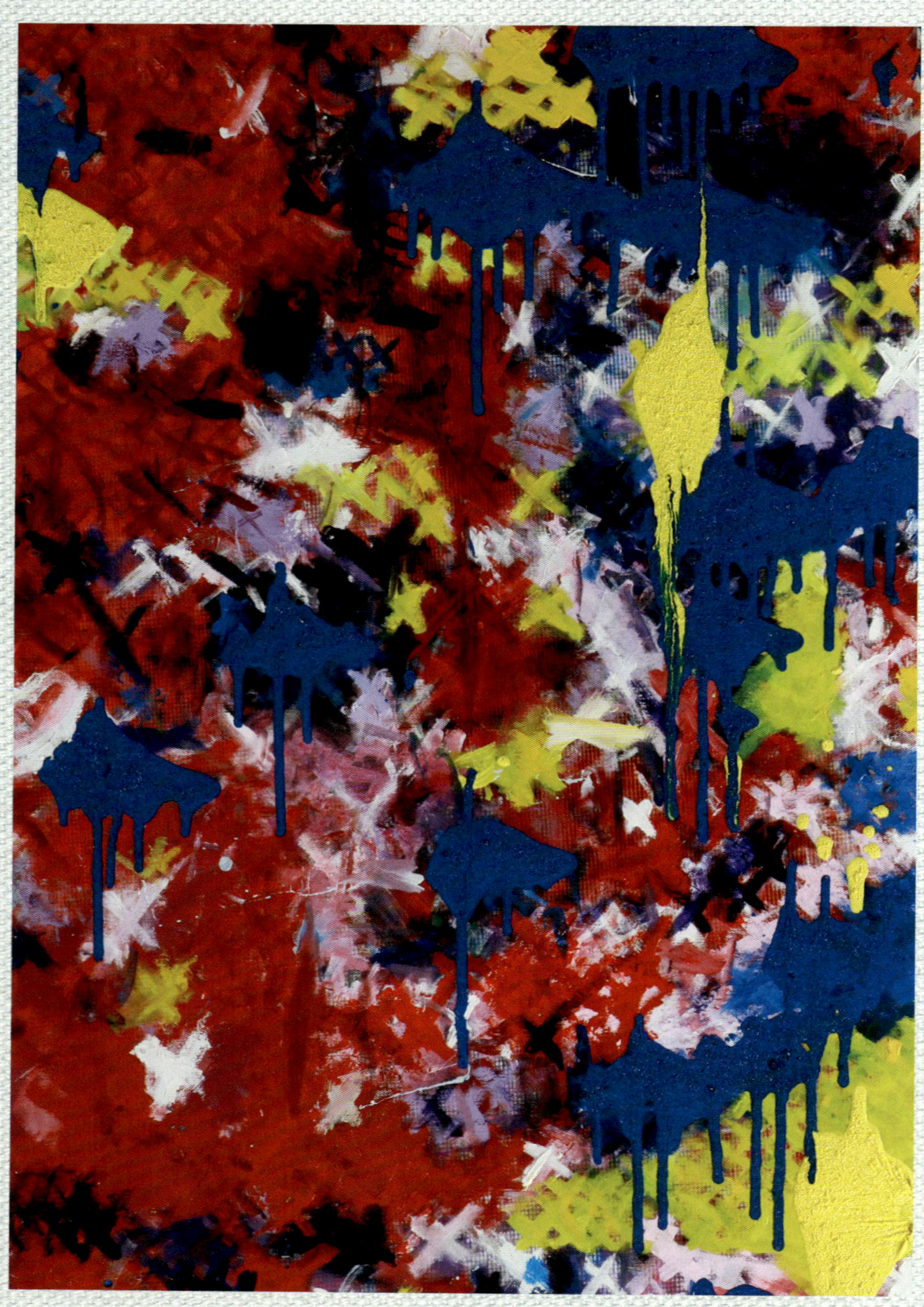

Nebula, 2014

"In these regions the formations of gas, dust, and other materials 'clump' together to form larger masses, which attract further matter, and eventually will become massive enough to form stars. The remaining materials are then believed to form planets and other planetary system objects."

*"The bright reds and yellows of this nebula represent gasses that have been heated by nearby stars to the point where they give off light.
The dark clouds consist of cold gas molecules and dust.
These clouds may be undergoing gravitational collapse to form small clusters of stars."*

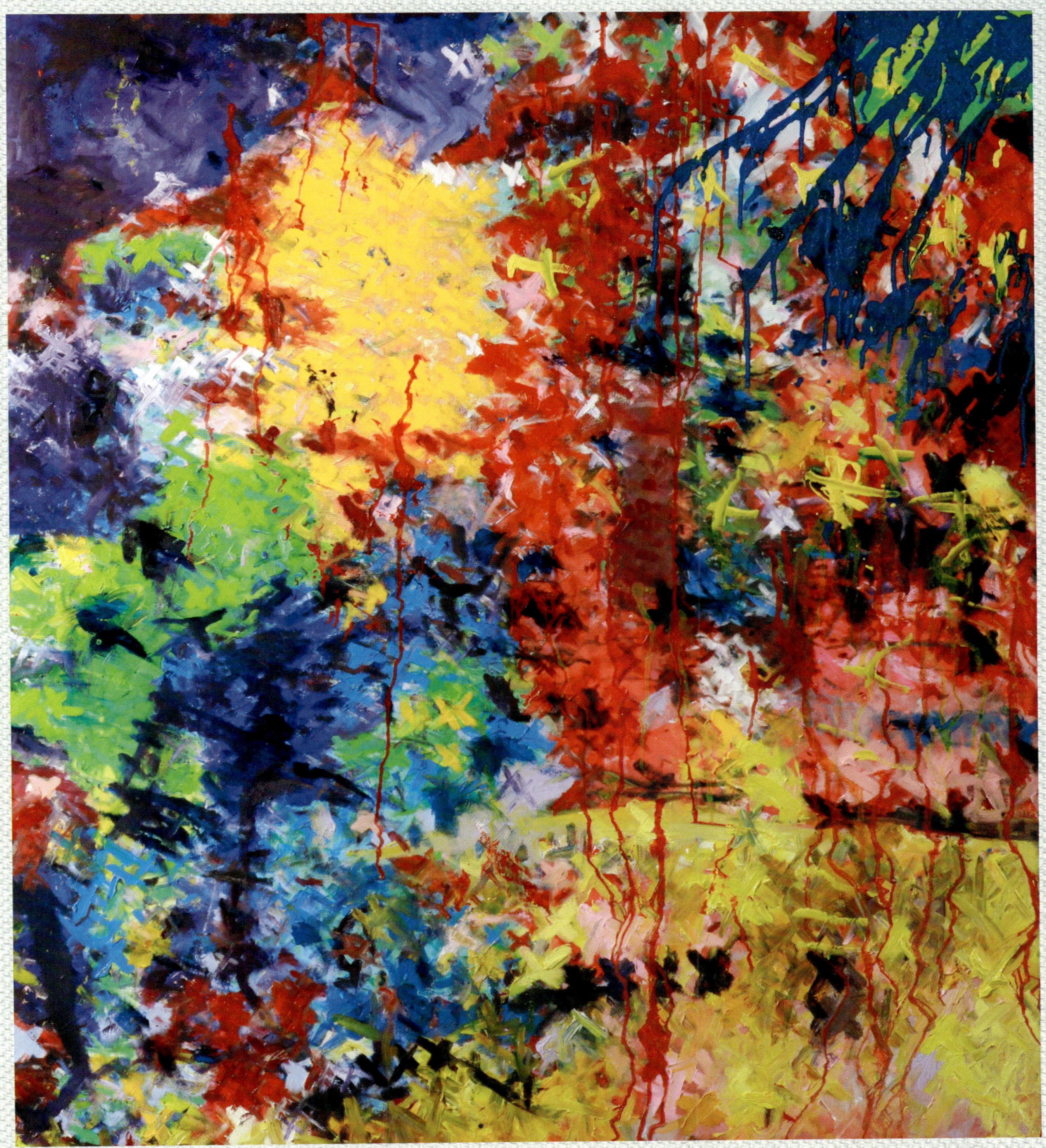

Grand Nebula (Key Hole), 2014

"A light pillar is an atmospheric optical phenomenon in the form of a vertical column of light which appears to extend above and below a light source. The effect, sometimes also called the crystal beam phenomenon, is created by the reflection of light from numerous tiny ice crystals suspended in the atmosphere or clouds. The light can come from the Sun in which case the phenomenon is called a sun pillar. Since they are caused by the interaction of light with ice crystals, light pillars belong to the family of halos. Their collective surfaces act as a giant mirror, which reflects the light source upwards and downwards into a virtual image."

Opposite: ***Sun Pillar*****, 2014**

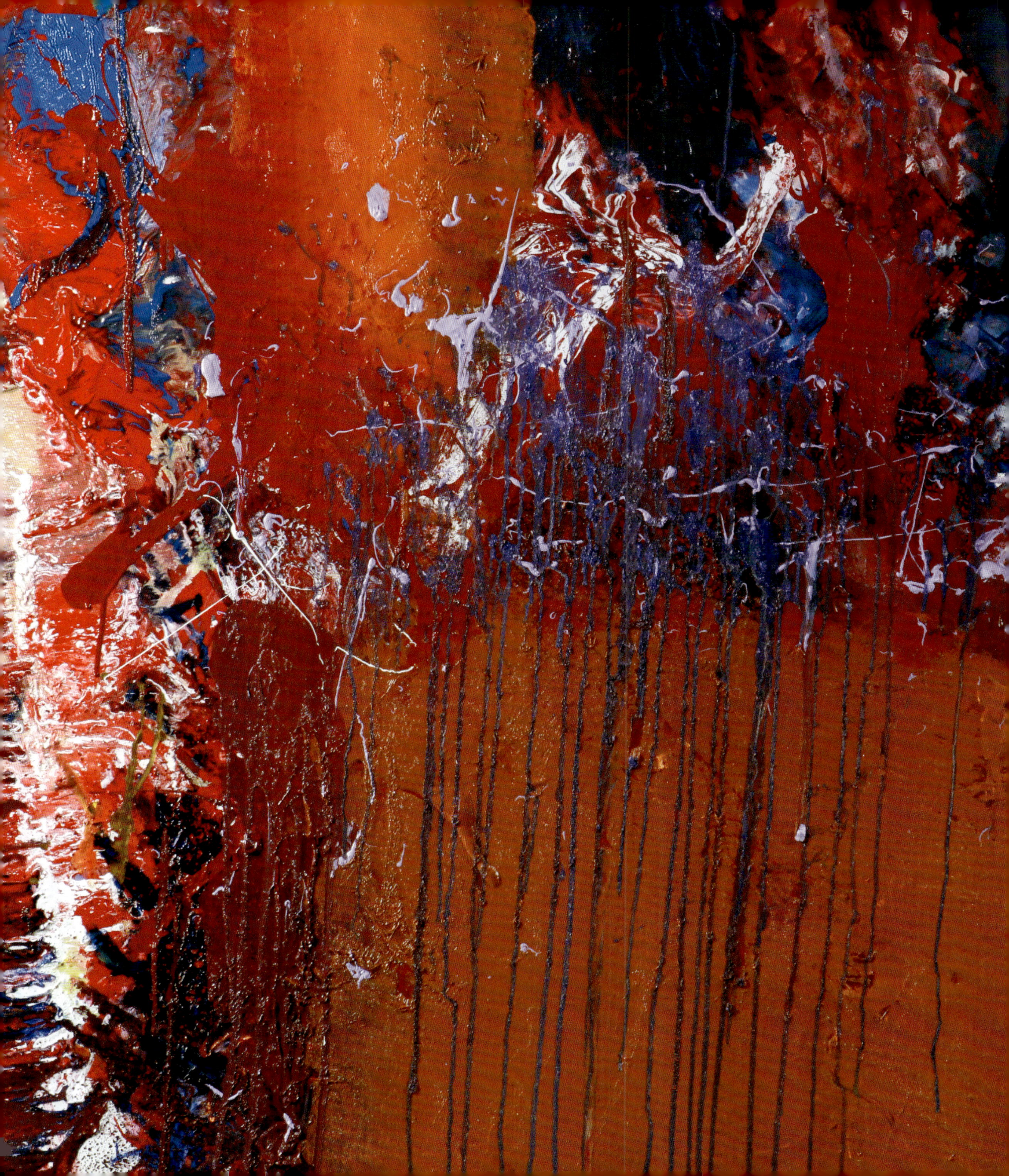

"With the help of a pulsar, astronomers have detected an Earth-size diamond in the sky. A pulsar is simply a spinning neutron star. But as a pulsar spins, lighthouse-like beams of radio waves stream from the poles of its powerful magnetic field. If they sweep past the Earth, they'll give rise to blips of radio waves, so regular that you could set your watch by them."

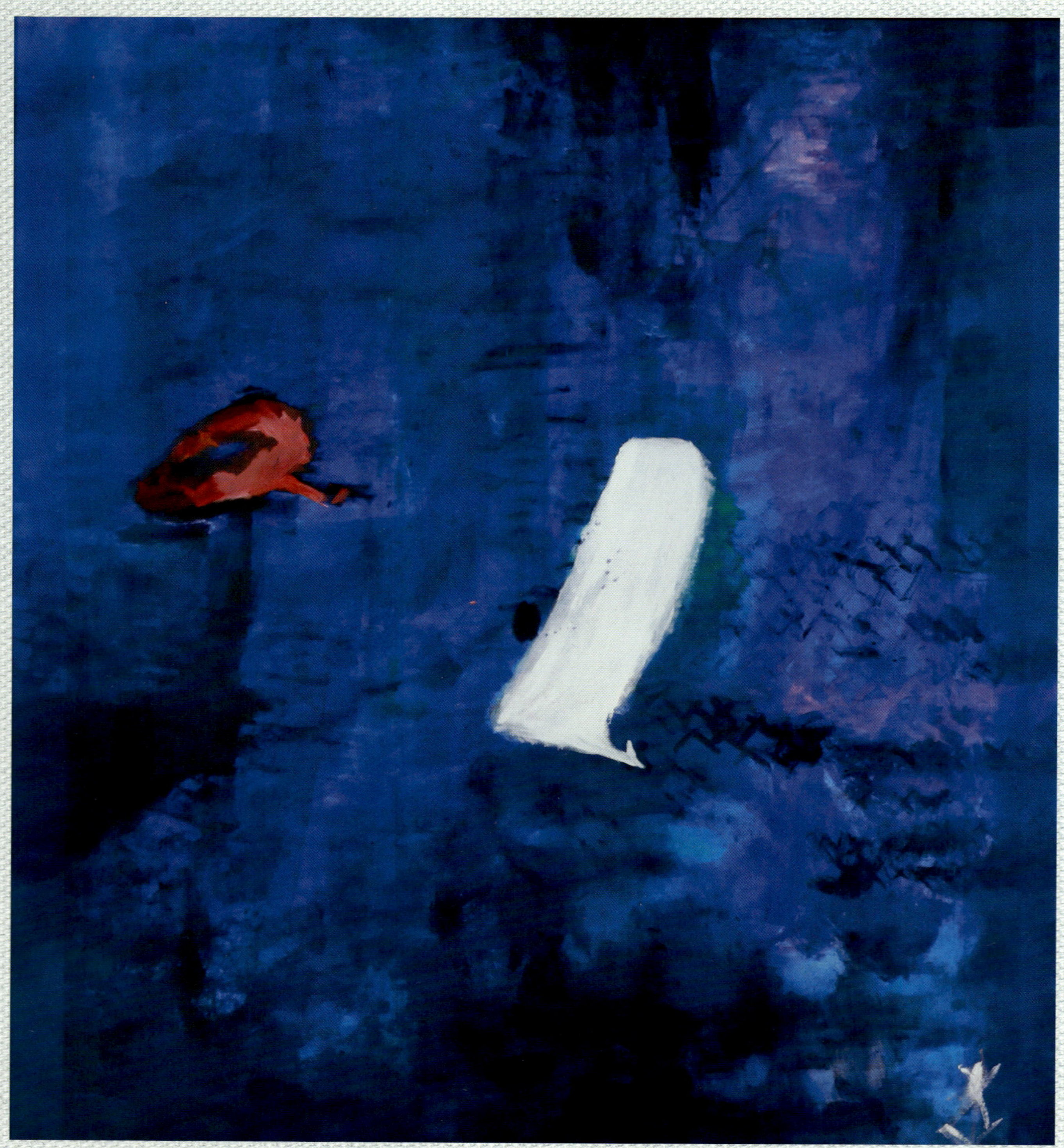

***Diamond in the Sky*, 2014**

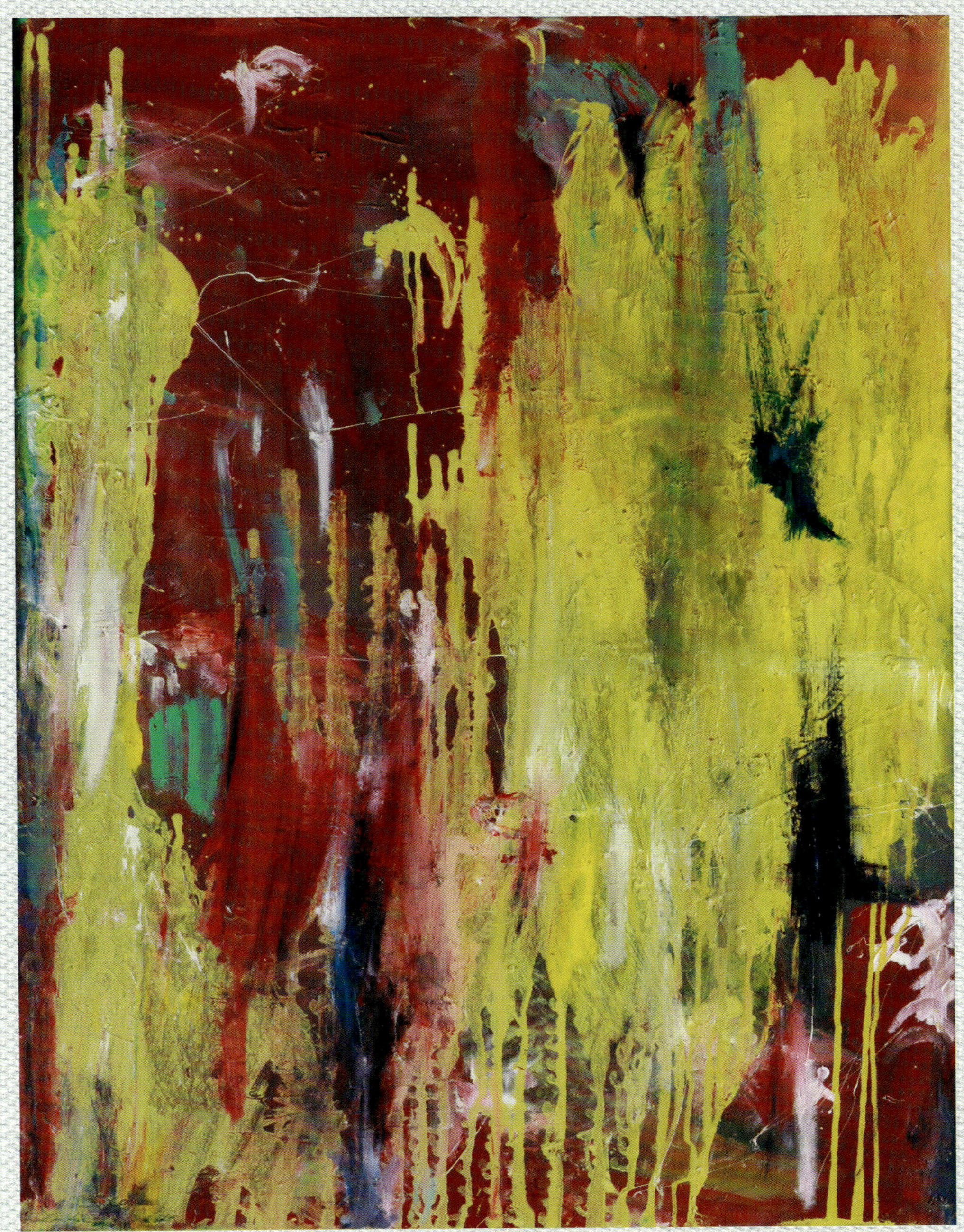

Staircase to Heaven, 2014

"And he dreamed. And behold, a ladder set up on the earth, and the top of it reached to heaven.
And behold, the angels of God ascending and descending on it."

—Genesis 28:12

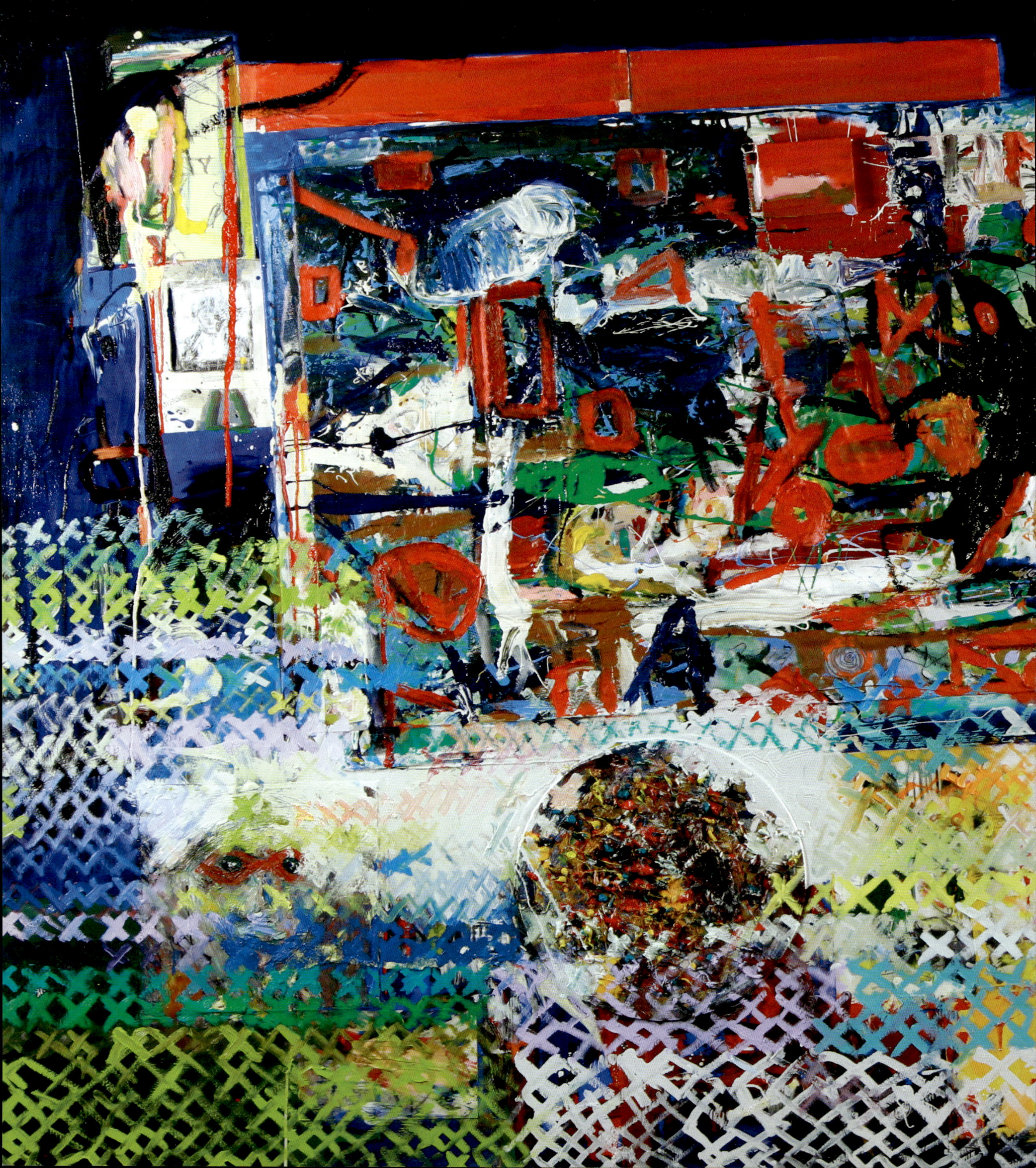

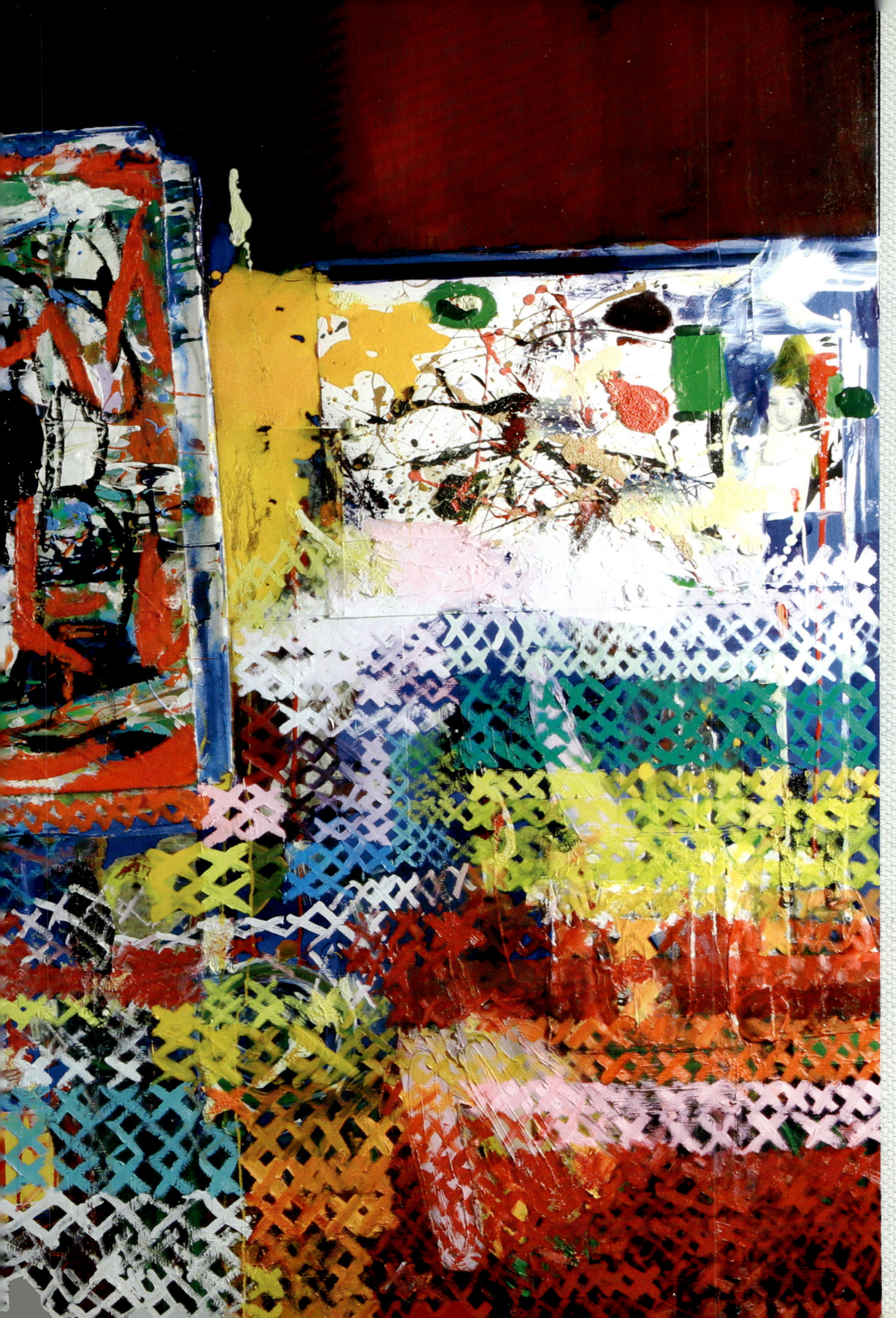

Insomnia, 2014

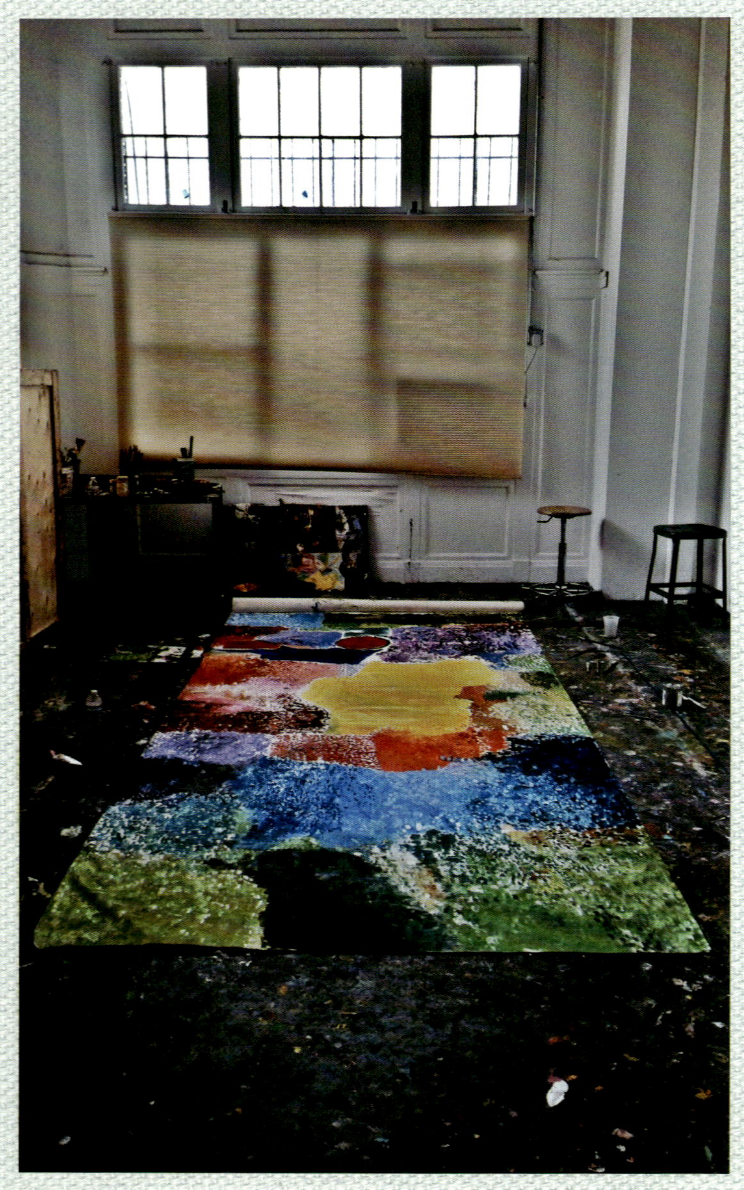

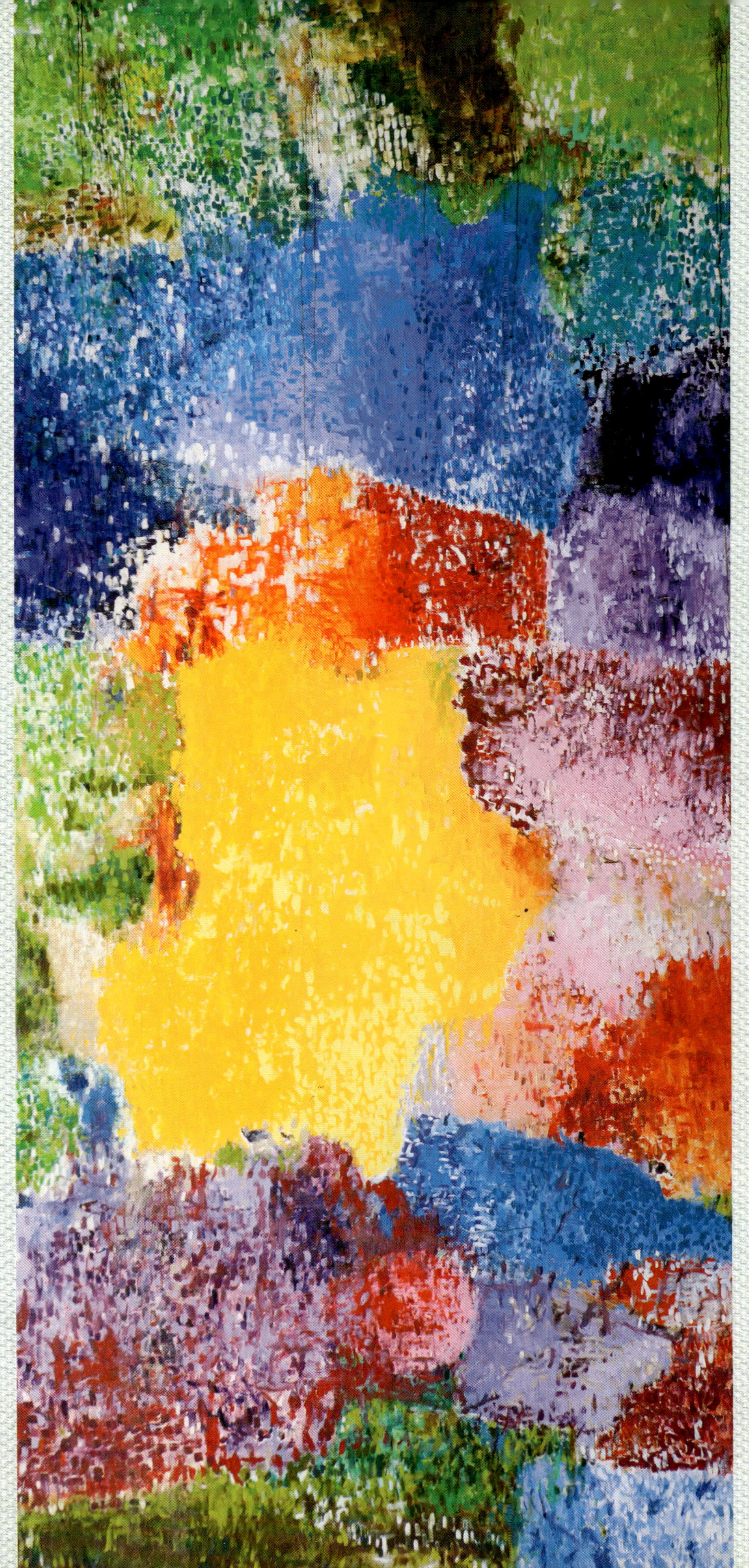

Four Last Songs, 2014
Based on a song cycle by Strauss

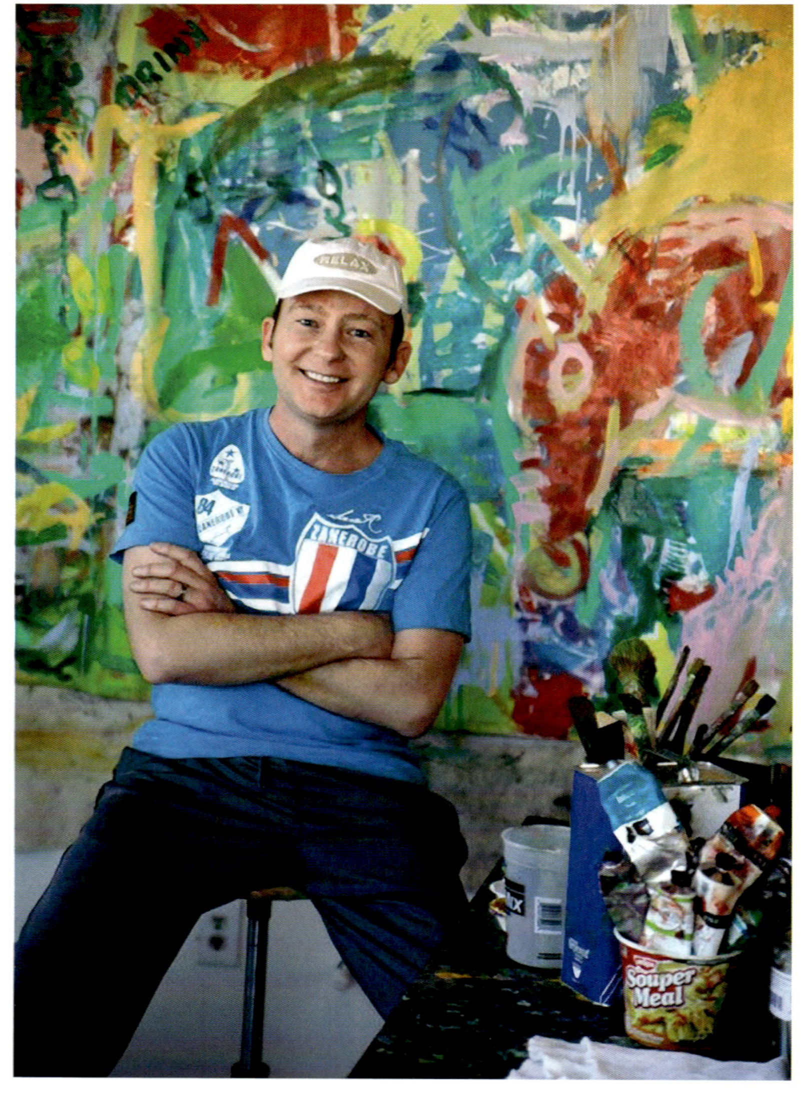

Approach, 2014

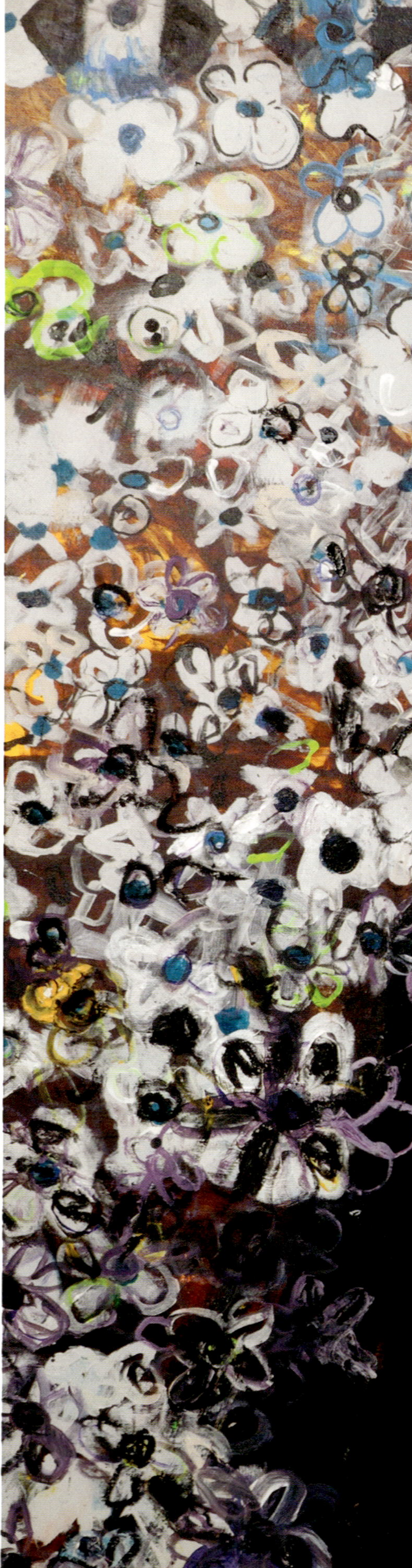

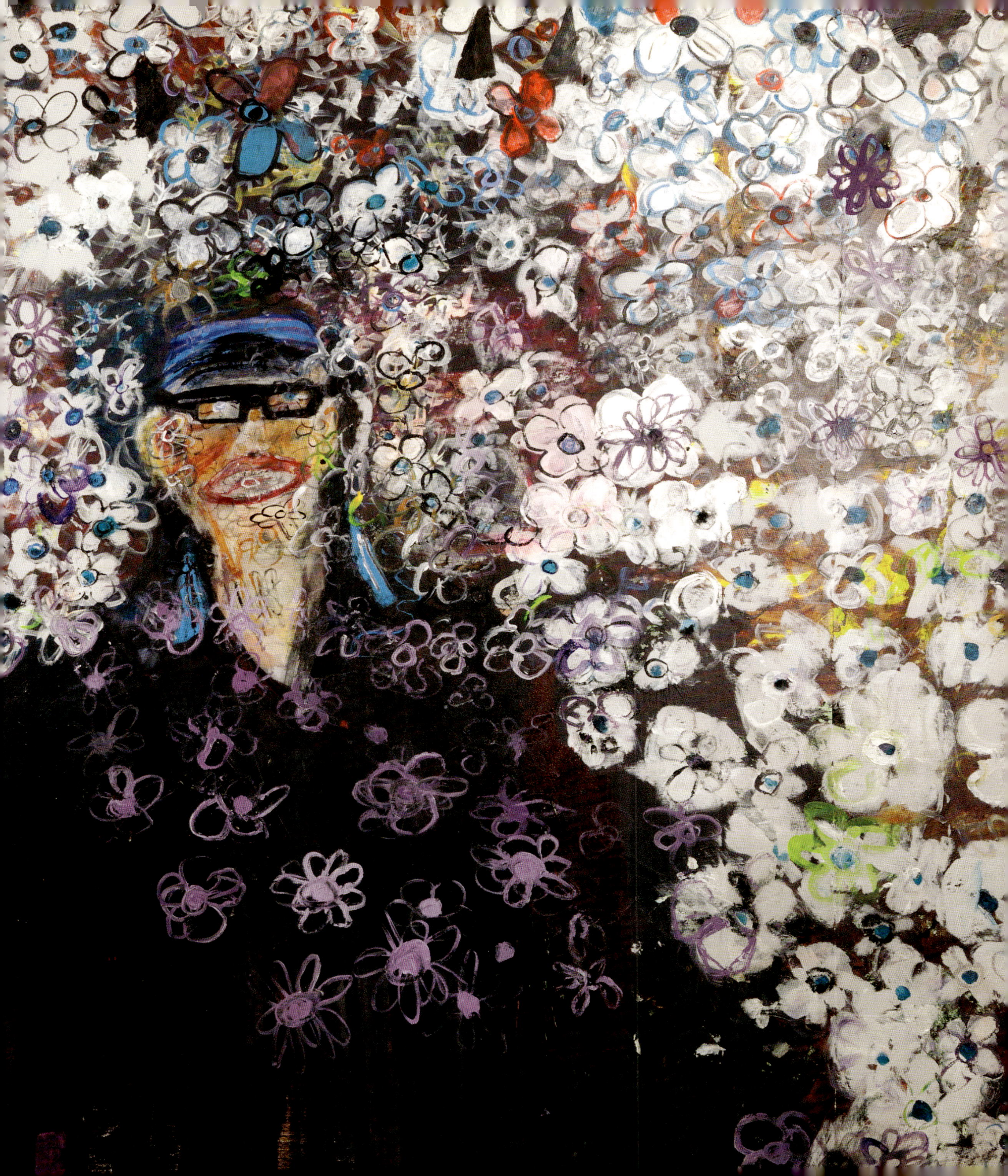

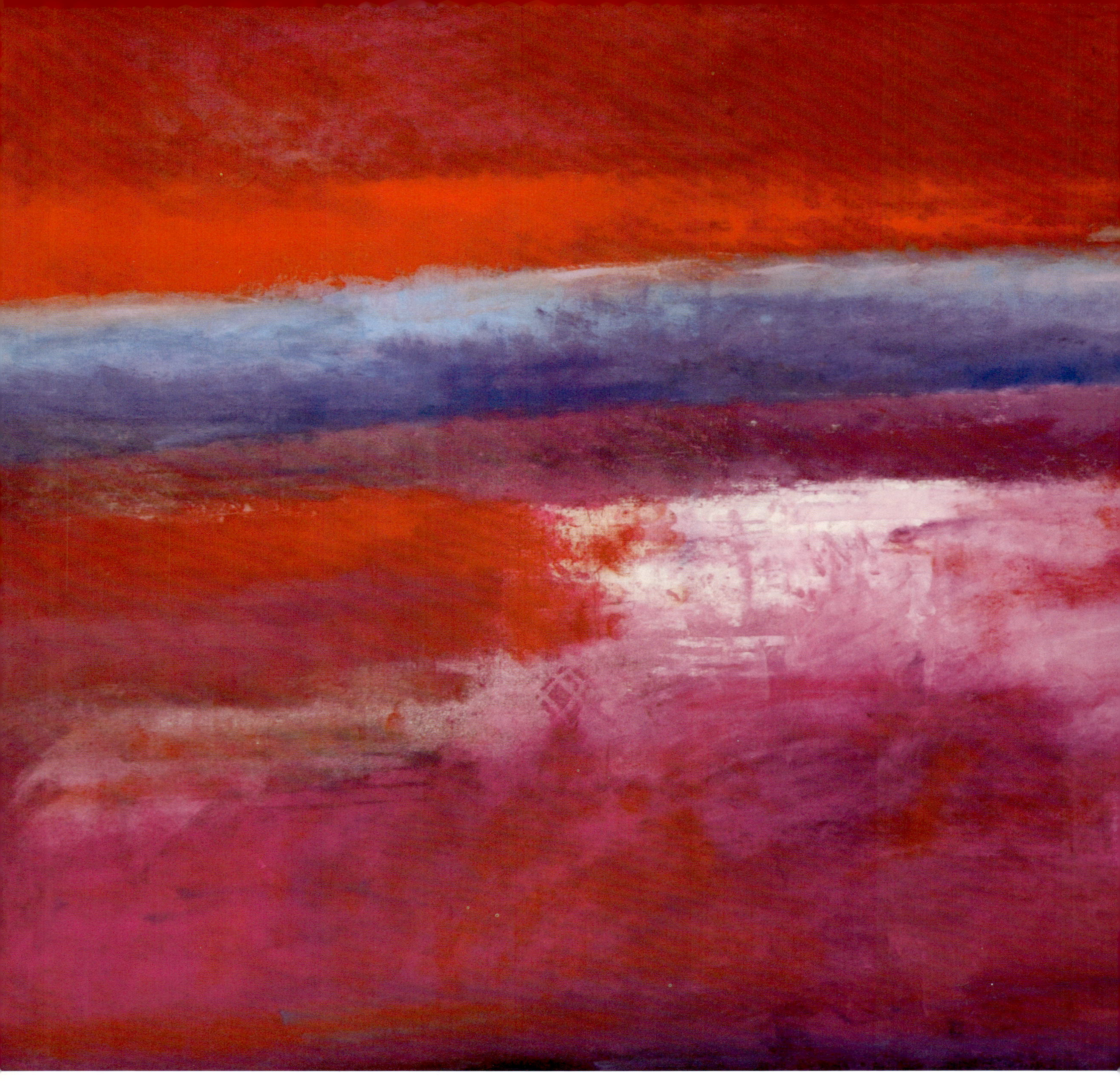

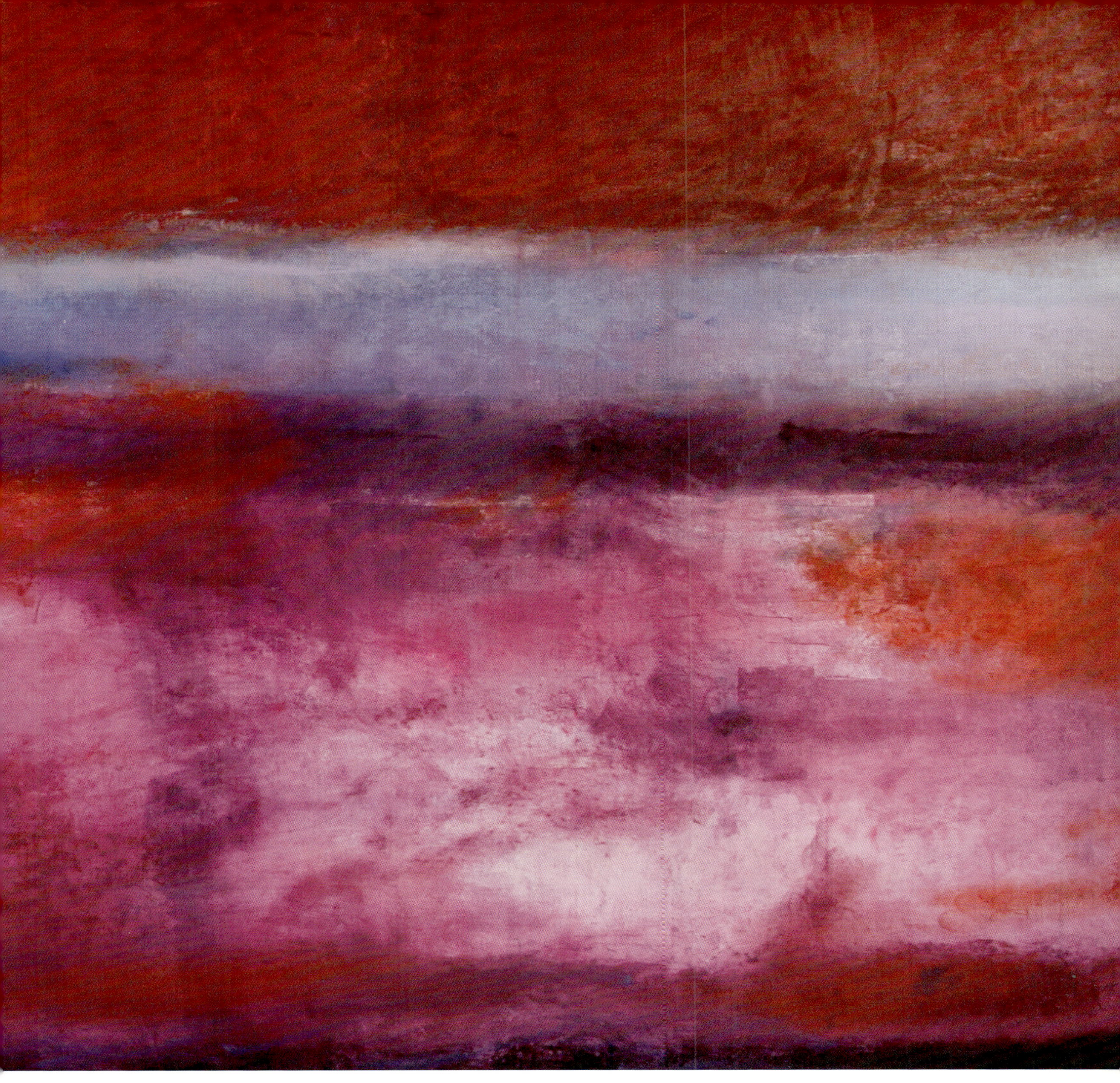

Promise, 2014

"Artists never really finish their work.
They just find good places to stop and continue their meditations."

—DW

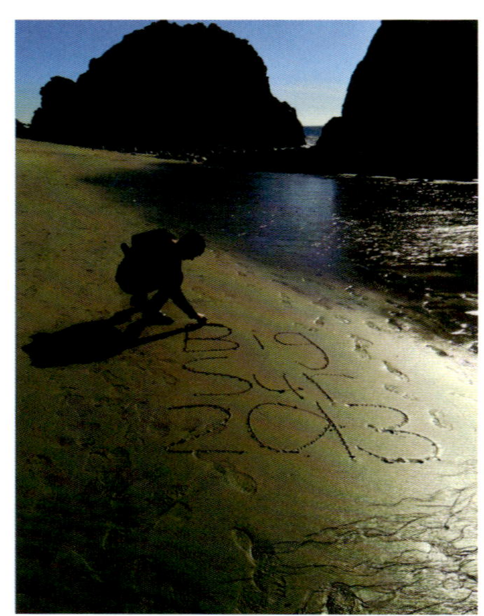

Big Sur, 2013

Davyd Whaley's ashes were spread in the surf of Pfeiffer Beach in Big Sur.

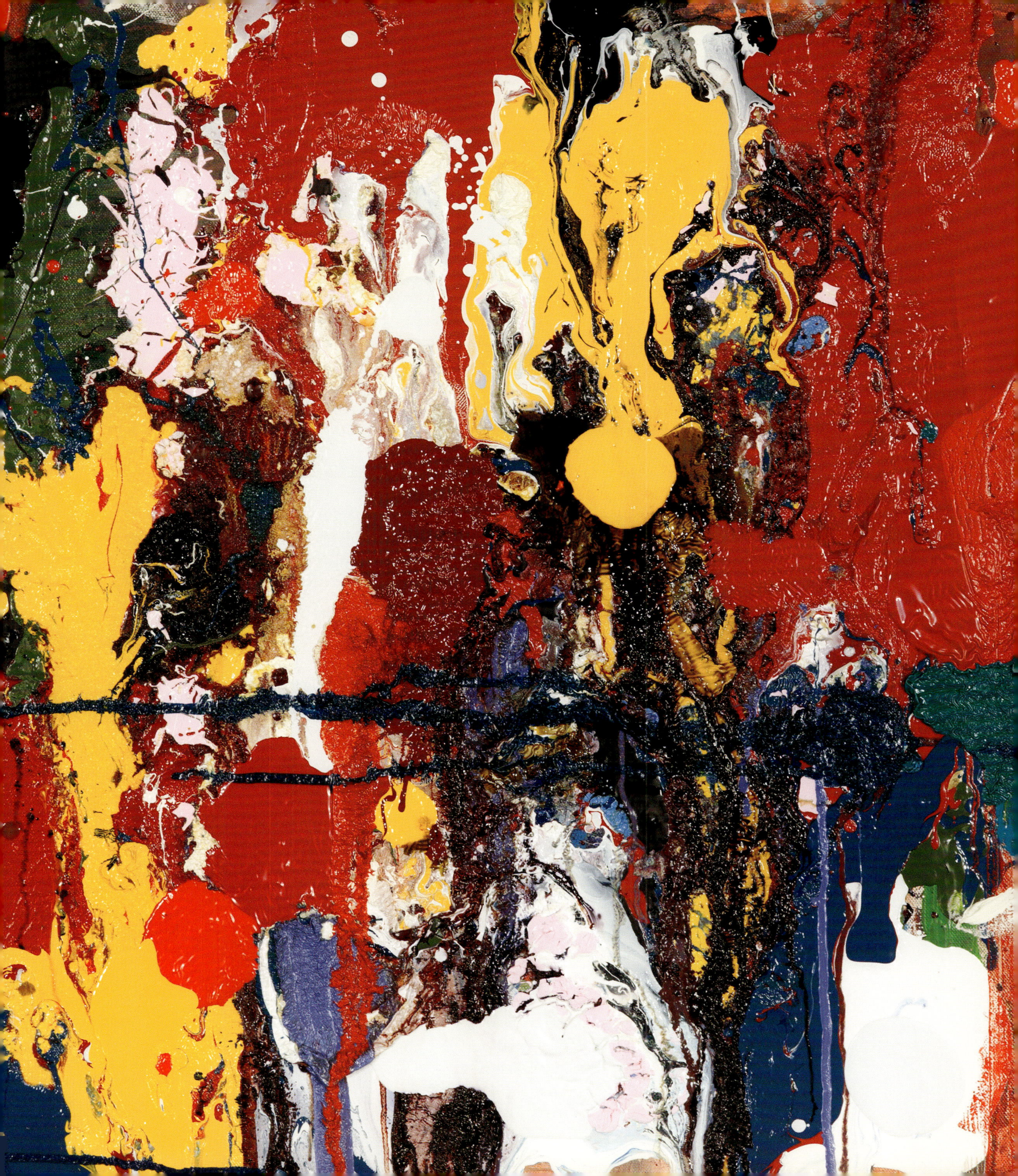

Endnotes

1. Norman Buckley, "Monkey, a Painting, and Children Who Are Different," blog entry, normanbuckley.com, December 21, 2014.
2. "The family I lived with in my youth did not encourage art; however I loved painting and drawing. One of my earliest memories is from about the age of four: I brought home a collage Thanksgiving turkey, with red and blue painted circles for feathers, and the smell of white glue. I was delighted and proud. 'I want to be an artist,' I said to the man who was my caretaker. I remember him telling me, 'That's stupid. Only girls are artists.' I remember feeling angry, sad and confused, so I retreated to my upstairs room with my turkey. But I also felt a sense of determination to prove him wrong." David Whaley, in response to interview questions from Jeanne-Marie Cilento for *Design & Art*, 20 March, 2013.
3. Jeanne-Marie Cilento, "Art and the American Dream: Interview with Painter Davyd Whaley," *Design & Art*, March 20, 2013.
4. Norman Buckley, interviewed by the author, December 21, 2015.
5. Davyd Whaley, website notes on the painting *Provider*. This and the following Davyd Whaley "notes" can be found below the images where they appear on the artist's website: www.davydwhaley.com.
6. Cited in the biographical note accompanying the artist's solo exhibition at Galerie Michael, February–March, 2014.
7. Ibid.
8. Erin Clark, "Davyd Whaley: Dream Chaser," *Artworks,* Spring 2011, 75.
9. Ibid., 74.
10. Ibid., 73.
11. Ibid.
12. Max Maslansky, email interview with the author, October 23, 2015.
13. Clark, 73.
14. Davyd Whaley, "Artist's Statement," Davyd Whaley Inaugural Exhibition, Galerie Michael, February–March 2013.
15. Whaley, notes on the painting *Relative Peace.*
16. Nick Brown, email interview with the author, October 28, 2015.
17. Ibid.
18. Franklyn Liegel, email correspondence with the artist, January 25, 2012.
19. Liegel, email, February 1, 2012.
20. Davyd Whaley, notes on the painting *Manna I* for Galerie Michael, undated.
21. Davyd Whaley, notes on the paintings *Manna I, II,* at Galerie Michael.
22. Davyd Whaley, "Presentation of Work." This document was likely prepared in 2012 by Whaley as a means of presenting his work for gallery consideration. Along with the text, it includes a number of images with accompanying commentary.
23. Whaley, notes on the painting *Journey*.
24. Davyd Whaley, notes on paintings prepared for Galerie Michael, 2013.

25. Curiously, the name of the artist who created this image has been confused with its German title *Schutzengel* (guardian angel). It seems likely that his name was Lindberg, but there appears to be no further information available.
26. Whaley, notes on the painting *Guardian Angel.*
27. Norman Buckley, notes on the painting *Guardian*, davydwhaley.com.
28. Whaley, notes on the painting *Nuclear Family.*
29. Ibid.
30. Whaley, notes on the painting *Atonement*.
31. Whaley, notes on the painting *Jiva and the Goddess.*
32. Davyd Whaley, Artist's statement, Galerie Michael exhibition, February–March 2013.
33. Whaley, notes on the painting *Santa Monica VII.*
34. Ibid.
35. *Anima* was included, along with other works completed at Art Students League, in a one-person show, *Anima Speaks,* Trestle Gallery, Brooklyn, NY, 2010.
36. Whaley, notes on the painting *Fertile Instinct.*
37. Whaley, notes on the painting *Sacred Heart.*
38. Whaley, notes on the painting *Fields of Play.*
39. Cited in Norman Buckley, "Illusion and Temporary States of Being," blog post, March 15, 2015, normanbuckley.com.
40. Ibid.
41. Ibid.
42. Ibid.
43. Buckley, "Meditations on the Light and Dark," blog post, October 14, 2015.
44. Ibid.
45. Davyd Whaley, notes on the painting *Relative Peace.*
46. It was after completing the *Blauw* series that Whaley came across a monochrome blue painting by Ad Reinhardt. "Blue, it's been done before," he wrote as a Tumblr post on April 9, 2014. "& his was better. I found this painting today of Ad Reinhardt's *Blue-Purple* hitting the auction [...] I think I may be out of my blue period for now."
47. Robert Creeley, "The Innocence."
48. Herman Hesse, "Going to Sleep": "Now that I am wearied of the day/my ardent desire shall happily receive/the starry night/like a sleepy child./Hands, stop all your work./Brow, forget all your thinking./All my senses now/Yearn to sink into slumber./And my unfettered soul/wishes to soar up freely/into night's magic sphere/to live there deeply and thousandfold." All four poems can be found posted in full at Whaley's Tumblr site: davydwhaley.tumblr.com/post/103383118287/each-year-for-the-last-several-years-davyd-painted.

Acknowledgments

FROM PETER CLOTHIER:

I'm deeply grateful, first, to Norman Buckley, for his many insights, his devotion to this project, and for sharing with me Davyd's private and extremely personal journals and sketchbooks on which many of my own observations are based. I'm grateful, too, to my wife, Ellie Blankfort, for her always helpful readings and comments as my text progressed. And to Davyd himself, whose struggles as a man and a painter proved so inspiring—and taught me much, along the way, about what it means to be a sensitive and vulnerable human being.

FROM NORMAN BUCKLEY:

There are many people who have been involved in the creation of this book and to whom I owe my deepest thanks. The idea to create such a work came within days after Davyd's death, in my conversations with his friends—Ellie Blankfort, Peter Clothier, and Anitra Kyees. I am grateful to each one of them for their contribution to this project and for their commitment to the formation of The Davyd Whaley Foundation, which seeks to promote the ideals and goals of Davyd by supporting Los Angeles area artists. I also want to thank Amy Inouye for the book's beautiful design. Thank you also to John Skalicky and Renee Rosso for photographing many of the paintings, and to Suzanne Steck, Stacy Schrier, Camila Hindell, Karen Huie, Kristan Bonde, Nick Brown, Max Maslansky, Fred Goldstein, and Davyd's half-brother David Whaley for their various contributions. I am very grateful to the collectors of Davyd's work and it's my hope that his art will continue to inspire them. I thank everyone at Galerie Michael, who brought his work to a wider public: Michael Schwartz, Robert Avellano, Renata De Aquino, Lisa Dickson, Jesse Glick, Sean Howse, Lynn Marks, Pablo Polanco, Richard Reiner, Richard Rice, Ralf Warneking, and Ashley Wynn. My gratitude to my family: my mother Betty Bob, my siblings Betty Lynn, Patrick, and Michael, for embracing Davyd as part of our family and for giving him the love he missed growing up. My very deep appreciation goes to Davyd's best friend of many years, Alesia Leingang. Alesia had saved many pieces of Davyd's art from his high school years, returned them to him later in his life, which then inspired his return to art as a full-time occupation. Davyd recycled much of that art into the work he created from 2009–2014. And finally, to Davyd Whaley, my whole heart, always.

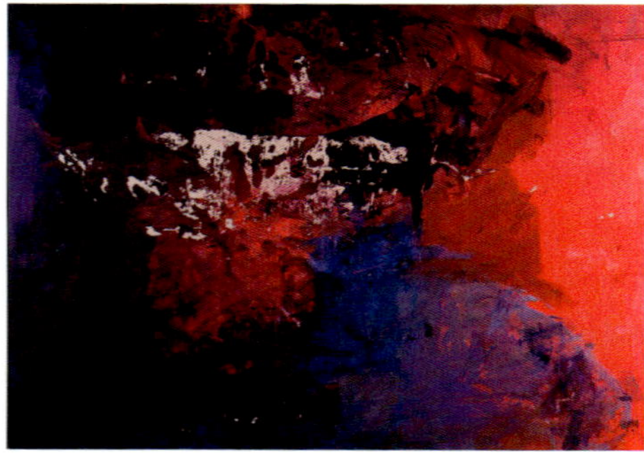

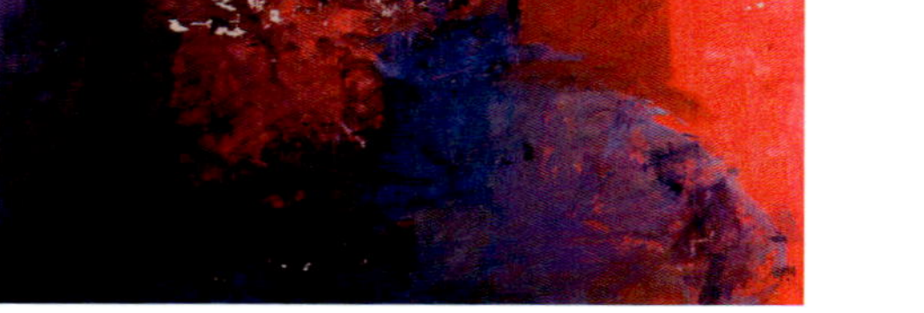

Little Joan, 2014

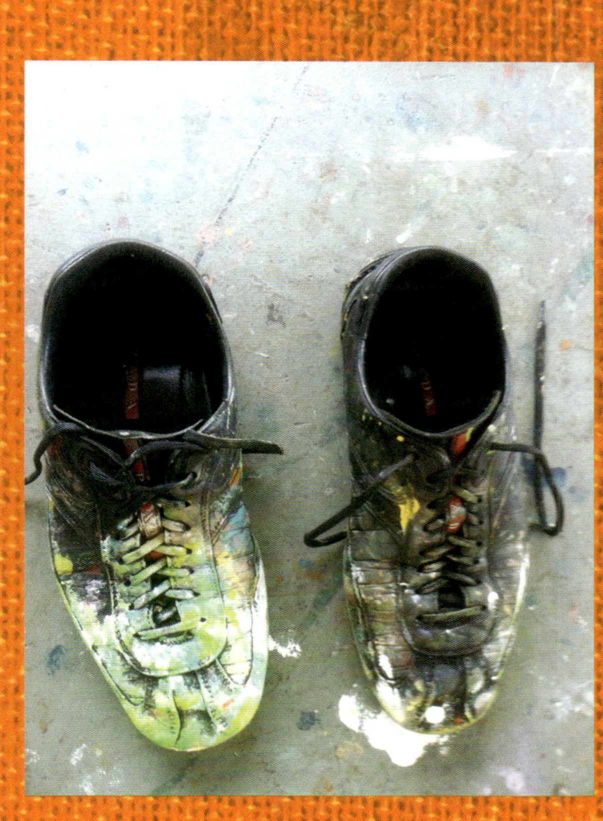

Index of Paintings

Endpapers (hardcover version only), Front: (top row) *Study for Initiate Principles,* 2012; *Untitled,* 2011; *Starfish Basic Symbols in Magic,* 2012; *Beat Me into Submission with Your Problems,* 2012; *Rise,* 2012; *Bear Cat,* 2014 • (row 2) *Virtue Holland,* 2012; *Abstract Figure,* 2013; *Meek,* 2012; *A Trip to MOMA,* 2008; *Saints and Mothers,* 2012 • (row 3) *Shaman,* 2011; *Love,* 2011; *Study for Approach,* 2014; *Alchemical Elements,* 2010; *Girl Breaks Bone,* 2012 • (bottom row) *Pandora*, 2012; *Liverpool,* 2013; *Do Not Despair,* 2012; *A Lesson about Van Gogh,* 2012; *Suspicion,* 2011
Front Endpapers (opposite title page): (top row) *Rhythm and Color,* 2011; *Hurt,* 2011; *Hail Mary,* 2014 • (row 2) *Self Portrait,* 2008; *Significance,* 2013; *Totem Muse,* 2010 • (row 3) *Nebuchadnezzar,* 2013; *Blue Green,* 2012; *Wooden Shoes,* 2012 • (bottom row) *Leonilla,* 2011; *Light and Darkness,* 2012; *Les Deux Magots,* 2012
Back Endpapers (opposite page 208): (top row) *Sophia,* 2010; *Boarding Ostrich,* 2012; *Tenant Meeting,* 2012 • (row 2) *Chaos,* 2012; *Home of the Brave #3,* 2013; *Wishbone,* 2012 • (row 3) *Control,* 2011; *Rest and Restitution,* 2012; *Untitled,* 2012; *Mireka Starr,* 2012 • (bottom row) *Dream Talk,* 2011; *Factory,* 2012; *Mama Ruth,* 2008; *Scroll #46,* 2012; *Inside the Mother,* 2012
Back Endpapers: (top row) *Nola,* 2013; *Home of the Brave #6,* 2013; *Still Life,* 2011; *Red Boy,* 2013; *Three Ladies,* 2012 • (row 2) *Grace,* 2013; *75,* 2013; *Build a Bigger Church,* 2009; *The Knife,* 2013; *Untitled,* 2014 • (row 3) *Spirit,* 2010; *Bob White,* 2013; *Untitled,* 2013; *Circles,* 2014; *Meek,* 2012; *Madonna in Sorrow,* 2014 • (bottom row) *Untitled Abstract,* 2013; *Untitled,* 2014; *Crone,* 2010; *Untitled,* 2012; *Study of Blue Tokyo,* 2013; *Analogy of Fishing,* 2011; *Untitled,* 2011

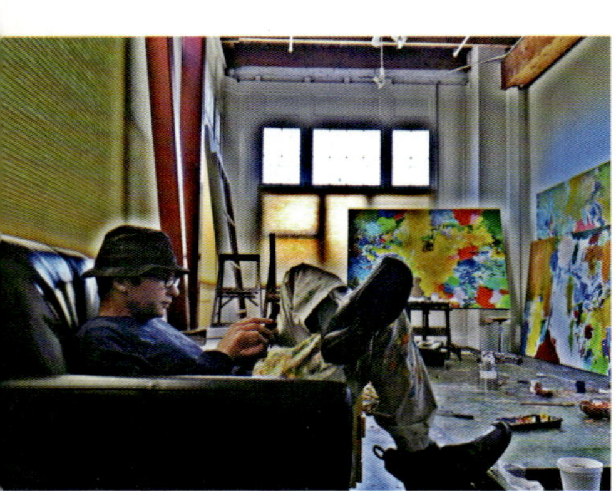

Hardcover ISBN-13: 978-0-692-72249-7
Paperback ISBN-13: 978-0-692-72250-3

Published by: The Davyd Whaley Foundation, Los Angeles California

Design by Amy Inouye, Future Studio Los Angeles

Library of Congress Control Number: 2016942757

Printed in Canada

PHOTO CREDITS: John Skalicky, Renee Rosso
ADDITIONAL PHOTOS BY: Norman Buckley, Brian Castle, Kristen Diou, Karen Huie, Davyd Whaley

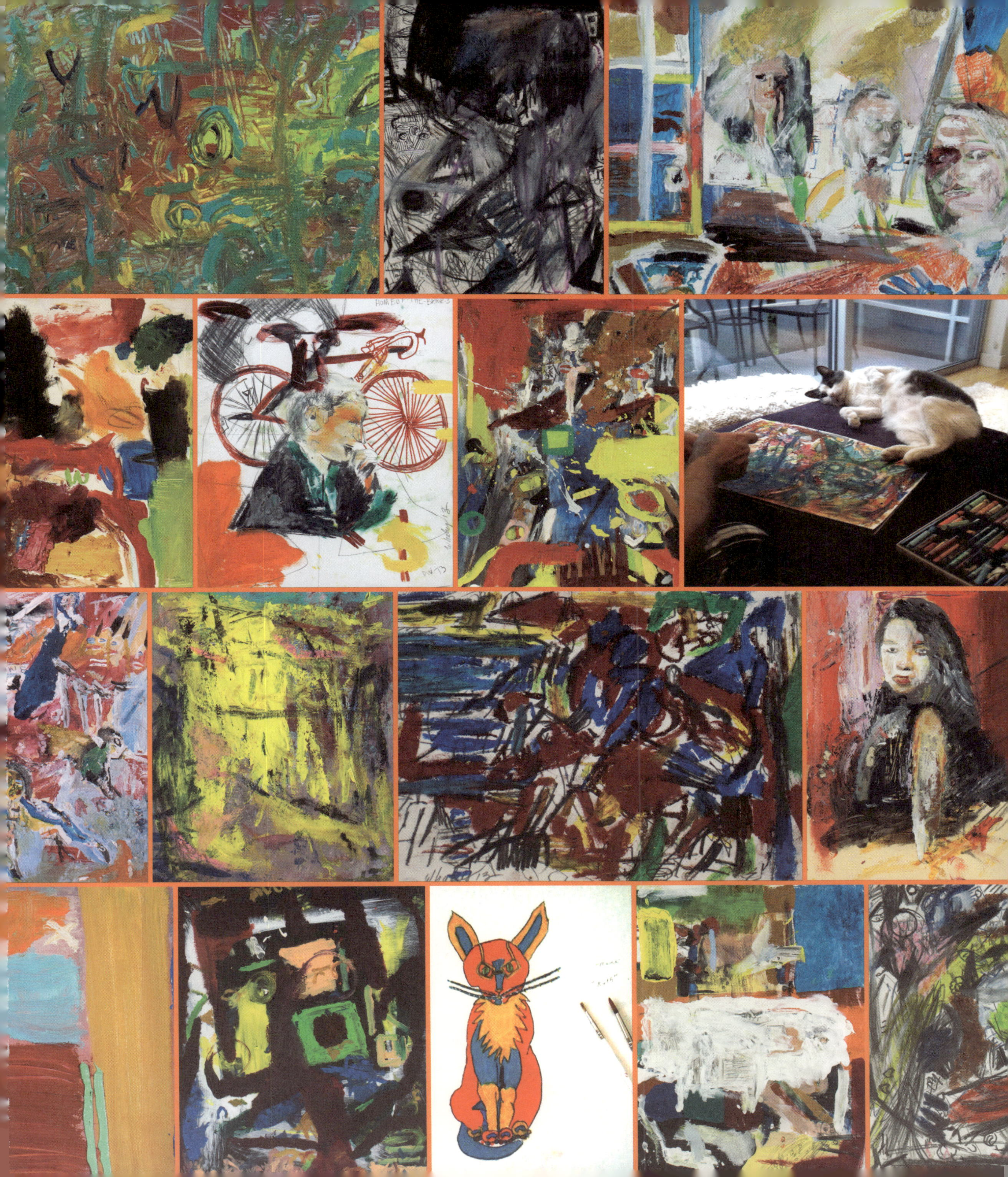

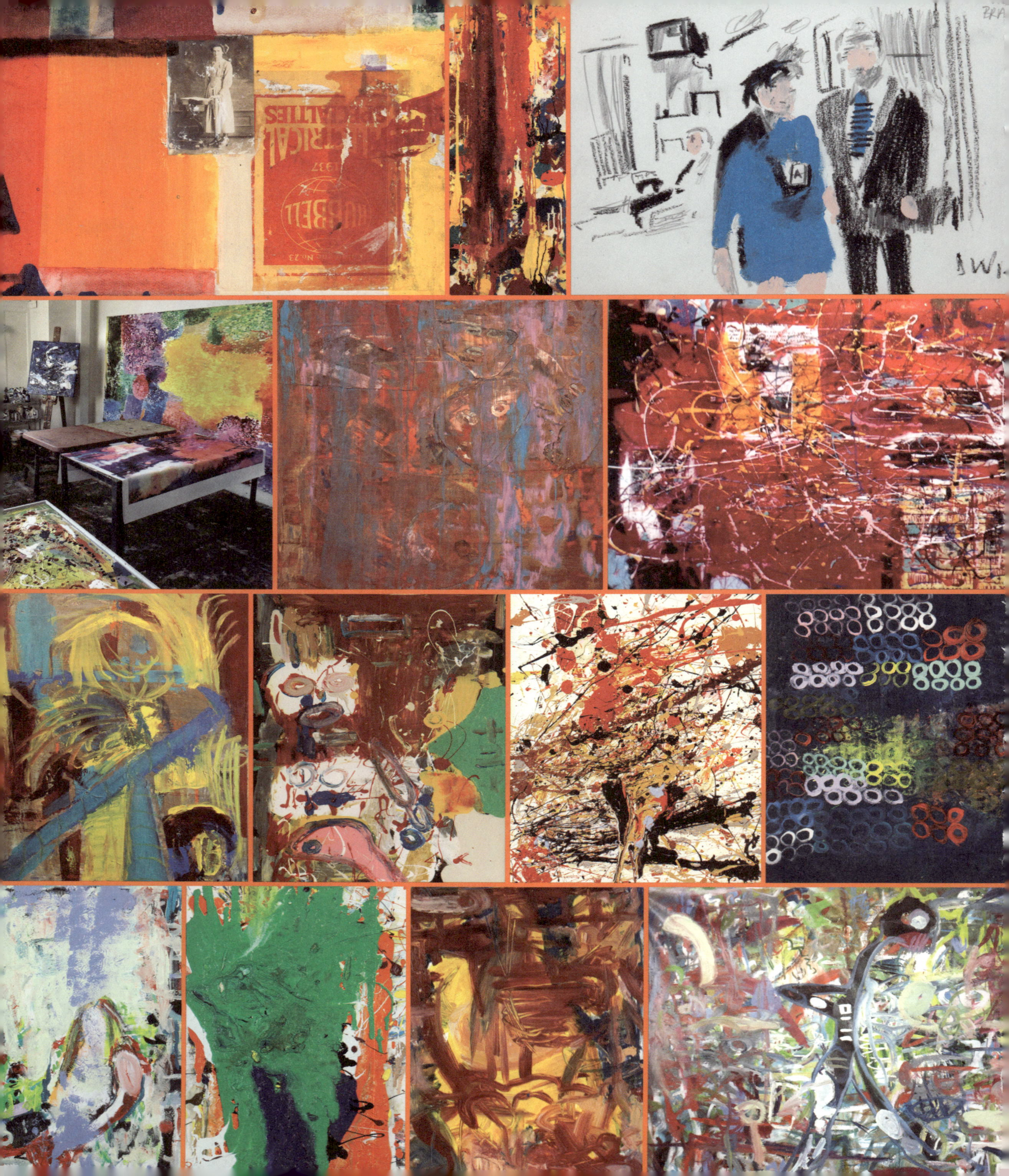